Programmed Learning Aid for

FINANCIAL MANAGEMENT

Programmed Learning Aid for

FINANCIAL MANAGEMENT

Revised Edition

J. FRED WESTON
Graduate School of Management
University of California, Los Angeles

Coordinating editor
ROGER H. HERMANSON
Georgia State University

LEARNING SYSTEMS COMPANY

A division of
RICHARD D. IRWIN, INC.   Homewood, Illinois   60430

Also available through
IRWIN-DORSEY LIMITED   Georgetown, Ontario   L7G 4B3

ISBN 0-256-02135-X
Printed in the United States of America

1 2 3 4 5 6 7 8 9 0 K 9 8 7 6 5 4 3 2

FOREWORD

Each of the books comprising the Programmed Learning Aid Series is in programmed learning format to provide the reader with a quick, efficient, and effective means of grasping the essential subject matter.

The specific benefits of the programmed method of presentation are as follows:

1. It keeps the reader *active* in the learning process and increases comprehension level.
2. Incorrect responses are *corrected immediately*.
3. Correct responses are *reinforced immediately*.
4. The method is *flexible*. Those who need more "tutoring" receive it because they are encouraged to reread frames in which they have missed any of the questions asked.
5. The method makes learning seem like a game.

The method of programming used in this PLAID on *Financial Management* and in most of the other PLAIDs is unique and simple to use. Begin by reading Frame 1^1 in Chapter 1. At the end of that frame answer the True-False questions given. To determine the correctness of responses, merely turn the page and examine the answers given in Answer Frame 1^1. The reader is told *why* each statement is true or false. Performance on the questions given is used as a measure of understanding of all the materials in Frame 1^1. If any of the questions are missed, reread Frame 1^1 before continuing on to Frame 2^1. This same procedure should be used throughout the book. Specific instructions are given throughout as to where to turn next to continue working the program.

The reader may desire to go through the PLAID a second time leaving out the programming questions and answers, or may desire to further test understanding by going through it a second time answering all of the questions once again and rereading only those frames in which comprehension is unsatisfactory.

PLAIDs are continuously updated in new printings to provide the reader with the latest subject content in the field.

I wish to express my thanks to Charles Robert Carlson, Assistant Professor of Finance at the University of Michigan for assisting in the programming of this PLAID.

The author of this PLAID on financial management is the coauthor of one of the most widely used textbooks in managerial finance. He has also been the author and coauthor of more advanced books and textbooks in finance as well as a large number of research papers and articles, and the editor or associate editor of a number of the finance journals, both theoretical and applied. He has been an officer of a number of finance associations including president of the American Finance Association. He has considerable practical experience in consulting in finance in both industry and government and in teaching applied finance in a number of executive programs.

Roger H. Hermanson
Coordinating Editor and Programmer

v

PREFACE

The author has prepared this Programmed Learning Aid in *Financial Management* as a supplement to standard textbooks and as a tool for systematic review. I believe it will be helpful to students in studying standard course materials, as a review for those entering MBA programs or executive programs, or simply as a fast and systematic review of the field for professionals on the job seeking to broaden their horizons. The PLAID is designed as a supplement and not as a text substitute for college level courses.

This PLAID covers the nature of financial management, how finance relates to the other functions of the business firm and how financial decisions can contribute to the maximization of stockholder wealth. The emphasis is on the review of the central concepts of business finance covering both the acquisition of assets and of funds and the internal financial management process of the firm. Each chapter is focused on the central decision areas of the topic that have an impact on the value of the firm. Risk and uncertainty are treated throughout the topics. In addition, modern developments in capital market theory are summarized clearly and succinctly. Difficult concepts are developed by brief case illustrations so that the applications of complex materials can readily be followed.

The organization of the subject matter falls into five major categories. The first section contains six chapters dealing with the finance function, the cash flow cycle, financial analysis, financial planning and control, financial forecasting, and budgeting and profit planning. This section provides the important analytical tools required as well as a guide to how financial activities interact with the other functions and general management responsibilities to contribute to more efficient operation of the firm. Part two deals with working capital management, the financial problems encountered continuously by financial managers. Part three completes the treatment of the left-hand side of the balance sheet by a consideration of asset investment decisions. It begins with the discussion of the role of the interest factor in financial decisions and then successively takes up capital budgeting decisions and investment decisions under uncertainty. This completes the first segment of the subject matter.

Part four covers the central theoretical valuation concepts in finance. It provides the background for decision areas covered in the subsequent chapters. This part begins with an analysis of valuation and rates of return. It then takes up leverage and the cost of capital, and concludes with an analysis of dividend policy in relation to valuation. Part five deals with long-term financing. It begins with a survey of the financial markets and their implications for the timing of financing. Then successively long-term financing decisions and intermediate-term financing decisions are analyzed. The financial tools and valuation principles previously developed are applied in these chapters. The long-term financing materials also include an analysis of adjustments achieved in financing patterns by the use of warrants and convertibles. The final chapter takes up financial strategies involved in the use of mergers and holding companies in the growth of the firm.

The foregoing sequence contains an interlocking and natural development. Most texts would agree with the placement of part one and part five. The other chapters and topics can be taken up in any desired sequence which follows the format for the course that the student is taking or which best fits the needs of the student or manager who is seeking to obtain an understanding of finance by self-study.

Using the programmed learning format, I subdivided the material into Frames, each of which is followed by a series of questions so that the student can be tested on the material just studied. The process is involving, reinforcing, flexible, and provides immediate correction when necessary. There are several aids to assist students in locating subject materials: First, there is a detailed table of contents which provides a chronological approach to the subject matter. Second, there is an alphabetically arranged topical outline of course content which provides an alphabetic approach to specific subject areas. Finally, there is a comprehensive glossary-index which defines terms and gives page references for more detailed coverage. Further, self-testing is provided through comprehensive examinations at the end of the PLAID which are arranged by chapter for maximum flexibility.

J. Fred Weston

TOPICAL OUTLINE OF COURSE CONTENT

CONTENTS

Guide to symbols used

a	The amount of an annuity.
A_t	Annual payments. Without the subscript, annual cash payments are equal.
$A_{\overline{n}\mid r}$	Present value of an annuity.
B	Value of the debt of a levered firm.
B_M	Value of a bond at maturity.
B_t	Value as a straight debt instrument at time t.
β_j	Beta coefficient, risk index.
c	Cash flows, most generally; *also* dollar amount of interest paid at coupon rate each year.
C	Carrying cost per unit (EOQ).
$C_{n,r}$	The repeated event or annuity compound interest factor.
CGS	Cost of goods sold.
Cor_{jk}	Correlation of returns between investments.
Cov_{jk}	The covariance of returns between investments $= \text{Cor}_{jk}\sigma_j\sigma_k$.
CPS	Cumulative percentage of sales.
CV_j	The coefficient of variation of the returns from investment j is $\sigma_j / E(R_j)$.
D	Dollar amount of dividends paid.
D_1	The expected end of year dividend.
DCF	Discounted cash flow.
DDB	Double declining balance method of depreciation.
e	The number of directors that are desired to be elected in cumulative voting.
EBIT	Earnings before interest and taxes.
EOQ	Economic order quantity in inventory management.
EPS	Earnings per share.
$E(R_j)$	The expected return from a security. $(\equiv \overline{R}_j)$
$E(\hat{R}_j)$	Expected after-tax return.
$E(R^*_j)$	Expected return on the common stock of an unlevered firm.
$E(R_p)$	The expected returns from a portfolio.

f Flotation costs as a percentage of gross proceeds.

F Fixed costs of placing and receiving an order (EOQ).

FC Fixed costs in break-even analysis.

FPD Financial policy decisions.

g The expected rate of growth or capital gain.

IRR Internal rate of return.

k Required rate of return on equity; *also* $E(R_j)$.

λ Slope of the capital market line for individual securities.

λ^* The slope of the market line or the market price of risk; $\lambda^* = \lambda\sigma_j$.

L_t The lease payment in period t.

Me Market value per share of stock, ex rights.

Mo Market value of stock, rights on.

MPR Market price of risk.

$\#$ The total number of directors to be elected.

n Number of years.

N Total number of shares of common stock outstanding; also used as the payback period, the number of years required to return the original investment.

N The number of shares each warrant entitles an owner to purchase.

$Nec.$ The number of shares required to elect a desired number of directors.

NOI Net operating income. Net operating income + Nonoperating income − Nonoperating expense = EBIT (earnings before interest and taxes).

NPV Net present value.

NR Number of rights required to purchase one share of common stock.

NTV Net terminal value.

O Option purchase price, used when purchasing stocks with warrants.

OI Operating income; *also* NOI, net operating income.

OL Operating leverage.

Π The probability assigned to various possible outcomes of an investment; also p.

p The probability assigned to various possible outcomes of an investment; *also* Π.

π Net income available to common stockholders.

P Present value, or beginning principal amount, or price per share of common stock as indicated by context.

P_0 The current price of common stock.

P_1	The expected end of year price per share of common stock.
$P_{n,r}$	The present value of an annuity factor for n years at r percent.
Q	Quantity sold (as used in calculation of OL).
r	Interest rate, in percent or cost of debt.
R_f	Risk-free return on debt.
ROI	Return on investment; when investment is gross total assets, return is net operating income; when investment is net total assets, return is net income or net income plus financial charges.
σ_j	The standard deviation of returns from a security; the square root of variance.
σ_p	The standard deviation of portfolio returns.
σ^2_j	Variance of the returns on investment j.
S	Equity value of the firm. (Less often, S refers to sales.)
S_b	Subscription price in rights offering.
S_n	Value at the end of n years at compound interest.
$S_{n\overline{m}|rm}$	The future sum to which an annuity will accumulate over n years at r rate of interest if compounded m number of times per year.
$S_{\overline{n}|r}$	The future sum to which an annuity will accumulate over n years at r rate of interest.
SYD	Sum-of-years-digits method of depreciation.
t	Time index or tax rate as indicated by context.
τ	Tax rate.
T	Original term to maturity of debt.
TVW	Theoretical value of a warrant.
V	Value as in the value of a firm.
V_L	Value of a levered firm.
V_u	Value of an unlevered firm.
VC	Variable costs of output (Q).
VR	Value of a stock subscription right.
w_j	Proportion of the total portfolio in one security or investment.
W	Wealth position of an investor.
WACC	Weighted average cost of capital.
$\widehat{\text{WACC}}$	After-tax weighted average cost of capital.

chapter 1

THE FINANCE FUNCTION

Frame 1[1]

THE EVOLVING ROLE OF FINANCE

The role of finance within the firm has shifted through time. At first, financial managers primarily had the responsibility for raising funds. Following the severe recession of 1929–33 with its wave of financial catastrophies, the preoccupation of finance was with capital structure. In the early 1950s emphasis shifted to a focus on the flow of funds in the internal management of the firm.

By the early 1960s the scope of finance was extended to policies and decisions which affect the value of the firm. The valuation of the business enterprise is determined by two fundamental factors: (1) its expected stream of future earnings and (2) the risk that actual earnings may be different from the expected earnings. The size and riskiness of expected future earnings are in turn influenced by such factors as the product-market mix of the firm, the size of the firm, its rate of growth, the type of assets in which it invests, the liquidity position of the firm, and the extent to which debt is used in its operations.

Beginning in 1966 the economy began to be greatly affected by inflation, tight money markets, and the high cost of funds. The effective use of scarce and expensive funds further increased in importance. The rise in debt ratios and the higher cost of debt made capital structures and the ability to meet debt interest payments important considerations. Increasing the value of the firm became critical for raising equity funds.

Four aspects are significant to the duties of the financial officer of the firm. One is the recognition of the simultaneous and interrelated flows of physical goods, information, and cash flows. The financial manager is not only responsible for controlling cash flows, but also has an important role in structuring and controlling information and physical flows.

A second element is the interaction between financial decisions and other management functions. For the effective functioning of the firm as a whole, financial managers must take into consideration their influence on research and development activities, the stimulation of product development, manufacturing systems, production, marketing, planning and control, personnel requirements, and so on.

A third highlight relates to the concept that in interacting with its external environment, the firm represents an adaptive and learning mechanism. The planning and control functions are part of a feedback and correction system designed to achieve a fast reaction time to miscalculations and environmental changes.

Fourth, because the financial executives are ultimately responsible for the design and operation of both the information and cash flow systems of the firm, they are also responsible for controlling the firm in its major profit centers, and from an overall viewpoint. Financial executives are involved in the review, evaluation, and adjustment of all aspects of the firm's operations; their objective is to contribute to maximizing the value of the firm. Since all the firm's policies are ultimately reflected in value maximization, the theory of the firm may be viewed as a financial theory of the firm.

1

FINANCE IN THE ORGANIZATION STRUCTURE

The financial manager of the firm often carries the title of treasurer. Sometimes he is called vice president-finance, controller, treasurer-controller, or secretary-treasurer. Whatever his title, the financial manager is usually close to the top of the organizational structure of the firm. Typically, he is a member of the first level of corporate staff in a large organization. In large firms, major financial decisions are often made by a finance committee. For example, finance committees are used in General Motors, United States Steel, and American Telephone and Telegraph. In smaller firms the owner-manager typically conducts the financial operations himself, although he may delegate many other management functions.

One reason for the high place occupied by the financial manager in the organizational structure is the importance of planning, analysis, and control operations for which he is responsible. Often a *financial control* staff reports directly to the president or operates as an analytical staff for vice presidents in charge of production, marketing, engineering, and other operations.

Another reason financial authority is rarely decentralized or delegated to subordinates is that many financial decisions are crucial to the survival of the firm. Decisions which have major financial implications—such as taking on a new product or discarding an old one, adding a plant or changing locations, floating a bond or a stock issue, or entering into sale and leaseback arrangements—are all major episodes in the life of a corporation.

Moreover, significant economies can be achieved through centralizing financial operations. A large corporation can float a $50 million bond issue at a much lower interest cost per dollar than the rate at which a small firm can borrow $1,000. The large corporation is likely to be able to borrow at a rate ranging from 7 to 9 percent. A small firm borrowing $1,000 will necessarily pay from 10 to 20 percent. It would be misleading, however, to imply that the advantages of centralization lie only in interest savings. The terms of the financial contract are also likely to be improved—a matter that may be of greater importance to the borrower than the interest rate. Contract terms refer to the extent to which borrowers may buy additional fixed assets, declare dividends, incur debt, and so forth.

Although the responsibility for carrying out major financial decisions is likely to be centered in the hands of a high-level official, a large number of day-to-day operations are conducted by the treasurer's office. These tasks include handling cash receipts and disbursements, borrowing from commercial banks on a regular and continuing basis, and formulating cash budgets.

IMPORTANCE OF FINANCIAL MANAGEMENT

Business finance has taken on increased social importance. If the economy is to function efficiently, resources must be allocated on a sound basis both by business firms and by other purposive organizations such as government agencies and even nonprofit institutions. Finance performs a central role in the operations of any purposive organization. The planning and control principles of business finance contribute to the efficient utilization of resources. Increasingly such principles must apply to social costs such as air and water pollution. The concepts of finance should be employed to recognize both internal and external (or social) costs in our economy. It thus contributes to the efficient use of resources in the economy and to the improvement of the quality of life.

Financial decisions also affect the size and variability of the earnings stream or profitability. Financial policy decisions affect risk and profitability, and these two factors jointly determine the value of the firm. Primary policy decisions relate to choosing the industry in which to operate—the product-market mix of the firm. Financial decisions influence risk and profitability in several ways. An increase in the cash position, for instance, reduces risk, but since cash is not an earning asset, converting other assets to cash also reduces profitability. Similarly the use of additional debt raises the rate of return, or the profitability of the firm. But at the same time, more debt means more risk. The task of finance is to strike the balance between risk and profitability that will contribute to the highest long-term value of the firm's securities.

In summary, therefore, finance performs a crucial role in the success and survival of the firm.

Financial decisions, both past and present, affect the viability and control of the firm. Financing is the critical management function in that it provides the means of remedying weak management in other areas. If production or marketing efforts, for example, have deteriorated, adequate financial means may be used to rehabilitate and restore the weak departments to renewed effectiveness. However, since money alone cannot substitute for other operating strength, finance is an interdependent part in the totality of managerial functions and responsibilities affecting an organization's performance.

Indicate whether each of the following statements is true or false by writing "T" or "F" in the space provided.

_____ 1. The role of finance within the firm is limited to that of raising funds.

_____ 2. The size and riskiness of expected future earnings determine the valuation of a firm.

_____ 3. The financial manager's role is to contribute to maximizing the value of the firm.

_____ 4. Financial authority is more often decentralized rather than centralized in a firm.

_____ 5. Liquidity and profitability are competing goals of the financial manager.

Now turn to Answer Frame 1¹, page 4, to check your responses.

Answer frame 1[1]

1. False. While this was the role of finance at first, the role has expanded over time to include concern with the capital structure of the firm, focus on the flow of funds, and involvement in the policies and decisions which affect the value of the firm.
2. True. These are the two fundamental factors that determine the value of a firm. These, in turn, are influenced by such factors as product-market mix of the firm, size and growth rate of the firm, the composition of the firm's assets and equities, and adjustment to changes in the external economic and financial environment.
3. True. He does this by being aware of the pervasiveness of the finance function throughout the firm. He is concerned with cash, information, and physical flows. He realizes the impact that financial decisions have on other decisions. His function in the planning and control area form part of the feedback mechanism of the firm. He is involved in the review, evaluation, and adjustment of all aspects of the firm's operations.
4. False. Financial authority is more often centralized since the decisions made are so crucial to the survival of the firm and economies can be achieved through centralization.
5. True. He must strike a balance between these two goals. Large cash balances on hand insure liquidity (the ability to pay bills when due), but idle cash balances also damage profitability.

An attempt is made in each frame to test the reader on the most important concepts within that frame. Therefore you should use your performance on the questions asked at the end of each frame as an indication of your comprehension of all the concepts in that frame. If you missed any of the above questions, you should go back and reread Frame 1[1] before turning to Chapter 2 on page 5. You should follow this same procedure throughout the PLAID.

chapter 2

CASH FLOW CYCLE

Frame 1[2]

An understanding of the nature of finance is facilitated by following the development of a cash flow cycle in a firm. Details will be omitted to focus on the basic financial flows. Thus, many important aspects that involve legal decisions, tax decisions, production, marketing, and personnel analysis are not considered in this initial brief summary.

A. Mr. Jones had been working as a machine operator in a metal fabricating plant for almost 20 years. From his years of experience, he had developed an idea for a special kind of metal fastener, and informal contacts with a number of potential customers indicated that he had a sound product idea. He was determined to start his own business.

Mr. Jones had accumulated personal savings over the years of $10,000. His home had been mortgage free, so he was able to obtain a first mortgage of $30,000, which enabled him to start out with a total of $40,000. He incorporated and issued himself $40,000 par value of capital stock. He rented a plant (with payment to be made at the end of each quarter), bought equipment in the amount of $25,000, and began business on January 1, 198A. His company's financial situation at this point is described by its balance sheet (Table 2–1).

B. Jones received some orders to manufacture 1,000 fasteners. To begin operations he was able to buy sheet metal in the amount of $10,000, with payment to be made within 20 days after purchase. His financial situation after this transaction is shown in the balance sheet for January 8 (Table 2–2).

The total assets of the Jones Company have

TABLE 2–1

JONES COMPANY
Balance Sheet
January 1, 198A

Assets

Current assets:	
Cash.................................	$15,000
Fixed assets:	
Plant and equipment..................	25,000
Total Assets........................	$40,000

Stockholders' Equity

Capital stock...........................	$40,000
Total Stockholders' Equity.........	$40,000

now increased to $50,000. This illustrates how the credit extended by the suppliers of the sheet metal have provided additional capital in the form of debt payable to the suppliers in the

TABLE 2–2

JONES COMPANY
Balance Sheet
January 8, 198A

Assets

Current assets:	
Cash.................................	$15,000
Raw materials inventory...............	10,000
Total Current Assets..................	$25,000
Fixed assets:	
Plant and equipment..................	25,000
Total Assets........................	$50,000

Liabilities and Stockholders' Equity

Current liabilities:	
Accounts payable......................	$10,000
Total Current Liabilities..............	$10,000
Stockholders' equity:	
Capital stock..........................	40,000
Total Liabilities and Stockholders' Equity............................	$50,000

5

TABLE 2–3

JONES COMPANY
Balance Sheet
January 16, 198A

Assets

Current assets:
Cash................................... $ 7,000
Inventory (work in process)............ 20,000
Total Current Assets.................. $27,000
Fixed assets:
Plant and equipment.................. 25,000
Total Assets....................... $52,000

Liabilities and Stockholders' Equity

Current liabilities:
Accounts payable..................... $10,000
Accrued wages payable................ 2,000
Total Current Liabilities.............. $12,000
Stockholders' equity:
Capital stock.......................... 40,000
Total Liabilities and Stockholders'
Equity........................... $52,000

amount of $10,000. The firm proceeds to cut all of the metal into pieces to prepare it for further fabrication into its final form. For $10,000 of labor used (which becomes part of the inventory cost), $8,000 is paid in cash, and $2,000 is payable at the end of a two-week period. The balance sheet on January 16 is now shown (Table 2–3).

Total assets have increased further to $52,000, representing an additional $2,000 from accrued wages payable. Raw material inventory has been changed to work-in-process inventory. From a financial standpoint the raw material inventory would have represented good collateral for a loan because the sheet metal could be resold for a number of uses. However, after it has been cut up in a particular shape, it is no longer likely to be acceptable as collateral.

C. Additional labor cost of $8,000 would be required to finish the manufacture of the fasteners, but the firm has only $7,000 in cash remaining. This illustrates how lack of financial planning can create problems for a business firm. Initially, until the firm has demonstrated that it can successfully produce and sell its final product, more of the equipment probably should have been rented or leased. It would be very risky for any lender to make a loan to the firm at this point because it has not yet demonstrated that it can in fact complete the manufacture of the fasteners to the satisfaction of the customer.

Even though Jones Company has an order, the transactions cannot be completed unless a satisfactory product is achieved.

But on the assumption that some lender has confidence in the experience and technical ability of Mr. Jones, we will assume that a loan is made. Assuming that the firm should have at least $4,000 of cash on hand, the firm can meet the additional labor expenses of $8,000 by borrowing $5,000 and drawing down its own cash by $3,000. At this stage the financial situation is depicted in the balance sheet for January 20 (Table 2–4).

The additional financing from a bank or finance company is represented by the item, notes payable of $5,000, in the balance sheet of January 20, 198A. All the fasteners have now been completed and are represented by finished goods inventory rather than work-in-process inventory.

D. The fasteners are now shipped to the purchaser with full payment at the selling price of $40,000 due in 10 days. Since shipment has been made, the Jones Company may record accounts receivable in the amount of $40,000. In the meantime the accrued wages of $2,000 must be paid, and the accounts payable incurred on January 8 must be paid by January 28 or they will be overdue. Thus, on January 28, if the Jones Company is to pay off its accrued wages of $2,000 and its accounts payable of $10,000, it must borrow an additional $12,000. If it were successful in doing so,

TABLE 2–4

JONES COMPANY
Balance Sheet
January 20, 198A

Assets

Current assets:
Cash................................... $ 4,000
Inventory (finished goods)............. 28,000
Total Current Assets.................. $32,000
Fixed assets:
Plant and equipment.................. 25,000
Total Assets....................... $57,000

Liabilities and Stockholders' Equity

Current liabilities:
Accounts payable..................... $10,000
Notes payable......................... 5,000
Accrued wages payable................ 2,000
Total Current Liabilities.............. $17,000
Stockholders' equity:
Capital stock.......................... 40,000
Total Liabilities and Stockholders'
Equity........................... $57,000

its notes payable would rise to $17,000. This again emphasizes that if it were possible the Jones Company should have rented or leased its plant and equipment to a greater extent in order to meet its working capital needs until it had completed its sale and receipt of cash for the fasteners. On the assumption that the $12,000 additional financing can be obtained, the balance sheet of January 28 is set forth (Table 2–5).

In the balance sheet for January 28, the finished goods inventory has become accounts receivable valued at the selling price of the goods sold. The difference between the cost of finished

goods of $28,000 and the selling price reflected in accounts receivable of $40,000 represents a profit which would increase retained earnings on the balance sheet. (Still to be recognized in determining earnings for the period are such expenses as depreciation expense on the equipment, rent expense on the building, and interest expense on notes payable.)

E. On January 30, the accounts receivable are paid as scheduled. With the $40,000 cash received the firm can pay off the notes payable. (Interest expense is ignored in the illustration.) The balance sheet as of January 30 would exhibit a strong cash position .(Table 2–6):

Thus at the completion of one cycle of production reflected in cash flows, the firm now has total assets of $52,000, representing the initial investment of $40,000 plus the profit of $12,000 on the initial order. This example illustrates the pure concept of the production and cash cycle.

TABLE 2–5
JONES COMPANY
Balance Sheet
January 28, 198A

Assets

Current assets:
Cash......................................	$ 4,000
Accounts receivable..................	40,000
Total...............................	$44,000

Fixed assets:
Plant and equipment..................	25,000
Total Assets......................	$69,000

Liabilities and Stockholders' Equity

Current liabilities:
Notes payable........................	$17,000
Total Current Liabilities..............	$17,000

Stockholders' equity:
Capital stock..........................	40,000
Retained earnings.....................	12,000
Total Stockholders' Equity...........	$52,000
Total Liabilities and Stockholders' Equity..........................	$69,000

TABLE 2–6
JONES COMPANY
Balance Sheet
January 30, 198A

Assets

Current assets:
Cash...................................	$27,000

Fixed assets:
Plant and equipment..................	25,000
Total Assets......................	$52,000

Stockholders' Equity

Capital stock...........................	$40,000
Retained earnings......................	12,000
Total Stockholders' Equity...........	$52,000

Indicate whether each of the following statements is true or false by writing "T" or "F" in the space provided.

_____ 1. Mr. Jones invested personal assets of $40,000 in the business.

_____ 2. Creditor capital was used to finance the purchase of raw materials.

_____ 3. The financial planning for the Jones Company was well executed.

_____ 4. By the end of January creditors' claims against assets were approximately 50 percent.

Now turn to Answer Frame 1², page 8, to check your responses.

Answer frame 1²

1. True. He invested accumulated personal savings of $10,000 and took out a mortgage of $30,000 on his home. This contributed capital is evidenced by capital stock of $40,000 which Mr. Jones received as a stockholder.

2. True. The sheet metal was acquired on account, which means that the suppliers of the materials extended credit to the company.

3. False. The company probably should have rented or leased the equipment. If it had not been able to borrow the funds to pay the additional labor to complete the products, the company might have had to cease operations. Its cash position was very tight.

4. False. By the end of January all of the liabilities had been paid, and the sole stockholder was the only claimant to the assets. (The $30,000 first mortgage on Mr. Jones' home is considered to be a personal liability rather than a liability of the Jones Company.)

If you missed any of the above, you should restudy Frame 1² before beginning Frame 2² below.

Frame 2²

This illustration is unrealistic in that a firm is not profitable in such a short period of time. The more typical experience of a small firm is unprofitable operations for one to two years even when its long-run prospects are good. This is because of heavy organizational costs incurred in setting up operations, selling expenses to obtain a flow of orders, and usually some "debugging" requirements in achieving efficient manufacturing operations.

However, it is purely the idea of the cash cycle that is being illustrated here. For this reason depreciation expense on the equipment and accrued rent on the building were ignored in determining "profit." The ideas involved can now be summarized and some of the first principles of financial management are also illustrated. These concepts are applicable whether a firm is just starting out or whether it is continuing ongoing operations. When an order is placed with a firm, the purchase of raw materials is required. Typically the supplier of raw material will sell the goods on credit so the firm initially receives financing in the form of accounts payable. To fabricate the materials into the finished product, machinery and labor will be required. The machinery will require either an initial investment outlay or a rental expense. As labor is used, wages must be paid.

When fabrication of goods is completed, they become finished goods inventory. When finished goods inventory are sold, it is usually, to some ex-

tent, a credit transaction. This gives rise to accounts receivable. Thus, in order to make sales, an investment or payment for the use of equipment is required; and payments for raw material and labor are also necessary. In addition, there is typically a lag between the sale of goods and the receipt of the actual cash for the sale.

This simple illustration emphasizes the need for budgeting, planning, and forecasting the relationship between the production operations of the firm, cash flows, and financing requirements. This is why a new firm starting operations, or a firm whose sales are likely to increase, must plan ahead on a monthly basis for at least one year and on an annual basis for three to five years to have at least a general understanding of what its financing needs will be.

In the illustration for the Jones Company, even though the operation was highly profitable, the firm could have failed for financial reasons at a number of points. The Jones Company has to utilize both accounts payable and notes payable from a financing source before the cycle of production, sales, and cash received is completed.

If the firm had not been able to obtain financing at any stage in the cycle of order-manufacturing-sale-collection of receivables, it could have become insolvent. The problem is particularly aggravated for new firms if major difficulties are encountered in the initial production activity. Costs may be higher, delays in completing the manufacture of the goods may occur, and the likelihood of the firm becoming insolvent is even greater. These are the reasons financial ratio analyses, budgeting, and financial forecasting are of such great importance in the financial management of business firms. These topics will therefore be developed in the following chapters.

Label each of the following statements as true or false.

_____ 1. Most firms tend to be profitable immediately after they begin business.

_____ 2. The $12,000 profit on the sale of the finished goods should be labeled as net earnings for the month of January.

_____ 3. A firm can be profitable and yet not be able to pay its debts as they come due.

_____ 4. New firms are particularly vulnerable if costs exceed estimates, delays are encountered, and so on.

Now turn to Answer Frame 2², page 10, to check your answers.

Answer frame 2²

1. False. It usually takes a while before new firms begin to show earnings. For most small firms this period is from one to two years even for those having good long-run prospects.

2. False. Certain expenses which were incurred have not been recorded. Specifically, no depreciation expense on the equipment nor rent expense on the building were recorded. These were ignored in the illustration since the objective was to il-lustrate the cash cycle. Also, no interest expense was recorded on the notes payable since this would only complicate the illustration.

3. True. New and expanding firms often have the problem of having to increase investments in inventory and fixed assets at an amount which exceeds cash generated from operations. Thus, even though they are profitable they are short of cash.

4. True. If costs and performance do not go according to schedule, new firms are particularly vulnerable to insolvency, since they often have limited assets and limited borrowing power.

If you missed any of the above, you should reread Frame 2² before beginning Chapter 3 below.

chapter 3

FINANCIAL ANALYSIS

Frame 1³

Financial managers have a major responsibility for planning and control within an organization. Planning is a process which involves a number of steps. First is analysis of the problem or opportunity. Second is searching for and formulating good alternatives for dealing with the problem or the opportunity. Third is analyzing and projecting the results of following each alternative. Fourth, a choice is made among the alternatives, resulting in the formulation of a plan.

A manager plans toward some specified objectives. The results of operations are compared with the objectives. The process of control is: (1) measuring performance, (2) comparing results with plans, and (3) taking action to improve performance. Both quantitative and qualitative factors are involved. Finance has primary responsibility for the quantitative aspects of controlling.

The processes of planning and controlling are complex. The quantitative techniques include a number of tools of financial analysis: (1) ratio analysis; (2) the formation of financial standards, objectives, and goals; (3) financial forecasting; and (4) budgeting. This chapter deals with financial ratio analysis; the remaining topics are treated in succeeding chapters.

THE LOGIC OF FINANCIAL ANALYSIS

Ratio analysis, like the other tools of financial analysis, is based on a logical relationship between underlying business operations and the accounting or financial representation of those activities. The analysis of the cash flow cycle demonstrated how various business activities, such as the purchase of raw materials, production and manufacturing activity, the sale of goods on credit, and the collection of accounts receivable, all were reflected in corresponding changes in the financial statements. In a like manner, the operations of a business firm generally follow the same logic in that the underlying production, sales, personnel, and the other operations of the firm are reflected in their financial consequences. Five types of ratios are discussed: activity, cost structure, leverage, liquidity, and profitability.

The logical relation between the financial ratios is shown in Figure 3–1. The top goal or objective which represents the keystone in the arch of planning and control is overall profitability. Here the term *profitability* is used in a broad, long-run sense. This is a result of two broad sets of forces. The first set represents standards of performance ratios. The activity ratios measure how effectively the firm is managing its investments in assets. The cost-structure ratios measure

FIGURE 3–1

Relations between financial ratios

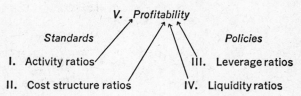

how effectively the firm is managing the control of its costs.

The second set is represented by financial policy ratios. Leverage ratios measure the extent to which the firm finances its investments and operations by the use of debt. Liquidity ratios measure the balance in the firm's cash flows. The liquidity and leverage ratios reflect management policies. Up to a point, decreasing liquidity and increasing leverage will increase the profitability of the firm. But if carried too far, leverage and illiquidity can lead to losses and insolvency of the firm. Profitability ratios measure the firm's overall effectiveness of operations and policies. Therefore, each individual ratio is first explained, and then a broad view of the use of ratios in the effective management and valuation of the firm will be discussed.

Indicate whether each of the following statements is true or false by writing "T" or "F" in the space provided.

———— 1. Finance has primary responsibility for the quantitative aspects of controlling.

———— 2. Activity, cost structure, leverage, and liquidity ratios relate to the underlying structure of a firm that determines its profitability.

———— 3. The activity ratios measure how effectively the firm is managing its liabilities while the cost-structure ratios measure how effectively the firm is managing its investment in assets.

———— 4. Leverage ratios measure the extent to which the firm finances its operations and investments by the use of debt while liquidity ratios measure the firm's ability to meet short-term obligations with cash.

Now turn to Answer Frame 1³, page 12, to check your answers.

Answer frame 1³

1. True. The processes of planning and controlling are complex. Among the quantitative techniques included in financial analysis are: (1) ratio analysis; (2) the formation of financial standards, objectives, and goals; (3) financial forecasting; and (4) budgeting.
2. True. The major objective of any enterprise is its long-term profitability. These sets of ratios assist in the understanding of the historical decision making in a firm and are the basis for predictions of future profitability results.
3. False. The activity ratios measure how effectively the firm is managing its investment in assets. These ratios all involve comparisons between the level of sales and the investment in various assets: cash, inventories, accounts receivable, and fixed assets. The cost-structure ratios measure how effectively the firm is managing the control of its costs.
4. True. The liquidity and leverage ratios reflect financial decision-making policies and are interrelated. For example, the increase in debt incurs additional interest payments which must be paid when due or the firm will be in default and subject to bankruptcy. As interest payments become larger the cash flows available for other commitments are reduced—which reduces the firm's liquidity cushion.

If you missed any of the above, reread Frame 1³ before starting Frame 2³, below.

Frame 2³

FINANCIAL RATIOS AND COMPUTATION PROCEDURES

For each financial ratio: first, the method of measurement or calculation will be described; second, the nature of the information conveyed by the financial ratio will be explained. To provide for a concrete illustration of the calculations, the Jones Company is assumed to have been in operation for several years and has reached a level of sales of $4 million per year. The financial statements of a firm are strongly influenced by its industry classification and by its size. In this initial presentation, the influences of size on the financial characteristics of a firm are emphasized. The ratios calculated for the Jones Company are based on the data in Table 3–1 which presents the balance sheet data as of December 31, 197A, and the income statement for the year ending December 31, 197A.

The balance sheet composition and the income statement relationships presented in Table 3–1 reflect the characteristic or normal pattern for a firm whose sales are in the $1- to $5-million range. (Note: The sources utilized were the Federal Trade Commission–Securities and Exchange Commission's *Quarterly Financial Report for Manufacturing Companies*, [U.S. Government Printing Office, 1971]; and Robert Morris Associates, *Annual Statement Studies* [Philadelphia· 1971].) Table 3–2 shows the method of calculating the ratios. Their measurement and implications are next set forth beginning with the activity ratios.

I. ACTIVITY RATIOS

Activity ratios measure how effectively the firm is managing the investment in its assets. The amount of sales represents the basic forecasting or causal variable in financial ratio analysis, budgeting, and financial forecasting.

1. Inventory turnover. If inventory turnover is low, it may have two undesirable consequences. One is that inventories are excessive, indicating that the firm is inefficient in inventory control. This will have a depressing effect on profitability. If inventory turnover is low, the risk is higher that some obsolete or otherwise unsalable inventories continue to be carried. If some inventories are obsolete, the current asset figure, which includes inventories and which is an overall indicator of liquidity, would be overstated. If the sales to inventory ratio is unusually high in relationship to the average for the industry, the firm might be losing sales because of lack of adequate

TABLE 3–1

JONES COMPANY
Balance Sheet
December 31, 198A

Assets				Liabilities and Stockholders' Equity		
		Amount	Percent		Amount	Percent
Current assets:				Current liabilities:		
1. Cash.............		$ 200,000	10	9. Accounts payable.............	$ 300,000	15
2. Receivables, net...		500,000	25	10. Notes payable 8%.............	200,000	10
3. Inventories........		500,000	25	11. Accruals.......................	80,000	4
4. Total Current				12. Provisions for federal income		
Assets...........		$1,200,000	60	taxes.......................	20,000	1
Fixed assets:				13. Total Current Liabilities........	$ 600,000	30
5. Gross plant and				Long-term liabilities:		
equipment......	$1,500,000			14. Long-term debt at 8%..........	$ 300,000	15
6. Less allowance for				15. Total debt....................	$ 900,000	45
depreciation.....	700,000			Stockholders equity:		
7. Net plant and				16. Common stock................	$ 300,000	15
equipment......		800,000	40	17. Retained earnings............	800,000	40
8. Total Assets.......		$2,000,000	100	18. Stockholders' Equity...........	$1,100,000	55
				19. Total Liabilities and Stock-		
				holders' Equity..............	$2,000,000	100

JONES COMPANY
Income Statement
Year Ending December 31, 198A

		Amount	Percent
Net sales...		$4,000,000	100
Less cost of sales excluding depreciation...........		2,800,000	70
Gross Profit.......................................		$1,200,000	30
Less operating expenses:			
Selling and delivery expense......................	$400,000		10
Officer's salaries.................................	120,000		3
Other general and administrative expense..........	200,000		5
Lease rentals.....................................	40,000		1
Total operating expenses excluding depreciation.....		760,000	19
Net operating profit excluding depreciation...........		440,000	11
Depreciation (8% of gross plant and equipment).....		120,000	3
Net Operating Income............................		$ 320,000	8
Add: Other income.................................			
Royalties.....................................		40,000	1
Earnings before Interest and Taxes..............		$ 360,000	9
Less:			
Interest on notes payable.........................	$ 16,000		
Interest on long-term debt........................	24,000	40,000	1
Earnings before income tax........................		$ 320,000	8
Tax at 40%..		128,000	
Net Income Available to Stockholders..........		$ 192,000	4.8

inventory stocks on hand. Undesirable consequences would include reduced sales and under-utilization of fixed assets.

2. Average collection period. To measure the average collection period, first determine credit sales per day by dividing total credit sales by 360. Then divide the resulting figure into accounts receivable. The result is the average col-

lection period which is compared to credit terms of the industry. An average collection period in substantial excess of the industry average term or duration of credit suggests the possibility that unsound credit policies exist, or that the firm is experiencing serious collection problems with at least some of its accounts. An average collection period in excess of the industry average will be

TABLE 3-2
Summary of financial ratios

A. Name of ratio	B. Formula for calculation	C. Calculation	D. Financial ratio
I. Activity ratios:			
1. Inventory turnover	$= \dfrac{\text{Sales}}{\text{Inventory}}$	$= \dfrac{\$4,000,000}{\$500,000}$	$= 8x$
2. Average Collection period	$= \dfrac{\text{Receivables}}{\text{Sales per day}}$	$= \$500,000 \Big/ \dfrac{\$4,000,000}{360}$	$= 45$ days
3. Fixed assets turnover	$= \dfrac{\text{Sales}}{\text{Fixed assets}}$	$= \dfrac{\$4,000,000}{\$800,000}$	$= 5x$
4. Total asset turnover	$= \dfrac{\text{Sales}}{\text{Total assets}}$	$= \dfrac{\$4,000,000}{\$2,000,000}$	$= 2x$
II. Cost structure ratios.			
5. Gross profit margin	$=$ Sales − Cost of sales (excluding depreciation and rentals) to Sales	$= \dfrac{\$4,000,000 - \$2,800,000}{\$4,000,000}$	$= 30\%$
6. Selling expense ratio	$=$ Selling expense to Sales	$= \dfrac{\$400,000}{\$4,000,000}$	$= 10\%$
7. G&A ratio	$=$ General and administrative expenses to Sales	$= \dfrac{\$320,000}{\$4,000,000}$	$= 8\%$
8. Depreciation plus lease rentals	$=$ Depreciation + Lease rentals to Sales	$= \dfrac{\$120,000 + 40,000}{\$4,000,000}$	$= 4\%$
III. Leverage ratios.			
9. Leverage ratio	$= \dfrac{\text{Total debt}}{\text{Total assets}}$	$= \dfrac{\$900,000}{\$2,000,000}$	$= 45\%$
10. Fixed charges coverage	$= \dfrac{\text{EBIT} + \text{Rentals}}{\text{Fixed charges}}$	$= \dfrac{\$360,000 + \$40,000}{\$105,000}$	$= 3.8x$
IV. Liquidity ratios:			
11. Current ratio	$= \dfrac{\text{Current assets}}{\text{Current liabilities}}$	$= \dfrac{\$1,200,000}{\$600,000}$	$= 2.0x$
12. Quick ratio	$= \dfrac{\text{Current assets} - \text{Inventories}}{\text{Current liabilities}}$	$= \dfrac{\$1,200,000 - \$500,000}{\$600,000}$	$= 1.2x$
V. Profitability ratios:			
13. Profit margin sales	$= \dfrac{\text{Net income}}{\text{Sales}}$	$= \dfrac{\$192,000}{\$4,000,000}$	$= 4.8\%$
14. Return on total assets	$= \dfrac{\text{Net income} + \text{Interest}}{\text{Total assets}}$	$= \dfrac{\$192,000 + \$40,000}{\$2,000,000}$	$= 11.6\%$
15. Return on net worth	$= \dfrac{\text{Net income}}{\text{Net worth}}$	$= \dfrac{\$192,000}{\$1,100,000}$	$= 17.5\%$

associated with a low receivables turnover. This may be an indicator of two potentially unfavorable developments. One is that bad debt writeoffs may occur. The second is that if some of the receivables are in fact uncollectible, the balance sheet value of the accounts receivable is overstated. Therefore, the firm may not be as liquid as the total current assets figure would ostensibly indicate.

3. Fixed asset turnover. The fixed asset turnover is measured by dividing the total net value of plant and equipment into sales. To the extent that a firm leases its plant or equipment, a substantial portion of its fixed assets will not show up on the balance sheet. Therefore, without a consideration of lease rentals in conjunction with other financial ratios, the fixed asset turnover of the firm cannot properly be evaluated. One method of taking into account the role of leases is to capitalize lease rentals and add the resulting figure to the firm's fixed assets and (as well as) to its debt.

4. Total asset turnover. The total asset turnover will be greatly influenced both by the size of the firm and by the nature of the industry. The largest firms tend to be found predominantly in capital-intensive industries—industries that require heavy investments in plant and machinery to produce their products, such as chemicals, petroleum, automobiles, and steel.

Small firms predominate in the least capital-intensive industries, so the ratios for small firms are likely to reflect their smaller use of fixed assets and their greater use of leased assets. Small firms would be expected to have a total asset turnover of two times or more. Large firms are more likely to have total asset turnovers of between one and one and a half times.

Label each of the following statements as true or false.

———— 1. Industry classification and size of the firm both strongly influence the financial statements of a firm.

———— 2. The inventory turnover ratio can never be too high.

———— 3. An average collection period substantially less than the industry average suggests the existence of outstanding credit management policies.

———— 4. Fixed asset turnover and total asset turnover ratios can assist in uncovering potential problem areas.

Now check your answers by turning to Answer Frame 2³, page 16.

Frame 3³

II. COST-STRUCTURE RATIOS

The cost-structure ratios are the most critical of all financial ratios. Costs represent a continuous flow which if out of control can quickly lead to an erosion of profitability and result in bankruptcy for the firm. However, costs are also amenable to corrective actions by the firm's managers. While relatively little information is provided on the structure of the income statement, analysis of the structure of costs is highly important in internal operations. (Information on cost structures for a relatively large number of industries is provided in the *Annual Statement Studies,* of Robert Morris Associates, previously mentioned.)

5. Gross profit margin. The first of the four cost-structure ratios is the gross profit margin. This ratio indicates the margin available for covering all of the other functions that have to be performed to achieve the final sale of the goods. Obviously the required gross profit margin figure will vary widely among industries. For firms that are too small to have their own selling operations and pay 15 to 25 percent for the use of sales representatives or sales agents, the gross profit margin necessarily must be somewhat higher than 30 percent if any profits are to remain. For those particular industries in which research and development as well as considerable selling effort have to be performed, the gross profit margin may need to be as high as 50 percent.

6. Selling and delivery expense ratio. This is likely to be in the range of 10 percent for large firms in most lines of business. If the firm has its own sales organization and the volume is high, and if technical engineering expenses involved in sales are relatively modest, the selling expense ratio may be somewhat less than 10 percent.

7. General and administrative expense ratio. This ratio measures the cost of the overall corporate level functions to be performed in the firm. It includes such items as officer's salaries, travel, and telephone. The control of general and administrative expenses is important because it involves a degree of self-regulation by the officers of the firm. Hence, it is a critical ratio in the analysis by outsiders seeking to appraise the firm's performance.

Answer frame 2³

1. True. The concrete illustration of the Jones Company emphasizes the financial character of a firm whose sales are in the $1 to $5 million range.
2. False. The firm might be losing sales because of a lack of adequate inventory stocks on hand which could lead to lost sales and underutilization of plant and equipment.
3. False. This is a possibility; however, loss of sales can occur because of too stringent and tight credit standards. Many times firms will extend credit as a marketing strategy to increase sales. As long as the additional cost of extending credit is less than the income on the additional sales generated, the policy will benefit the firm.
4. True. Total asset turnover ratios can assist in evaluating how effectively the firm is managing its total assets; whereas, the fixed asset turnover isolates the evaluation of the investment required in fixed assets. For example, a total asset turnover ratio could be in a satisfactory range when compared to its industry composite, while at the same time a poor fixed asset turnover ratio may be offset by an exceptionally good inventory turnover ratio.

If you missed any of the above, reread Frame 2³ before starting Frame 3³, page 15.

Frame 3³ continued

8. Depreciation plus lease rentals. This represents major elements of expense involved in the utilization of the firm's fixed assets. If most fixed assets have long lives, the ratio of depreciation to gross plant and equipment and to sales will be somewhat lower than for short lives, assuming the same ratio of sales to fixed assets. The rentals have been added to the depreciation figure because they represent a cost of obtaining the use of assets.

True or false?

_____ 1. Among the most critical financial ratios are the cost-structure ratios.

_____ 2. The gross profit margin indicates the profits available for covering all the functions necessary to achieve the final sale of goods, and the ratio usually does not vary among industries.

_____ 3. The general and administrative expense ratio usually varies very little from year to year, and hence it is not too important.

_____ 4. Depreciation plus lease rentals will be somewhat high if the fixed assets have short lives and the lease obligations of a firm are quite high.

Now check your answers by turning to Answer Frame 3³, page 18.

Frame 4³

III. LEVERAGE RATIOS

Leverage and liquidity policies will be influenced by how fully the firm has utilized its assets and by how well the firm has managed the control of its costs. To some extent the liquidity and leverage ratios are interrelated. For example, if a firm uses a considerable amount of current debt this will decrease the current ratio, but it will also increase the total debt unless long-term debt is offset to an equal degree. This also illustrates that liquidity ratios are not the same as leverage ratios. If a firm substituted long-term debt for short-term debt, its current ratio would be increased; but if it had an excessive amount of long-term debt, it might face insolvency problems because of large fixed interest requirements.

Short-term creditors of the firm are most concerned with liquidity ratios because they provide the key to the firm's ability to meet its maturing short-term obligations. Longer term creditors of the firm are more concerned about the firm's total debt and the performance of the activity and cost-structure ratios which will greatly influence the firm's long-term profitability—the ultimate source of paying its long-term obligations.

Creditors also have a direct interest in leverage ratios because the percent of total assets financed by the owners represents the margin of safety by which the value of total assets can decline on liquidation and still meet the obligations to creditors. Thus, for the Jones Company balance sheet set forth, the owners' funds have financed 55 percent of total assets. Therefore, on liquidation, total assets could decline in value by 55 percent and still meet all obligations owed to creditors. Creditors are also interested in the ability of the firms to meet their fixed obligations, which explains the use of the fixed charge coverage ratio.

9. Leverage ratio. The debt ratio, or the degree of leverage employed by the firm, is the ratio of total debt to total assets. A broad rule of thumb is that the owners should have at least as much funds in the business as the creditors. The Jones Company is approaching this limit. Creditors obviously prefer lower debt ratios since they provide a greater cushion against losses in the event of liquidation. Owners may seek high leverage in order to control more assets and to magnify earnings. Extremely high debt ratios may result in irresponsible shoestring operations by the owners. Thus, while owners may seek to have very high debt ratios, the market may be unwilling to provide debt beyond a safe limit.

10. Fixed charge coverage. The fixed charge coverage ratio (also called times fixed charges earned or times interest earned) is calculated by dividing the income available for meeting fixed charges by the total fixed charges. The total amount of fixed charges includes interest payments, lease payments, and before-tax sinking fund payments. It is assumed that the sinking fund requirement on the Jones Company long-term debt is $15,000 per year. The numerator represents earnings before interest and taxes (EBIT) plus fixed charges such as lease rentals.

A sinking fund is a requirement of a bond issue that an annual amount be set aside in connection with the repayment of the bond. Sinking fund payments represent repayment of a debt and therefore do not represent an expense deductible for income tax purposes. Therefore, the firm must earn enough profit before taxes to be able to pay its taxes and then be able to meet the sinking fund requirements with the remainder. With a tax rate of 40 percent, $25,000 must be earned to meet the sinking fund requirement of $15,000:

$$\text{Before-tax income required for sinking fund payment} = \frac{\text{Sinking fund payment}}{1.0 - \text{Tax rate}}$$
$$= \frac{\$15,000}{1.0 - 0.4} = \frac{\$15,000}{0.6}$$
$$= \$25,000$$

A broad rule of thumb of fixed charge coverage for a manufacturing company is that it should range from four to seven times. This allows for some decline in gross income before financial embarrassment might be encountered from inability to meet fixed charges.

Is each of the following true or false?
_____ 1. Liquidity ratios are not the same as leverage ratios but they are interrelated.
_____ 2. Both short-term and long-term creditors are primarily concerned with the firm's long-term profitability.
_____ 3. Leverage ratios represent the margin of safety by which the value of total assets can decline on liquidation and still meet the obligations to creditors.
_____ 4. Owners and creditors both seek high-leverage ratios since high leverage magnifies earnings.

Now check your answers with those in Answer Frame 4³, page 18.

Answer frame 3³

1. True. Costs represent a continuous cash outflow which can result in the firm being unable to meet its fixed commitments and lead to bankruptcy. Effective management cost controls are necessary for firms to achieve their profit goals.
2. False. The gross profit margin does indicate the profits necessary for covering all the functions necessary to achieve the final sale of goods, but it usually does vary among industries. Some firms (usually small) have no sales organization while others have a large sales organization in addition to a large research and development organization.
3. False. The general and administrative expense may or may not vary but its level is important. The control of officer's salaries, travel, telephoning, and so on is important as it provides insight into the degree of self-regulation by the officers or top managers of the firm.
4. True. Short lives of assets result in relatively high annual depreciation charges. Also in recent years lease rentals in particular have become sizable in relation to total assets.

If you missed any of the above, restudy Frame 3³ before beginning Frame 4³, page 16.

Answer frame 4³

1. True. They are interrelated because the desired mix on the use of long-term versus short-term debt will affect the current ratio. The current ratio is a measure of liquidity whereas the debt-to-equity ratio measures the leverage of a firm.
2. False. Both short-term and long-term creditors are concerned with long-term profitability, but short-term creditors are *primarily* concerned with liquidity. They depend on receiving cash payments in the short run.
3. True. For example, the total assets of the Jones Company on liquidation could decline in value by 55 percent and still meet all obligations owed to creditors.
4. False. Owners do generally prefer higher debt ratios since earnings can be enhanced. But creditors prefer lower debt ratios since they provide a greater protection against failure to meet large fixed interest charges.

If you missed any of the above, reread Frame 4³ before starting Frame 5³, below.

Frame 5³

IV. LIQUIDITY RATIOS

Liquidity ratios measure the firm's ability to meet its maturing obligations. A large number of liquidity ratios could be employed, but most aspects of liquidity are conveyed by two ratios.

11. Current ratio. The current ratio is current assets divided by current liabilities. A widely employed bankers' rule of thumb is that the current ratio should be at least 2. This provides for a shrinkage in the value of the current assets by 50 percent before the firm is unable to meet its maturing short-term obligations.

12. Quick ratio. In calculating the quick ratio, inventories are deducted from current assets and the remainder is divided by current liabilities. The logic of this calculation is that inventories are likely to be the least liquid of a firm's current assets in that the loss ratio is likely to be higher on inventories if forced liquidation is required. A widely used rule of thumb for the quick ratio is 1, implying that inventories are normally about half of current assets.

V. PROFITABILITY RATIOS

The profitability ratios reflect the results of the preceding four sets of ratios. They measure the joint effects of the extent to which the firm has met its standards with regard to activity and cost-structure performance, balanced against the policies the firm selects with regard to liquidity and leverage ratios. At least three profitability measures should be utilized because of variability in accounting measures of revenues and costs as well as variability in the measurement of balance sheet values.

13. Profit margin on sales. The profit margin on sales is net income after taxes available to the owners of the firm divided by total sales. It measures the percent by which the selling price of the firm's products could decline before the firm suffers losses.

14. Return on total assets. The return on total assets is measured by adding back interest to net income after taxes and dividing by total as-

sets. It is a measure of the after-tax profitability with which the firm's total resources have been employed. This is sometimes referred to as the return on investment (ROI), but Chapter 4 gives a preferred method of calculating ROI.

15. Return on net worth. The return on net worth (stockholders' equity) measures the overall results of operations from the owners' standpoint. The return on net worth reflects both the profitability with which total investment or total assets have been employed and how effectively the firm has utilized leverage. Since the numbers in Table 3–1 were chosen to reflect the characteristics of firms with $4 million of sales, the resulting ratios in Table 3–2 correspond to a broad set of standards or norms.

Label each of the following statements as true or false.

———— 1. The current ratio is a liquidity ratio that is widely employed by bankers as it primarily provides an indication of the firm's ability to meet its long-term obligations.

———— 2. If inventories, the most liquid of the current assets, are costly and of a specialized nature, the quick ratio is of little assistance in evaluating a firm's liquidity condition.

———— 3. Profit margin (before interest but after taxes) on sales multiplied by the total asset turnover yields the return on total assets.

———— 4. Profit margin on sales, return on investment, and return on net worth measure the extent to which the firm has met its standards with regard to activity and cost-structure performance, balanced against the policies the firm selects with regard to liquidity and leverage ratios.

Now check your answers with those in Answer Frame 5[3], page 20.

Frame 6[3]

EVALUATION OF FINANCIAL RATIOS

The preceding discussion raises the question of how the ratios for individual companies are to be evaluated. Two broad methods are utilized: One is to make a comparison with industry composites; a second is to analyze historical trends.

The use of industry composites. Two types of industry composites are widely used. The first is from Dun & Bradstreet (D&B) published periodically in *Dun's*, a monthly magazine. Fourteen ratios similar to those described in this chapter are calculated. The ratios are compiled from

financial statements collected by Dun & Bradstreet's reporters in connection with establishing the ratings reported in Dun & Bradstreet's reference books, organized by individual industries.

A second set of ratios is provided by Robert Morris Associates (RMA), the National Association of Bank Loan and Credit Officers. While RMA's annual statement studies do not provide an analysis by quartiles as do the D & B ratios, it groups the ratios by size of firm and presents 11 financial ratios similar to those described in this chapter.

A comparison of individual ratios with industry

Answer frame 5³

1. False. The current ratio is a liquidity ratio primarily designed to assist in the evaluation of the firm's ability to meet its short-term obligations.
2. False. Inventories are usually the least liquid of current assets, which is precisely why they are removed or subtracted from current assets in the quick ratio calculation. The quick ratio is widely used by bankers for this reason.
3. True. When the return on total assets ratio is low it is useful to trace back through the total asset turnover ratio and/or the profit margin (before interest but after taxes) on sales for possible corrective action to try to improve the profitability of the firm.
4. True. These three profitability ratios are the end results of all the preceding ratios. Or rather, these profitability ratios measure the end results of the major decision making in the firm.

If you missed any of the above, restudy Frame 5³ before turning to Frame 6³, page 19.

Frame 6³ continued

composites is useful as a starting point. It is not determinate, however. The product characteristics of the individual firm may differ somewhat from those of the industry as a whole. In addition, there may be specific policies followed by the firm which make its situation somewhat different from that of the industry. But an important value of comparing the individual firm with the industry is that if differences are observed, there is a basis for raising the significant analytical questions. Why are the ratios different? What distinct and different policies are being followed? What is the basis for these different policies? Under what economic conditions would these policies be particularly advantageous? Under what economic and financial circumstances would different policies of the firm be undesirable or unfavorable? These are the kinds of questions that can be raised by a comparison of the individual firm's ratios with those of industry composites.

The analysis of historical trends. Trends in the industry composite ratios are compared with trends in the ratios of the individual firm, the Jones Company. An error in any management policy will show up in many individual firm's ratios as compared with trends in composite ratios for the industry. Suppose, for example, that the average collection period for the Jones Company went up sharply due to the lengthening of credit terms or to slow collections in 197A. The inventory turnover would not be affected, but the total asset turnover would decline. With the excessive investment in receivables, the gross

profit margin would probably decline. Excessive receivables are likely to result in a higher bad debt ratio and possibly increased office personnel expenses in the effort to return collections to normal. Thus, the general and administrative expense ratio might also rise.

If the excessive receivables were financed by current debt, the current ratio would also decline, even if receivables and current debt increased by the same amount. The quick ratio would also decline for similar reasons. The total debt to total assets ratio would increase because current debt would have increased without a corresponding increase in stockholders' equity. Furthermore, if the gross profit margin has decreased and the amount of debt (and therefore the amount of interest) has increased, it is likely that the times interest earned ratio will also decline. With the lower profit margins, the return on total assets will also decline, and in addition the ratio of net profits to sales will decline. Whether the return on net worth declines depends upon the influence of the two opposing pressures. If profit margins decrease, it will tend to reduce the return on net worth. Thus unsound management policies in one single area are reflected in most of the other individual financial ratios as compared with the time trend of industry composites.

But comparisons with industry composites need not be determinative. Since there may be valid reasons why the financial ratios of an individual firm depart from those of its industry, such divergences do not necessarily indicate a pathological condition on the part of the individual firm. Much importance is placed on the comparative time trend of the individual firm's ratios. If over time the ratios are deteriorating in relation to the industry composites, the basis for inquiry and analysis is increased.

The two main uses of financial ratios are comparisons with industry averages and time trend analysis. Financial ratio analysis has many uses.

An important function is its use by the chief executive and financial managers for overall planning and control and for control of divisional operations. Financial analysis is also used by outside creditors and by security analysts. Financial ratio analysis has many applications and is used throughout the development of subsequent topics of financial management.

True or false?

_____ 1. When comparing the individual firm's ratios with industry composites, differences can point out significant problem areas.

_____ 2. When trends in the industry composite ratios are compared with trends in the ratios of the individual firm, a specific management policy may be reflected in many of the firm's ratios.

_____ 3. Divergences of a firm's ratios from industry trend composites may indicate a strengthened financial condition for the firm.

_____ 4. Financial ratio analysis has very little use as industry classifications become less and less clear.

Now turn to Answer Frame 6³, page 22, to check your answers.

Answer frame 6³

1. True. Comparisons with industry composites and the analysis of historical trends are the two primary methods used in ratio analysis. In addition, firms will sometimes select several close competitors with which to compare their performance.

2. True. For example, the average collection period for the Jones Company increased, and this effect was apparent in the total asset turnover ratio, the gross profit margin, general and administrative expense ratio, the current ratio, the quick ratio, the total debt to total assets ratio, the times interest earned ratio, the profit margin on sales, and the return on total assets.

3. True. Industry composites or industry averages incorporate, in many cases, a large number of firms. Extreme values or a large number of unprofitable firms may distort the average. Ratios of individual firms and industry averages are tools of financial analysis and should only be used to indicate weaknesses or strengths. Further detailed analysis is usually necessary to uncover the reasons for any significant deviation.

4. False. Financial ratio analysis is used by many chief executives, financial managers, investment analysts, and many others in evaluating the comparative performances of firms. Merger activity and diversification efforts in the last decade have complicated the industry classifications, but financial ratio analysis is still an extremely valuable financial tool.

If you missed any of the above, restudy Frame 6³ before beginning Chapter 4, page 23.

chapter 4

FINANCIAL PLANNING AND CONTROL

Frame 1[4]

As explained in Chapter 3, financial ratio analysis is one of the important tools in developing a planning and control system. The next step is the use of historical patterns and other information to develop standards for planning and control as illustrated in what is widely referred to as the *du Pont system.*

I. ROI PLANNING AND CONTROL

An extension of traditional financial ratio analysis is the return on investment (ROI), or du Pont chart system of planning and control. The du Pont chart system was developed with emphasis on the effective managerial control of divisional operations. But even in nonprofit operations similar types of control problems are found. A planning and control system provides a framework for improving managerial control of investments or costs.

The basic du Pont chart (Figure 4–1) presents an analysis of not only the asset side of the balance sheet but also elements of the income statement. Since the corporate level of the firm is responsible for policies with regard to leverage and liquidity and its related tax effects, these policies are not involved in the analysis of divisional performance. The fundamental principle involved in the analysis is that division managers should be held responsible only for those areas of activity for which they have authority.

In Figure 4–1 the data presented in Table 3–1

are now utilized with an emphasis on control of divisional operations. The total asset, or total investment, figure is the total of current assets plus the gross fixed assets ($1,200,000 + $1,500,000 = $2,700,000). In the control of divisional operations, the fixed asset figure used is gross rather than net. The use of net assets would create an incentive not to replace assets because the longer fixed assets are held, the lower their net value will be. Therefore, the less the total investment, the higher their turnover would be and the higher the indicated "profit" would be.

This principle can be applied to evaluating firms as well as divisions. For a given line of business, there should be an appropriate relationship between the net plant and equipment and gross plant and equipment. If the ratio of net to gross plant and equipment is less than 30 percent, the firm has been laggard in replacing its assets; a danger signal. In this case there is a high probability that the firm or a division has obsolete fixed assets. If the ratio is high, it would indicate either that the firm is new or that it has recently undertaken considerable replacement of its gross plant and equipment.

The cost elements shown in the du Pont chart are similar to those shown on the income statement. Since the corporate level is responsible for all interest expenses, they are not included in the total cost figure shown in the chart. Sales less total costs before interest expenses represents net operating income, the appropriate figure for use in control in divisional operations. The ratio of

23

FIGURE 4–1
Du Pont System Of Financial Control Of Divisions

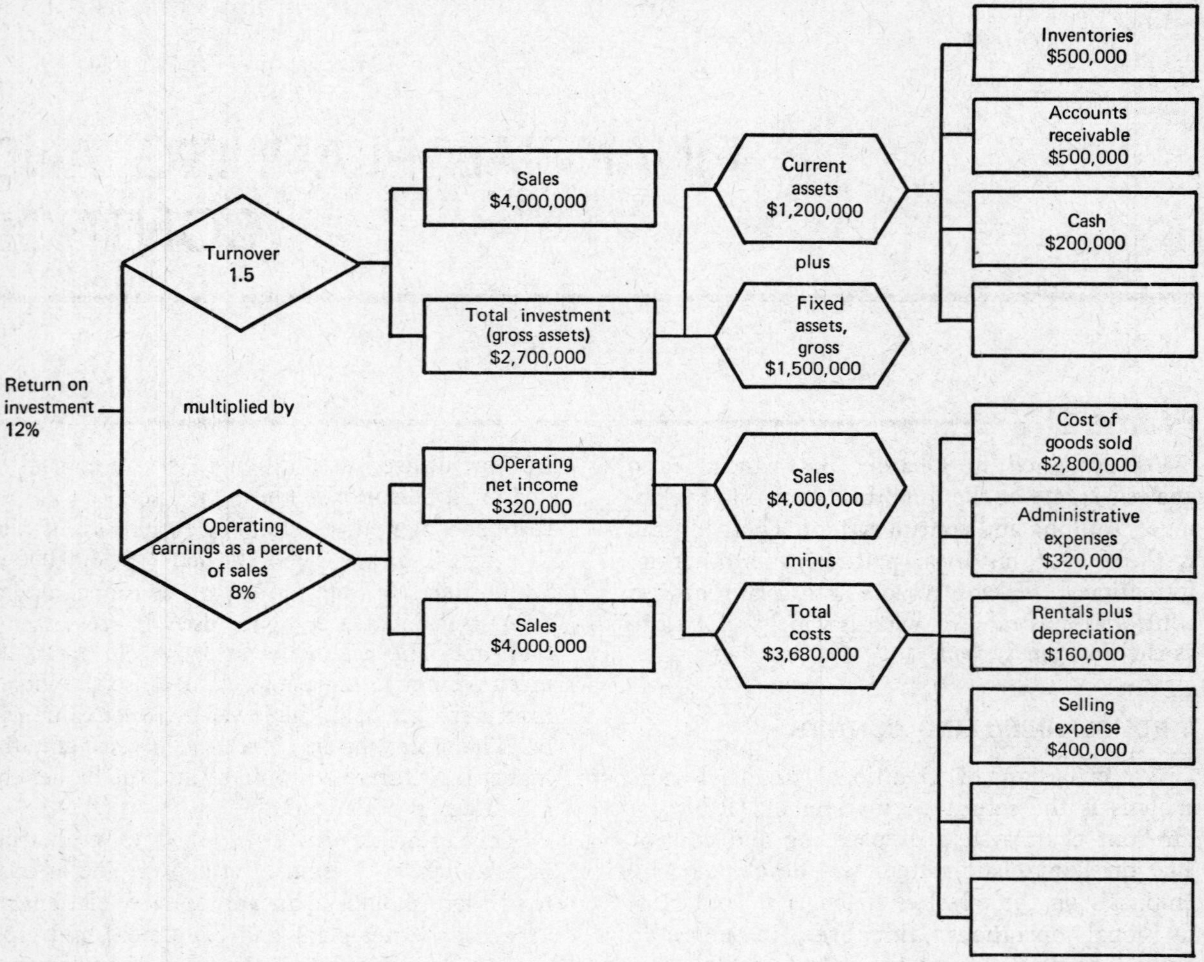

net operating income to sales is the net operating profit margin on sales.

The Turnover multiplied by Operating Margin on Sales is the return on investment (ROI). This return on investment figure of 12 percent cannot be compared with the ratio of return on total assets figure usually calculated from the firm's standpoint since it is on gross assets. Suppose that there is an overinvestment in current assets so that it becomes $2,500,000. Total investment would then become $4,000,000. Turnover would drop to 1.0 times, and ROI would drop to 8 per cent. This example illustrates one of the values of the du Pont chart of control. It illustrates all factors that measure the efficiency of managing

the company's investments and the efficiency of controlling its costs.

If the excess investment of $1,300,000 were in gross fixed assets, two adverse effects on ROI result from raising that figure to $2,800,000. The turnover would drop to 1.0 times, as before. And, in addition, if depreciation continued to average 8 percent of gross fixed assets, the depreciation charge would be increased by $104,000 so that depreciation and rentals would become $264,000. Total costs would rise and net operating income would decline to $216,000, or 5.4 percent of sales. At the turnover of 1.0 times, the ROI would drop from 12.0 percent to 5.4 percent.

IMPLEMENTATION OF PLANNING AND CONTROL PROCESSES

It should be emphasized that the du Pont chart is not to be employed in a static or mechanical way; it should be employed as a dynamic process. For example, sales expense might rise because a rival firm has engaged in a strong advertising campaign or has given its salesmen extra commissions to stimulate additional efforts. It may be necessary for the division to meet this new competitive threat and therefore the division's selling expenses may rise, temporarily causing ROI to decline. The competitive alternative may be a substantial decline in sales and perhaps a loss of a "share of the market," which is generally difficult to recover.

Alternatively, during a given quarter selling prices might drop because of an influx of lower price imports. Thus, at the same volume the total dollar sales might drop. The most effective competitive response to this may involve policy changes beyond the scope of divisional responsibility. A longer range view should also be taken into account. Suppose the firm incurs a large amount of additional applications-engineering ex-

penses in a given quarter. This would cause current costs to rise and current profitability to drop, but it would provide the basis for an increase in future profits from an improved product which produces increased sales in the longer term.

Thus, the targets and standards by which managers seek to make the goals of the firm operational are not ends in themselves. Rather, they should be viewed as management instruments for engendering healthy processes in the firm. Targets and standards can be employed to contribute to an information and feedback process that is dynamic in quality, has favorable effects on the development on the firm's personnel, and can facilitate quick reaction to change.

The ROI system of planning and control is a useful vehicle for assembling relevant information. It is not critical whether that information is focused on ROI or on other "organization objectives." ROI is useful in providing information on every element of the balance sheet and income statement as a basis for further analysis. For these reasons the ROI approach is the most widely used system for developing effective planning and control processes.

Indicate whether each of the following statements is true or false by writing "T" or "F" in the space provided.

_____ 1. The du Pont chart system is an extension of financial ratio analysis for use in evaluating managerial control of divisional operations, but it should not be used for not-for-profit operations.

_____ 2. Fundamental in the analysis of division managers' performance is to include only that data on areas for which they have direct authority.

_____ 3. The reason for using gross fixed assets rather than net fixed assets is to encourage divisional managers to maintain a modern plant.

_____ 4. The turnover multiplied by operating margin on sales is the return on total assets as usually presented on balance sheets.

_____ 5. One of the values of the du Pont chart of control is that it measures the efficiency of managing the company's investments and the efficiency of controlling its costs.

Now turn to Answer Frame 1⁴, page 26, to check your answers.

Answer frame 1⁴

1. False. The ROI approach is the most widely used system for developing effective planning and control processes for both profit *and* not-for-profit organizations, since it is a framework for guiding the efficient use of resources.

2. True. Division managers should be held responsible only for those areas of activity for which they have authority. The exclusion of interest charges on debt in the ROI process, since this is a corporate responsibility, is an example of adhering to this fundamental principle.

3. True. The use of net assets would create an incentive not to replace assets because the longer fixed assets are held, the lower their net value will be. Therefore, the less the total investment, the higher their turnover and the greater the profits. The ratio of net to gross plant can provide an indication of the obsolescence of fixed assets.

4. False. The turnover multiplied by operating margin on sales is the "return on gross total assets or investment" and not return on net total assets. This is because we are using gross assets in the turnover ratio and operating net income in our profit margin ratio.

5. True. It shows their interrelationship and is helpful in tracing or pinpointing areas in need of correction to improve the profitability of the firm. It should be emphasized that the du Pont chart be used as a dynamic process and as a supplemental or prescreening type of device. ROI is useful in providing information on every item on the balance sheet and income statement as a basis for further analysis.

If you missed any of the above, restudy Frame 1⁴ before beginning Chapter 5 on page 27.

chapter 5

FINANCIAL FORECASTING

Frame 1[5]

Financial forecasting is a central responsibility of financial managers. Financial planning is essential to assure that the required funds are available for new facilities and for the personnel necessary for the growth and strengthening of the firm. Long-range planning is required both for assets and for other capabilities the firm will need in the future and for the financing required to obtain them. Long-term growth will generally require that funds be obtained from outside the firm through selling additional ownership stock and by incurring additional long-term debt. The cost and terms under which funds are obtained have major effects upon the firm's profitability and health, so they must be planned and analyzed carefully. Financial forecasting provides an important framework for all planning activities of the firm.

DEVELOPING STANDARDS FOR MAKING FORECASTS

To achieve sales which give rise to accounts receivable, a firm must have assets such as inventories and fixed plant with which to carry on manufacturing operations. Cash is required to carry on the transactions and operations of the business firm. Since assets are requisite to sales, a relation between sales volume and asset requirements will exist. Thus the underlying causal mechanism in financial forecasting is sales.

The well-known financial ratio composites provided by Dun & Bradstreet and by Robert Morris Associates in its *Statement Studies* can be used as standards for control and standards for forecasting. For example, suppose that the Dun &

Bradstreet median financial ratio composites for an industry are the following:

TABLE 5–1
Illustrative Dun & Bradstreet ratios

1.	Sales to net worth...............	4 times
2.	Average collection period..........	30 days
3.	Net sales to inventory..............	6 times
4.	Current ratio......................	2 times
5.	Fixed assets to net worth..........	80%
6.	Current debt to net worth..........	60%
7.	Total debt to net worth............	100%
8.	Profit to sales....................	5%
9.	Profit to net worth................	20%

Nine of the 14 ratios provided by Dun & Bradstreet are presented in Table 5–1. From these ratios a pro forma balance sheet can be developed for a sales volume of $120,000 (see Table 5–2).

In developing the pro forma balance sheet, the ratios were employed as standards or guides. In the same manner in which they were used to develop the balance sheet, they could also be used for financial planning and forecasting. Before illustrating this, it is useful to recognize that a

TABLE 5–2
Pro forma balance sheet

Cash.........................	$ 6,000	
Accounts receivable............	10,000	
Inventory.....................	20,000	
Current assets.................		$36,000
Fixed assets..................		24,000
		$60,000
Current debt..................		$18,000
Long-term debt................		12,000
Net worth....................		30,000
		$60,000

number of different ways of expressing these relationships are equivalent.

For example, the first three ratios listed in Table 5–1 are types of activity ratios. These are shown in Table 5–3, based on 360 days per year. The ratios are first expressed as turnovers. Thus, net worth is turned over into sales four times. Accounts receivable are turned over into sales 12 times. Inventory is turned over into sales six times.

But each of these turnovers can also be expressed as a percentage of sales. Net worth is 25 percent of sales. Accounts receivable are 8.3 percent of sales. In turn, each can be expressed as the number of days' sales in the item. For example, there are 90 days' sales in net worth and 30 days' sales in accounts receivable.

TABLE 5–4
Pro forma balance sheet number 2

Cash...........................	$ 9,000	
Accounts receivable...........	15,000	
Inventory.....................	30,000	
Current assets.................		$54,000
Fixed assets..................		36,000
		$90,000
Current debt..................		$27,000
Long-term debt...............		18,000
Net worth....................		45,000
		$90,000

These standards can be employed in forecasting the firm's financial requirements. If sales increase from $120,000 to $180,000 per annum, the balance sheet of Table 5–2 would change to the levels presented in Table 5–4.

The same type of logic can be employed for analyzing the cost elements in the income statement. By analyzing the cost-to-sales relationships over time, standards for cost control can also be developed.

TABLE 5–3

	Turnover (times)	Percent of sales	Number of days' sales
Sales to net worth............	4	25.0%	90
Sales to accounts receivable...................	12	8.3	30
Net sales to inventory.......	6	16.7	60

Indicate whether each of the following statements is true or false by writing "T" or "F" in the space provided.

_____ 1. The underlying causal requirement or the most important variable in financial forecasting is sales.

_____ 2. Since industry ratio composites are averages derived from a large number of firms, they are of little value in setting up standards for control and forecasting for an individual firm.

_____ 3. It is important to recognize that ratios can be expressed in many different ways, which makes them useful to evaluate efficiency of investment management, to calculate pro forma financial statements, and so on.

_____ 4. When using industry composites from Dun & Bradstreet, Robert Morris Associates, and others, it is not too important to verify how the calculation was made since ratio calculation is well developed and uniform in interpretation and use.

Now turn to Answer Frame 1[5], page 30, to check your answers.

Frame 2[5]

PERCENT OF SALES METHOD

The nature of the relationship between the firm's level of activity and its financing requirements is illustrated by the percent of sales method of forecasting financial requirements. Because the firm's assets, personnel, and other requirements are determined by the level of operations as indicated by total sales activity, financial planning in the firm starts with a forecast of sales.

The technique of forecasting sales is a subject developed at some length in economics and marketing books. Here it is assumed that a good sales forecast has been made by the responsible managers in the firm, recognizing that the financial manager may also participate in sales forecasting. Sound financial forecasting is dependent upon the reliability of the sales forecasts.

The percent of sales method of forecasting financial requirements is a powerful and useful tool. In Table 5–5, selected items from the balance sheet of the Jones Company are presented. The balance sheet of December 31, 198A, is related to sales of $4 million for the year 198A. For all items that are directly determined by sales, a percentage relationship is expressed. These relationships follow from the financial ratio analysis discussed previously in Chapter 2. Cash in the amount of 5 percent of sales is required to carry

TABLE 5–5

JONES COMPANY
Balance Sheet Items Expressed as a
Percentage of Sales*
December 31, 198A

Cash.....................................	5.0%
Receivables.............................	12.5
Inventories.............................	12.5
Fixed assets (net).......................	20.0
Total...............................	50.0%
Accounts payable........................	7.5%
Accrued taxes and wages.................	2.5
Other debt..............................	FPD
Common stock...........................	FPD
Retained earnings.......................	CPS
Total...............................	10.0%
Assets as a percentage of sales.........	50%
Less: Spontaneous increase in liabilities.......................	10
Percentage of Additional Sales to be Financed.................	40%

* Sales for the year 198A equal $4,000,000

on the transactions of the firm. Receivables and inventories each represent 12.5 percent of sales, while net fixed assets are 20 percent of sales.

Similarly, the Jones Company purchases materials and parts on credit, resulting in accounts payable shown as 7.5 percent of sales. Accrued taxes and wages represent 2.5 percent of sales. The remaining items in the liabilities or net worth section of the balance sheet are not directly determined by the current year's sales. For mortgage bonds and common stock the abbreviation FPD is employed to indicate that these amounts were determined by financial policy decisions.

Retained earnings are influenced by three factors: level of sales, profit rate, and dividend payout ratio. If the firm's profit is a constant percentage of sales and the dividend payout ratio is a constant percentage of profit, retained earnings will be a cumulative percentage of sales, as indicated by the abbreviation, CPS. For illustration, if profits after taxes are 5 percent of sales and the dividend payout is 50 percent of profit, each year retained earnings will be increased by 2.5 percent of that year's total sales.

A basis for forecasting financial requirements is thereby provided. Table 5–5 shows that for every $100 increase in sales, the investment in net assets will increase by $50. This is the basic amount that must be financed by the firm. Accounts payable and accruals, which also spontaneously increase with increases in sales, represent 10 percent of sales. These current liability items automatically increase with sales to provide $10 of additional funds for each $100 increase in sales. As a result, for each $100 increase in sales, the Jones Company must finance $40 from either retained earnings or external sources. Whether the Jones Company will be required to use external financing sources depends upon the dollar amount of increase in retained earnings as compared with the dollar amount of financing required.

Answer frame 1⁵

1. True. Since assets such as inventories and fixed plant are a requisite to sales, a relationship between sales volume and asset requirements will exist.
2. False. Even though the industry averages are derived from a large number of firms they are useful as guides and as one of many tools used in financial forecasting.
3. True. Ratio analysis uses financial data in many different ways depending upon the intended purpose of the user. The average collection period and the accounts receivable turnover ratio both use the same basic data and are intended to give insight into the credit and collection policies of a firm. They can be used also to assist in forecasting future levels of accounts receivable—as was done in the preceding development of a pro forma balance sheet.
4. False. Most finance textbooks recommend dividing average inventory into cost of goods sold rather than into sales. (The reason behind this is that the sales figure includes the profit margin, and the inventory turnover ratio is intended to measure or evaluate only inventory management.) Dun & Bradstreet divides average inventory into sales as they are unable, in many cases, to obtain comparable cost of goods sold figures across many firms.

If you missed any of the above, reread Frame 1⁵ before starting Frame 2⁵ on page 28.

Frame 2⁵ continued

Label each of the following statements as true or false.

——————— 1. The percentage of sales method for financial forecasting is primarily a method or technique used to forecast sales.

——————— 2. FPD is an abbreviation indicating items on the balance sheet that remain constant and are not forecasted as a percentage of sales.

——————— 3. Retained earnings will be a CPS whenever the firm's dividend payout ratio is a constant percentage of profit.

——————— 4. Spontaneous increases in financing are the growth in accounts payable and accruals with increases in sales.

Now turn to Answer Frame 2⁵, page 32, to check your answer.

Frame 3⁵

To illustrate these concepts further, suppose that the sales of the Jones Company increase by 10 percent, or $400,000. The percentage of incremental sales to be financed is 40 percent, or $160,000. If the after-tax rate of profit on sales is 5 percent, the total amount of profit on sales of $4,400,000 would be $220,000. If one half of profits after taxes are paid out in dividends, retained earnings would increase by $110,000. Financing requirements before retained earnings are $160,-000. Hence, the Jones Company will require additional financing of $50,000. This analysis suggests a number of principles. (1) The higher the asset turnover, the less external financing will be required for a given growth rate in sales. This is because less assets are required per dollar of sales. (2) The higher the growth rate in sales for a given asset turnover and profit rate on sales, the greater the net outside financing needed to support that growth. This result follows because with larger sales, more assets are required. (3) For a given growth rate in sales and for a given asset turnover, the higher the profit rate on sales, the less additional external financing will be required. The higher profits provide a greater amount of internal financing.

True or false?

_____ 1. The higher the asset turnover, the greater the amount of external financing that will be required for a given growth rate in sales.

_____ 2. The higher the growth rate in sales for a given asset turnover and profit rate on sales, the greater the net outside financing needed to support that growth.

_____ 3. If the growth rate in sales and the asset turnover are constant and the profit rate on sales decreases, the external financing required will be decreased.

_____ 4. If a small firm does not have access to external financing, its growth rate could cause it to have severe cash flow problems.

Now check your answers in Answer Frame 3[5], page 32.

Frame 4[5]

III. REGRESSION METHOD OF FINANCIAL FORECASTING

The percentage of sales method is flexible and adaptable for forecasting relatively short-term changes in financing needs. However, for a number of reasons it may be defective for longer term forecasts. To remedy some of the deficiencies of the percentage of sales method, the regression technique may be employed. When there is a base stock inventory, the line of best fit between the causal variable and the dependent variable will have a positive intercept as illustrated by Table 5–6 and Figure 5–1. (This presentation will limit itself to the use of graphic techniques of the regression method).

The sales forecast is the causal variable, graphed on the horizontal axis. Inventory is the dependent variable. For each year both sales and inventory are plotted as a single point with the appropriate year designated. Thus the regression method permits the analysis of three variables on a single chart. The line of best fit between the points illustrates the relation between sales and inventory. When the line of relationship is a straight line, the equation of the regression line may be easily determined. First the slope of the line is calculated by relating the change in inventories to the change in sales over some time interval. For example, when sales increase by $1,000,000, inventories increase by $100,000. The slope is the ratio of these changes:

$$\frac{\text{Change in inventories}}{\text{Change in sales}} = \frac{\$100,000}{\$1,000,000}$$
$$= 0.10$$
$$= \text{Slope of the line}$$

The intercept of the regression line can be estimated by taking a point on the vertical axis on the regression line drawn in Figure 5–1, using the slope calculated, and solving for a in the following equation of a straight line:

$$Y = a + bX$$

In this instance X is sales and Y is inventory or any other asset item whose level is being determined. For sales of $3,000,000 in 197F, the related inventory was $400,000. The slope of the line, b, is 0.10 which can be utilized in the equation to solve for a:

$$\$400,000 = a + 0.10\ (\$3,000,000)$$
$$\$400,000 = a + \$300,000$$
$$a = \$100,000$$

TABLE 5–6
Relations between inventories and sales

Year	Sales	Inventory	Inventory as a percentage of sales
197A.	$ 500,000	$150,000	30.0%
197B.	1,000,000	200,000	20.0
197C.	1,500,000	250,000	16.6
197D.	2,000,000	300,000	15.0
197E.	2,500,000	350,000	14.0
197F.	3,000,000	400,000	13.3
197G.	3,500,000	450,000	12.8
197H.	4,000,000	500,000	12.5

Answer frame 2⁵

1. False. The percentage of sales method is used to forecast the level of balance sheet items. It should be recognized that the forecast of sales must be accurate since it is used as a base for forecasting many other amounts.
2. False. FPD indicates that the amounts were determined by financial policy decisions. This was true for mortgage bonds and common stock in Table 5–5. In essence, they are related to sales in the long term but do not bear a direct percentage relationship to sales on a year-to-year basis. They may remain constant or fluctuate dramatically in a given year, but this is a topic that will be covered in subsequent chapters.
3. False. CPS, or cumulative percentage of sales, will be the correct retained earnings only if the firm's profit is a constant percentage of sales in addition to the dividend payout ratio being a constant percentage of profit.
4. True. In the example presented in Table 5–5, $10 of additional funds for each $100 increase in sales was provided by the increase in accounts payable and accrued taxes and wages.

If you missed any of the above, reread Frame 2⁵ before turning to Frame 3⁵, page 30.

Answer frame 3⁵

1. False. As the asset turnover ratio increases, a smaller amount of dollars is needed to invest in assets, thereby requiring less total funds and less external financing for a given growth rate in sales.
2. True. The percentage of additional sales to be financed will remain the same, but the percentage of retained earnings provided will decline while the amount of external funds needed will increase. For example, if the growth in sales increases from 10 percent to 20 percent for the Jones Company, the funds needed from external financing increase from $50,000 to $200,000.
3. False. If the profit rate on sales decreases, the effect will be to reduce profits and retained earnings, providing a greater need for external financing. Obviously, we are assuming that the tax rate and dividend policy remains unchanged.
4. True. As can be seen by the change in the growth rate in sales from 10 percent to 20 percent as illustrated in the answer to question 2, the funds needed from external financing increased. Since small firms generally do not have access to capital markets or to large sources of external financing, an unusually high growth in sales gives them severe cash flow problems. Many small firms therefore stretch accounts payable and at the same time speed collections on accounts receivable as much as possible. In addition, they may increase prices on their products in order to control the growth rate in sales—while hoping the additional profit margins will increase the total amount of internally generated funds.

If you missed any of the above, restudy Frame 3⁵ before starting Frame 4⁵ page 31.

Frame 4⁵ continued

The value of *a*, the intercept term, is highly important from the practical standpoint of establishing financial controls. The inventory of $100,-000 is the base to which additional amounts of inventory are added as sales increase. The slope of the line is constant in that for any amount of increase in sales, inventory requirements will increase by 10 percent of that amount. But using the percentage of sales method, the inventory-to-sales ratio declines as sales increase. The inventory-to-sales relation declines from 30 percent in 197A when sales were $500,000 to 12.5 percent in 197H when sales are $4,000,000. If inventory as a percentage of sales was used as a control

FIGURE 5–1
Illustration of relation between inventories and sales

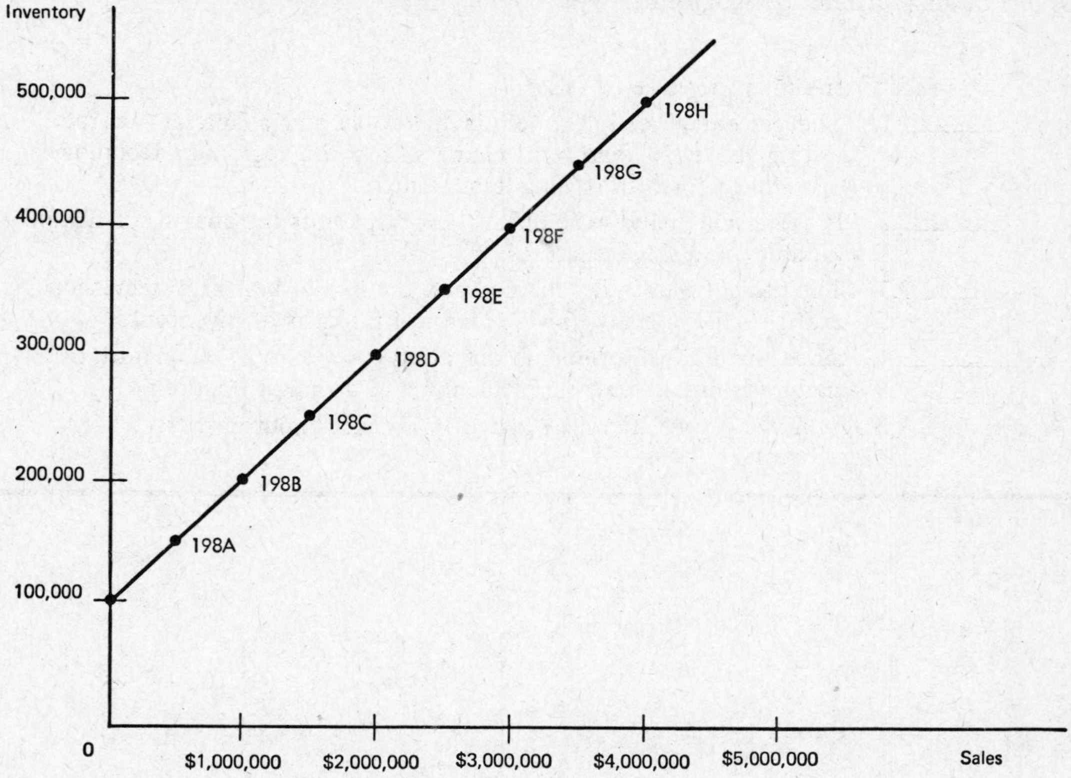

standard, based on some prior year or on an early year in the series or some average of the historical ratios or percentage of inventory to sales, it would represent too high a standard (too lax). The correct result is provided by the regression method.

IV. ESTABLISHING STANDARDS FOR FORECASTS

We need two items of information to forecast the financing needs of the particular firm. One, we need to know in what industry the firm operates. Two, we need an estimate of its sales volume. We can then predict what the balance sheet of the firm will be if it is to conform to the norms for its line of business, or with other established standards.

The use of quantitative relationships provides reference guides. Initial estimates can be based on standards. At this point, judgment, qualitative

factors, and other special elements that may be utilized in financial planning and forecasting should be considered. However, the value of purely quantitative relationships is that the fundamental cause and effect factors are initially isolated. Subsequently, other influences that may disturb these historical or comparative relationships can be brought in. Despite the many influences that may distort these relationships, first-stage approximations can be achieved by the use of the relatively mechanical approaches presented.

This methodology provides a useful framework for encompassing both the quantitative relationships and any qualitative factors that may be brought in. In this analysis of the financial system, the standards can be modified to take into account special or changing factors and circumstances. Nevertheless, such changes are made from a base of established fundamental quantitative relations. Thus standards provide checkpoints that can be utilized in postaudits of forecasts.

Without such a foundation for making altera-tions, planning may become an amorphous process of making qualitative judgments. The weakness in such judgments is that they do not make explicit the cause and effect relationships involved.

Is each of the following true or false?

_____ 1. The percentage of sales method is flexible and adaptable for fore-casting relatively short-term changes, and the regression technique is useful in forecasting long-term changes.

_____ 2. In regression analysis the line of best fit permits the analysis of three variables on a single chart.

_____ 3. The percentage of sales method and the line of best fit in regression analysis will generally provide identical forecasts of inventories.

_____ 4. Since qualitative judgments are always necessary, the quantitative analysis is usually only supplemental and of minor importance.

Now turn to Answer Frame 4[5], page 36, to check your answers.

chapter 6

BUDGETING AND PROFIT PLANNING

Frame 1[6]

Once the firm's broad financial plans have been established, the next step is to set up detailed plans of operations—the budget. A complete budget system encompasses all aspects of the firm's operations over the planning horizon; modifications in plans as required by variations in factors outside the firm's control, especially the level of economic activity, are accounted for by use of flexible budgets.

The budget system provides an integrated picture of the firm's operations as a whole. Therefore, the budget system enables the manager of each division to see the relation of his part of the enterprise to the totality of the firm. For example, a production decision to alter the level of work-in-process inventories, or a marketing decision to change the terms under which a particular product is sold, can be traced through the entire budget system to show its effects on the firm's overall profitability.

THE BUDGET SYSTEM

Budgets are developed for every significant activity of the firm. Within each budget program are individual budgets such as a materials budget, a personnel requirements budget, and a facilities or long-run capital expenditures budget. Projections of revenue and cost elements result in the budgeted or pro forma income statement. The projected balance sheet builds on the forecasts of the requirements for the various types of assets to support the anticipated sales. Of particular interest is the cash budget.

CASH BUDGETING

The cash budget indicates the combined effects of the budgeted operations on the firm's cash flow. If an increase in the volume of operations results in a negative cash flow, the cash budget will show the amount of additional financing required and its timing as well. The cash budget indicates the amount of funds needed month by month, or even week by week or day by day (for a firm with widely fluctuating receipts and disbursements), and is one of the financial manager's most important tools. An illustrative case example is therefore provided for the Textile Company.

The Textile Company is analyzing the seasonal nature of its cash flows to formulate a proposal for a credit line from its commercial banks. The pattern of its sales is as follows: January through July, November, and December at $100,000; August at $200,000, September at $300,000, and October at $400,000.

Cash received on sales amounts to 10 percent in the current month of sales, 70 percent in the month following the sales, and 20 percent during the second month following the sales. Obligations for labor, both direct and indirect, incurred each month are $10,000 per month plus 20 percent of sales in the current month plus 10 percent of sales in the following month. Raw materials purchases are $30,000 plus 20 percent of next month's sales. Salaries for general administrative expenses are $6,000 per month. Selling expenses are 10 percent of current monthly sales. De-

Answer frame 4⁵

1. True. Regression analysis is a more sophisticated type of quantitative analysis which has led to improved predictions of forecasted results over a longer period of time. Canned computer programs are available and the technique can be extended to include several independent variables.

2. True. The three variables are inventory, sales, and their relationships over time. The intercept is the base amount of inventories to which additional amounts of inventory are added as sales increase. The relationship of inventory to sales is expressed as the slope of the line.

3. False. This is precisely why the percentage of sales method should only be used for short-term changes. The example as illustrated in Table 5–6 shows how inventory as a percentage of sales declines while the slope of the line of best fit remains constant.

4. False. The use of quantitative relationships provides reference guides, shows the fundamental cause and effect relationships, and provides checkpoints that can be utilized in postaudits of forecasts. As more and more data necessary for decision making are quantified, the possibility for error in the qualitative area may be reduced.

If you missed any of the above, reread Frame 4⁵ before beginning Chapter 6 on page 35.

Frame 1⁶ continued

preciation charges are $5,000 per month. Estimated quarterly income tax payments of $11,000 are paid in January, April, July, and October and are one fourth of estimated annual current profits. Cash on hand on January 1 is $50,000. A minimum cash balance of $20,000 needs to be maintained for transaction purposes.

The nature of the Textile Company's business is highly seasonal. The pattern of cash flows is set out in the cash budget developed in Table 6–1. In the top portion a work sheet is used to determine the collections on sales and the payments for labor and raw materials. The data from the work sheet are used in the cash budget, which begins with the receipts from collections. Next, each payment category is listed for each month. The difference between cash receipts and cash payments is the net increase or decrease in cash during the month. For January, the net decrease in cash is $17,000. The initial cash of $50,000 is reduced by $17,000 to an end of month amount of $33,000. Since the desired level of cash is 20,-000, the firm has excess cash of $13,000 as of the end of January. This same type of analysis is carried out for each month. The bottom line, "excess cash or borrowing needed," represents the cumu-

lative borrowing requirements for the firm at the end of each month.

Because collections are made during the two months following sales, the rise in sales volume from August through October causes the cash position to become negative, causing a maximum borrowing need of $167,000 by the end of September. As the accounts receivable are collected, the firm moves into a positive cash position by November, ending the year with excess cash of $154,000. Thus, although the firm has a negative cash change during each of the first nine months of the year, it ends the year with a positive cash position. It begins the year with an initial amount of cash in excess of the desired level because of the negative cash change for each month. On the basis of the pattern revealed by the cash budget, it will be necessary for the firm to make arrangements for financing at least $167,000 by September. But it will be able to repay the loan by the end of November. During the months the firm has cash in excess of its requirements, the Textile Company uses the funds in short-term investments that will provide interest or other forms of return. Note that depreciation is a noncash expenditure.

TABLE 6–1

Cash Budget–198A
(in $000)

	Jan.	Feb.	Mar.	Apr.	May	June	July	Aug.	Sept.	Oct.	Nov.	Dec.
Worksheet												
Sales..................................	100	100	100	100	100	100	100	200	300	400	100	100
Collections:												
1st month...........................	10	10	10	10	10	10	10	20	30	40	10	10
2d month...........................	70	70	70	70	70	70	70	70	140	210	280	70
3d month...........................	20	20	20	20	20	20	20	20	20	40	60	80
Total.............................	100	100	100	100	100	100	100	110	190	290	350	160
Labor.................................	40	40	40	40	40	40	50	80	110	100	40	40
Payments...........................	40	40	40	40	40	40	50	80	110	100	40	40
Raw materials.....................	50	50	50	50	50	50	70	90	110	50	50	50
Payments...........................	50	50	50	50	50	50	50	70	90	110	50	50
Cash budget												
Receipts:												
Collections..........................	100	100	100	100	100	100	100	110	190	290	350	160
Payments:												
Labor.................................	40	40	40	40	40	40	50	80	110	100	40	40
Raw materials.....................	50	50	50	50	50	50	50	70	90	110	50	50
G&A salaries.......................	6	6	6	6	6	6	6	6	6	6	6	6
Selling expense....................	10	10	10	10	10	10	10	20	30	40	10	10
Income taxes.......................	11			11			11			11		
Total Payments...............	117	106	106	117	106	106	127	176	236	267	106	106
Net cash gain (loss)................	(17)	(6)	(6)	(17)	(6)	(6)	(27)	(66)	(46)	23	244	54
Initial cash..........................	50	33	27	21	4	(2)	(8)	(35)	(101)	(147)	(124)	120
EOM cash...........................	33	27	21	4	(2)	(8)	(35)	(101)	(147)	(124)	120	174
Desired cash........................	20	20	20	20	20	20	20	20	20	20	20	20
Excess cash:												
(Borrowing Needed)...............	13	7	1	(16)	(22)	(28)	(55)	(121)	(167)	(144)	100	154

Indicate whether each of the following statements is true or false by writing "T" or "F" in the space provided.

_____ 1. A detailed plan of operations providing an integrated picture of the firm's operations as a whole for various levels of sales is called a flexible budget.

_____ 2. A cash budget is used to prevent a firm from temporarily being out of cash and unable to meet its short-term obligations such as payroll.

_____ 3. A month by month or quarterly cash budget interval is sufficient for a firm with widely fluctuating receipts and disbursements.

_____ 4. The cash budget as shown in Table 6–1 shows that borrowing of $16,000 is needed during April and that borrowing of an additional $22,000 is needed during May.

Now turn to Answer Frame 1⁶, page 38, to check your answers.

Answer frame 1⁶

1. True. The budget system does provide plans for every significant activity of the firm, and a flexible budget does provide for different sales projections for different levels of economic activity.
2. True. To run out of cash may cause disaster for a firm. Hence, a cash budget is one of the most important tools used in determining its short-term cash needs.
3. False. Often a day by day cash budget interval is necessary. In cash budgeting it is important to carefully screen all assumptions as to the receipt and disbursement of funds. For example, cash sales may amount to a given percentage each month but may be received near the end of the month, whereas, purchases may be made and paid for early in the month in order to take advantage of purchase discounts. A monthly cash budget would not show this shortage of cash during the month.
4. False. Borrowing of $16,000 is needed during April, but then only $6,000 additional borrowing is necessary in May.

If you missed any of the above, reread Frame 1⁶ before starting Frame 2⁶, below.

Frame 2⁶

THE NATURE OF THE BUDGETING PROCESS

Historically, budgeting was treated as a device to limit expenditures. The more modern approach is to view the budgeting process as a tool for obtaining the most productive and profitable use of the company's resources. Budgets are reviewed to compare plans and results—a process called "controlling to plan." It is a continuous monitoring procedure, reviewing and evaluating performance with reference to previously established standards.

Budgets imposed in an arbitrary fashion may represent impossible targets at the one extreme, or standards that are too lax at the other. If standards are unrealistically high, frustrations and resentment will develop. If standards are unduly lax, costs will be out of control, profits will suffer, and morale will become flabby. However, a set of budgets based on a clear understanding and careful analysis of the firm's operations can play an important positive role.

Budgets, therefore, can provide valuable guides to both high-level executives and middle-management personnel. Well-formulated and effectively developed budgets make subordinates aware of the fact that top management has a realistic understanding of the nature of operations in the business firm. Thus, the budget also becomes an important communication link between top management and the divisional personnel whom they guide.

PROFIT PLANNING—BREAK-EVEN ANALYSIS

In a sense, all topics of financial management are concerned with profit planning. All decisions are oriented to improving sales, improving efficiency, controlling costs, and making the most effective utilization of investments. Hence, all of these decisions contribute to profit improvement and are a part of profit planning. Break-even analysis has a particular function to perform: It is a type of profit planning approach for studying the relationships among sales, fixed costs, and variable costs.

In general, by incurring fixed costs, the firm can reduce costs of operations if a sufficient volume of business is generated. For example, many operations in manufacturing, such as cutting pieces of metal or punching out holes from pieces of metal, can be performed less expensively with machinery if a sufficient volume of business is involved. Therefore, if only two pieces of metal are to be cut, or only three holes punched out of a piece of metal per day, it would be cheaper to have a worker do it as a part of his other duties. On the other hand, if millions of pieces of metal or millions of holes must be punched out per day, the job will be done less expensively by automating it. However, if machinery is purchased to perform the function, and then the expected volume of cuttings and stampings is substantially reduced, the firm may suffer losses.

Therefore, the essence of break-even analysis is to provide a guide for making decisions among alternative ways of doing things. Four types of decisions may be involved: (1) When a firm is planning a general expansion in the level of operations, it has to make a choice between the extent to which additional fixed plants will be purchased or whether additional facilities will be rented or leased. (2) A similar type of decision is involved in connection with new products. The basic question here is how large must the sales volume on a new product be if the firm is to break even. (3) In analyzing whether to modernize or automate its operations, the firm has to choose between the use of fixed costs versus variable costs. (4) The most general and central aspect is involved in competitive strategies. At a sufficient volume of operation and with a sufficient investment, the firm may be able to reduce its costs so that it may reduce its prices. Thus, break-even analysis is a tool to be used in the firm's effort to achieve cost leadership in its industry. This is in part a matter of cost efficiency and in part a matter of utilizing fixed costs and equipment that will reduce per unit cost at higher volumes of operation.

Label each of the following statements as true or false.
———— 1. A budget is primarily a control device to limit expenditures.
———— 2. If budgets have the support of top-level management and if middle- and first-level management have an opportunity to participate in the development of budgets, deviations from overall company plans will be minimized.
———— 3. An important aspect of financial management is the process of financing investments for the purpose of improving profits for the firm.
———— 4. Break-even analysis is a technique for determining whether or not a given production process should be automated.

Now turn to Answer Frame 2⁶, page 40, to check your answers.

Frame 3⁶

The central ideas involved in break-even analysis are illustrated by Table 6–2. Here the situation for three firms is set forth. In each case they have the same selling price of $6/unit. Firm A has the smallest dollar amount of fixed costs, but the highest variable cost per unit. Firm C has the highest amount of fixed costs but the lowest amount of variable costs per unit. As would be expected, Firm C achieves its break-even point at the largest sales volume, 50,000 units, or a total of $300,000. Firm A, in contrast, achieves a breakeven at 30,000 units with sales of $180,000. At a low volume of 10,000 units, Firm C achieves the greatest loss of the three. Thus, different degrees of fixed and variable costs represent different degrees of operating leverage (discussed below).

The nature of break-even analysis may be illustrated by a series of charts reflecting the data for each of the three firms as shown in Figure 6–1. The nature of the break-even charts can be explained by using the data for Firm B. Its fixed costs are $120,000. Volume produced is measured on the horizontal axis. Income is measured on the vertical axis. The revenue line is constructed by graphing the units sold on the horizontal axis against sales dollars on the vertical axis. For the corresponding volume of units sold, total costs are

Answer frame 2[6]

1. False. Although at one time budgets were regarded in this way, the more modern approach is to view the budgeting process as a tool for obtaining the most productive and profitable use of the company's resources.
2. True. This is primarily what is meant by well-formulated and effectively developed budgets. Therefore, the budget becomes an important communication device among the management personnel of the firm.
3. True. All decisions are designed to generate the amount of sales that will maximize profits over the long term. This means making the most effective use of assets as well as improving efficiency and controlling costs.
4. True. But break-even analysis is more extensive in scope. It is a type of profit planning method for evaluating the relationships among sales, fixed costs, and variable costs. Thus, it can assist in developing new products, price determination, and predicting competitive actions, to mention a few.

If you missed any of the above, reread Frame 2[6] before starting Frame 3[6], on page 39.

Frame 3[6] continued

FIGURE 6–1

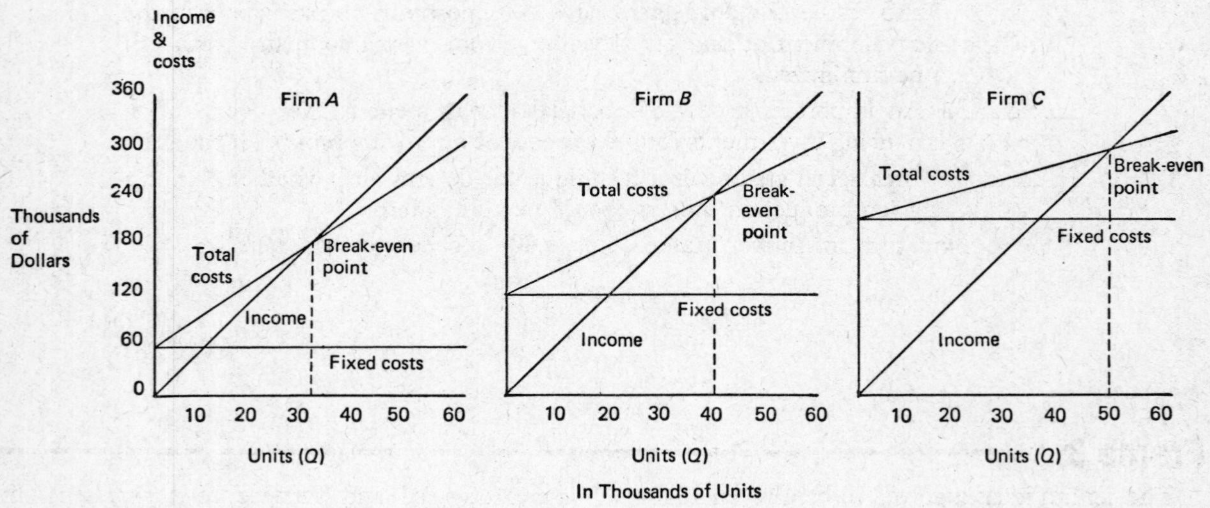

In Thousands of Units

graphed from the corresponding column of figures from Table 6–2. The slope of the total income line is $6 per unit; the slope of the total cost line is the variable cost per unit, which is $3. Thus, in the illustration for Firm B, the slope of the selling price line is twice as steep as the slope of the total cost line; but the total cost line starts from a higher position on the vertical axis. Thus some required volume has to be achieved before the greater slope of the total revenue line over-

comes the higher starting point of the total cost line. The point at which the two lines intersect is the break-even point.

By contrasting the three different combinations of fixed costs and variable costs, we have illustrated different degrees of operating leverage. The degree of operating leverage, starting from some specified level of units sold, is defined as the percentage change in operating income resulting from the percentage change in units sold.

$$\text{Degree of operating leverage} = \frac{\text{Percent change in operating income (OI)}}{\text{Percent change in units sold } (Q)} \quad (6\text{--}1)$$

Thus for Firm B in Figure 6–1, the degree of operating leverage at 50,000 units of sales is:

$$\text{Degree of OL}_B = \frac{\dfrac{\Delta(\text{OI})}{\text{OI}}}{\dfrac{\Delta Q}{Q}}$$

$$= \frac{\dfrac{\$60,000 - \$30,000}{\$30,000}}{\dfrac{60,000 - 50,000}{50,000}} = \frac{\dfrac{\$30,000}{\$30,000}}{\dfrac{10,000}{50,000}}$$

$$= \frac{100\%}{20\%} = 5.0$$

A simplified formula for calculating the degree of operating levelage can also be set forth.

$$\text{Degree of operating leverage at point } Q = \frac{S - VC}{S - VC - FC} \quad (6\text{--}2)$$

Thus the degree of operating leverage is sales minus variable costs divided by sales minus variable costs minus fixed costs. Using the formula set forth in equation (6–2), the degree of operating leverage at 50,000 units is:

$$OL = \frac{\$300,000 - \$150,000}{\$30,000} = \frac{\$150,000}{\$30,000} = 5$$

The two methods, of course, give the same answer: the operating leverage is 5. The significance of the result 5 is that having moved past its break-even point at 50,000 volume of units sold, any percentage change in units sold will magnify the percentage change in profits by a multiple of 5.

CASH BREAK-EVEN ANALYSIS

Of particular interest is to translate ordinary break-even analysis into cash break-even analysis. Some of the firm's revenues may be in receivables, so that not all sales will represent cash inflows. Some of the firm's fixed costs may be noncash outflows, such as depreciation. The concept of a cash break-even chart will be illustrated by as-

TABLE 6–2

Profit planning

Firm A
Selling price = $6
Fixed costs = $60,000
Variable costs = $4

Firm B
Selling price = $6
Fixed costs = $120,000
Variable costs = $3

Firm C
Selling price = $6
Fixed costs = $200,000
Variable costs = $2

Units sold (Q)	Sales	Costs	Profit
Firm A			
10,000	$ 60,000	$100,000	−$ 40,000
20,000	120,000	140,000	− 20,000
30,000	180,000	180,000	0
40,000	240,000	220,000	20,000
50,000	300,000	260,000	40,000
60,000	360,000	300,000	60,000
90,000	540,000	420,000	120,000
Firm B			
10,000	$ 60,000	$150,000	−$ 90,000
20,000	120,000	180,000	− 60,000
30,000	180,000	210,000	− 30,000
40,000	240,000	240,000	0
50,000	300,000	270,000	30,000
60,000	360,000	300,000	60,000
90,000	540,000	390,000	150,000
Firm C			
10,000	$ 60,000	$220,000	−$160,000
20,000	120,000	240,000	− 120,000
30,000	180,000	260,000	− 80,000
40,000	240,000	280,000	− 40,000
50,000	300,000	300,000	0
60,000	360,000	320,000	40,000
90,000	540,000	380,000	160,000

suming that $50,000 of fixed costs for Firm C are depreciation charges. If $50,000 of the $200,000 fixed costs of Firm C are depreciation, the cash fixed costs are only $150,000. The cash break-even point would therefore be lower than the 50,000 units of profit break-even point. The cash break-even point drops to $37,500.

Break-even analysis using straight line relationships is useful as a first-approximation to understand the general nature of the problem. More sophisticated analysis will require modifications in the relationships set forth. However, even in more complex situations, the basic concepts and principles involved are often indicated by linear break-even analysis.

True or false?

_____ 1. As fixed costs are increased, the break-even level of operation is decreased.

_____ 2. The degree of operating leverage is defined as the percentage change in net income resulting from the percentage change in units sold.

_____ 3. The degree of operating leverage for Firm C in Figure 6–1 at 60,000 units of sales is 6.

_____ 4. When a large amount of the firm's revenues are in receivables and the depreciation expense is very large, a cash break-even analysis is very useful.

Now turn to Answer Frame 3⁶, page 44, to check your answers.

chapter 7

CURRENT ASSET MANAGEMENT

Frame 1[7]

The next three chapters discuss working capital policy and management. Gross working capital has traditionally been defined as the firm's total current assets. The term has a double meaning: (1) an investment requirement and (2) liquid assets. Current assets represent the amount of *near-cash* or liquid investment a firm must have in order to support its sales volume. Cash, marketable securities, accounts receivable, and inventories constitute assets that are relatively more liquid than fixed assets to meet the claims of short-term creditors. The current asset-debt relationship is conveyed by the concept of net working capital, defined as current assets minus current liabilities. Thus, the management of working capital requires an understanding of the principles both of determining the correct amount and mix of current assets as well as of raising funds to finance these assets. The short-term financing aspect will be covered in Chapter 8. Chapter 9, "Working Capital Policy," seeks to draw the various ideas together.

Investments in current assets are important for at least three reasons. (1) Current assets generally represent more than one half the total assets of a business firm. Since current assets is the largest category of investment by the firm, changes in working capital policies may cause substantial variations in financing required. If a firm's average collection period is 30 days and its credit sales are $2,000 per day, its investment in accounts receivables will be $60,000. If its average collection period increases to 50 days, its investment in receivables will rise to $100,000. But with an average collection period of 10 days, its investment-in receivables would be $20,000. Thus a re-

duction in investment from $100,000 to $20,000 is equivalent to avoiding $80,000 in financing that otherwise would be required. (2) There is a direct relationship between the growth of sales and the need to finance additional assets of the firm. For example, if the standard for an industry is an average collection period of 30 days and credit sales are $2,000 per day, the initial situation above, the investment in accounts receivable will be $60,000. If sales rise to $3,000 per day, the investment in accounts receivable would increase to $90,000. The growth of sales also produces requirements for additional inventories and for cash balances. (3) Investments in current assets are especially important for small firms. A small firm can reduce its investments in fixed assets by buying used equipment and by renting or leasing plant and equipment, but it is not possible to reduce the investment in current assets to the same degree.

CASH MANAGEMENT

Cash management is the first task of controlling the investment in current assets. *Cash* refers to the firm's holdings of currency and demand deposits (checking accounts) at commercial banks. Since demand deposits are used in about 90 percent of the volume of business transactions, it is likely to be the major type of cash item.

Sound working capital management requires investment in cash for a number of reasons. Holding cash for transactions enables the firm to conduct its ordinary business of purchasing, selling, and so on. Another reason for holding cash has been referred to as the precautionary motive,

Answer frame 3[6]

1. False. As fixed costs are increased the break-even level of operation is *increased*.
2. False. It is defined as the percentage change in operating income resulting from the percentage change in units sold. Net income is derived after the fixed interest charges on debt and income taxes are subtracted from operating income.
3. True. The degree of operating leverage at 60,000 units of sales is:

$$\text{Degree of OL}_C = \frac{\dfrac{\$160,000 - \$40,000}{\$40,000}}{\dfrac{90,000 - 60,000}{60,000}} = \frac{\dfrac{\$120,000}{\$40,000}}{\dfrac{30,000}{60,000}} = 6$$

Using the simplified formula, the degree of operating leverage at 60,000 units is:

$$\text{Degree of OL}_C = \frac{S - VC}{S - VC - FC} = \frac{\$360,000 - \$120,000}{\$360,000 - \$120,000 - \$200,000} = 6$$

This means in this illustration at this particular level of output, that any percentage change in units sold will magnify the percentage change in profits six times.

4. True. But even cash break-even analysis does not fully represent cash flows. It is still useful because it provides a picture of the flow of funds from operations. A cash budget would be required to obtain a detailed analysis of cash flows.

If you missed any of the above, reread Frame 3[6]. Before beginning Chapter 7 on page 43, turn to page 189 to work Examination 1, which covers Chapters 1–6.

Frame 1[7] continued

similar to the idea of "safety stocks" discussed in inventory management below. Also, it is essential that the firm have sufficient funds to take cash discounts. Since the current and quick ratios are key items in credit analysis, the firm must meet the financial standards or norms of the line of business in which it is engaged in order to maintain its credit standing. A strong credit standing enables the firm to purchase goods from trade suppliers on favorable terms and to maintain its line of credit with banks and other sources of financing. The firm should have sufficient liquidity to meet emergencies such as strikes, fires, or the marketing campaigns of its competitors. This in turn affects the borrowing flexibility of the firm, determining the firm's ability to borrow additional cash as required. The speculative motive (the third reason) for holding cash involves being ready for favorable business opportunities that may come along from time to time.

Building upon his knowledge of cash flows (developed in the preceding chapters), the financial manager may be able to improve the inflow-out-flow pattern of cash. He can do so by better synchronization of flows and by reduction of float. Float refers to funds in transit. For example, checks received from customers in distant cities are subject to two types of delays: the time required for the check to travel in the mail and the time required for clearing through the banking system.

To reduce these two types of float, a *lock-box plan* can be used. If a firm makes sales in large amounts at far distances, it can establish a lock box in a post office located in the customer's area. It can arrange to have customers send payments to the postal box in their city and then have a bank pick up the checks and deposit them in a special checking account. The bank then has the checks cleared in the local area and remits by wire to the firm's bank of deposit.

Mathematical models have been developed to help determine the optimal cash balances. These models are variations on basic inventory models, whose nature will be conveyed by the discussion of inventory models in the last section of this chapter.

Indicate whether each of the following statements is true or false by writing "T" or "F" in the space provided.

_____ 1. Current assets are important because of the size or proportion of total assets they represent, the increase in size necessary as sales grow, and their particularly significant role in managing a small firm.

_____ 2. The major type of cash item is the firm's holdings of currency.

_____ 3. Of the three main reasons for holding cash—transaction, precautionary and speculative—the speculative reason is by far the most important.

_____ 4. Float refers to excess cash held for speculative reasons, and to optimize this balance a lock-box plan is used.

Now turn to Answer Frame 1[7], page 46, to check your answers.

Frame 2[7]

MARKETABLE SECURITIES

Individual firms report varying amounts of marketable securities among their current assets. One motive for holding marketable securities or *near-monies* is to use them as a buffer or safety stock against cash shortages. Alternatively, a firm may have cash which is temporarily invested in marketable securities for a number of reasons such as seasonal or cyclical business fluctuations. Also because of uncertainties as to future needs, a firm may have cash funds to invest in temporary investments for a few weeks to several years, or indefinitely.

Depending on how long he anticipates holding the funds, the financial manager decides upon a suitable maturity pattern for his holdings. The numerous alternatives can be selected and balanced in such a way that he obtains the maturities and risks appropriate to the financial situation of his firm. Commercial bankers, investment bankers, and brokers provide the financial manager with detailed information on alternative forms of investments. Since the characteristics of potential investments change with shifts in financial market conditions, the financial manager must keep up to date on changing opportunities.

MANAGEMENT OF INVESTMENT RECEIVABLES

In recent years firms' investments in accounts receivable have been growing. This has been true particularly of larger firms who have access to capital markets and utilize their greater fundraising ability to extend credit to their customers.

The major determinants of the level of receivables are (1) volume of credit sales, (2) seasonality of sales, (3) rules for credit limits, (4) terms of sales and credit policies of individual firms, and (5) collection policies. The ratio of receivables to sales generally ranges from 8 to 12 percent, or on the average, approximately one month's sales are in receivables. However, wide variations are experienced among firms, reflecting the differential impact of the factors listed above.

The basis of a firm's credit policy is its industry's characteristic credit terms; generally, a firm must meet the terms provided by other firms in the industry. However, a central task in formulating credit policy is an evaluation of the credit worthiness of the potential customer.

To evaluate the credit risk, the credit manager considers the five Cs of credit: character, capacity, capital, collateral, and conditions. (1) *Character* refers to the probability that the customer will try to honor his obligations. This factor is of considerable importance because every credit transaction implies a promise to pay. Experienced credit men frequently emphasize that the moral factor is the most important issue in a credit evaluation. (2) *Capacity* refers to the ability of the customer to pay. This is judged by reviewing his past record of payments, observing the customer's plant or store, evaluating his business methods. (3) *Capital* is measured by the

Answer frame 1⁷

1. True. Current assets usually represent more than one half of total assets, and the growth in accounts receivable is usually directly related to the growth in sales as in cash and inventory. The success of small firms depends primarily on current asset management since they usually have more alternatives available to them in obtaining the use of fixed assets—leasing for example.
2. False. Demand deposits in banks are used for about 90 percent of the volume of business transactions. Companies do not usually hold large amounts of cash on hand.
3. False. The transaction requirement (in order for the firm to conduct its ordinary business) is the most important reason for holding cash. The speculative motive is the least important. If firms have favorable business opportunities they usually have time to negotiate for their financing. If these business opportunities are fairly regular, a firm may want to provide for these occurrences through the use of a short-term marketable security portfolio.
4. False. Float refers to funds in transit to the firm and is caused by the time required for a check to travel in the mail plus the time required for clearing through the banking system. Since these funds are "nonearning" current assets, a lock-box plan is used to reduce the size of the float.

If you missed any of the above, reread Frame 1⁷ before beginning Frame 2⁷, page 45.

Frame 2⁷ continued

general financial position of the firm as indicated by financial ratio analysis, with special emphasis on the tangible net worth of the enterprise. (4) *Collateral* is represented by assets that the customer may offer as a pledge for security of the credit extended to him. (5) Finally, *conditions* refer to the impact of general economic trends on the firm, or to special developments in certain areas of the economy that may affect the customer's ability to meet his obligations.

The five C's of credit represent the factors by which the credit worthiness of a customer is judged. Information on these items is obtained from the firm's previous experience with the customer, supplemented by a well-developed system of information-gathering groups. Two major sources of external information are available for this purpose. The first is the work of the local credit associations. By periodic meetings of local groups and by direct communication, information on experience with debtors is exchanged. More formally, credit interchange, a system developed by the National Association of Credit Management for assembling and distributing information of debtors' past performance, is also provided. The interchange reports show the paying record of the debtor, industries from which he is buying,

and the trading areas in which his purchases are being made. The second source is the work of the credit-reporting agencies, the best known of which is Dun & Bradstreet. Agencies that specialize in coverage of a limited number of industries also provide credit information.

The terms of credit set forth the conditions under which a discount may be granted and the date payment is due. Terms of 2/10, net 30, means that a 2 percent discount from the sales price is granted if payment is made within 10 days; if the discount is not taken, the entire amount is due 30 days from the invoice date. Terms of net 60 indicate that no discount is offered. A toy manufacturer may utilize season dating such as 2/10, net 30, Nov. 1 dating. These terms indicate that the effective invoice date is Nov. 1, so the discount may be taken until Nov. 10, or the full amount paid on Nov. 30. Season dating may induce some customers to buy early, reducing storage costs for the toy manufacturer and giving earlier indications as to total sales for the season.

Collection policy describes the processes by which the firm seeks to obtain payment of its accounts receivable. Collection policies should seek a balance between pressure to avoid excessive investment in receivables and maintaining customers' goodwill. Collection policies should seek to expand sales to the point at which incremental sales equal incremental costs. The collection processes are also an opportunity to provide customer counseling to help increase his ability to pay his bills.

Label each of the following statements as true or false.

———— 1. The maturity pattern of marketable securities is one of the least important components in the financial manager's decision-making process as far as deciding on his portfolio of marketable securities.

———— 2. The moral integrity of a potential customer is probably the most important factor in credit evaluation.

———— 3. Character, capacity, credit, collateral, and conditions are the five C's of credit by which credit worthiness of a customer is judged.

———— 4. Collection policies should be designed so as to minimize bad debt losses.

Now turn to Answer Frame 2[7], page 48, to check your answers.

Frame 3[7]

MANAGING INVENTORY INVESTMENTS

The major determinants of investment in inventory are level of sales, length and technical nature of production processes, durability versus perishability or style factor in the end product, ordering costs, and storage costs. Although wide variations occur, inventory-to-sales ratios are generally concentrated in the 12 to 20 percent range. Within limits set by the economics of a firm's industry, there exists a potential for improvement in inventory control by use of computers and operations research.

Managing assets of all kinds is basically an inventory-type problem—the same method of analysis applies to cash, receivables, and fixed assets as applies to inventories themselves. First, a basic stock must be on hand to balance inflows and outflows of the items, with the size of the stock depending upon the patterns of flows, whether regular or irregular. Second, because the unexpected may always occur, it is necessary to have safety stocks on hand. These safety stocks represent the little extra necessary to avoid the cost of not having enough to meet current needs. Third, additional amounts may be required to meet future growth needs. These are anticipation stocks. Related to anticipation stocks is the recognition that there are optimum purchase sizes, defined as economical ordering quantities (EOQ). In borrowing money, in buying raw materials for production, or in purchasing plant and equipment, it is usually cheaper to buy more than just enough to meet immediate needs.

The basic inventory model recognizes that certain costs (carrying costs) rise as average inventory holdings increase, but that other costs (ordering costs and stock-out costs) fall as average inventory holdings rise. These two sets of costs comprise the total cost of ordering and carrying inventories, and the economic ordering quantity model is designed to locate an optimal order size that will minimize total inventory costs.

The data required in formal procedures determining the optimal order quantity and the associated considerations are set forth in Table 7–1.

From the data in Table 7–1 an analysis of cost

TABLE.7–1

Inventory problem scenario

1. Existing inventory: (10,000 units)($12 cost) = $120,000 investment
2. Estimated annual sales = 490,000 units (S)
3. Safety stock = 5,000 units
4. Ordering costs = $400 per order (F)
5. Holding costs (per unit) (C)
   Interest costs (10%)($12)   = $1.20
   Storage, safety, spoilage, etc. =   .80
                                     _____
                                     $2.00 per unit per year

Answer frame 2[7]

1. False. It is one of the most important decision variables along with risk and return considerations. Financial managers should select those securities having maturities that match their specific need for funds.
2. True. However, it is probably the most difficult of all the factors to measure.
3. False. The third C is not credit but capital. Capital refers to the financial position of the firm and in particular to the tangible net worth of the firm. Tangible net worth is the net worth or stockholders' equity minus intangible assets such as patents and goodwill. Financial ratio analysis was covered in Chapter 3 and is one of the most commonly used methods of ascertaining a firm's financial condition.
4. False. The firm should try to extend credit to the point where the contribution of sales to an additional higher risk category of customers just equals the additional cost of selling to that category of customer. In other words, the firm should extend credit to additional risk categories of customers to the point where the marginal revenue equals the marginal cost of those additional sales.

If you missed any of the above, restudy Frame 2[7] before starting Frame 3[7], page 47.

Frame 3[7] continued

patterns for a range of order sizes is set forth in Table 7–2. The logic of Table 7–2 is conveyed by explaining the numbers in the column which begins with an order size of 14,000 units. The estimated annual sales of 490,000 units is divided by the order size of 14,000 to obtain the number of orders, 35. Average inventory is the safety stock of 5,000 units plus one half the order size of 14,000, or 7,000, to total 12,000 units. Holding costs of $2 per unit multiplied times the average inventory of 12,000 gives the total holding costs of $24,000. The ordering costs of $400 per order multiplied by the number of orders, 35, equals the total ordering costs, or $14,000. The total costs represent the sum of ordering costs of $14,000 plus holding costs of $24,000, for a total of $38,000.

As the order size is increased, average inventory rises; consequently holding costs increase. As the order size increases, ordering costs decline. As shown in Table 7–2, the lowest total cost is achieved at an order size of 14,000 units. The EOQ formula can also be used to obtain the same result for the optimal order quantity.

Holding costs (carrying costs) represent storage costs, insurance, depreciation, and the cost of funds tied up in the inventory. The cost of ordering inventories consists of the cost of placing orders, shipping and handling, and so on. They are the fixed costs of purchasing and recording an order. The total cost of inventories is obtained by combining these rising and declining elements of cost, as illustrated in the total cost curve in Figure 7–1. The total cost of holding inventories is minimized by choosing an optimal ordering quantity. The economic order quantity (EOQ) represents the minimum point on the total cost curve associated with various sizes of ordering quantities. As illustrated in Figure 7–1, as the order quantity size is increased, holding costs rise while ordering costs fall.

We can then verify that EOQ represents that

TABLE 7–2
Numerical solution for EOQ

Order size	1,000	5,000	10,000	14,000	49,000	245,000
1. Number of orders (N).......	490	98	49	35	10	2
2. Average inventory* (A)......	5,500	7,500	10,000	12,000	29,500	127,500
3. Holding costs ($2 × A)......	$ 11,000	$15,000	$20,000	$24,000	$59,000	$255,000
4. Ordering costs ($400 × N)....	$196,000	$39,200	$19,600	$14,000	$ 4,000	$ 800
Total costs (3 + 4).....	$207,000	$54,200	$39,600	$38,000	$63,000	$255,800

* Average inventory = (A) = Safety stock plus [(Order size)/2].

FIGURE 7–1
Inventory costs in relation to order size

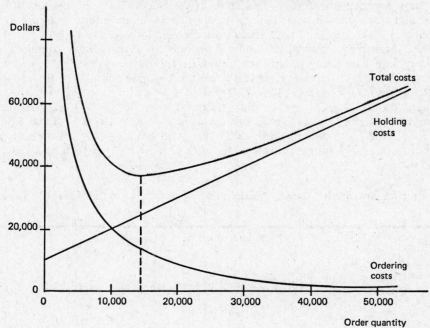

order quantity that achieves the minimum total inventory costs. The EOQ formula is:

$$EOQ = \sqrt{\frac{2FS}{C}}$$

Where:

EOQ = Economic ordering quantity, or the optimum quantity to order each time an order is placed.

F = Fixed costs of placing and receiving an order (ordering costs).

S = Annual sales in units.

C = Carrying cost per unit of inventory (holding costs).

Using the EOQ formula, the solution to the problem posed is as follows:

$$\text{Optimal order quantity} = \sqrt{\frac{(2)(400)(490,000)}{2.00}}$$
$$= 14,000 \text{ units}$$

The result is the same as illustrated in Figure 7–1 and is the order quantity with the minimum cost.

True or false?

_____ 1. The lack of a good inventory control system (particularly in a small firm) is the reason why so many firms fail soon after they begin operations.

_____ 2. The concepts applied to inventory control usually are not applicable to cash management.

_____ 3. An EOQ model is designed to locate an optimal order size that will minimize total costs associated with inventory management (which represent carrying costs, ordering costs, and stock-out costs).

_____ 4. In the chapter illustration, total costs at the EOQ point are $39,600, and average inventory is 10,000 units.

Now turn to Answer Frame 3⁷, page 50, to check your answer.

Answer frame 3[7]

1. True. It is important to manage inventories efficiently since they usually represent a large percentage of current assets. The policy of many small firms seems to be to avoid a stock-out. This can lead to excessive levels of inventory, resulting in low levels of profitability and large losses from obsolete inventories.

2. False. Managing assets of all kinds is basically an inventory-type problem, and many firms have even applied the EOQ model to cash management.

3. True. Figure 7–1 shows that when these three costs are considered, the economic order quantity (EOQ) is 14,000 units.

4. False. At the EOQ of 14,000 units, the total costs are $38,000 and the average inventory is 12,000 units. Total costs represent holding costs of $24,000 ($2.00 × 12,000 units) and ordering costs of $14,000 ($400 × 35 orders). The average inventory of 12,000 units is equal to safety stock plus the EOQ divided by 2 (5,000 + $\frac{14,000}{2}$).

If you missed any of the above, reread Frame 3[7] before beginning Chapter 8, below.

chapter 8

SHORT-TERM FINANCING

Frame 1[8]

Short-term credit is defined as debt originally scheduled for payment within one year. Ranked by their relative importance in supplying credit to business, the main sources of short-term financing are: (1) trade credit, (2) commercial banks, and (3) commercial paper.

TRADE CREDIT

In the ordinary course of events, a firm buys its supplies and materials on credit from other firms, recording the debt as an account payable. Accounts payable, or trade credit as it is commonly called, is the largest single category of short-term credit, representing about 40 percent of the current liabilities of nonfinancial corporations. The percentage is somewhat larger for smaller firms, since they may not qualify for financing from other sources.

Calculation of the cost of trade credit is set forth in Table 8–1. In the first example the terms are 2/10 days, net 30. If the firm fails to take the

TABLE 8–1

Cost of trade credit

1. First example
    Terms: 2/10, net 30 for $1,000 invoice

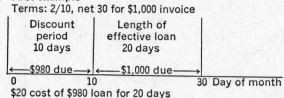

$20 cost of $980 loan for 20 days

$$\frac{\$20}{\$980} \times \frac{365 \text{ days}}{20 \text{ days}} = 37.2\% \text{ annual cost}$$

2. Second example
    Terms: 2/10, net 60 for $1,000 invoice

$$\frac{\$20}{\$980} \times \frac{365 \text{ days}}{50 \text{ days}} = 14.9\% \text{ annual cost}$$

Sometimes 360 days is used in the second fraction in computing the effective annual rate of interest. Also, using percentages in the first fraction, $2/(100 - 2)$, often makes the computations easier.

cash discount, it has received a loan for 20 days on a discounted basis. That is, if the firm had taken the cash discount, it would have paid $980, and it must repay $1,000 at maturity. The annual cost is 37.2 percent. In example 2, the terms are 2/10, net 60, and by similar reasoning the annual cost would have been 14.9 percent.

Whether trade credit costs more or less than other forms of financing is a moot question. If the buyer does not have forms of financing alternative to trade credit, the costs to the buyer may be commensurate with the risks to the seller. However, in some instances, trade credit is used simply because the user may not realize how expensive it is. In such circumstances, careful financial analysis may lead to the substitution of alternative forms of financing for trade credit.

Indicate whether each of the following statements is true or false by writing "T" or "F" in the space provided.

_____ 1. Trade credit or accounts payable is short-term credit which is probably the most important source of financing for a small firm.

_____ 2. The cost of not taking discounts (on an annual basis) can be found as follows:

$$\text{Cost} = \frac{\text{Discount percent}}{(100 - \text{Discount percent})} \times \frac{365}{(\text{Final due date} - \text{Discount period})}$$

_____ 3. Using 360 days in the computation, the cost of credit terms of 1/10, net 20 is 36.36 percent and of 2/10, net 20 is 42.84 percent.

_____ 4. If a firm stretches accounts payable 40 days beyond the terms of 2/10, net 30 its cost is 15.34 percent (using 360 days in the computation).

Now turn to Answer Frame 1⁸, page 52, to check your answer.

Frame 2⁸

COMMERCIAL BANKS

Commercial bank lending appears on the balance sheet as notes payable and is second in importance to trade credit as a source of short-term financing. Banks occupy a pivotal position in the short-term and intermediate-term money markets. Measurement of the effective (true) rate of interest depends upon the method of charging interest by the lender, as shown by Table 8–2. If the interest is paid at the maturity of the loan,

the stated rate of interest is the effective rate of interest, or 8 percent. If the bank deducts the interest in advance (discounts the loan), the effective rate of interest is increased to 8.7 percent.

A compensating balance of 20 percent raises the effective interest rate to 10 percent. If the loan is repaid in 12 monthly installments, the effective rate of interest is doubled. The borrower has the full amount of money only during the first month, and by the last month he has already repaid 11/12 of the loan, so he has the use of

Answer frame 1[8]

1. True. Smaller firms (nonfinancial) usually do not have access to capital or money markets and rely almost exclusively on credit granted them by their suppliers.

2. True. The denominator in the first term (100 − Discount percent), equals the funds made available by not taking the discount. Using this method is sometimes easier than using dollar amounts in the first fraction. Also, sometimes 360 days are used rather than 365 in the second fraction.

3. False. The cost of 1/10, net 20 is 36.36 percent but the cost of 2/10, net 20 is 73.47 percent. They are calculated as follows:

$$\text{Cost of 1/10, net 20} = \frac{1}{(100 - 1)} \times \frac{360}{(20 - 10)} = 36.36 \text{ percent}$$

$$\text{Cost of 2/10, net 20} = \frac{2}{(100 - 2)} \times \frac{360}{(20 - 10)} = 73.47 \text{ percent}$$

4. False. The cost is 12.24 percent calculated as follows:

$$\text{Cost of 2/10, net (30 + 40)} = \frac{2}{(100 - 2)} \times \frac{360}{(70 - 10)} = 12.24 \text{ percent}$$

Stretching accounts payable could eventually cause a deterioration in a firm's credit standing. It could even cause sellers to quote a higher price to the firm.

If you missed any of the above, reread Frame 1[8] before starting Frame 2[8], page 51.

Frame 2[8] continued

TABLE 8–2

Cost of bank credit

Amount of loan = $100,000
Annual interest = $8,000
Compensating balance = $20,000

1. Simple interest method

$$\text{Cost} = \frac{\$8,000}{\$100,000} = 8.0\%$$

2. Effect of discount

$$\text{Cost} = \frac{\$8,000}{\$100,000 - \$8,000} = 8.7\%$$

3. Effect of compensating balance

$$\text{Cost} = \frac{\$8,000}{\$100,000 - \$20,000} = 10\%$$

4. Interest rate on average amount of amortized loan

$$\text{Cost} = \frac{\$8,000}{\$50,000} \cong 16\%$$

5. Interest rate on discounted amortized loan

$$\text{Cost} = \frac{\$8,000}{\$92,000/2} \cong 17.39\%$$

only one half the face amount of the loan. Under the discounting method, the effective cost of the installment loan would be 17.39 percent.

A potential borrower seeking to establish a relationship with a bank should recognize the important differences among banks as potential sources of funds. Banks now have close relationships with their borrowers. Since there is considerable personal contact over the years, the borrower's business problems are frequently discussed; thus the bank often provides informal management counseling services. With heightened competition between commercial banks and other financial institutions, the aggressiveness of banks has increased. Modern commercial banks now offer a wide range of financial business services. In addition, most large banks have business development departments that provide counseling to firms and serve as intermediaries on a wide variety of their requirements.

Label each of the following statements as true or false.

_____ 1. The effective rate and the rate of interest stated by banks are identical when the loan is discounted.

_____ 2. A compensating balance of 30 percent raises the effective interest to 11.4 percent in the example illustrated in Table 8–2.

_____ 3. Under the discounted method, the effective cost of the installment loan with a compensating balance requirement of $20,000 is 17.39 percent.

———— 4. With heightened competition between commercial banks and other financial institutions the amount of management counseling services will probably be increased.

Now turn to Answer Frame 2⁸, page 54, to check your answers.

Frame 3⁸ ————————————————————————————

COMMERCIAL PAPER

Commercial paper consists of promissory notes of large firms and is sold primarily to other business firms, insurance companies, pension funds, and banks. Maturities of commercial paper vary from two to six months, with an average of about five months. The rates on prime commercial paper vary, but they are generally about one half of 1 percent below those on prime business loans.

Several advantages may be achieved by use of the commercial paper market. (1) It permits the broadest and most advantageous distribution of paper. (2) It provides more funds at lower rates than do other methods. (3) The borrower avoids the inconvenience and expense of financing arrangements with a number of institutions, each possibly requiring a compensating balance. (4) Publicity and prestige accrue to the borrower as his product and his paper become more widely known. (5) Finally, the commercial paper dealer frequently offers valuable advice to his clients.

A basic limitation of the commercial paper market is that the amount of funds available is limited to the excess liquidity that corporations, the main suppliers of funds, may have at any particular time. Another disadvantage is that a debtor who may be experiencing temporary financial difficulties will not be able to obtain credit extensions because commercial paper dealings are impersonal.

USE OF SECURITY IN SHORT-TERM FINANCING

Sometimes a potential borrower's credit rating is not sufficiently strong to justify an unsecured loan. If the borrower can pledge some forms of collateral as security to be claimed by the lender in the event of default, the lender may extend credit to an otherwise unacceptable firm. The most common types of collateral used for short-term credit are inventories and accounts receivable.

Accounts receivable financing can be done either by pledging the receivables or by selling them outright—factoring. When the receivables are pledged, the borrower retains the risk that the person or firm who owes the receivable will not pay; but this risk is typically passed on to the lender when factoring is involved. Because the factor takes the risk of default, he will typically investigate the purchaser's credit. Therefore, the factor can perform three services—a lending function, a risk-bearing function, and a credit-checking function. When receivables are pledged, the lender typically performs only the first of these three functions. Consequently, factoring is more expensive than is pledging accounts receivable.

The nature of factoring can be conveyed by an illustrative example. The selling Firm A receives an order of $12,000 payable in 30 days after delivery. The factor checks and approves the order. After the goods are shipped, the factor makes funds available to the seller. The factoring commission for credit checking is 2 percent of the invoice price, or $240. If the interest expense is computed at the prime rate plus a 2 percent premium, for example, at a 16 percent annual rate on the invoice price, it would be:

$$1/12 \times 0.16 \times 12,000 = \$160$$

The factor will, in addition, hold back a reserve (in this instance assumed to be 10 percent of the invoice) until the account has been collected to provide for disputes over damaged goods, goods returned by the buyers, and so on. When funds are received from the factor, the accounting entry on the seller's books will be:

Answer frame 2⁸

1. False. The effective or true rate of interest is equal to the stated rate when interest is paid at the *maturity* or termination of a single payment loan.

2. True. It is calculated as follows:

$$\text{Cost} = \frac{\$8,000}{\$100,000 - \$30,000} = 11.4 \text{ percent}$$

3. False. It is 22.2 percent and is calculated as follows:

$$\text{Cost} = \frac{\$8,000}{(\$92,000 - \$20,000)/2} = 22.2 \text{ percent}$$

4. True. Management counseling services and a wide range of other financial and business services will probably be increased since one way of reducing the effective price is by expanding the product—in this instance—funds plus counseling.

If you missed any of the above, reread Frame 2⁸ before turning to Frame 3⁸, page 53.

Frame 3⁸ continued

Cash.......................... 10,400	
Interest expense............... 160	
Factoring commission.......... 240	
Reserve due from factor on	
collection of account......... 1,200	
Accounts Receivable.....	12,000

When the factor collects the face of the invoice at the end of the 30 days, the reserve held back would be paid to the seller. The process is a continuous one, so the amount actually remitted by the factor occurs when the reserve exceeds some specified percentage of accounts receivable on which the factor has made advances.

Loans may also be secured by inventories. When inventories are held in public warehouses, a trust receipt is issued and conveyed to a lender in a loan transaction. When the technique, known as a field warehousing arrangement, is used, the inventory pledged for a loan is under the physical control of a warehouse company, which releases the inventory only on order from the lending institution. Payments are then remitted to the lender by the seller of goods when received from the buyers. Canned goods, lumber, steel, coal, and other standardized products are the type of goods usually covered in field warehouse arrangements.

Short-term financing is particularly important for meeting the fluctuating needs of business firms and particularly important for new and smaller firms. The risks and limited financing alternatives available to new and smaller firms make it difficult for them to obtain long-term financing. The main reason for this is that a lender on a long-term basis is committing himself to the future of the firm, and repayment depends upon the firm's success over an extended period of time. Hence, since the risks of newer and smaller firms are large, lenders may be unwilling to make long-term commitments. Thus, short-term financing (often secured) is generally the lifeblood of new and smaller firms.

True or false?

———— 1. Commercial paper is an IOU exchanged or sold primarily between small- and medium-sized firms.

———— 2. Commercial paper provides funds at lower rates than most other short-term methods.

———— 3. Fixed assets are the most common type of collateral used for short-term credit due to their large dollar value.

———— 4. A factor typically performs a lending function and a risk-bearing function, but the credit-checking function is retained by the seller.

Now turn to Answer Frame 3⁸, page 56, to check your answers.

Now turn to Answer Frame 3⁸, page 56, to check your answers.

chapter 9

WORKING CAPITAL POLICY

Frame 1⁹

The decision criteria for analysis of investment in current assets have been set forth, and the nature and costs of alternative sources of short-term financing were described. These two streams of analysis are now brought together by a consideration of working capital policy. Working capital policy involves decisions with respect to (1) the mix of current versus fixed assets, (2) the mix of short-term debt versus long-term debt, and (3) the relation between current assets and current liabilities. The third aspect has already been covered in connection with financial ratio analysis as the current ratio, which is a measure of the firm's liquidity or solvency. The first two will now be analyzed.

Although both current and fixed assets are functions of expected sales, only current assets can readily be adjusted to actual sales in the short run. Hence, the burden of making adjustments to short-run fluctuations in sales must be carried by working capital management. The investment in fixed assets can be reduced by renting or leasing rather than owning fixed assets.

The effects of alternative approaches to working capital policies can be illustrated by a numerical example. Three alternative working capital policies are set forth in Table 9–1a and 9–1b: conservative (slack), optimal, and aggressive (tight). In Table 9–1a the analysis of alternative working capital policies is reflected in the balance sheet. Fixed assets are shown to be the same amount, $25,000, under the three alternative policies. However, the amount of current assets and, therefore, the ratio of current assets to fixed assets differs under the three policies. In some respects, life is made easier for the managers

of a firm by following a slack policy with regard to investment in current assets. For example, if inventories are ample, the risk of loss of sales due to stock-out is lower. If credit terms are more liberal or if collections are lax, a firm may be able to increase sales, but only at the expense of greater investment in current assets and possibly higher bad debt loss ratios. This slack or conservative approach is reflected in the $35,000 investment in current assets illustrated in Table 9–1a.

Alternatively, a firm could follow a very tight or aggressive policy toward investment in current assets. Inventories could be held to a minimum, credit terms could be very tight and collections very vigorously pursued. Thus, under the aggressive or tight working capital policy there is a $15,000 investment in current assets. The optimal policy is assumed to represent a balance, resulting in an investment of $25,000 in current assets.

These alternative working capital policies are likely to have an effect on sales. This is indicated by the sales volume set forth in the income statement portion of Table 9–1b. Average sales are increased by $10,000 from the $90,000 for the "tight" policy as the investments in current assets are increased. When the economy is weak or strong, sales are assumed to be another $10,000 lower or higher under each of the three alternative working capital policies. However, a tight working capital policy in a weak economy, in which buyers have more alternatives available, results in stronger negative reactions to inventory stock-outs and aggressive credit actions; hence, a $20,000 sales decline is indicated.

Another impact of alternative credit policies is reflected in the cost functions. The total cost

Answer frame 3[8]

1. False. Commercial paper consists of promissory notes of large, well-established (blue chip) firms that are sold to other large, well-established firms as well as to pension funds, banks, and insurance companies.

2. True. The rates are at or below the prime rate. Firms which issue commercial paper are generally required by commercial paper dealers to have unused bank lines of credit equal to about 10 percent of their outstanding volume of commercial paper. The usual compensating balance on regular bank loans is 15 to 20 percent; consequently, there is still an advantage to commercial paper.

3. False. Pledging accounts receivable, factoring accounts receivable (selling them outright), and the use of inventories are the most common types of collateral used for short-term credit.

4. False. A factor will usually perform all three services and will charge a commission for credit checking. Even though this service is expensive, it may be cheaper for a small firm to factor than to provide its own credit department. This is an area that aggressive banks are now entering.

If you missed any of the above, restudy Frame 3[8] before beginning Chapter 9 on page 55.

Frame 1[9] continued

functions excluding interest expenses are as follows:

$$CGS = FC + VC$$

Slack:	$CGS = \$30,000 + 0.6S$
Optimal:	$CGS = \$25,000 + 0.6S$
Tight:	$CGS = \$20,000 + 0.7S$

where:

CGS is the cost of goods sold.
FC is the fixed costs.
VC is variable costs.
S is sales.

Slack working capital is indicated to have higher fixed costs because of excessive investment in inventory associated with greater warehousing expenses, and so on. Thus, tight working capital policy is associated with lower fixed costs. However, tighter working capital policy will have higher variable costs because there will be more frequent ordering of goods for inventory. Also, on inventory stock-outs greater expenses may be incurred to attempt to obtain inventory under emergency conditions. The cost conditions for the optimal policy are indicated to be between these two extremes.

TABLE 9–1a

Effects of alternative working capital policies on the balance sheet

Balance sheet	Conservative policy (slack)	Optimal policy	Aggressive policy (tight)
Current assets.....................	$35,000	$25,000	$15,000
Fixed assets......................	25,000	25,000	25,000
Total assets..................	$60,000	$50,000	$40,000
Current liabilities (8%).............	$ 5,000	$10,000	$20,000
Long-term debt (10%)..............	25,000	15,000	—
Total debt...................	$30,000	$25,000	20,000
Equity...........................	30,000	25,000	20,000
Total Liabilities and Net Worth..	$60,000	$50,000	$40,000
Current Ratio.....................	7/1	2.5/1	0.75/1

TABLE 9–1b

Effects of alternative working capital policies on the income statement and rates of return

Income statement	Conservative policy (slack)			Optimal policy			Aggressive policy (tight)		
	Strong economy	Average economy	Weak economy	Strong economy	Average economy	Weak economy	Strong economy	Average economy	Weak economy
Sales......................	$120,000	$110,000	$100,000	$110,000	$100,000	$90,000	$100,000	$90,000	$70,000
Less: CGS..............	102,000	96,000	90,000	91,000	85,000	79,000	90,000	83,000	69,000
EBIT........................	18,000	$ 14,000	$ 10,000	$ 19,000	$ 15,000	$11,000	$ 10,000	$ 7,000	$ 1,000
Less: Interest...........	2,900	2,900	2,900	2,300	2,300	2,300	1,600	1,600	1,600
Taxable income...........	$ 15,100	$ 11,100	$ 7,100	$ 16,700	$ 12,700	$ 8,700	$ 8,400	$ 5,400	$ (600)
Less: Taxes (50%).......	7,550	5,550	3,550	8,350	6,350	4,350	4,200	2,700	—
Net Income..........	$ 7,550	$ 5,550	$ 3,550	$ 8,350	$ 6,350	$ 4,350	$ 4,200	$ 2,700	($600)
Rates of return									
EBIT to total assets.......	30.0%	23.3%	16.7%	38.0%	30.0%	22.0%	25.0%	17.5%	2.5%
Return on equity..........	25.2%	18.5%	11.8%	33.4%	25.4%	17.4%	21.0%	13.5%	(3.0%)

Indicate whether each of the following statements is true or false by writing "T" or "F" in the space provided.

_____ 1. The burden of making adjustments for short-run fluctuations in sales can be reduced by leasing fixed assets.

_____ 2. An aggressive working capital policy is more likely to result in frequent stock-outs than a conservative working capital policy.

_____ 3. In forecasting future sales and economic conditions it is important to evaluate several working capital strategies in order to determine the policy that will maximize earnings.

_____ 4. A slack working capital policy in a strong economy and an aggressive working policy in a weak economy is good strategy.

Now turn to Answer Frame 1⁹, page 58, to check your answers.

Answer frame 1⁹

1. False. Only current assets can readily be adjusted to actual sales in the short run; whereas leasing of fixed assets is a long-term type of commitment.
2. True. An aggressive policy involves a smaller investment in current assets (including inventory). Thus, stock-outs are likely to be more frequent than under a conservative policy.
3. False. The firm should evaluate several working capital strategies, but its objective should be to look at *two* parameters—risk and return. Looking only at profitability could place the firm in an extremely risky position and even jeopardize its solvency.
4. False. Such a generalization cannot be made. The optimal policy depends upon the gains and costs involved and may vary among industries and even among individual companies in a given industry.

If you missed any of the above, reread Frame 1⁹ before beginning Frame 2⁹ below.

Frame 2⁹

We next return to the balance sheet section in Table 9–1a to observe differences in the proportion of current to long-term debt. The assumptions under this analysis are that the total debt to equity ratio remains unchanged at 1 to 1. (The leverage ratio as measured by the ratio of debt to total assets is 50 percent.) Thus, under the slack working capital policy in which total assets are higher than under the other two working capital policies, both the total amount of debt and the total amount of equity are higher than in the other two cases.

The larger the percentage of funds obtained from long-term sources, the more conservative the firm's working capital policy. But short-term debt normally carries a lower interest rate than long-term debt. During periods of tight money, however, short-term interest rates may be higher than long-term interest rates. The more the short-term debt, the greater the probability that during a period of tight money the firm may not be able to renew its short-term debt. On the other hand, the use of short-term debt provides the firm with added flexibility under those circumstances when the need for funds is temporary. When the need for funds is seasonal, for example, short-term loans are liquidated within the year, and it would be more expensive to cover such financing by long-term debt.

Three alternative short-term debt policies are illustrated in Table 9–1a. Under the conservative policy, the ratio of current liabilities to long-term debt is 1 to 5. Under the aggressive policy, all debt is in short-term debt. Under the optimal policy, current debt is two thirds of long-term debt. The current ratio follows as a consequence of the two sets of assumptions about investment in current assets and the current debt to long-term debt ratio. Under the slack or conservative capital policy, the current ratio is 7 to 1. Under the aggressive or tight working capital policy, the current ratio is 0.75 to 1. Under the optimal working capital policy, the current ratio is 2.5 to 1.

With the data provided to this point, Table 9–1b can be developed on the basis of the interest rate assumptions shown in Table 9–1a. We have previously set forth the sales and cost of goods sold assumptions and can compute earnings before interest and taxes (EBIT). From the information given, we can also calculate interest expenses, taxable income, taxes, and net income. In the last section of Table 9–1b, rates of return are calculated. The average rate of return is shown to be higher for the optimal credit policy than for the two alternative policies. Thus, we observe that both the return on total assets and the return on equity is higher for the optimal working capital policy. However, this fact alone is not definitive since we have to take into consideration the range of variability in returns under the alternative working capital policies.

Label each of the following statements as true or false.

_____ 1. Under an aggressive working capital policy, total assets required to support a given volume of sales is less than under an optimal or conservative working capital policy.

_____ 2. Although the conservative working capital policy achieves the highest level of sales for all states of the economy, it may not achieve the highest level of profitability.

_____ 3. The larger the percentage of liabilities from long-term sources the more aggressive the firm's working capital policy. (Assuming the leverage ratio of debt to total assets remains the same as is the case in Table 9–1a.)

_____ 4. If we were able to quantify the range of variability in returns under the alternative working capital policies, our optimal working capital strategy could be either more conservative or more aggressive.

Now turn to Answer Frame 2[9], page 60, to check your answers.

chapter 10

THE INTEREST FACTOR

Frame 1[10]

Financial decisions require comparisons among the alternatives of receiving payment immediately, periodically over a number of months or years, or at the end of a period of years. Therefore, sound decisions must take into consideration the influence of interest costs. The situations involving compound interest can be handled by utilizing a small number of basic formulas.

ANNUAL COMPOUND INTEREST RATES

Suppose that your firm is negotiating a sale. Two alternatives are being explored as to how the customer will pay for his purchase: either he will make one payment now, or one somewhat higher payment after a period of time. For example, suppose that you are offered $1,000 today or $1,200 at the end of the fifth year. Which should you take? We assume that if the company received the money immediately it could earn a 6 percent return on those funds. We can state the problem as follows:

P = Principal, or beginning amount = $1,000
r = Interest rate = $6\% = 0.06$
n = Number of years = 5
S_n = The value at the end of the year n

Answer frame 2⁹

1. True. The total asset turnover for an average economy for slack, optimal, and tight working capital policies are 1.83, 2.00, and 2.25, respectfully. Consequently, we see that the tight working policy provides the highest total asset turnover ratio, but not necessarily the best rates of return.

2. True. As shown by Table 9–1b, the overinvestment in current assets reduces profit margin on sales, asset turnover, and hence the return on total assets and equity under the conservative (slack) working capital policy.

3. False. The aggressive firm would use a larger percentage of short-term funds as they are usually less expensive than long-term funds (8 percent versus 10 percent), and the funds would only be borrowed when needed. This type of action, though, increases the risk of not being able to obtain funds when needed due to tight monetary conditions.

4. True. If a working capital policy involves a high probability of loss under some economic conditions, even if it offers a higher average return, the favorable difference in the average return may not, in the view of top management, be worth the additional risk.

If you missed any of the above, reread Frame 2⁹. Before beginning Chapter 10 on page 59, turn to page 193 to work Examination 2, which covers Chapters 7–9.

Frame 1¹⁰ continued

The formula that applies is the compound interest formula.

$$S_n = P(1 + r)(1 + r)(1 + r)(1 + r)(1 + r) \quad (1)$$
$$= P(1 + r)^n$$

Next the data are inserted in the formula.

$$S_5 = \$1,000(1.06)^5$$

We then look in Table A–1 on page 185 to find that at 6 percent, a dollar over a five-year period grows to $1.338. Since the amount we would have now is $1,000, it is multiplied times the interest factor:

$$S_5 = \$1,000(1.338) = \$1,338$$

Therefore, if the firm can earn 6 percent with the money, it is worthwhile for it to receive the $1,000 today rather than $1,200 at the end of the fifth year.

FUTURE AMOUNTS AND THEIR PRESENT VALUES

There is an equivalent way of viewing the situation where a company is offered an amount to be received in the future. It is desirable to compare that amount with the value of whatever amount could be received today. This requires the computation of the present value of the amount to be received in the future. The determination of present values involves the same formula except that it is solved for P, representing present value, instead of for S_n, which is known. By simple algebra the required formula would be:

$$P = S_n/(1 + r)^n \quad (1.1)$$

Using our previous example, we determine S_n to be $1,338. Since the appropriate interest rate is 6 percent and the number of years is five, we would be dividing $1,338 by 1.338 to obtain the result $1,000. But there is a simpler method. We can use a present value interest table (Table A–2 on page 186), which is the reciprocal of a compound interest table. In this case the formula is:

$$P = S_n(1 + r)^{-n} \quad (2)$$

We can now insert the illustrative numbers:

$$P = \$1,338 \, (0.747)$$
$$P = \$1,000$$

Compound interest and present value computations are two different ways of looking at the same relationship.

Indicate whether each of the following statements is true or false by writing "T" or "F" in the space provided.

———— 1. $1,000 invested at 8 percent compounded annually will yield $1,800 at the end of year 10.

———— 2. Table A–2 on page 186 is compiled by taking the reciprocal of all the interest factors in Table A–1 on page 185.

———— 3. The present value of $2,000 to be received four years from now discounted at 12 percent is $1,272.

———— 4. The interest factor for the compound sum of $1 is less than one; whereas the interest factor for the present value of $1 is greater than one.

Now turn to Answer Frame 1^{10}, page 62, to check your answer.

Frame 2^{10}

THE PRESENT VALUE OF AN ANNUITY

Income flows are a series of periodic payments made over a span of time. This type of compound interest situation is probably the one most frequently encountered by a business firm. For example, a firm may sell some goods that will be paid for in three installments of $1,000 payable at the end of each year. At a 10 percent interest rate, what is the present value of those installment payments? The situation can be depicted as follows:

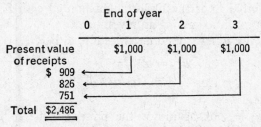

	End of year		
	0	1	2	3
Present value of receipts		$1,000	$1,000	$1,000
	$ 909			
	826			
	751			
Total	$2,486			

Thus the present value of an annuity is the sum of the present value of the amount to be received at the end of each year. But a present value of an annuity table (Table A–3, page 186) will give the amount directly, which is convenient when more than two or three years are involved.

Consider the situation where the firm makes an investment from which it expects to receive a series of cash returns over a period of years. At an appropriate discount rate, what would the series of future income receipts be worth today? The firm needs this information in order to determine whether it is worthwhile to make the investment. For example, the firm makes an investment promising the payment of $1,000 a year for 10 years with an interest rate of 10 percent. What is the present value of such a series of payments?

$$A_{\overline{n}|r} = \frac{a}{(1+r)} + \frac{a}{(1+r)^2} + \cdots + \frac{a}{(1+r)^n} \quad (3)$$

$$= a\left[\frac{1-(1+r)^{-n}}{r}\right],$$

where:

$A_{\overline{n}|r}$ is the present value of an annuity.
a is the amount of the annuity.
r is the interest rate.
n is the number of years.

Equation (3) represents the present value of an annuity factor of $1 at an interest rate, r, for n periods. Note that it is the sum of a series of present value of $1 expressions. Values for equation (3) can be found directly in Table A–3 on page 186 for the designated interest rate and number of years. Since the expression in brackets is somewhat cumbersome, for convenience the symbol $P_{n,r}$ is used where: $P_{n,r}$ is the present value of an annuity factor for n years at r percent. Equation (3) above can, therefore, be rewritten as:

$$A_{\overline{n}|r} = a\,P_{n,r} \quad (3.1)$$

Substituting actual numbers and using the present value of an annuity from the interest table (Table A–3 in the Appendix), we obtain:

Answer frame 1¹⁰

1. False. Using the following formula and table A–1, the result is as follows:

$$S_n = P(1 + r)^n$$
$$S_{10} = 1,000(1 + 0.08)^{10} = 1,000(2.159) = \$2,159$$

2. True. For example, the compound interest factor of $1 for five years at 6 percent is 1.338, which is found in Table A–1 on page 185. The reciprocal of 1.338 is $1/1.388 = 0.747$; which is the present value of $1 located in Table A–2 on page 186 for five years at 6 percent.

3. True. It is calculated as follows:

$$P = Sn(1 + r)^{-n}$$
$$P = 2,000(1 + 0.12)^{-4} = 2,000 \times 0.636 = \$1,272$$
(Use Table A–2)

4. False. It is useful to remember that the present value factor of a single amount is always less than 1 while the compound factor is always greater than 1. This will eliminate the occasional reference to the wrong table.

If you missed any of the above, reread Frame 1¹⁰ before beginning Frame 2¹⁰, page 61.

Frame 2¹⁰ continued

$$A_{\overline{10}|10\%} = \$1,000(6.145) = \$6,145$$

In other words, a series of payments of $1,000 received for 10 years, applying an interest factor of 10 percent, would be worth $6,145 today. Hence, if the amount of investment the firm were required to make was $8,000, for example, or any amount greater than $6,145, the firm would be receiving a return of less than 10 percent on its investment. Conversely, if the investment necessary to earn annual payments of $1,000 for 10 years at 10 percent were say, $5,000 or any amount less than $6,145, the firm would be earning a return greater than 10 percent.

A number of other questions can be answered using these same relationships. Suppose the decision facing the firm requires determining the rate of return on an investment. For example, suppose we would have $6,145 to invest and that an investment opportunity promises an annual return of $1,000 for 10 years. What is the indicated rate of return on our investment? Exactly the same relationship is involved, but now the equation is solved for the interest rate. Rewriting the equation gives:

$$P_{10,r} = A_{\overline{10}|r}/a, \qquad (3.2)$$

where r is the unknown interest rate.
We can now substitute the appropriate figures.

$$P_{10,r} = \$6,145/\$1,000 = 6.145$$

In Table A–3 on page 186, showing present value of periodic payments received annually, we look across the year 10 row until we find the interest rate that corresponds to the interest factor 6.145. This is 10 percent.

Now let us consider another situation. Suppose that we are going to receive a return of $2,000 per year for five years from an investment of $8,424. What is the return on our investment? This is generally referred to as the internal rate of return on investment, or it is also sometimes referred to as the DCF, or discounted cash flow approach to valuing an investment.

We follow the same procedure as before.

$$P_{5,r} = A_{\overline{5}|r}/a$$
$$P_{5,r} = \$8,424/\$2,000$$
$$= 4.212$$

We look again for the present value of an annuity in Table A–3 along the row for year 5 to find the interest factor 4.212. We then look at the interest rate at the top of the column to find that it is 6 percent. Thus, the return on that investment is 6 percent. If our required rate of return was 8 percent, we would not find this investment attractive. On the other hand, if the required return on our investment were only 5 percent, we would consider the investment attractive.

Suppose that the firm has made an investment of $30,725 and will be repaid in annual installments at an interest rate of 10 percent. What is the annual amount the firm will receive for each of the 10 years? The general equation for this problem is

$$a = A_{\overline{n}|r}/P_{n,r} \qquad (3.3)$$

Inserting the amounts given for the problem we have:

$$a = \$30,725/6.145$$
$$= \$5,000$$

The result is exactly $5,000. Suppose the question is, what amount should we have to receive $5,000 for 10 years at a 10 percent interest rate?

In this instance we would solve the general expression for the present value as shown:

$$A_{\overline{n}|r} = a\, P_{n,r}$$

In this problem the annual annuity of $5,000 is given, and the interest factor is determined by the knowledge that the interest rate is 10 percent and the annuity will continue over a 10-year period. When we insert the numbers, we have the following result:

$$= \$5,000(6.145)$$
$$A_{\overline{n}|r} = \$30,725$$

Label each of the following statements as true or false.

_____ 1. The present value of an eight-year annuity of $2,000 discounted at 14 percent is $4,639.

_____ 2. If we invest $12,117 and receive an annual return of $3,000 each year for seven years, our discount rate or rate of return on this investment is 16 percent.

_____ 3. When a firm makes an investment of $25,000 and expects to receive at least a 14 percent rate of return over 10 years, the necessary annual returns or cash inflows are at least $6,000.

_____ 4. The internal rate of return on a $5,000 annuity for six years with an initial cash outflow of $23,115 is 8 percent.

Turn to Answer Frame 2¹⁰, page 64, to check your answers.

Frame 3¹⁰

COMPOUND SUM OF AN ANNUITY

We may also need to know the future value or future sum to which a series of payments will accumulate. The reason may be to determine whether we have enough funds to repay an obligation in the future. The sum of an annuity can be determined from the following basic relationship:

$$S_{\overline{n}|r} = a[(1 + r)^{n-1} + (1 + r)^{n-2} + \cdots + (1 + r)^1 + 1]$$

$$S_{\overline{n}|r} = a\left[\frac{(1 + r)^n - 1}{r}\right] = aC_{n,r} \qquad (4)$$

where:

S is the future sum to which an annuity will accumulate.

a is the annuity.

$C_{n,r}$ is the repeated event or annuity compound interest factor.

Suppose the firm were to receive annual payments of $1,000 a year for five years and is charging an interest rate of 8 percent. What will be the amount that the firm will have at the end of five years? We can solve this problem by consulting Table A–4 on page 187. Utilizing our equation we would have:

$$S_{\overline{n}|r} = \$1,000(5.867)$$
$$S_{\overline{n}|r} = \$5,867$$

The pattern of compounding can be shown by the following illustration:

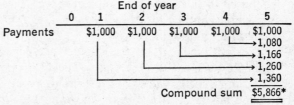

	End of year				
	0	1	2	3	4	5
Payments		$1,000	$1,000	$1,000	$1,000	$1,000
						1,080
						1,166
						1,260
						1,360
				Compound sum		$5,866*

* Difference due to rounding.

Answer frame 2¹⁰

1. False. It is calculated as follows:

$$A_{\overline{n}|r} = a\left[\frac{1 - (1 + r)^{-n}}{r}\right] = aP_{n.r}$$
$$A_{\overline{8}|14\%} = 2{,}000P_{8.14\%} = 2{,}000 \times 4.639 = \underline{\$9{,}278}$$

Use Table A–3 on page 186 to obtain the interest factor for the eight-year annuity at 14 percent. Note: The interest factors in Table A–3 are always less than the number of years for the annuity.

2. True. The return is calculated as follows:

$$A_{\overline{n}|r} = aP_{n.r}$$
$$P_{n.r} = A_{\overline{n}|r}/a$$

or

$$P_{7.r} = A_{\overline{7}|r}/a$$
$$P_{7.r} = 12{,}117/3{,}000 = 4.039$$

In Table A–3 we look across the year seven row until we find the interest factor 4.039. The column that this appears in has a 16 percent interest rate—our return on this project.

3. False. Annual cash inflows are calculated as follows:

$$A_{\overline{n}|r} = aP_{n.r}$$

solving for a we have

$$a = A_{\overline{n}|r}/P_{n.r} = A_{\overline{10}|14\%}/P_{10.14\%} = \$25{,}000/5.216 = \underline{\$4{,}793}$$

At $6,000 annual cash flow our return is higher than 14 percent and would be acceptable and preferable, but $4,793 is also acceptable since at this amount our rate of return is exactly 14 percent.

4. True. The internal rate of return (IRR) is calculated as follows: $r = $ IRR

$$P_{n.r} = A_{\overline{n}|r}/a$$
$$P_{6.r} = A_{\overline{6}|r}/a = \$23{,}115/5{,}000 = 4.623$$

In Table A–3 we look across the year six row until we find the interest factor 4.623. Reading up the column we find our IRR = 8 percent.

If you missed any of the above, reread Frame 2¹⁰ before starting Frame 3¹⁰, page 63.

Frame 3¹⁰ continued

The calculation of the compound sum of an annuity is the sum of five single compound sum terms. (It will be observed that in this presentation we are assuming that the payments are made at the end of each year. This is called a regular annuity or a deferred annuity. If the payment is made at the beginning of the year, it is referred to as an annuity due.) However, these steps are performed for us in Table A–4, the sum of an annuity of $1 for n years.

The five payments of $1,000 each would accumulate to $5,867 by the end of the fifth year. Thus, if we had obligated the firm to repay a $5,000 obligation in five years, it would be able to do so. On the other hand, if the obligation

were more, say $7,000, there might be a problem of insufficient funds.

Sometimes the same question is asked in a different way. Suppose we need to have a specified amount of money, such as $5,867, by the end of five years. How much would we have to set aside each year at an interest rate of 8 percent in order to have that amount? We would solve the equation above for a, the annuity. We would have:

$$a = S_{\overline{n}|r}/C_{n.r} \tag{4.1}$$

Since we know that we need to have $5,867, we look in the interest table for the sum of an annuity, Table A–4, to see what the interest factor is at 8 percent for five years. This is 5.867. Therefore, we would need to set aside $1,000 each year.

Now that the basic idea has been set forth, let us take a more complex example. Suppose the amount of money that the firm must have at the end of 10 years is $29,000. The applicable interest rate is 8 percent. We wish to know how much we would have to set aside each year in order to accumulate the required amount. The general expression is:

$$a = S_{\overline{10}|8\%}/C_{10,8\%} \qquad (4.2)$$

Inserting the numbers given in the illustration we would have:

$$a = \$29,000/14.487 = \$2,002$$

It would be necessary to set aside slightly over $2,000 each year in order to have the required amount.

OVERVIEW

The following formulas have been used:

$$S_n = P(1 + r)^n \qquad (1)$$
$$P = S_n(1 + r)^{-n} \qquad (2)$$
$$A_{\overline{n}|r} = a\left[\frac{1 - (1 + r)^{-n}}{r}\right] = aP_{n,r} \qquad (3)$$
$$S_{\overline{n}|r} = a\left[\frac{(1 + r)^n - 1}{r}\right] = aC_{n,r} \qquad (4)$$

The two expressions for the compound future sum and for the present value of a sum that will be received in the future can be regarded as one equation. For annuities there are different expressions for the interest factor in calculating the present value as compared with the future sum. Thus, in total, only three basic equation relationships are involved.

These three basic equations enable us to solve at least 12 types of problems. We have three equations and we can solve each one of them for any of the four terms in the equation (present value, future sum or annuity, interest rate, number of years) given the other three. Thus, with a relatively small number of relationships, and the help of the compound interest tables, a variety of problems involving the time value of money can be handled. Before closing we will consider three variations on the basic themes set forth.

True or false?

_____ 1.   A bank receiving payments of $2,000 a year, compounded at an annual interest rate of 12 percent will have $30,000 at the end of nine years.

_____ 2.   We would have to set aside $1,974 each year in order to have $10,000 at the end of four years at a 16 percent interest rate.

_____ 3.   The internal rate of return on a six-year annuity which provides $3,000 annual receipts and a $22,008 terminal value is 8 percent.

_____ 4.   Tables A–3 and A–4 are reciprocals.

Now turn to Answer Frame 3¹⁰, page 66, to check your answers.

Frame 4¹⁰

COMPOUNDING PERIODS WITHIN ONE YEAR

In the illustrations set forth thus far, the examples have been for returns that were received once a year (annually). For compounding within one year, we simply divide the interest rate by the number of compoundings within a year and multiply the annual periods by the same factor.

For example, in our first equation for compound interest we had the following:

$$S_n = P(1 + r)^n \qquad (1)$$

This was for annual compounding. For semiannual compounding (or m number of times per year), we would follow the rule just set forth. The equation would become:

Answer frame 3¹⁰

1. False. The terminal amount is calculated using the following formula and Table A–4.

$$S_{\overline{n}|}r = a\left[\frac{(1+r)^n - 1}{r}\right] = aC_{n,r}$$

$$S_{\overline{9}|12\%} = \$2,000 \times 14.776 = \$29,552$$

Note: The interest factors in Table A–4 are always greater than the number of years for the annuity.

2. True. The calculation is as follows:

$$a = S_{\overline{n}|r}/C_{n,r} = S_{\overline{4}|16\%}/C_{4.16\%} = \$10,000/5.066 = \$1,974$$

3. True. The calculation is as follows ($r = $ IRR):

$$C_{n,r} = S_{\overline{n}|r}/a$$
$$C_{6,r} = S_{\overline{6}|r}/a = \$22,008/3,000 = 7.336$$

Using Table A–4 and reading across the year-6 row we find 7.336. Looking up the column we find IRR is 8 percent.

4. False. Tables A–1 and A–2 are reciprocals but Table A–3 and A–4 are not. The reason they are not is because they are annuities which provide for a constant cash flow at the end of each year. An example will clarify this point. Assume a two-year annuity of receipts of $100 at a 10 percent interest rate.

$$S_{\overline{2}|10\%} = aC_{2.10\%} = \$100 \times 2.100 = \$210.00$$
$$A_{\overline{2}|10\%} = aP_{2.10\%} = \$100 \times 1.736 = \quad 173.60$$

If the Tables A–3 and A–4 were reciprocals then

$$A_{\overline{2}|10\%} = a/C_{2.10\%} = 100 \times \frac{1}{2.100} = \$47.60$$

Therefore, they are not reciprocals. Thus, the need for the three basic equations or Tables A–1 or A–2, A–3, and A–4.

If you missed any of the above, reread Frame 3¹⁰ before starting Frame 4¹⁰, on page 65.

Frame 4¹⁰ continued

$$S_{n/m} = P\left(1 + \frac{r}{m}\right)^{nm}, \tag{5}$$

where m is the number of compoundings during a year.

We may apply this to the first numerical illustration employed. The question originally was how much would $1,000 at a 6 percent interest rate accumulate over a five-year period. The answer was $1,338. Now, we apply semiannual compounding. The equation would appear as follows:

$$S_{5/2} = \$1,000\left(1 + \frac{0.06}{2}\right)^{5(2)}$$

Thus, the new expression is equivalent to compounding the $1,000 at 3 percent for 10 periods.

Looking in the compound interest table (Table A–1 on page 185) for 10 years, the interest factor would be 1.344. The equation would read:

$$S_{5/2} = \$1,000(1 + 0.03)^{10}$$
$$= \$1,344$$

With semiannual compounding the future sum amounts to $1,344 as compared with the $1,338 we had before. Frequent compounding provides compound interest paid on compound interest, so the result is higher. Thus, we would expect that daily compounding, as some financial institutions advertise, or continuous compounding, as is employed under some assumptions, would give somewhat larger amounts than annual or semiannual compounding. But, the basic ideas are unchanged.

The same logic is equally applicable to all categories of relationships we have described. For example, in the first illustration on the present value of an annuity, the problem was stated as the payment of $1,000 a year for 10 years with an interest rate of 10 percent, compounded annually. If the compounding is semiannual we would employ an interest rate of 5 percent and apply the compounding to 20 periods. When compounding semiannually, it is also necessary to divide the annual payment by the number of times the compounding takes place within the year. Then, utilizing our previous example we would have the following expression:

$$
\begin{aligned}
A_{\overline{nm}|r/m} &= \$500(P_{r/m,nm}) \\
&= \$500(P_{10\%/2,10(2)}) \\
&= \$500(P_{5\%,20}) \\
&= \$500(12.462) \\
&= \$6,231
\end{aligned}
$$

It will be noted that with annual compounding the present value of the annuities is $6,145, but with semiannual compounding the present value is $6,231. With more frequent compounding, the results will be somewhat higher because interest is compounded on interest.

CALCULATIONS FOR A SERIES OF UNEQUAL RECEIPTS OR PAYMENTS

In all previous illustrations we have assumed that the receipts flowing in or the payments to be made are of equal amounts, which simplifies the calculations. However, if unequal receipts or unequal payments are involved, the principles are again the same, but the calculations must be extended somewhat. For example, suppose that the firm makes an investment from which it will receive the following amounts:

Year	Receipts	× Interest factor (15%)	= Present value
1........	$100	.870	$ 87.00
2........	200	.756	151.20
3........	600	.658	394.80
4........	300	.572	171.60
		PV of the investment =	$804.60

Using the present value interest table (Table A–2), at an interest rate of 15 percent we obtain the amounts indicated above. The interest factor multiplied times the receipts is the present value. The amounts for each year are then summed to determine the present value of the investment, which in this example is $804.60. This example illustrates how an annuity of unequal payments which could not be computed directly from the present value of an annuity table can be handled by breaking the problem into a series of one-year payments received at successively later time periods.

This illustrates a general technique that can be employed in using compound interest relationships. A particular business problem or decision involving the time value of money, no matter how complex, can usually be handled by compound interest methods. The technique is to take a complex problem and break it into a series of simple ones. Then the results of the simple problems can be combined to arrive at the overall solution.

THE DETERMINATION OF THE APPLICABLE INTEREST RATES

A number of sources can be used to determine the applicable interest rate in a particular business decision. One broad reference is the general level of interest rates in the economy as a whole. Individual interest rates in the economy generally differ by the maturity (the period of time over which the obligation runs) as well as the degree of risk of the obligation. Short-term U.S. government securities generally bear the lowest rate of interest, while the debt obligations of a small company with an uncertain future usually carry a relatively high rate of interest.

In addition, the levels of interest rates are affected by business conditions in the economy at a particular time and by economic developments in foreign countries. For guidance on interest rate levels in the economy, financial managers may refer to readily available publications such as the *Survey of Current Business*, published by the United States Department of Commerce; the *Federal Reserve Bulletin*, published by the Board of Governors of the Federal Reserve System; *International Financial Statistics*, published by the International Monetary Fund; and *Economic Indicators,* available from the United States Government Printing Office. All of these publications are available at nominal subscription rates.

Another guide in the determination of which interest rate should be applied in making com-pound interest decisions is consideration of what the firm could earn if it used the money in some alternative investment opportunity. This is generally referred to as the opportunity cost of an investment. The opportunity cost of investments is the yield on the best alternative use of the funds.

Is each of the following true or false?

_____ 1. A lump sum of $2,000 at 8 percent interest compounded quarterly accumulates over five years to a $9,322 terminal value.

_____ 2. We would have to set $2,850 aside each quarter in order to have $10,000 at the end of three years at a 16 percent interest rate (interest to be compounded quarterly).

_____ 3. A firm investing the indicated receipts at the end of each year at 15 percent will receive $1,406.50 at the end of year 4.

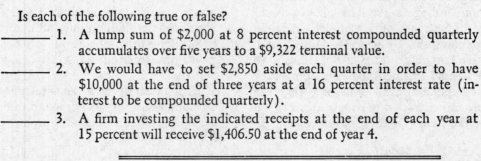

Year	Receipts	× Interest factor (15%)	= Terminal value
1.............	$100	1.521	$ 152.10
2.............	200	1.322	264.40
3.............	600	1.150	690.00
4.............	300	1.000	300.00
		$S_n =$	$1,406.50

_____ 4. The opportunity cost of an investment is the applicable cost of capital on the best equivalent risk investment alternative foregone.

Now turn to Answer Frame 4¹⁰, page 70, to check your answers.

chapter 11

CAPITAL BUDGETING DECISIONS

Frame 1[11]

Capital budgeting represents the process of planning expenditures whose returns extend over a period of time. Examples of capital outlays for tangible or physical items are expenditures for land, buildings, and equipment. Outlays for research and development, advertising, or promotion efforts may also be regarded as investment outlays when their benefits extend over a period of years. While capital budgeting criteria are generally discussed in relation to investment in fixed assets, the concepts are equally applicable to investment in cash, receivables, or inventory. Selection of the criteria for making such investments is the subject matter of this chapter.

ADMINISTRATIVE ASPECTS

Investment decisions and their evaluation by capital budgeting analysis are important for a number of reasons. (1) The consequences of the decision continue for a number of years. Thus to some degree after making an investment decision, some flexibility for the future is reduced. (2) Capital budgeting requires effective planning, including accurate sales forecasts, to assure the proper timing of asset asquisitions. This means that capital assets should be available when needed, and yet not too early to avoid the extra cost of having them idle until required. (3) Since asset expansion involves substantial outlays, the required financing must be arranged in advance. (4) Since the dollar amounts of outlays on investments are large, the success or failure of an enterprise may result from excessive investments, inadequate amounts of investment, or undue de-

lay in replacing obsolete assets with modern assets.

Individual firms usually have formal administrative procedures for reviewing capital budgeting requests. Small items can be approved by individual department heads while larger dollar amounts require approval from officers at higher levels in the organizational structure. Major investment outlays require the review and approval of the company's Finance Committee or, in some instances, the Board of Directors.

The Finance Department generally coordinates its activities with other departments to develop systematic records on the use of investment funds. Records are also compiled on revenues and savings from equipment purchased. An important aspect of the record keeping is postaudits, which provide a comparison between the initial estimates and the actual results. The postaudits review past decisions to aid in improving decisions on new investment outlays.

ALTERNATIVE CRITERIA

Three major methods for the evaluation and ranking of investment proposals are utilized. They are (1) the payback period (N), (2) the net present value (NPV), and (3) the internal rate of return (IRR). Each criterion will be defined, the numerical computation process will be illustrated, and the characteristics of the method will be described. For illustration, we will utilize Investment A, which provides cash flows (profit after taxes plus depreciation) of $300 for six years and requires an investment outlay of $900.

Answer frame 4^{10}

1. False. The calculation for the terminal value is as follows:

$$S_{n/m} = P\left(1 + \frac{r}{m}\right)^{nm} = \$2,000\left(1 + \frac{0.08}{4}\right)^{5 \times 4} = 2,000 \times 1.486 = \$2,972$$

The interest factor is obtained in Table A–1 on page 185 for 2 percent for 20 periods.

2. False. The calculation for the quarterly payment is as follows:

$$S_{\overline{nm}|\ r/m} = aC_{nm,r/m}$$
$$S_{\overline{3 \times 4}|\ 16/4} = aC_{3 \times 4, 16/4}$$
$$a = S_{\overline{12}|\ 4\%}/C_{12,4\%} = \$10,000/15.026 = \$665.5$$

The interest factor is obtained in Table A–4 on page 187 for 12 periods at 4 percent.

3. True. Using the compound sum table (Table A–1), at an interest rate of 15 percent we obtain the amounts indicated. For example, the $100 receipt at the end of year one is compounded annually three years at 15 percent giving a terminal value of $152.10.

4. True. The opportunity cost of an investment is the yield on the best alternative use of the funds. We will use this concept again in a later chapter.

If you missed any of the above, restudy Frame 4^{10} before beginning Chapter 11, page 69.

Frame 1^{11} continued

Indicate whether each of the following statements is true or false by writing "T" or "F" in the space provided.

_____ 1. Capital budgeting is a discounted cash flow analysis used to make decisions on capital outlays for fixed assets only.

_____ 2. The administrative aspects of capital budgeting that are probably the most crucial are the gathering of accurate source data (cash flow estimates) and the post-audits review of actual results versus predicted results.

_____ 3. Since the approval level for small investment outlays in capital budgeting is usually delegated to the lower levels of management in an organization, it is a good practice in post-audits review to determine if large jobs have been sectionalized into many individual components.

_____ 4. The accounting return on investment (net income divided by total assets) is one of the three major methods for evaluating and ranking investment proposals.

Now turn to Answer Frame 1^{11}, page 72, to check your answers.

Frame 2[11]

The payback period is defined as the number of years required to return the original investment.

$$\text{Payback period } (N) = \frac{\text{Initial fixed investment}}{\text{Annual cash inflows}}$$

$$N(A) = \frac{900}{300} = 3 \text{ years}$$

The main value of the payback period is that it provides information on the risk and liquidity of the project. The shorter the payback period, the greater the liquidity of the project and the less risky in terms of the number of years required before the investment is recovered. For a firm with cash flow or liquidity problems, the payback period may be given very heavy weight. The principal drawbacks of the payback period are (1) It fails to consider cash flows after the payback period and consequently cannot be regarded as a measure of profitability. (2) It fails to consider the timing of cash flows during the payback period, ignoring the time value of money. (3) It is an incomplete measure of risk because, by focusing only on the expected outcomes relative to the original investment, it does not take into account the dispersion of possible outcomes. In the illustration, Investment A has a payback period of three years. In sum, using the payback method for evaluating alternative investments may lead to the wrong decision in that a project may be chosen which does not maximize the net present value of cash flows.

The second criterion, the net present value (NPV), is the present value of all future cash flows discounted at the cost of capital, minus the cost of the investment, also discounted at the cost of capital. Assuming a cost of capital of 10 percent, the calculation of the NPV for the project proceeds as follows:

$$\text{Net present value (NPV)}$$
$$PV(A) = 300.00(4.355) = \$1,306.50$$
$$NPV(A) = \$1,306.50 - 900.00 = \$406.50$$

The 4.355 for Project A represents the present value of an annuity of $1 at 10 percent for six years. The annual net inflows multiplied by the respective annuity factors gives the total present value of the flows for each. The cost of the investment is subtracted from the total present value to obtain the net present value of Project A, $406.

The three distinguishing characteristics of the net present value criterion are: (1) It accounts for the time value of money. (2) The present time is used as the reference point. (3) The NPV approach implies reinvestment at the cost of capital.

The third investment criterion is the internal rate of return. The internal rate of return represents the discount rate at which the net present value or net terminal value of all cash flows is zero. The calculation procedure is shown in the next frame.

Label each of the following statements as true or false.

_____ 1. The payback period is used in addition to discounted cash flow methods in capital budgeting as it does provide information on the risk and liquidity of the project.

_____ 2. Assuming the cost of funds to be 8 percent for a project requiring an initial investment of $2,000 which provides net cash flows of $600 each year for six years, the net present value is $2,773.80.

_____ 3. In question 2 the net present value (NPV) methodology assumes that the net cash flows of $600 each year are reinvested to year 6 in other investment opportunities yielding an 8 percent return.

_____ 4. The internal rate of return (IRR) is a special case of our more general NPV methodology where NPV must be zero.

Now turn to Answer Frame 2[11], page 72, to check your answers.

Answer frame 1[11]

1. False. Capital budgeting is a discounted cash flow analysis used to make decisions on capital outlays for fixed assets and also for investments in current assets. Many serious errors are made in capital budgeting analysis of long-term investments when working capital effects are ignored.

2. True. In computer lingo—GIGO means garbage-in-garbage-out. The original cash flow estimates and the monitoring of results in capital budgeting are crucial to the effectiveness of the capital budgeting process.

3. True. Without any planned control feature to guard against sectionalization in the capital budgeting process, a natural tendency is for lower levels of management to divide a big job into many individual components. They do this in order to eliminate the necessity of obtaining higher level management approval and to avoid the greater amount of paper work involved. Almost always sectionalization of a job will be more costly, and in addition many unprofitable or marginal projects will be implemented.

4. False. The three methods are (1) the payback period (N), (2) the net present value (NPV), and (3) the initial rate of return (IRR). The accounting return does not use basic cash flow data and therefore does not directly deal with the time value of money. Net income is derived from the general accrual process of accounting.

If you missed any of the above, review Frame 1[11] before starting Frame 2[11], page 71.

Answer frame 2[11]

1. True. This is particularly true of small, fast-growing firms with cash flow or liquidity problems. The discounted cash flow methods are used also because they overcome the primary disadvantages posed by the payback period.

2. False. NPV is calculated as follows:

$$\text{NPV} = aP_{n,r} - \$2,000 = \$600 \times 4.623 - \$2,000 = \$773.80$$

The interest factor (4.623) for a six-year annuity at 8 percent is found in Table A–3 on page 186. Since NPV > 0, the project is acceptable.

3. True. To clarify this point we can do the following:

Step 1: Calculate the terminal value.

$$S_{\overline{6}|8\%} = aC_{6,8\%}$$
$$S_{\overline{6}|8\%} = \$600 \times 7.336 = \$4,401.60$$

Step 2: Calculate the present value (P) of the terminal value.

$$P = S_6(1+r)^{-6} = \$4,401.60(1+0.08)^{-6}$$
$$P = \$4,401.60 \times 0.630 = \$2,773$$

Step 3: Deduct the investment outlay.

$$\text{NPV} = \$2,773 - \$2,000 = \$773$$

We obtain the same NPV by first calculating the total terminal value by assuming the intermediate net cash flows to be reinvested at the cost of funds rate, then discounting back at the 8 percent cost of funds, and subtracting the initial investment. This proves that the intermediate net cash flows must be reinvested at the cost of funds rate.

4. True. We set NPV = 0 or NTV = 0 and solve for the rate of return that satisfies the equation.

If you missed any of the above, reread Frame 2[11] before beginning Frame 3[11], page 73.

Frame 3¹¹

Calculation procedure for internal rate of return (IRR): Equate net present values of revenues and costs and solve for r.

IRR(A)

$$900 = 300 (P_{6,r}) \quad (\text{use } r = 24\%)$$
$$900 = 300 (3) \quad (r \cong 24\%)$$

Equate net terminal values of revenues and costs and solve for r.

IRR(A)

$$900 (1 + r)^6 = 300 (C_{6,r}) \quad (\text{use } r = 24\%)$$
$$900 (3.635) = 300 (10.980)$$
$$3,272 \cong 3,294 \quad (r \cong 24\%.)$$

In equating net present values, we need to obtain the present value of an annuity factor of $1 such that the present value of cash inflows will equal the investment outlay. This is obtained by dividing the annual cash flows into the investment. For Investment A the interest factor for an annuity of $1 for six years is 3.000, which represents an interest rate of approximately 24 percent. The same result is obtained by equating net terminal values. The procedure requires that the investment outlays be multiplied by the compound sum of $1, the interest factor for the appropriate number of years. These are equated respectively to the annual cash inflows multiplied by the compound sum of an annuity factor for the appropriate number of years. The interest rate that (approximately) equates these two streams is the internal rate of return.

The internal rate of return accounts for the time value of money. It implies reinvestment at the internal rate of return. From a practical or operational standpoint, it has the value of providing a result expressed as a percentage factor or as an interest factor, which conveys meaning as a rate-of-return figure. A drawback of the IRR method is that if, after a series of net inflows has begun, in one or more years a net outflow occurs, multiple solutions may result. For this and other reasons the IRR criterion will sometimes lead to inconsistent results: that is, more than one discount rate may equate the present value of cash inflows to the present value of investment costs.

True or false?

_____ 1. The internal rate of return for net cash flows of $700 for six years with an initial investment outlay of $2,448.60 is 18 percent.

_____ 2. In question #1 the IRR methodology assumes that the $700 net cash flows are reinvested to year 6 in other investment opportunities yielding a return equal to the cost of capital.

_____ 3. The IRR and NPV methodologies are discounted cash flow (DCF) processes that account for the time value of money and will always result in accurate investment decisions.

_____ 4. IRR methodology is usually superior to NPV methodology because the assumption about the reinvestment rate is probably more realistic in actual business operations.

Now turn to Answer Frame 3¹¹, page 74, to check your answers.

Frame 4¹¹

NPV VERSUS IRR CRITERIA

To understand more fully the superiority of the NPV approach as compared to the IRR criterion requires use of the calculation procedure when the amounts of cash flows each year are unequal, which will be illustrated for Projects B and D. The dollar amount of investment outlay remains the same, $900. However, the net inflows follow the pattern indicated in Table 11–1. The total amount received over future time periods is $1,200 for Investment B with larger inflows in the earlier years. For Investment D, the total inflows are $1,300 with larger inflows in the later

Answer frame 3¹¹

1. True. The IRR when NPV = 0 is calculated as follows:

$$\$2,448.60 = \$700P_{6,r}$$

where r is IRR; $P_{6,r}$ is 3.498 (using Table A–3 on page 186), we find r equals IRR, or 18 percent. Alternatively, we could find IRR when NTV = 0 as follows:

$$\$2,448.60(1 + r)^6 = 700C_{6,r}$$

Using $r = 18$ percent and Tables A–1 on page 185 and A–4 on page 187, we have

$$\$2,448.60 \times 2.7 \cong 700 \times 9.442$$
$$6611.22 \cong 6609.40$$

Thus,

$$\text{IRR} = 18 \text{ percent.}$$

2. False. The IRR methodology assumes that the intermediate net cash flows of $700 are reinvested at the IRR of 18 percent. It was the NPV methodology that assumed that the intermediate cash flows are reinvested at the cost of capital rate of return.

3. False. The IRR method may lead to incorrect decisions in cases where in one or more years a reversal (positive net cash flow, negative net cash flow, positive net cash flow, and so on) of cash flow occurs. In these cases, multiple IRR may result. The solution to this problem is to explicitly determine what reinvestment rate is applicable to the intermediate cash flows.

4. False. The NPV assumption that the intermediate net cash flows are reinvested at the cost of capital is usually a more realistic rate of return and is consistently applied to all projects. The reinvestment rate for IRR methodology will be different for every project IRR. In addition, even though a particular project has an abnormally high IRR the reinvestment rate is probably not that high.

If you missed any of the above, reread Frame 3¹¹ before starting Frame 4¹¹, page 73.

Frame 4¹¹ continued

years. Because of the different time patterns of net inflows, the discount factor has a different weighting influence.

Table 11–1 illustrates the calculations of the net present values of Project B and Project D. The present values for each of the two projects are first calculated. Since the net cash flows are different for each year the calculations must be made for each year individually. Then the present value interest factor for each year for each interest rate illustrated is multiplied times the net cash inflows for each year to obtain the present values of each net cash inflow. These present values are totaled for the six years to obtain the row labeled "Present values." The net present values are obtained by subtracting the investment cost of $900 from each present value amount.

In Table 11–2 the net present values for Project B and Project D are tabulated for all of the interest rates utilized in Table 11–1, which range from 1 percent to 16 percent. Note that at the

very low interest rate of 1 percent, the present values of the inflows exceed the investment outlay by substantial amounts. At the 16 percent interest rate, the present values of the inflows are less than the initial investment outlay.

The net present values are calculated by subtracting the cost of the investment from the present values of the net cash inflows. The data in Table 11–1 demonstrate that the internal rate of return (IRR) is the special case when the net present value (NPV) is zero. For Project D the net present value at a 9 percent interest rate is $5 but at an interest rate of 10 percent is a negative $27. Hence the net present value of Project D would be zero at slightly more than 9 percent. Similarly, for Project B at an interest rate of 12 percent the net present value is $15, but at an interest rate of 13 percent the net present value is a negative $2. Hence the internal rate of return for Project B is slightly under 13 percent. Table 11–2 shows that the investment worth of a proj-

TABLE 11–1

Calculations of net present values
(C_o = Initial investment = $900)

Net cash inflows

Year	B	D
1....................................	$400	$100
2....................................	300	100
3....................................	200	200
4....................................	150	200
5....................................	100	300
6....................................	50	400

	Interest factor = 1%			Interest factor = 9%			Interest factor = 10%		
		Present values			Present values			Present values	
Year	Percent	B	D	Percent	B	D	Percent	B	D
1................................	.990	$ 396	$ 99	.917	$367	$ 92	.909	$364	$ 91
2................................	.980	294	98	.842	253	84	.826	248	83
3................................	.971	194	194	.772	154	154	.751	150	150
4................................	.961	144	192	.708	106	142	.683	102	137
5................................	.951	95	285	.650	65	195	.621	62	186
6................................	.942	47	377	.596	30	238	.564	28	226
Present values................		$1,170	$1,245		$975	$ 905		$954	$ 873
Net present values...........		$ 270	$ 345		$ 75	$ 5		$ 54	$ (27)

	Interest factor = 12%			Interest factor = 13%			Interest factor = 16%		
		Present values			Present values			Present values	
Year	Percent	B	D	Percent	B	D	Percent	B	D
1................................	.893	$ 357	$ 89	.885	$354	$ 89	.862	$345	$ 86
2................................	.797	239	80	.783	235	78	.743	223	74
3................................	.712	142	142	.693	139	139	.641	128	128
4................................	.636	95	127	.613	92	123	.552	83	110
5................................	.567	57	170	.543	54	163	.476	48	143
6................................	.507	25	203	.480	24	192	.410	21	164
Present values................		$ 915	$ 811		$898	$ 784		$848	$ 705
Net present values...........		$ 15	$ (89)		$ (2)	$(116)		$(52)	$(195)

ect is measured by its net present value which in turn depends upon the cost of capital appropriately used in discounting the net cash inflows. In addition, the net present values for a zero cost of capital are also included, simply representing the total net cash inflows less the initial investment of $900. At low costs of capital, the NPV of Project D is greater than the NPV of Project B. However, at higher rates of interest the NPV of Project D is less than the NPV of Project B. In general, the projects whose returns are largest in the earlier years will have higher net present values at higher costs of capital. Conversely, projects whose larger returns are realized in later years will have lower net present values at higher costs of capital. This is because the projects with higher returns in the later years are penalized by the lower values of the discount factors (the larger degree of discounting) applied in later years.

The foregoing relationships are depicted graphically in Figure 11–1. At a 0 cost of capital, Project D has a higher net present value and it remains higher until an interest rate of about 5 percent. At a higher applicable cost of capital, the NPV of Project B exceeds the NPV of Project D by increasing amounts.

Figure 11–1 also enables us to observe graphi-

TABLE 11–2
Influence of cost of capital on net present values

| Cost of capital | Net present values for various cost of capital rates | |
	B	D
0.....................	$300	$400
1%..................	270	345
9.....................	75	5
10.....................	54	(27)
12.....................	15	(89)
13.....................	(2)	(116)
16.....................	(52)	(195)

cally the definition of the internal rate of return. The internal rate of return is the cost of capital at which the present value of a project is zero—the point at which the NPV lines cross the horizontal axis. In Figure 11–1 we can observe graphically that the internal rate of return of Project D is slightly above 9 percent and for Project B is slightly below 13 percent. However, we cannot say unambiguously that Project B is superior to Project D because its internal rate of return is higher. At a cost of capital of 4 percent, for example, the net present value of Project D exceeds the net present value of Project B; however, at costs of capital greater than 5 percent, Project B is superior. Only the net present value method provides an unambiguous rule for evaluating projects.

Using the NPV approach implicitly assumes that the funds generated during the life of a project can be reinvested at the firm's marginal cost of capital. The IRR approach implies that the funds generated by a particular investment can be reinvested at the calculated IRR. Note that the IRR is not a market return, but rather a "number" that results from the firm's evaluation of a given project. On the other hand, the firm's cost of capital is the market price the firm must pay for capital. Clearly it is much more realistic to assume that the firm can reinvest its revenues at a rate of return equal to that currently available in the capital market, rather than at a rate of return which happens to make the discounted net present value of a particular investment equal to zero.

ANALYSIS OF REPLACEMENT DECISIONS

A systematic procedure is set forth for the analysis of equipment replacement decisions. The concepts will be developed through the use of illustrative examples, data for which are set forth in Table 11–3. A tax rate of 40 percent is used to distinguish between the factor multiplied by $(1 - t)$ and the factor multiplied by t. For a

FIGURE 11–1

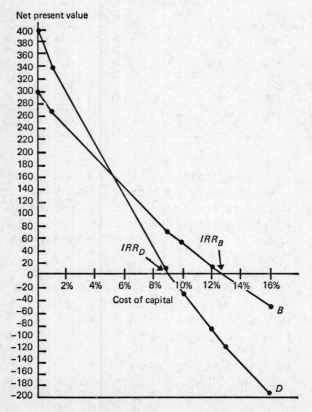

TABLE 11–3
Facts for analysis of equipment replacement

	Old machine	New machine
Purchase time......	5 years before	This year
Cost.................	$10,000	$12,000
Estimated life..... .	10 years	10 years
Expected end-of-life salvage value.....	0	$ 2,000
Sales level..........	$15,000	$16,500
Operating costs.....	$11,000	$ 9,500
Tax rate............	40%	40%
Cost of capital......	12%	12%
Current value.......	$ 3,000	$12,000
Book value at end of 5 years (straight-line depreciation).	$ 5,000	

small firm, an average or marginal tax rate of 40 percent is not unrealistic, but for a large firm a more accurate tax rate would be 48 percent. However, the aim is to make these illustrations relatively simple so that most of them can be followed by mental calculations. For actual situations, hand calculators or even computer programs can be employed. The aim here is simply an understanding of the principles involved.

In Table 11–4, a work sheet for systematic analysis of replacement investment decisions is shown. The outflows are identified by reference to the time at which the investment is made in order to indicate the total amount of funds required to initiate the action. Thus the first item is the $12,000 outlay on the new equipment. If investment is made in the new equipment and a salvage value of $3,000 is realized on the disposal of the old equipment, the amount realized on the sale is $3,000. Since this would reduce the net amount of cash required to purchase the new equipment, the salvage value of the old machine, which is an inflow, is treated in the work sheet as a negative outflow. When the old equipment is sold at a price below its book value, a tax loss is established. Under the assumption of straight-line depreciation, the book value at the time the old machine is sold is $5,000. The tax loss on the sale of old equipment, the third item of out-

flow, reflects a set of relatively complicated tax principles, the upshot of which is that a tax loss on the sale of capital equipment can be charged against ordinary income. Hence in the present example the $2,000 tax loss establishes an after-tax saving represented by multiplying the 40 percent tax rate times the amount of the tax loss. Thus another negative outflow is the tax loss of $800.

Benefits and inflows are represented by an increase in sales and reduction of costs of $1,500 each or $3,000. It is clear that the benefits of $3,000 per year would be subject to the ordinary income tax of 40 percent. The amount of the benefit after tax would be obtained by multiplying the annual benefits by $(1 - t)$. Since the tax rate is 0.4, the value of $(1 - t)$ would be 0.6; when 0.6 is multiplied times $3,000, the amount after tax is $1,800. This is multiplied by the present value of an annuity factor at 12 percent, which is 5.650, to give $10,170.

Since the new machine has a depreciable value of $10,000 and a 10-year life, the depreciation is $1,000 per year. On the other hand, the undepreciated portion, or the book value of the old machine, will also be decreasing $1,000 a year for its remaining five years of life. Since the depreciation on the old is calculated over the remaining 5-year life, it may be argued that the comparison

TABLE 11–4

Analysis of investment replacement*

	Amount before tax	Amount after tax	Year event occurs	Present value factor at 12%	Present value
Outflows at time investment is made					
Investment in new equipment..........................	$12,000	$12,000	–	1.000	$12,000
Salvage value of old.......................................	(3,000)	(3,000)		1.000	(3,000)
Tax loss on sale...	(2,000)	(800)	0	1.000	(800)
Total outflows (present value of costs)..............					$ 8,200
Inflows, or annual returns					
Benefits...	3,000	1,800	1–10	5.650	$10,170
Depreciation on new (annual)...........................	1,000	400	1–10	5.650	2,260
Depreciation on old (annual)............................	(1,000)	(400)	1–5	3.605	(1,442)
Salvage value on new.....................................	2,000	2,000	10	0.322	644
Total inflows (present value of benefits)............					$11,632
Present value of inflows..................................					$11,632
Present value of outflows................................					8,200
Net present value of inflows minus outflows..............					$ 3,432

* Straight-line depreciation used on both the old and new equipment

is of a 5-year flow for the old equipment and a 10-year flow for the new. While there are some technical niceties that might be explored here, the fact is that the new machine has a remaining life of 10 years and the old machine of only 5 years. An equivalent annual cost analysis could be made but would not be necessary in view of the margin of error to which the estimates of sales increases or reduction in operating cost are subject.

The reason that the after-tax depreciation amounts are included in inflows is that the depreciation expense results in a reduction of taxes. Since taxes represent an outflow, a reduction in taxes is a negative outflow and can be treated as a positive inflow. Just as the tax loss was multiplied by t, the tax rate, the annual depreciation expense is also multiplied by t (to determine the amount of the annual tax that is avoided or sheltered by the depreciation expense). The depreciation on the new machine of $1,000 is multiplied by 0.4 to establish a tax shelter of $400 per year for 10 years. The depreciation on the old machine of $1,000 per year under a straight-line depreciation method is also $400; however, it represents a loss of a tax shelter extending over the remaining five-year life of the old machine.

The final item in the inflows section of Table 11–4 is the salvage value on the new machine. The new machine is expected to have a salvage value of $2,000 at the end of 10 years. This amount is discounted over the 10-year period back to the present.

In this illustration, the sum of the outflows is found to be $8,200 and the sum of the inflows is $11,632. The difference represents a net present value of $3,432, at the firm's cost of capital of 12 percent, in favor of investing in the new machine to replace the old machine.

This work-sheet method is a convenient procedure for systematically organizing the outflows and inflows, and is applicable to all types of investment decisions such as new product analysis, expansion decisions, and so on. The basic idea is to analyze the present value of outflows as compared with the present value of inflows obtained, utilizing the firm's cost of capital to discount both streams.

In the above example, straight-line depreciation was used to simplify the calculations. How-

ever, two accelerated depreciation methods are now widely used by business firms: either the sum-of-the-years' digits method (SYD) or the double declining balance method (DDB). These two methods will be illustrated by reference to a machine purchased for $1,200 with an estimated useful life of 10 years and a scrap value of $200 at the end of a 10-year period. Table 11–5 compares the depreciation charges under straight-line depreciation compared with SYD and DDB. The following discussion explains how each column is calculated.

The straight-line depreciation is simply the $1,200 outlay less the $200 salvage value which equals $1,000, representing the depreciable value of the asset. Its life is 10 years. The annual depreciation over the asset's depreciable life is therefore $100 per year.

Under the DDB method of accelerated depreciation, the annual straight-line rate is doubled and then applied to the undepreciated value of the asset as of the end of the previous year. In the present example, since the annual straight-line rate is 10 percent per year, the double declining rate would be 20 percent. The rules provide that the DDB rate can be applied to the full purchase price of the machine, not the cost less salvage value. Also, a company can switch from DDB to straight line whenever the straight-line depreciation on the remaining book value of the asset exceeds the DDB depreciation. For

TABLE 11–5

Comparison of depreciation methods for a 10-year, $1,200 asset with a $200 salvage value

| Year | Depreciation methods | | |
	Straight line	Sum-of-the-years digits	Double declining balance
1	$ 100	$ 182	$ 240
2	100	164	192
3	100	145	154
4	100	125	123
5	100	109	98
6	100	91	79
7	100	73	78
8	100	55	78
9	100	36	78
10	100	18	78
	$1,000	$1,000	$1,198

our example, the calculation under the DDB method would be as follows:

Year	DDB	Straight line	Undepreciated amount under DDB
0.....			$1,200
1.....	.20(1,200) = $ 240		$1,200 — $240 = 960
2.....	.20(960) = 192		960 — 192 = 768
3.....	.20(768) = 154		768 — 154 = 614
4.....	.20(614) = 123		614 — 123 = 491
5.....	.20(491) = 98		491 — 98 = 393
6.....	.20(393) = 79		393 — 79 = 314
7.....	.20(314) = 63	$ 78	314 — 63 = 251
8.....	.20(251) = 50	78	251 — 50 = 201
9.....	.20(201) = 40	78	201 — 40 = 161
10.....	.20(161) = 32	78	161 — 32 = 129
	$1,071	$1,198	

Check on shift to straight-line method:

Year	Remaining book value DDB method	Number of years remaining	Depreciation
6..............	$393	5	$79
7..............	314	4	78
8..............	251	3	84

In the sixth year, shifting to the straight-line depreciation method would result in the same depreciation of $79 as under DDB, so there would be no advantage to shifting. In the seventh year there is an advantage of 78 less 63 which equals 15. There is no reason to wait until the eighth year to shift.

EVALUATION RULES UNDER ALTERNATIVE SITUATIONS

Some additional distinctions are required to set forth appropriate investment ranking or selection rules. First, several different types of investment proposals are encountered. *Mutually exclusive proposals* are alternative methods of performing the same function. Examples would be a steel bridge versus a wooden bridge, or the selection of fork-lift trucks versus conveyor belts for moving materials in a factory. *Independent proj-*

ects are not related. For instance, mechanization of a firm's accounting system, the purchase of loading docks, and the addition of power facilities are mutually independent proposals. *Contingent proposals* are those for which the consideration of one proposal is dependent upon first adopting a prior proposal. For example, a firm may need additional equipment, but has no remaining factory floor space. In order to purchase additional equipment, the firm must either lease or buy additional floor space—thus, the investment in additional equipment is contingent upon prior investments in additional floor space.

Second, we distinguish whether the situation is one of *capital rationing* or of no capital rationing. Capital rationing means that the firm does not have sufficient funds to finance all the proposals for investments that have been developed by the managers of the firm. In the extreme case of "strict" capital rationing, the firm may be unable to raise more than some specific amount of funds, for example, $10 million for a large firm or $200,000 for a small firm. In other words, at some dollar amount the firm is unable to obtain additional funds. Hence, under strict capital rationing, the total of investment outlays cannot exceed the absolute amount specified. If there is no capital rationing, the firm is able to raise all funds required for its available investment opportunities at its cost of capital. In the more realistic intermediate case, beyond some quantity of investments the firm's cost of capital curve is no longer horizontal, but begins to have a positive slope.

With *no capital rationing*, the acceptance of a single proposal and multiple independent or multiple contingent proposals is the same. The rule is to accept all projects if the net present value (NPV) or net terminal value (NTV), using the cost of capital as the discount rate, is positive. For mutually exclusive proposals, select the proposal with the highest positive NPV or NTV.

Under capital rationing, or a rising cost of capital curve, there is no simple selection rule. The theoretically correct result can be obtained only by the utilization of one of the mathematical programming techniques—linear programming, integer programming, dynamic programming, or variations on these basic types. The correct result under capital rationing (particularly if the projects are independent in time sequence) can be approximated by developing a ranking of the investment opportunities by their NPV's. This schedule is then related to the availability of funds at a range of costs of capital. Alternatively, the internal rate of return approach can be used.

Projects can be ranked by their internal rates of return (to obtain a marginal efficiency of capital schedule), relating this prospective investments schedule to the firm's marginal cost of capital curve. This procedure is illustrated in Chapter 14, after the cost of capital functions have been discussed.

Is each of the following true or false?

_____ 1. NPV is also superior to IRR methodology when amounts of net cash flow each year are unequal because the calculation procedure for NPV is much more simple.

_____ 2. As illustrated by Table 11–1 on page 75, when the cost of capital is high, projects that have large cash flows later in the investment planning horizon will have a relatively low NPV.

_____ 3. If an additional $2,000 is necessary for set-up cost in the example in Table 11–4, our NPV would be $1,432.

_____ 4. Mutually exclusive projects are those for which the consideration of one proposal is dependent upon first adopting a prior proposal.

Now turn to Answer Frame 4^{11}, page 82, to check your answers.

chapter 12

INVESTMENT UNDER UNCERTAINTY

Frame 1¹²

In this chapter the following will be covered: (1) return and risk measures, (2) the use of decision trees, (3) portfolio diversification, and (4) the role of utility in investment choices.

RETURN AND RISK MEASURES

An index of investment worth is developed by comparing its expected return with the possibilities that the actual return may be different from the expected return. The symbols employed in the development of the concepts introduced in this chapter are summarized in Table 12–1.

The returns from any investment will be in-

TABLE 12–1

Explanation of symbols used

s = Alternative future states of the world.

π_s = The probability assigned to various possible outcomes of an investment.

$E(R_j) = \bar{R}_j$ = The expected return on investment j; this is the weighted average or actuarial return with weights determined by the probabilities.

σ_j^2 = Variance of the returns on investment j from their average; a measure of dispersion.

σ_j = The standard deviation of returns; the square root of variance.

CV_j = The coefficient of variation of the returns from investment $j = \sigma_j/E(R_j)$.

$Cov(R_j,R_k)$ = The covariance of returns between investments = $Cor(R_j,R_k)\sigma_j\sigma_k$ or $Cor_{jk}\sigma_j\sigma_k$.

$Cor(R_j,R_k)$ = Correlation of returns between investments = $Cov(R_j,R_k)\sigma_j\sigma_k$ or $Cov_{jk}/\sigma_j\sigma_k$.

$E(R_p)$ = The expected return from a portfolio.

σ_p = The standard deviation of portfolio returns or risk of the portfolio.

w_j = Proportion of the total portfolio in the jth security or investment.

fluenced by developments that take place during the life of the investment. Wars, international tensions, government economic policies, crop yields, and so on will all influence the future states of the world. Many alternative states may occur from various combinations of many different influences. For practical illustration, we consider three alternatives in Table 12–2.

In Table 12–2, some illustrative probability factors and related investment returns are set forth. Multiplying each possible return by its associated probability and adding over all future states gives the expected or mean return from the investment.

Table 12–2 then proceeds to illustrate the calculation of a measure of dispersion. In column (5), the deviation of each possible return from the average return is calculated. We are seeking a measure of the average deviation, so in column (6) we square the deviations as the next step, to avoid cancelling out positive and negative deviations. Finally, in column (7), each probability factor is multiplied times the associated squared deviation, and then summed over all states to obtain the variance.

To place the measure of dispersion in the same dimensions as the mean value, we "unsquare" the variance by taking its square root to obtain the standard deviation. The coefficient of variation standardizes the risk measure by dividing it by the mean value expressed in the same units, resulting in a "pure" number which can be directly compared with other pure numbers $[\sigma_j/E(R_j)]$. It gives risk per unit of returns

Answer frame 4[11]

1. True. This point is illustrated by Projects B and D (see page 75).
2. True. This is because the projects with higher returns in the later years are penalized more by the lower discount factors applied in later years. Graphical analysis of this point is illustrated in Figure 11–1 on page 76.
3. False. The only change in Table 11–4 is a $2,000 outflow at $t = 0$ and a change in the depreciation on new machine to $1,200 before tax and $480 after tax for years 1–10. NPV is calculated as follows:

$$NPV = 10,170 + 2,712 + 644 - 1,442 - 10,200 = \$1,884$$

4. False. Mutually exclusive proposals are alternative methods of performing the same function. The question describes a contingent proposal.

If you missed any of the above review Frame 4[11] before beginning Chapter 12 on page 81.

Frame 1[12] continued

TABLE 12–2
Calculation of the expected return and dispersion of the returns from investment *j*

(1) Alternative future states of the world s	(2) Prob-ability factor π	(3) Possible returns from he investment R_j	(4) Calculation of expected return πR_j	(5) Calculation of dispersion $[R_j - E(R_j)]$	(6) $[R_j - E(R_j)]^2$	(7) $\pi[R_j - E(R_j)]^2$
1............................	.3	−.020	−.006	−.120	.0144	.0043
2............................	.5	.200	.100	.100	.0100	.0050
3............................	.2	.030	.006	−.070	.0049	.0010
	1.0		$E(R_j) = .100$		$\sigma_j{}^2 =$	.0103
			$CV_j = \sigma_j/E(R_j) = 10.2\%/10\% = 1.02$		$\sigma_j =$	10.2%

and for our example illustrated in Table 12–2 it is calculated to be 1.02.

Assuming that variations from the mean return are as likely to be downward as upward, (such as a normal or bell-shape distribution) the smaller dispersion of possible returns from their expected return, the better. The smaller the variance, standard deviation or coefficient of variation, the better. Thus, the mean return is a "good," and the standard deviation or coefficient of variation is a "bad." Therefore, the mean-variance approach seeks to achieve the greatest return per unit of risk incurred, or for a given return seeks to minimize the risk incurred.

Indicate whether each of the following statements is true or false by writing "T" or "F" in the space provided.

_____ 1. An index of investment worth is the mean-variance approach which quantitatively measures both risk and return.

_____ 2. The expected return for the following probability distribution of possible returns is 7 percent.

Probability Factor π	Possible returns from the investment R_i
.05	−.10
.10	0
.20	.04
.30	.08
.20	.12
.10	.16
.05	.26
1.00	

_____ 3. The measure of dispersion is either variance ($\sigma_j^2 = .00516$ or standard deviation ($\sigma_j = 7.18$ percent) for the preceding data.

_____ 4. The coefficient of variation standardizes the risk measure, and for the preceding data we obtain a CV $\approx$ .9.

Now turn to Answer Frame 1^{12}, page 84, to check your answers.

Frame 2^{12}

THE USE OF DECISION TREES

Thus far a comparison has been made between the returns and risks of individual projects. But many important decisions do not have to be made at any one point in time: sometimes decisions may be made in stages. For example, a firm considering the possibility of locating a plant in another section of the country might take the following steps: (1) spend $50,000 for a survey of supply and demand conditions in the new region; (2) if the survey results are favorable, spend $1 million on a pilot plant to determine whether market penetration can be achieved; (3) upon the basis of this initial experience, plan for (a) enlarging the existing plant, (b) building a larger plant to meet expectations of future growth in sales, or (c) if the prospects are unfavorable, abandoning the regional expansion efforts entirely. The sequence of judgments can be mapped out in a pattern similar to the branches of a tree. Hence, the analysis has been termed decision tree analysis.

An illustration is set forth in Figure 12–1. The

FIGURE 12–1

Illustrative decision tree

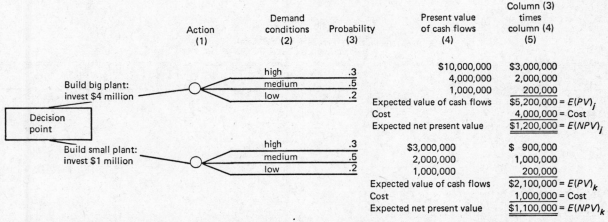

Note: The figures in column 4 are the annual cash flows from operations—sales revenues minus cash operating costs—discounted at the firm's cost of capital. The above analysis combines the calculation of present values from Chapter 11 with the application of probabilities to determine expected values and their dispersion described in the first section of the present chapter. By assuming that the present values have already been calculated, the more cumbersome procedures for combining both types of calculations have been avoided.

Answer frame 1[12]

1. True. An index of investment worth is developed by comparing its expected return with the possibilities that the actual return may be different from the expected return. The mean-variance approach seeks to achieve the greatest return per unit of risk or the greatest reduction in risk for a given level of return.

2. False. The expected return is 8.0 percent and is calculated as follows: $.05(-.10) + .10(0) + .20(.04) + .30(.08) + .20(.12) + .10(.16) + .05(.26) = .08$, or 8.0 percent.

3. True. The variance (σ^2) and standard deviation (σ) are calculated as follows:

    Variance: $\sigma_j^2 = .05(-.10 - .08)^2 + .10(0 - .08)^2 + .20(.04 - .08)^2 + .30(.08 - .08)^2 + .20(.12 - .08)^2 + .10(.16 - .08)^2 + .05(.26 - .08)^2 = .00516$.

    Standard deviation: $\sigma_j = \sqrt{.00516} = .0718$, or 7.18 percent.

4. True. The coefficient of variation (CV) is calculated as follows:

$$CV_j = \frac{\sigma_j}{\bar{R}_j} = \frac{.0718}{.0800} = .8975 \approx .9$$

This project then has less risk than the project illustrated in Table 12–2 since its $CV_j = 1.02$.

If you missed any of the above, reread Frame 1[12] before beginning Frame 2[12], page 83.

Frame 2[12] continued

firm has decided to build another plant. It faces two choices: building a $4 million plant or a $1 million plant. The probabilities for a high, medium, and low growth of sales over the next five years are set forth in Column (3). Column (4) sets forth the present value of cash flows. Column (5) represents the multiplication of the probabilities by the present value of the cash flows. The expected net present value for the $4 million plant is $1.2 million, and for the $1 million plant it is $1.1 million. Thus, the expected net present value is higher for the large plant than for the smaller plant. The coefficient of variation $[CV_j = \sigma_j / E(R_j)]$ for the large plant's expected net present values is 2.78 but only 0.64 for the smaller plant. Thus, the risk to return ratio is smaller for the small plant than for the larger one. By this criterion the smaller plant should be built instead of the larger plant. However, as explained later in this chapter, decisions involving risk ultimately depend on the decision makers' attitude about bearing risk.

TABLE 12–3
Return and risk analysis
(dollar amounts in 000,000)

π	NPV	πNPV	NPV–E(NPV)	[NPV–E(NPV)]²	π[NPV–E(NPV)]²
0.3	$6	$1.8	$4.8	$23.04	$6.912
0.5	0	0.0	(1.2)	1.44	0.720
0.2	(3)	(0.6)	(4.2)	17.64	3.528
		$E(NPV)_i = \overline{1.2}$			$\sigma_i^2 = \overline{11.160}$
					$\sigma_i = 3.340$
					$CV_i = \sigma_i/E(NPV)_i = 2.780 = \dfrac{3.34}{1.20}$
0.3	2	0.6	0.9	0.81	0.243
0.5	1	0.5	(0.1)	0.01	0.005
0.2	0	0	(1.1)	1.21	0.242
		$E(NPV)_k = \overline{1.1}$			$\sigma_k^2 = \overline{0.490}$
					$\sigma_k = 0.700$
					$CV_k = \sigma_k/E(NPV) = 0.636 = \dfrac{.7}{1.1}$

Label each of the following statements as true or false.

_____ 1. Many important capital investment decisions which require large sums of money are made in stages—and an excellent tool frequently used for these types of decisions is a "decision tree."

_____ 2. If we change the probabilities in Figure 12–1 for high, medium, and low growth in sales anticipated by building a big plant to 0.2, 0.5, and 0.3, respectfully, the $E(NPV)_j$ equals \$500,000 ($j =$ \$4 million plant).

_____ 3. With the changes made in Question 2, our risk is greater since the $CV_j = 10.5$.

_____ 4. Our choice, now based on the risk to return ratio, is to build the larger plant.

Now turn to Answer Frame 2^{12}, page 86, to check your answers.

Frame 3^{12}

PORTFOLIO DIVERSIFICATION

The return-risk analysis is not complete if confined to a single investment. We must consider the interactions of the return-risk patterns for one investment with the return-risk patterns of other investments. In particular, we must take into consideration the covariation between the patterns of possible returns between investments: the covariance. Covariance is defined as:

$$Cov\ (R_j, R_k) = Cor(R_j, R_k)\sigma_j\sigma_k$$

Thus, covariance is defined by multiplying the standard deviations of the returns from each of the projects by a measure of the degree of correlation between the returns from the two investments.

The correlation between returns is another basic concept taken from statistics. The values of the correlation coefficient range from plus 1 for perfect positive correlation to minus 1 for perfect negative correlation. A zero correlation coefficient indicates no relationship between the returns

TABLE 12–4
Relation between corvariance and correlation

Basic facts:

π_s	R_{sj}	R_{sk}
.1	10	−10
.4	− 5	5
.5	12	−12

Formula

$$Cor_{jk} = \frac{Cov_{jk}}{\sigma_j\sigma_k} \qquad \text{Equation (12–1)}$$

Computations

π_s	R_{sj}	πR_{sj}	$(R_{sj} - \bar{R}_j)$	$(R_{sj} - \bar{R}_j)^2$	$\pi_s(R_{sj} - \bar{R}_j)^2$	R_{sk}	πR_{sk}	$(R_{sk} - \bar{R}_k)$	$(R_{sk} - \bar{R}_k)^2$	$\pi(R_{sk} - \bar{R}_k)^2$
.1	10	1	5	25	2.5	−10	−1	− 5	25	2.5
.4	− 5	−2	−10	100	40.0	5	2	10	100	40.0
.5	12	6	7	49	24.5	−12	−6	− 7	49	24.5
		$\bar{R}_j = 5$			$\sigma_j^2 = \overline{67.0}$		$\bar{R}_k = \overline{-5}$			$\sigma_k^2 = \overline{67.0}$
					$\sigma_j = \sqrt{67}$					$\sigma_k = \sqrt{67}$

π_s	$(R_{sj} - \bar{R}_j)(R_{sk} - \bar{R}_k)$	$\pi_s(R_{sj} - \bar{R}_j)(R_{sk} - \bar{R}_k)$
.1	(5)(− 5) = − 25	− 2.5
.4	(−10)(10) = −100	−40.0
.5	(7)(− 7) = − 49	−24.5
		$Cov_{jk} = \overline{-67.0}$

$$Cor_{jk} = \frac{Cov_{jk}}{\sigma_j\sigma_k} = \frac{-67}{\sqrt{67}\sqrt{67}} = \frac{-67}{67} = -1$$

Answer frame 2¹²

1. True. A graphic illustration like the one shown in Figure 12–1 is of great assistance in visualizing this more complicated decision process.

2. False. $E(NPV)_j$ is calculated as follows:

$$
\begin{array}{rcl}
.2 \times \$10,000,000 &=& \$2,000,000 \\
.5 \times \ \ \ 4,000,000 &=& \ \ 2,000,000 \\
.3 \times \ \ \ 1,000,000 &=& \ \ \ \ \ 300,000 \\
\hline
&& \$4,300,000 \ E(PV) \\
&& \ \ 4,000,000 \ Cost \\
\hline
&& \$ \ \ \ 300,000 \ E(NPV)_j
\end{array}
$$

3. True. CV_j is calculated as follows, $j = \$4$ million plant:

π	NPV	πNPV	NPV − E(NPV)	[NPV − E(NPV)]²	π[NPV − E(NPV)]²
.2......	6	1.2	5.7	32.49	6.498
.5......	0	0	−0.3	0.09	0.045
.3......	−3	−0.9	−3.3	10.89	3.267
	$E(NPV)_j =$	0.3		$\sigma_j{}^2 =$	9.810
				$\sigma_j =$	3.132

$$
CV_j = \frac{\sigma_j}{E(NPV)_j} = \frac{3.132}{0.300} = 10.44
$$

Thus, our risk measure (CV) increased to 10.50 from 2.78.

4. False. The decision to build the small plant is further reinforced because with the new probabilities, $E(NPV)_k = 0.9$ and $\sigma_k = 0.7$. Hence $CV_k = 0.78$ which is a much smaller increase than for CV_j. In addition, when $E(NPV)_k > E(NPV)_j$ and $CV_k < CV_j$, our decision is clear cut as both the return and risk measures favor the building of a \$1 million plant.

If you missed any of the above, reread Frame 2¹² before starting Frame 3¹², page 85.

Frame 3¹² continued

from the two investments. Hence two investments with a correlation of zero may be regarded as independent investments.

The relation between covariance and correlation is illustrated in the following example for a correlation of negative 1. We can employ the expression for calculating the correlation coefficient as shown in equation (12–1) and utilized in the computations in Table 12–4. The data in Table 12–4 demonstrate the relation between return, risk, the measure of covariance, and the correlation coefficient.

Three relationships, utilizing the symbols defined in Table 12–1, will be employed in the analysis of risk reduction by portfolio diversification (Recall also that $Cov_{j,k} = Cor_{j,k}\sigma_j\sigma_k$):

$$E(R_p) = w_i E(R_j) + (1 - w_i)E(R_k) \qquad (12\text{--}2)$$

$$\sigma_p = [w_i{}^2\sigma_j{}^2 + (1 - w_i)^2\sigma_k{}^2 + 2w_i(1 - w_i)Cov_{jk}]^{\frac{1}{2}} \qquad (12\text{--}3)$$

$$w_j = \frac{\sigma_k{}^2 - Cov_{jk}}{\sigma_j{}^2 + \sigma_k{}^2 - 2Cov_{jk}} \qquad (12\text{--}4)$$

Equation (12–4) gives the proportion w_j of a portfolio in security j that will minimize the standard deviation of portfolio returns. In practical application for two security cases, we designate as security j, the security with the lowest standard deviation. Then the variance term in the numerator is the variance of the other security which has the larger variance.

While we will illustrate the concepts for the two-asset portfolio, the principles are exactly the same for the multi-asset portfolio. For many investment portfolios, more complex matrices of variance and covariance relationships are involved computationally, but the concepts are the same as those that will be illustrated here.

The illustrative calculations are now presented. We begin with example 1 in which the basic facts are presented first.

Facts given for example 1:

$$E(R_j) = 10\% \quad \sigma_j = 6\% \quad w_j = 0.5$$
$$E(R_k) = 12\% \quad \sigma_k = 10\% \quad \text{Cor}_{jk} = -1$$

The correlation of negative 1 assumes that when one investment does well the other does poorly and vice versa. The numbers given in the illustration indicate that investment k has a somewhat higher return, but an even greater degree of risk. The two investments are assumed to be combined equally in the portfolio, $w_j = 0.5$.

Calculations for example 1 $(\text{Cor}_{jk} = -1)$:

$$E(R_p) = .5(10) + .5(12) = 11\%$$
$$\sigma_p = [(.5)^2(6)^2 + (.5)^2(10)^2$$
$$+ 2(.5)(.5)(-1)(6)(10)]^{\frac{1}{2}}$$
$$= [.25(36) + .25(100) - .5(60)]^{\frac{1}{2}}$$
$$\sigma_p = 2\%$$

The expected return on the portfolio is seen to be the average of the expected returns from the two individual investments. However, the standard deviation or risk of the portfolio is only 2 percent, which is much below the 6 percent for the j investment and 10 percent for the k investment.

Example 1 illustrates the power of portfolio diversification. The expected return is the simple average weighted by the proportion of the investments in the portfolio. However, the standard deviation or risk of the portfolio is greatly reduced. This reduction occurs because of the perfect negative correlation between the returns from the two investments. Indeed, with a correlation of negative 1, the risk or standard deviation of the portfolio can be eliminated.

A reasonable alternative possibility would be that the correlation between the two investments is zero (example 2). This would indicate that they are independent investments, and that the economic influences on the two investments stem from independent and unrelated sources or causes. The weights remain 0.5 of the portfolio in each security $(w_j = 0.5)$.

Calculations for example 2 $(\text{Cor}_{jk} = 0)$:

$$E(R_p) = 11\%$$
$$\sigma_p = [9 + 25]^{\frac{1}{2}}$$
$$\sigma_p = 5.8\%$$

The expected return from the portfolio remains 11 percent since the proportions of the two investments have been unchanged. However, because the correlation between the returns from the two investments is now zero, the standard deviation of the portfolio rises to 5.8 percent, but the risk of the portfolio is still lower than the risk from either of the individual investments.

We can now utilize Equation (12–4) to determine that proportion in which to combine the investments in the portfolio in order to reduce risk as much as possible.

Calculations for example 3 $(\text{Cor}_{jk} = -1)$:

$$w_j = \frac{10[10 - (-1)(6)]}{(10)^2 + (6)^2 - 2(-1)(6)(10)}$$
$$= \frac{10(16)}{100 + 36 + 120} = \frac{160}{256} = .625$$
$$w_j = .625 \qquad E(R_p) = 10.75\%$$
$$(1 - w_j) = .375 \qquad \sigma_p = 0$$

Calculations for example 4 $(\text{Cor}_{jk} = 0)$:

$$w_j = \frac{10(10 - 0)}{(10)^2 + (6)^2}$$
$$= \frac{100}{100 + 36} = \frac{100}{136} = .735$$
$$w_j = .735 \qquad E(R_p) = 10.53\%$$
$$(1 - w_j) = .265 \qquad \sigma_p = 5.14\%$$

Example 3 shows that the best proportion is 0.625 when the correlation coefficient is negative one. For example 4, in which the correlation coefficient is zero, the best proportion would be 0.735.

We can summarize the pattern of relations shown by these simple examples. Table 12–5 shows the effects on the portfolio return (E_p) and portfolio risk (σ_p) by moving to the portfolio proportions which minimize portfolio risk. When the correlation between the returns from the two securities is a negative one, placing 0.625 of the portfolio in security j will reduce the portfolio

TABLE 12–5
Summary of influence of portfolio proportions on return and risk

Example number	Correlation coefficient	Weights	$E(R_p)$	σ_p
1.......	$Cor_{jk} = -1$	$w_j = .500$	11.00%	2.00%
2.......	$Cor_{jk} = 0$	$w_j = .500$	11.00%	5.80%
3.......	$Cor_{jk} = -1$	$w_j = .625$	10.75%	0
4.......	$Cor_{jk} = 0$	$w_j = .735$	10.53%	5.14%

standard deviation to zero. However, the portfolio return is also reduced, from 11 percent to 10.75 percent. Similarly, when the correlation between the returns from the two securities is zero, the proportion of portfolio in security j which minimizes the portfolio standard deviation is 0.735.

These examples make clear what is meant by achieving the best portfolio. *Best* is here defined as minimizing the portfolio standard deviation. However, it is clear that a tradeoff is involved. To reduce the portfolio standard deviation requires giving up some portfolio return.

True or false?

_____ 1. A favorable portfolio effect is where the deviation of the returns from the steel company subsidiary (σ_j) and the deviation of the returns from the residential construction subsidiary (σ_k) result in a combined deviation of the returns from both (σ_p) less than either of σ_j and σ_k.

_____ 2. Covariance and correlation coefficient are synonymous terms.

_____ 3. Since most projects in capital budgeting are positively correlated, the opportunity for risk reduction through diversification is very slight indeed.

_____ 4. With a correlation coefficient of negative 1, the risk or standard deviation of a portfolio can be eliminated.

Now turn to Answer Frame 3¹², page 90, to check your answers.

Frame 4¹²

Thus even for portfolios, a combination may involve more risk and more return or less risk and less return. A portfolio is defined as *efficient* if it combines investments in those proportions which provide the highest return for a given amount of risk, or the lowest amount of risk for its return class. These proportions of investments represent the set of efficient portfolios.

This is illustrated in Figure 12–2. The boundary AB describes the portfolio combinations that satisfy the condition just stated. This can be demonstrated by comparisons with the portfolio risks and return combinations on every part of the figure portrayed in the chart. For example, portfolios whose risk-return results fall on the boundary from A to C involve less return and greater risk, so they are less efficient than portfolios on the boundary segment A to B. Portfolios in the boundary segments CD and EB are characterized by an increased amount of return for a

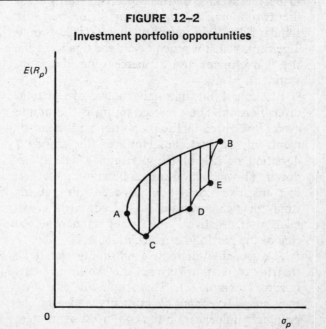

FIGURE 12–2
Investment portfolio opportunities

greater amount of risk. However, all of the points on the boundary *CDEB* are dominated by combinations interior to those portfolios, and the interior portfolios are in turn dominated by all of those portfolios on the boundary *AB*.

Which combination of risk and return on the boundary segment *AB* is best? The question cannot be answered for all investors. Every point on the boundary segment *AB* is efficient.

The combination of risk and return preferred depends upon the decision-makers' preferences between risk and return combinations. Thus to analyze the decision as to risk-return combinations, we must necessarily bring into the analysis a consideration of utility theory and reactions or attitudes of the decision maker toward bearing risk. Hence the subject of utility theory is considered next.

Is each of the following true or false?

——— 1. The efficient set in Figure 12–2, representing all the investment portfolio opportunities, is the entire shaded area bounded by *A B E D C*.

——— 2. Point *A*, representing one investment portfolio opportunity, dominates an investment portfolio opportunity represented as point *D*.

——— 3. Diversification can only be achieved by including a large number of assets in a portfolio.

——— 4. Generally, firms can diversify more efficiently than individuals because of their expertise, level of sophistication, synergy in merger activity, and full-time application of management know-how.

Now turn to Answer Frame 4^{12}, page 90, to check your answers.

Frame 5^{12}

RISK AND UTILITY THEORY

Since utility is a psychological attitude or preference, its measurement involves the same kind of problems as measuring temperature. An arbitrary choice of origin and unit of measurement is made, and then useful comparisons can be made and utility functions developed. A procedure associating utility with various levels of income has been developed:

Select any two incomes, say $500 and $1,000. Assign any arbitrary utilities to these incomes, say 0 utiles and 1 utile, respectively. This corresponds to an arbitrary choice of origin and unit of measure. Select any intermediate income, say $600. Offer the consumer unit the choice between (1) a chance α of $500 and $(1 - \alpha)$ of $1,000 or (2) a certainty of $600, varying α until the consumer unit is indifferent between the two. . . . Suppose this indifference value of α is 40 percent chance of obtaining $500 and a 60 percent chance of obtaining $1,000. If the hypothesis is correct, it follows that: $U(600) =$

$2/5 U(500) + 3/5 U(1,000) = 2/5 \times 0 + 3/5 \times 1 = 3/5 = 0.60$ utiles. Thus, the utility attached to every income between $500 and $1,000 can be determined in this way.

By the procedure described in the quotation above, the relationship between utility and income or wealth can be developed over a range of values as illustrated in Table 12–6. The data in Table 12–6 can then be graphed as shown in Figure 12–3.

While the quantity of utility (utiles) is arbitrary, the shape of the curve illustrated in Figure

TABLE 12–6

Illustration of decision maker's utility for range of returns

Dollar payoff	Utility
$1,000	1.000
900	.975
800	.925
700	.800
650	.720
600	.600
500	.000

Answer frame 3¹²

1. True. When the economy is booming, the returns for steel are high, whereas the returns for residential construction are low. The relationship is countercyclical (a negative correlation coefficient), and when the two subsidiary returns are combined, a stable pattern of returns results. Thus, the deviations of returns on the portfolio of assets, σ_p, may be less than the sum of the deviations of the returns from the individual assets. This risk reduction is defined as the portfolio effect.
2. False. Covariance is defined as:

$$\text{Cov}(R_j, R_k) = \text{Cor}(R_j, R_k)\sigma_j\sigma_k$$

The correlation coefficient is the degree of correlation between the returns of j and k and is only one of the terms needed to calculate the broader term (used in calculating σ_p) covariance.
3. False. It is true that most projects are positively correlated but they are not perfectly positively correlated. Any correlation coefficient less than $+1$ will reduce the risk of the portfolio—and the nearer the coefficient of correlation is to -1 the greater the reduction in portfolio risk.
4. True. The elimination of portfolio risk is illustrated in example 3 with $\text{Cor}_{jk} = -1$, where the portfolio standard deviation is calculated as follows:

$$\sigma_p = [(.625)^2(6)^2 + (.375)^2(10)^2 + 2(.625)(.375)(-1)(6)(10)]^{\frac{1}{2}}$$
$$\sigma_p = 14.08 + 14.08 - 2(14.08) = 0$$

However, the expected return is as follows:

$$E[R_p] = .625(10) + .375(12) = 10.75\%$$

Example 1, using $w_j = .5$, had a $\sigma_p = 2$ percent and a $E(R_p) = 11$ percent. Therefore, we have reduced portfolio risk from 2 percent to 0, but our expected return for the portfolio has also been reduced from 11 percent to 10.75 percent. Our choice then will have to be made based on a utility curve incorporating the consideration of risk and return. The utility curve will be developed later in the chapter.

If you missed any of the above, reread Frame 3¹² before beginning Frame 4¹², page 88.

Answer frame 4¹²

1. False. The shaded area in Figure 12–2 is represented by all the attainable sets of risky assets. Portfolios on boundary AB are the efficient set. A portfolio on the efficient set dominates all other attainable sets since it represents either the greatest return for a given level of risk or the least amount of risk for a given level of return.
2. True. Point A represents a portfolio compared to which there are no other feasible combinations of investment opportunities that will provide a smaller standard deviation for that given level of return. Point A is on the efficient frontier.
3. False. Portfolio diversification or reduction of portfolio risk can be achieved with a relatively small number of assets. The most important consideration is the covariance of possible returns between investments.
4. False. It is generally believed that investors can diversify more efficiently than business firms. Individual investors can buy any security traded on public markets—a far wider choice than the investment opportunities available to the firm's management, and the individual investor has the opportunity to switch investments with far greater ease than the firm's management.

If you missed any of the above, reread Frame 4¹² before starting Frame 5¹², page 89.

Frame 5[12] continued

FIGURE 12–3

Relation between utility and dollar payoffs

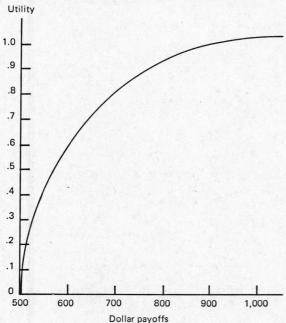

FIGURE 12–4

Relation between utility and money

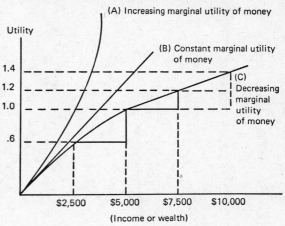

12–3 is of significance. The curve illustrates an individual investor for whom the utility of income or wealth increases at a decreasing rate as his income or wealth increases. The increments of utility or the marginal utility of income or wealth decreases as the level of income or wealth increases. Other possibilities are that the marginal utility of money is an increasing function of income or wealth, or that the marginal utility of income or wealth is constant. These alternatives are graphed in Figure 12–4, where dollars of income or wealth are shown on the horizontal axis and utility is shown on the vertical axis. If an individual has a constant utility for money, his utility rises linearly with wealth (curve B). If he has an increasing utility of money, his utility rises more than proportionately as wealth increases (curve A). If his marginal utility of money is declining, each additional dollar brings less satisfaction than the previous one (curve C).

Most investors appear to have a declining marginal utility for money, and this affects their attitude toward risk. Risk means the probability that a given return will turn out to be lower than

was expected. Someone who has a constant marginal utility for money will value each dollar of "extra" returns just as highly as each dollar of expected returns not earned in the event of the "bad" outcome. On the other hand, someone with a diminishing marginal utility for money will get more pain from a dollar lost than pleasure from a dollar gained. Because of his utility of money function, the second individual will be averse to risk, and he will require a higher return on an investment that is subject to much risk.

The shape of the investor's utility function will influence the shape of the curves expressing the relation between return and risk that he requires as shown in Figure 12–5. A person with decreasing marginal utility of money (curve C in Figure 12–4) will require increasing increments of expected return for bearing additional units of risk as measured by the standard deviation of portfolio returns. Line B represents the risk averter; line A represents an even higher degree of risk aversion. Line C in Figure 12–5 corresponds to line B in Figure 12–4, representing an individual who is willing to receive a constant proportional increase in return for increases in risk. D actually prefers risk. For a standard deviation of 4 percent, A requires an 11 percent expected return; B, 8 percent; C, 6 percent; and D, 3 percent ex-

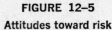

FIGURE 12–5

Attitudes toward risk

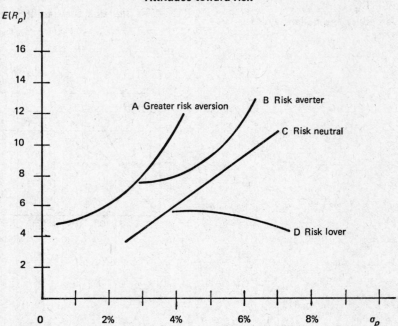

pected return. Individual C is said to be risk neutral, individuals A and B illustrate risk aversion, and D prefers to bear risk. It is generally held that individuals are risk averters. In general, the more risk, the greater return individuals will require.

In Figure 12–6, we bring together the influences of portfolio opportunities provided by the market, illustrated in Figure 12–2, and the influence of the utility functions of the decision maker as reflected in the return-risk requirements shown in Figure 12–5 for individuals with different marginal utility functions. Since individuals are generally risk averse, we shall utilize curves A and B, representing different degrees of risk aversion from Figure 12–5. Curve A from Figure 12–5 is shown as the utility indifference curve U_A in Figure 12–6. Curve B from Figure 12–5 is shown as the utility indifference curve U_B in Figure 12–6.

The curves are called utility indifference curves because they portray combinations of risk and return that are equally satisfactory to the individual. There are a series of utility indifference curves parallel to U_A and U_B that are drawn

tangent to the line segment AB boundary of efficient portfolios. The indifference curves above U_A and U_B are more desirable since they provide higher returns for a given amount of risk or less risk for a given amount of returns. Indifference curves that lie below U_A and U_B are less desirable, so we can dismiss them from further consideration. But only U_A and U_B can be attained by the market opportunities available as reflected in the line segment AB. Hence for individual A, the risk-return combination at point M is an equilibrium situation. For individual B, the equilibrium combination of risk and return is the point N.

For individual A, the trade-off between risk and return is such that his equilibrium position is a portfolio with a standard deviation of 2 percent and an expected return of 6 percent. The line U'_A, which represents the tangent between the utility curve for individual A and the efficient portfolio boundary AB, has a steeper slope than the slope of U'_B, which is also drawn tangent to the point of equilibrium for individual B. By steeper slope, we mean that individual A for a given amount of increase in risk requires a greater

FIGURE 12–6
Utility and portfolio selection

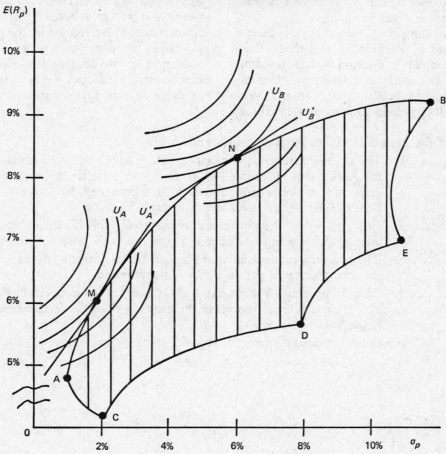

amount of compensation in the form of expected return. The less-steep slope of the utility curve for individual B indicates that he requires less compensation in the form of an increase in expected return for a given increase in risk.

Figure 12–5 therefore presents a framework for understanding how decisions involving risk are ultimately resolved. We cannot say in general that point M for individual A is better than point N for individual B or vice versa. All of the points on the portfolio boundary segment AB are efficient in the sense that has already been defined as achieving the highest return for a given amount of risk or for a given return minimizing the amount of risk. The choice of portfolios that

carry different combinations of risk and return reflects the shape of the individual's utility curve for the trade-offs between risk and return. If the individual has a high degree of risk aversion as illustrated by individual A in Figure 12–4, his equilibrium position is represented by point M in Figure 12–6. He is willing to bear only a small amount of risk and he earns a relatively small amount of return. Individual B who is less risk averse is willing to accept more risk (6 percent); he is compensated for bearing more risk by an expected return of 8.25 percent. Note that individual A who is more risk averse is receiving three units of return for every unit of risk, whereas B is receiving approximately 1.4 units of return per unit or risk that is being borne. This reflects the situation originally depicted in Figure 12–5 where it was shown that B has a smaller degree of risk aversion than individual A.

Therefore a complete framework for determining the kind of portfolio of investments that will be selected by a decision maker requires knowledge of the underlying utility function of the decision maker for choices involving risk. We can also see why portfolio analysis is essential for an analysis of how decision makers arrive at choices involving different combinations of risk and returns. The efficient portfolio of investments that will be selected by an individual decision maker is determined by the point at which his utility function which relates risk and return is tangent to the efficient boundary of portfolio choices which indicates the best combination of available market opportunities.

Label each of the following statements as true or false.

_____ 1. The rational investor in the market place appears to have a declining marginal utility for money—more pain from a dollar lost than pleasure from a dollar gained—which is represented by curve C in Figure 12–4 and curves A and B in Figure 12–5.

_____ 2. In Figure 12–6 the shape of utility curves U_A and U_B indicates that investor A has a higher degree of risk aversion than does investor B.

_____ 3. The optimum amount of risk to be taken by a firm is achieved when the expected return per unit of risk is maximized.

_____ 4. Risk is important in financial analysis because it directly influences almost every decision process in the firm as well as the final valuation of the firm.

Now turn to Answer Frame 5^{12}, page 96, to check your answers.

chapter 13

VALUATION AND RATES OF RETURN

Frame 1[13]

In the discussion of capital budgeting in Chapter 11, it was seen that the discount rate used in the calculations is of vital importance. Changes in the discount rate produce significant changes in computed net present values and sometimes cause a reversal in the decision to accept or to reject a particular project. In the discussion of capital budgeting, it was assumed that the cost of capital (the discount rate used in the present value process) was known, and this known rate was used in the calculations. Chapters 13 and 14 analyze the factors influencing the cost of capital. Two categories of influences must be considered: (1) general market forces and (2) specific characteristics and policies of the individual firm. The general market relationships and how they affect the rates of return on individual securities are discussed in this chapter. The following chapter examines how the firm's overall cost of capital may be determined by financing-mix decisions.

THE CAPITAL MARKET THEORY

Portfolio theory, briefly summarized in the previous chapter, has led to theoretical developments with useful applications to business finance. It is now possible to analyze rates of return, valuation, asset expansion decisions, capital structure, and other financial policies in a broader framework. Portfolio analysis provides theories of how individuals choose securities under uncertainty and how the market prices of securities are determined. These theories, in turn, provide a general market equilibrium framework to which

the financial decisions of managers of individual firms must relate to maximize owners' wealth.

In equilibrium, the capital market pricing mechanism can be described by a linear equation showing the relationship between expected return and risk for efficient portfolios:

$$E(R_p) = R_f + \lambda^* \sigma_p, \qquad (13\text{--}1)$$

where:

$E(R_p)$ is expected return on efficient portfolios.
R_f is risk-free interest rate.
λ^* is the price of risk for efficient portfolios.
λ^* is $[E(R_m) - R_f]/\sigma_m$, where the subscript, m, refers to the market.
σ_p is the standard deviation of returns on efficient portfolios.

Equation (13–1) and Figure 13–1 indicate that the expected return on an efficient portfolio in

FIGURE 13–1

Expected return on an efficient portfolio

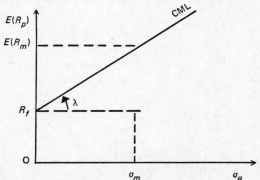

95

Answer frame 5¹²

1. True. Line A represents an increasing marginal utility of money in Figure 12–4. In Figure 12–5 individual B is also a risk averter who has a declining marginal utility for money—but with a smaller degree of risk aversion than A.
2. True. Essentially the slope of the utility curve at any point will determine the degree of risk aversion. Investor A, at point of tangency, M, requires a ratio of three units expected return per unit of portfolio risk. Investor B, at point N, requires only slightly above one (percent) unit of expected return per unit of portfolio risk.
3. False. On the efficient boundary of the market opportunities curve the ratio of return to risk declines as the amount of risk increases. But the optimum point is determined as shown in Figure 12–6 by the point of tangency between the utility preference curve (for different combinations of return and risk) with the market opportunities represented by the efficient boundary of the alternative portfolio combinations. In other words, if a decision maker is less disturbed by risk, he will seek a higher expected return and be willing to bear greater risk to achieve the higher return. For a decision maker who is risk averse, he will accept a lower return in order to avoid bearing a higher amount of risk.
4. True. In order to make choices among risky investments and to maximize the value of the firm, key management personnel should explicitly think through the return to risk criteria they are employing in decision making.

If you missed any of the above, reread Frame 5¹². Before beginning Chapter 13 on page 95, turn to page 196 to work Examination 3, which covers chapters 10–12.

Frame 1¹³ continued

equilibrium is equal to a risk-free return plus the market price of risk multiplied by (or weighted by) the standard deviation of the portfolio returns. The capital market line is drawn as a straight line with the intercept at R_f, the risk-free return, and its slope is equal to the market price of risk. The market price of risk is defined as the risk premium measured by the expected return on the market less the risk-free return divided by (that is, normalized by) the standard deviation of the market return. Ultimately, of course, the market price of risk reflects the attitudes of individuals in the aggregate (that is, all individuals in the market) toward risk of all securities in the market or a market portfolio. The market price of risk fundamentally reflects, therefore, a composite of the utility functions of all individuals.

Indicate whether each of the following statements is true or false by writing "T" or "F" in the space provided.

_____ 1. Portfolio theory explains how individuals choose securities under uncertainty and also explains how the market prices of securities are determined.

_____ 2. For an efficient portfolio in an equilibrium condition, the expected return is equal to a risk-free return plus the market price of risk multiplied by the standard deviation of the portfolio returns.

_____ 3. The slope (λ^*) of the market line is the market price of risk. It essentially represents the aggregate attitudes toward risk of all the individuals in the market who are buying and selling securities.

_____ 4. The following equation is valid in equilibrium: $E(R_p) = R_f + \lambda^* \sigma_p$ where: $\lambda^* = [E(R_m) - R_f]/\sigma_m$.

Now turn to Answer Frame 1¹³, page 98, to check your answers.

Frame 2[13]

To convey some of the basic ideas involved in connection with the market price of risk and the empirical magnitudes involved, some procedures for calculating the market parameters are next described. In Table 13–1, data and procedures for estimating the market parameters are set forth. Four states of the world conditions are illustrated (SD = strong depression, WD = weak depression, WU = weak upturn, and SU = strong upturn) with their associated probabilities. The expected return and standard deviation of the market portfolio then are calculated to be $E(R_m) = 0.10$ and $\sigma_m = 0.20$.

The return on an efficient portfolio can then be calculated by using the market parameters calculated in Table 13–1 and assuming a risk-free interest rate of 5 percent and a portfolio standard deviation of 0.4. The expected return on an efficient portfolio would be:

$$E(R_p) = .05 + \frac{(.10 - .05)}{.20}\ .40$$
$$= .05 + .25(.40) \qquad (13\text{-}1.1)$$
$$= .05 + .10 = .15 = 15\%$$

Thus far we have developed the market parameters. Our ultimate interest is in developing materials for use in arriving at the cost of capital and valuation of individual securities and individual projects.

THE SECURITY MARKET LINE RELATIONS

The equation for individual securities may also be developed from the capital market line:

$$E(R_j) = R_f + \lambda \text{Cov}(R_j, R_m), \qquad (13\text{-}2)$$

where: λ = Price of risk for securities = $[E(R_m) - R_f] / \sigma_m^2$; $\text{Cov}(R_j, R_m)$ = Covariance of the returns from individual securities with market returns; i.e., $\text{Cov}(R_j, R_m) = \text{Cor}(R_j R_m)\ \sigma_j \sigma_m$; and $E(R_j)$ = Expected return on an individual security.

In Table 13–2 the data provided by the market relationships are utilized along with R_j data for the Mostin Company to calculate the expected return and covariance for the Mostin Company. The procedures for the individual company parallel those through column (5) in Table 13–1 for

TABLE 13–1
Calculation of expected return and variance for the market

(1) State	(2) p	(3) R_m	(4) pR_m	(5) $R_m - E(R_m)$	(6) $[R_m - E(R_m)]^2$	(7) $p[R_m - E(R_m)]^2$
SD	.1	−.30	−.03	−.40	.16	.016
WD	.2	−.10	−.02	−.20	.04	.008
WU	.3	.10	.03	0	0	0
SU	.4	.30	.12	.20	.04	.016
	1.0		$E(R_m) = $ .10			Var $R_m = $ .040, $\sigma_m = $ .20

TABLE 13–2
Calculation of expected return and covariance for the Mostin Company

(1) State	(2) p	(3) R_j	(4) pR_j	(5) $[R_j - E(R_j)]$	(6) $[R_m - E(R_m)]$	(7) $[R_j - E(R_j)] [R_m - E(R_m)]$	(8) $p[R_j - E(R_j)] [R_m - E(R_m)]$
SD	.1	−.40	−.04	−.60	−.40	.240	.0240
WD	.2	−.20	−.04	−.40	−.20	.080	.0160
WU	.3	.00	.00	−.20	−.00	.000	.0000
SU	.4	+.70	.28	.50	.20	.100	.0400
			$E(R_j) = $ .20				$\text{Cov}(R_j, R_m) = $ .0800 = 8%

Answer frame 1[13]

1. True. This is the primary focus of the chapter. It provides a general market equilibrium framework which is useful in analyzing rates of return, valuations of possible acquisitions, asset expansion decisions, capital structure decisions, and many other financial decisions.
2. True. The expected return on efficient portfolios is equal to a risk-free return plus the market price of risk weighted by the standard deviation of the *portfolio* returns.

$$E(R_p) = R_f + \lambda^* \sigma_p \text{ (capital market price equation)}$$

3. True. Algebraically it is represented as follows:

$$\lambda^* = [E(R_m) - R_f]/\sigma_m$$

It is a composite of the utility functions of all individuals in the market place.
4. True. Equation 13–1 is the most general relationship for efficient portfolios. The market portfolio is one of a number of possible efficient portfolios.

If you missed any of the above, reread Frame 1[13] before starting Frame 2[13], page 97.

Frame 2[13] continued

calculating the market parameters. In column (6) we repeat the deviations of the market returns as calculated in Table 13–1. In column (7) the deviations of the firm's returns are multiplied by the deviations of the market returns. In column (8) the probability factors are multiplied times the results in column (7) and summed to obtain the covariance of the Mostin Company's returns with the market returns.

While the risk measure for portfolios is the standard deviation of portfolio returns, the risk factor for individual securities is the covariance and not the standard deviation. The reason for using covariance rather than the standard deviation is that part of the risk reflected in the standard deviation can be diversified away. The market will not be willing to pay a premium for that portion of risk which can be diversified away in portfolios.

Label each of the following statements as true or false.

_____ 1. If the risk-free rate is 6 percent, the expected return on an efficient portfolio with a standard deviation of 0.6 is 7.2 percent. (Use market parameters illustrated in Table 13–1.)

_____ 2. In equation form, the algebra carried out in Table 13–2 would be as follows:

$$\text{Cor}(R_j, R_m) = \sum_{t=1}^{n} \left(\frac{R_{tj} - E(R_j)}{\sigma_j} \right) \left(\frac{R_{tm} - E(R_m)}{\sigma_m} \right) p_t$$

$$\text{Cov}(R_j, R_m) = \text{Cor}(R_j, R_m) \sigma_j \sigma_m$$

Substituting, we have

$$\text{Cov}(R_j, R_m) = \sum_{t=1}^{n} [R_{tj} - E(R_j)][R_{tm} - E(R_m)] p_t$$

_____ 3. The correlation coefficient for the Mostin Company is equal to 0.5 when $\sigma_m = 0.2$ and $\sigma_j = 0.5$.

_____ 4. The reason for using covariance rather than standard deviation as our risk measure for individual securities is because part of the risk reflected in the standard deviation can be diversified away.

Now turn to Answer Frame 2[13], page 100, to check your answers.

Frame 3[13]

Hence, for individual securities, the security market line relates the covariance of the returns on the individual securities with the market to the expected return on the individual security as shown in Figure 13–2. For individual securities, the independent variable is the covariance instead of the standard deviation. Conceptually this is important because it indicates that the risk of an individual security or firm depends on the portfolio into which it is placed.

In addition, the price of risk is the market price of risk with the variance of market returns in the denominator instead of the standard deviation. The effect is to change the slope of the capital market line for individual securities. For example, using the data we had developed on market parameters, if we divide by the variance instead of the standard deviation, the slope of the line becomes 1.25 instead of 0.25:

$$\lambda = \frac{.10 - .05}{.04} = 1.25$$

Using 1.25 as the slope of the SML for individual securities with a covariance of 8 percent, the risk premium would be 10 percent, which added to the risk-free return of 5 percent, gives a required return of 15 percent. This result follows from the use of equation 13–2.

$$E(R_j) = R_f + \lambda \, \text{Cov}(R_j, R_m) \qquad (13\text{–}2)$$
$$= .05 + 1.25(.08)$$
$$= .05 + .10 = .15 = 15\%$$

Recall that in Table 13–2, the covariance of the Mostin Company security is calculated to be .08 or 8 percent, but the $E(R_j)$ shown in Table 13–2 is 20 percent. This difference will result in market readjustments. The data in Table 13–2 represent investors' expectations about the probable results of investing in the security of the Mostin Company. If some investors expect that the security of the Mostin Company will yield a return of 20 percent when the market relationship indicates that only a 15 percent return is required for the risk level involved, they will purchase the stock. Their purchases of the stock cause its price to increase. When the price of the stock increases to the level where it yields only a 15 percent return, the security will then have reached its market equilibrium relation.

Alternatively, we could reason that if investors expected a range of possible returns from the Mostin Company security that resulted in a calculation of a covariance of 12 percent, this would also represent an equilibrium relation. If the covariance of the Mostin security were 12 percent, its risk premium would be 15 percent (1.25 times 12 percent) and the required yield would be 20 percent, which is equal to the expected return shown in Table 13–2.

The risk index can also be expressed in terms of the "beta coefficient,"

$$\beta_j = \frac{\text{Cov}(R_j \, R_m)}{\sigma^2_m}$$

β_j is measured by the ratio of the covariance of the returns of the individual security with market returns, divided by the variance of market returns. The market line relationship for individual securities using betas is:

$$E(R_j) = R_f + [E(R_m) - R_f]\beta_j \qquad (13\text{–}3)$$

Equation 13–3 multiplies the firm's normalized risk index, the beta coefficient, by the market risk premium to obtain the risk adjustment factor. When we add the risk adjustment factor to the risk-free return, we obtain the same results as for the use of covariance to determine the required return on the individual security.

One of the values of the capital asset pricing model is that it conveys what lies behind the risk-adjusted returns. Both the covariance and beta concepts are helpful in explaining the source and nature of the risk adjustment factor and at the same time provide a summary of the concepts of

FIGURE 13–2
The SML for individual securities

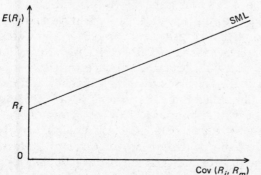

Answer frame 2¹³

1. False. The expected return is calculated as follows:

$$E(R_p) = R_p + \lambda^* \sigma_p$$

$$E(R_p) = R_f + \frac{[E(R_m) - R_f]}{\sigma_m} \sigma_p$$

$$E(R_p) = .06 + \frac{(.10 - .06)}{.20} .60$$

$$= .06 + .20(.60) = .06 + .12 = .18 = 18\%$$

2. True. This is merely showing in equation form the algebra carried out in Table 13–2.

3. False. The correlation coefficient is calculated as follows:

$$\text{Cov}(R_j, R_m) = \text{Cor}(R_j, R_m) \sigma_j \sigma_m$$

$$.08 = \text{Cor}(R_j, R_m) .50 \times .20$$

$$\text{Cor}(R_j, R_m) = \frac{.08}{.10} = .80$$

A correlation coefficient of .80 indicates that the returns from the Mostin Security would vary positively and almost in the same proportion as the returns from the market.

4. True. The market will not be willing to pay a premium for that portion of risk which can be diversified away in portfolios. This was illustrated in Chapter 12 where we showed the greatest reduction in portfolio risk occurred when the correlation coefficient was equal to a negative one.

If you missed any of the above, restudy Frame 2¹³ before starting Frame 3¹³, page 99.

Frame 3¹³ continued

the market model. It is useful to begin by setting forth the general order of magnitudes of the elements in equation 13–3. As indicated, the average return on the market over a representative time period would approximate 10 percent. We may use 5 percent for the risk-free return. Thus the market risk premium would be 5 percent (10% minus 5%). A plausible estimate of the variance of the market returns is 1% or 0.01; hence, 0.10 would be the related standard deviation of market returns. The slope of the capital market line would be the market risk premium divided by the standard deviation of market returns which is .05/.10 = .50. The slope of the security market line based on the same numbers is the market risk premium divided by the variance of market returns, or .05/.01 = 5.00.

The range of observed values of beta for representative (long) time periods is from 0.5 to 1.5 (recall that beta is Cov (R_j, R_m) divided by the variance of market returns). Taking 0.01 as the variance of market returns, the order of magnitude of the covariances for the individual securities would be the product of the betas times the market variance, giving a 0.005 to 0.015 range or 0.5% to 1.5%.

The range of market variance and security beta values set forth reflects empirical studies of the capital market relations. These values can be used to indicate the nature of the risk adjustment factor. We begin with the risk-free return of 5 percent which is also referred to as the "pure rate of interest" on a security with no risk of default on payment of interest and principal. A security with a beta of 1.2 would have a risk adjustment factor of 1.2 times the market risk premium of 5 percent which equals 6 percent. Thus the required return on a security with a beta of 1.2 would be 11 percent (5% plus 6%). Given a market variance of 0.010, a security with a beta of 1.2 would have a covariance with the market of 0.012; the slope of the security market line is 5, multiplied times the covariance of 0.012 results in a risk adjustment factor of 0.06 or 6%, the same result as when beta was used. Thus either covariance and the slope of the security market line or beta and the market risk premium can be used to calculate the risk adjustment factor.

In both instances the nature of the risk adjustment factor becomes clear. The risk adjustment factor for an individual security is a market risk factor multiplied (weighted) by the risk index computed for the individual security. The risk adjustment factor also influences required rates of return for different classes of securities. Thus in the following section in which rates of return on different types of securities are discussed, the differences in the levels of required rates of return will reflect differences in the applicable risk adjustment factors.

True or false?

_____ 1.   The market line for individual securities relates the standard deviation to the expected return on the individual security.

_____ 2.   The slope of the capital market line for individual securities and other inefficient portfolios is steeper than the slope of the capital market line for an efficient portfolio.

_____ 3.   A risk adjusted return or a required return used in developing a cost of capital is an area where we can use the capital market equilibrium approach to assist us in the measurement process.

_____ 4.   A beta coefficient (β_j), the firm's normalized risk index, is calculated as follows:

$$\beta_i = \frac{\text{Cov }(R_i, R_m)}{\sigma_m}$$

Now turn to Answer Frame 3^{13}, page 102, to check your answers.

Frame 4^{13}

VALUATION OF DIFFERENT TYPES OF SECURITIES

The capital asset pricing model has been used to establish the relationships between return, risk, and valuation. With the framework so provided, we now turn to the valuation of individual forms of securities. Here the emphasis is on how different patterns of income flows and growth over a number of years affect valuation.

We begin with the discussion of a bond which has no maturity. The value of a bond which has no maturity is determined by the amount of interest payment promised each year divided by the appropriate discount factor (determined by an analysis of risk-return relationships).

$$\text{Value} = V = \frac{\text{Constant annual receipts}}{\text{Capitalization rate}} = \frac{X}{r}$$
$$(13\text{--}4)$$

Assume that the annual receipts (X) are $70 and that the going capitalization rate (r) for this type of risky bond (consol) is 7 percent:

$$V = \frac{\$70}{.07} = \$1,000$$

If the capitalization rate rises to 10 percent, the value of the bond will fall:

$$V = \frac{\$70}{.10} = \$700$$

If the capitalization rate falls to 5 percent, the value of the bond will rise:

$$V = \frac{\$70}{.05} = \$1,400$$

The present value of a bond with a three-year maturity can be calculated by two methods shown below in equation 13–5 and 13–6. In equation 13–5 the first term is the present value of an annuity A, which represents the dollar amount of interest paid on the bond reflecting the coupon rate on the bond. The interest rate in the first term is the current interest rate; n is the maturity term of the bond. The second term is the maturity value of the bond discounted back to its present value. The second method shown in

Answer frame 3¹³

1. False. The security market line relates the *covariance* of the returns to the expected return on the individual security as shown in Figure 13–2. This is a *crucial* point as it shows that the risk of the individual security of the firm depends on the portfolio into which it is placed.

2. True. The price of risk is the market price of risk with the variance of market returns in the denominator instead of the standard deviation:

$$\lambda = [E(R_m) - R_f]/\sigma_m^2 = (.10 - .05)/.04 = 1.25 \text{ (for individual securities)}$$
$$\lambda^* = [E(R_m) - R_f]/\sigma_m = (.10 - .05)/.20 = 0.25 \text{ (for efficient portfolios)}$$

3. True. This is a rather new development in computing cost of capital and should improve the capital budgeting process. In the past, and even with some firms today, the risk adjusted returns were arrived at subjectively—or by merely guessing.

4. False. $\beta_j = \text{Cov}(R_j, R_m)/\sigma_m^2$.

   Beta is equal to the covariance of the returns of the individual security with market returns divided by the *variance* of market returns. An individual security's required return is calculated by multiplying beta times the market risk premium to obtain the risk adjustment factor which we add to the risk-free return.

If you missed any of the above, reread Frame 3¹³ before beginning Frame 4¹³, page 101.

Frame 4¹³ continued

equation 13–6 has the same final term, but expresses the annual interest payments by a series of present value terms.

$$P = A \frac{1 - (1 + r)^{-n}}{r} + \frac{M_n}{(1 + r)^n} \quad (13\text{–}5)$$

$$P = \frac{A}{(1 + r)} + \frac{A}{(1 + r)^2} + \cdots + \frac{A}{(1 + r)^n} + \frac{M_n}{(1 + r)^n} \quad (13\text{–}6)$$

These two expressions will now be illustrated for the three year bond with a face value of $1,000 ($M$), and a coupon rate of 7 percent, so that the annual interest payment is $70; the current rate of interest is 8 percent. The indicated value of the bond is below its face value because the current rate of interest exceeds the coupon rate on the bond.

$$P = 70 \frac{1 - (1 + .08)^{-3}}{.08} + \frac{1,000}{(1 + .08)^3} \quad (13\text{–}5a)$$
$$= 70 (2.57) + 1,000 (.794)$$
$$= 180 + 794$$
$$= \$974$$

$$P = \frac{70}{(1 + .08)} + \frac{70}{(1 + .08)^2} + \frac{1,070}{(1 + .08)^3} \quad (13\text{–}6a)$$
$$= 70(.926) + 70(.857) + 1,070(.794)$$
$$= 65 + 60 + 849$$
$$= \$974$$

Table 13–3 and Figure 13–3 show that a $70 coupon consol bond fluctuates in price much more sharply at different interest rate levels than the three-year bond. As a general principle, the longer the maturity of a security, the greater its price change as a consequence of a change in low capitalization rates. However, for "deep-discount" bonds (selling at 20 to 30 percent below their par value because interest rates have risen), this relationship may be reversed.

TABLE 13–3

Effect of bond maturity on current bond prices at different interest rate levels

Interest rate	Current price $1,000 consol paying 7%	3-year bond paying 7%
.05	1,400	1,055
.06	1,167	1,027
.07	1,000	1,000
.08	875	974
.09	778	949
.10	700	925
.12	583	880

FIGURE 13–3

**Effects of varying interest rates on the
value of bonds with different maturities**

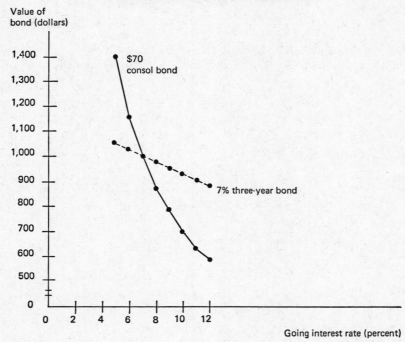

Is each of the following true or false?

_____ 1. If a firm expects to earn $3 million after taxes indefinitely and investors capitalize the earnings stream at 15 percent, the value of the firm is $45 million.

_____ 2. A three-year bond with a face value of $1,000 and a 9 percent coupon rate will be valued at $1,000 when the current rate of interest is 9 percent.

_____ 3. A 10-year bond with a 9 percent coupon rate when the current rate of interest is 8 percent will be valued at $966.90.

_____ 4. As a general principle, the shorter the maturity of a security the greater its price change as a result of a change in the discount or capitalization rate.

Now turn to Answer Frame 4¹³, page 104, to check your answers.

Frame 5¹³ ━━━━━━━━━━━━━━━━━━━━━━━━━━━━━━━━━━

Since preferred stocks carry no maturity, their value is calculated using the same formulation as for a consol. Hence, an equivalent of equation 13–4 would be used to arrive at the valuation of a preferred stock.

The principles for valuation of fixed income securities can also be applied to the valuation of common stock. Common stock earnings and dividends are variable, so the valuation formulas must take this into account. The expected return on common stock is equal to the dividend yield plus the market appreciation yield as shown in equation 13–7:

Return on common stock = Dividend yield
+ Market appreciation yield   (13–7)

Answer frame 4¹³

1. False. The value is $20 million calculated as follows:

$$\text{Value} = \frac{\text{Constant annual receipts}}{\text{Capitalization rate}} = \frac{\$3 \text{ million}}{.15} = \$20 \text{ million}$$

It is called the capitalization of income method of valuation.

2. True. Using equation 13–6, the value of the bond (P) is computed as follows:

$$P = \frac{90}{(1 + .09)} + \frac{90}{(1 + .09)^2} + \frac{90}{(1 + .09)^3} + \frac{1,000}{(1 + .09)^3}$$
$$P = 90 \times .917 + 90 \times .842 + 90 \times .772 + 1,000 \times .772$$
$$P = \$1,000$$

Using equation 13–5 we have:

$$P = 90 \frac{1 - (1 + .09)^{-3}}{.09} + \frac{1,000}{(1 + .09)^3}$$
$$P = 90 \times 2.531 + 1,000 \times .772$$
$$P = \$1,000$$

3. False. The value of the bond is calculated as follows:

$$P = 90 \frac{1 - (1 + .08)^{-10}}{.08} + \frac{1,000}{(1 + .08)^{10}}$$
$$P = 90 \times 6.71 + 1,000 \times .463$$
$$P = \$1,066.90$$

Thus, the bond will sell at a premium. See Figure 13–3.

4. False. See Figure 13–3.

If you missed any of the above, reread Frame 4¹³ before starting Frame 5¹³, page 103.

Frame 5¹³ continued

In equation 13–7 the dividend yield is measured by the expected dividend divided by the current price. The market appreciation yield is the expected increase in price divided by the current price:

Expected return on common stock

$$= \frac{\text{Expected dividend}}{\text{Current price}} \quad (13\text{–}7a)$$
$$+ \frac{\text{Expected increase in price}}{\text{Current price}}$$

In equations 13–7b and 13–7c the relationships in equation 13–7a are set forth in symbols:

$$k = \frac{D_1}{P_0} + \frac{P_1 - P_0}{P_0} \quad (13\text{–}7b)$$

$$k = \frac{D_1}{P_0} + g \quad (13\text{–}7c)$$

where

k is the rate of return on equity $[\equiv E(R_j)]$.

E_0 is the current year's earnings.

D_1 is the expected end of year dividend.

P_0 is the current price.

P_1 is the expected end of year price.

g is the expected rate of capital gain or growth in dividends.

Solving equation 13–7c for P_0, we obtain:

$$P_0 = \frac{D_1}{k - g} = \frac{D_0(1 + g)}{k - g} \quad (13\text{–}8)$$

Equation 13–8 has a high degree of versatility which can be illustrated by numerical examples.

Assume: $D_0 = 3.81$; dividend payout ratio $= 50\%$; $k = 10\%$; and $g = 5\%$.

Then $P_0 = \$4/(.10 - .05) = \$4/.05 = \$80$. Thus we have a basic formula for determining the value of a security whose dividend grows at a constant rate.

Label each of the following statements as true or false.

———— 1.   The price of a share of $100 par value preferred stock which pays an $8 dividend which the market capitalizes at 10 percent is $100.

———— 2.   The Carlson Milling Machine Company pays a $2.25 annual dividend and is expected to have a dividend growth rate of 5 percent over the next several years. If it is capitalized at 20 percent, the price of the share then is $15.

———— 3.   In Question 2 the dividend yield is 15 percent and the capital gain or market appreciation yield is 5 percent.

———— 4.   The cost of debt capital to the firm is the bondholder's rate of return, and the cost of funds to a firm raised through an issue of preferred stock is the preferred sharcholder's rate of return.

Now turn to Answer Frame 5^{13}, page 106, to check your answers.

Frame 6^{13}

Next, we will continue to assume $E_0 = 7.62$; $D_0 = 3.81$, and $k = 10\%$, but will make four alternative assumptions about g, the growth rate. The four assumptions are that $g_m = -6\%$; $g_0 = 0$; $g = 5\%$; and $g_s = 15.5\%$ for 5 years, 5% thereafter. Table 13–4 sets forth common stock values under the alternative growth rate assumptions, and the computation procedures for arriving at common stock values under these alternative assumptions are illustrated for the data presented. For negative and constant "normal" growth, equation 13–8 is employed. For zero growth, equation 13–4, which is used in evaluating a bond with a constant return and no maturity, is applicable.

The expected dividend at the end of the period under *negative growth* would be $3.81 multiplied by a .94 factor (a decrease of $.23). Thus, for negative growth, the lower dividend of $3.58 divided by the capitalization factor of .16 results in a current price of $22.38. For *zero growth*, $3.81 is divided by .10 to give a price of $38.10. Since we assume a dividend of $3.81 in the previous period, at the *normal* 5 percent *growth* rate, it will be $4.00 at the end of the period. For constant normal growth, a dividend of $4 is divided by a capitalization factor of $[(.10 - .05) = .05]$ to give $80, representing a multiplier of 20.

The expression for valuing the growth stock is

TABLE 13–4

Common stock values for alternative assumptions about the growth rate

Negative growth

$$P_0 = \frac{D_1}{k - g_m} = \frac{3.58}{.10 + .06} = \frac{3.58}{.16} = \$22.38 \quad (13\text{-}8)$$

Zero growth

$$P_0 = \frac{D_1}{k} = \frac{3.81}{.10} = \$38.10 \quad (13\text{-}4)$$

Constant normal growth

$$P_0 = \frac{D_1}{k - g} = \frac{4.00}{.10 - .05} = \$80.00 \quad (13\text{-}8)$$

Temporary supernormal growth

$$P_0 = \sum_{t=1}^{n=5} \frac{D_0(1 + g_s)^t}{(1 + k)^t} + \frac{D_0(1 + g_s)^n(1 + g)^1}{(k - g)(1 + k)^n} \quad (13\text{-}9)$$

Also,

$$P_0 = \sum_{t=1}^{n=5} \frac{D_0(1 + g_s)^t}{(1 + k)^t} + \frac{P_5}{(1 + k)^n}$$

Where:

$$P_5 = \frac{D_6}{k - g} = \frac{D_5(1 + g)^1}{k - g} = \frac{D_0(1 + g_s)^5(1 + g)^1}{k - g} \quad (13\text{-}9a)$$

$$P_0 = \sum_{t=1}^{n=5} \frac{3.81(1.155)^t}{(1.10)^t} + \frac{3.81(1.155)^5(1.05)^1}{(.10 - .05)(1.10)^5}$$

$$= 3.81 \sum_{t=1}^{n=5} (1.05)^t + \frac{3.81(1.05)^5(1.05)}{.05} \quad (13\text{-}9b)$$

$$= 3.81(5.802)^* + 3.81[20(1.276)(1.05)] \quad (13\text{-}9c)$$

$$= 3.81(5.802)^* + 3.81(26.796) \quad (13\text{-}9d)$$

$$= 22.11 + 102.09$$

$$= 124.20$$

* This is the sum of an annuity of $1 for five years times 1.05.

Answer frame 5^{13}

1. False. The value of each share of preferred stock is calculated to be $80. It is computed as follows:

$$\text{Value} = P_0 = \frac{D_1}{r} = \frac{8}{.10} = \$80.$$

The par value of the preferred stock would be $100 with an 8 percent coupon rate.

2. True. The price is calculated as follows:

$$P_0 = \frac{D_1}{k-g} = \frac{2.25}{.20-.05} = \$15$$

3. True. The dividend yield is calculated as follows:

$$\text{Dividend yield} = \frac{D_1}{P_0} = \frac{2.25}{15} = .15 = 15\%$$

The market appreciation yield is equal to the growth rate of 5 percent.

4. False. If a bondholder received an 8 percent return and the firm had a corporate marginal tax rate of 50 percent, its cost of debt capital would be 4% [8% (1 − .5)]. This is because interest (or coupon payments) is deductible for income tax purposes. But dividend payments are not deductible by the corporation for tax purposes, so the cost to the firm would be the full cost of the preferred stock. Also there may be a difference between the coupon cost of bonds or preferred stock and the current yield that the market requires.

If you missed any of the above, reread Frame 5^{13} before beginning Frame 6^{13}, page 105.

Frame 6^{13} continued

somewhat more complex, but can be simplified. The initial expression is equation (13–9). The first term is the present value of dividends during the supernormal growth period. The second term is the present value of the dividends received during the subsequent period of normal growth (equal to the present value of the price of the stock at the end of the supernormal growth period). The components of the price at the end of the five years of supernormal growth are shown in equation (13–9a) representing a form of equation 13–8 described above.

The computation procedure starts with equation (13–9b). By choosing a supernormal growth return of 15.5 percent and a required return for investors of 10 percent, when we divide, we obtain 1.05 [1.155/1.10 = 1.05]. For the period of supernormal growth this expression is the sum of an annuity factor. This represents a short cut. The individual steps would be to apply the supernormal growth rate to each year's dividend and discount each individual year's term back to its

present value and sum the present values. The same result is accomplished by dividing the present value factor into the sum of an annuity factor as illustrated here.

We now have 1.05 times the sum of an annuity for five years at a 5 per cent interest factor or 1.05 times 5.5256 to obtain 5.802. The 5.802 multiplied times $3.81 gives us the first part of the price for the supernormal growth of $22.11.

For the subsequent normal growth period the 1.05 factor is a compound sum which is 1.276 for five years. (Another short cut to obtain the equivalent of a present value factor.) The four elements in the second part of equation (13–9c) are: [20 (3.81) (1.276) (1.05)]. Each is briefly explained: 20 is the multiplier for normal growth; $3.81 is the dividend at period zero; 1.276 is the compound sum factor at 5 percent for five years; 1.05 moves the fifth year dividend of $4.86 to period six. The last three factors represent a sixth year dividend of $5.105 to which the multiplier of 20 is applied to give a total of $102.09 for the

TABLE 13–5

Prices, dividend yields, and price earnings ratios under different growth rates

	P_0 *Price*	D_0/P_0 *Current dividend yield*	P_0/E_0 *ratio*
Negative growth..........................	$ 22.38	3.81/22.38 = 17.02%	22.38/7.62 = 3X
Zero growth...............................	38.10	3.81/38.10 = 10.00%	38.10/7.62 = 5X
Constant normal growth.................	80.00	3.81/80.00 = 4.80%	80.00/7.62 = 10.5X
Temporary supernormal growth..........	124.20	3.81/124.20 = 3.07%	124.20/7.62 = 16.3X

value of the normal growth segment. The sum of the two price elements gives a current price for the growth stock of $124.20. The results are summarized in Table 13–5, showing dividend yields and price earnings ratios under different growth rate assumptions.

The current dividend yield would be obtained by dividing the initial dividend of $3.81 by the current price. The dividend yields range from 17 percent for the negative growth situation to 3 percent for the positive growth stock. The price-earnings ratio ranges from 3 to 16.3 times. An important point is emphasized by the results in Table 13–5. We set forth in advance that the *expected return* or required return on equity capital for the investor under each of the four situations was 10 percent. For the negative growth stock, the current dividend yield was over 17 percent. The current dividend yield overstates the return to the investor and has to be reduced to give effect to the percent negative growth rate to give the 10 percent yield. Only for the zero growth stock does the current dividend yield represent the actual return to the investor. For the constant normal growth stock, the current dividend yield is almost 5 percent, and additionally, a capital gains growth yield of 5 percent is expected. For the temporary supernormal growth stock, since the current dividend yield is 3 percent, the capital

gains growth must average about 7 percent per annum to give a total return of 10 percent.

The current earnings-price ratio (reciprocal of current price-earnings ratio) does not represent the "cost of equity capital." The earnings-price ratio varies with the expected future growth rate. But the equity cost of capital, or the required yield to the investor, is the same for all four stocks: it is 10%. The current earnings-price ratio will be high for a negative growth stock and will be low for a positive growth stock. However, the required return to investors remains the same, 10 percent in this example.

Finally, it should be recognized that the approach to valuation employed in the present chapter is not the only one in use. The concept employed has been referred to as the economic or intrinsic value of an asset measured by the capitalization of prospective income flows or net revenues. Among the other concepts of value employed are: (1) *Liquidating value*—the amount realizable if assets are sold separately from the organization that has been using them; (2) *Going concern value*—the amount realizable if an enterprise is sold as an operating business: (3) *Book value*—the accounting value at which an asset is carried; and (4) *Market value*—the actual price at which an asset (or firm) can be sold at a particular point in time.

True or false?

_____ 1. If we change D_0 only from $3.81 to $2.00 for the problem illustrated in Table 13–4, we obtain the following prices, dividend yields, and P_0/E_0 ratios.

Growth	P_0 Price	D_0/P_0 Current dividend yield	P_0/E_0 Price-earnings ratio
Negative growth.....................	$11.75	17.0%	2.94X
Zero growth.........................	20.00	10.0	5.00X
Constant normal growth.............	42.00	4.8	10.50X
Temporary supernormal growth...........................	65.20	3.1	16.30X

_____ 2. The results of question #1 show that in each growth case the return to the common stockholder is a combination of the dividend yield and capital gains.

_____ 3. The cost of equity capital in question #1 for the temporary supernormal growth situation is much higher than the cost of equity capital for the zero growth situation and can be measured by the reciprocal of the price-earnings ratio.

_____ 4. The capitalization of prospective income flows is a far superior method to valuation than any other method yet devised.

Now turn to Answer Frame 6¹³, page 110, to check your answers.

chapter 14

LEVERAGE AND THE COST OF CAPITAL

Frame 1[14]

In Chapter 13 on valuation and rates of return, the cost of capital was defined for an all-equity financed firm. This chapter analyzes the effects of the use of debt on the firm's cost of capital.

The definitions of terms frequently used are first reviewed. Asset structure is the left-hand side of the balance sheet—the assets or investments of the firm which must be financed. Financial structure is the right-hand side of the balance

TABLE 14–1

Return on common stock under alternative leverage and profitability conditions

	Profitability conditions						
	Very poor	Poor	Marginal	Below average	Normal	Good	Very good
Rate of return on total assets.............	2%	6%	8%	12%	18%	22%	25%
(EBIT).....................................	$2	$6	$8	$12	$18	$22	$25
Firm A: Leverage factor 0%							
EBIT......................................	$2	$6	$8	$12	$18	$22	$25
Less: Interest expense..................	0	0	0	0	0	0	0
Taxable income.........................	$2	$6	$8	$12	$18	$22	$25
Taxes....................................	1	3	4	6	9	11	12.5
Profit after taxes......................	$1	$3	$4	$ 6	$ 9	$11	$12.5
Return on equity........................	1%	3%	4%	6%	9%	11%	12.5%
Firm B: Leverage factor 50%							
EBIT......................................	$2	$6	$8	$12	$18	$22	$25
Less: Interest expense..................	4	4	4	4	4	4	4
Taxable income.........................	($2)	$2	$4	$ 8	$14	$18	$21
Taxes....................................	(1)	1	2	4	7	9	10.5
Profit after taxes......................	($1)	$1	$2	$ 4	$ 7	$ 9	$10.5
Return on equity........................	(2%)	2%	4%	8%	14%	18%	21%
Firm C: Leverage factor 80%							
EBIT......................................	$2	$6	$8	$12	$18	$22	$25
Less: Interest expense..................	6.40	6.40	6.40	6.40	6.40	6.40	6.40
Taxable income.........................	($4.40)	($ .40)	$1.60	$ 5.60	$11.60	$15.60	$18.60
Taxes....................................	(2.20)	(.20)	.80	2.80	5.80	7.80	9.30
Profit after taxes......................	($2.20)	($ .20)	$ .80	$ 2.80	$ 5.80	$ 7.80	$ 9.30
Return on equity........................	(11%)	(1%)	4%	14%	29%	39%	46.5%

Answer frame 6¹³

1. True. The calculations are as follows:

Negative growth

$$P_0 = \frac{D_1}{k - g_m} = \frac{1.88}{.10 + .06} = \frac{1.88}{.16} = \$11.75$$

$$D_0/P_0 = \frac{2.00}{11.75} = .17 = 17\%; \; P_0/E_0 = \$11.75/\$4.00 = 2.94 \text{ X}$$

Zero growth

$$P_0 = \frac{D_1}{k} = \frac{2.00}{.10} = \$20.00$$

$$D_0/P_0 = \frac{\$ 2.00}{\$20.00} = 10\%; \; P_0/E_0 = \$20.00/\$4.00 = 5 \text{ X}$$

Constant normal growth

$$P_0 = \frac{D_1}{k - g} = \frac{2.10}{.10 - .05} = \frac{2.10}{.05} = \$42.00;$$

$$D_0/P_0 = 2.00/42.00 = .048 = 4.8\%; \; P_0/E_0 = \$42.00/\$4.00 = 10.5 \text{ X}$$

Temporary supernormal growth

$$P_0 = \sum_{t=1}^{n=5} \frac{D_0(1 + g_s)^t}{(1 + k)^t} + \frac{D_0(1 + g_s)^n(1 + g)^1}{(k - g)(1 + k)^n}$$

$$P_0 = \sum_{t=1}^{n=5} \frac{2.00(1.155)^t}{(1.10)^t} + \frac{2.00(1.155)^5(1.05)^1}{(.10 - .05)(1.10)^5}$$

We can now apply equation (13–9d) from Table 13–4, substituting the $2.00 dividend for the $3.81 dividend.

$$= 2.00(5.802) + 2.00(26.796)$$
$$= 11.604 + 53.592 = 65.20$$
$$D_0/P_0 = 2.00/65.20 = .031 = 3.1\%; \; P_0/E_0 = \$65.20/\$4.00 = 16.3 \text{ X}$$

2. True. The negative growth situation shows a dividend yield of 17 percent minus a capital loss of 7 percent. The temporary supernormal growth stock represents a dividend yield of approximately 3 percent and an expectation of an average capital gains growth averaging approximately 7 percent. The normal growth stock represents a dividend yield of approximately 5 percent and a growth of 5 percent.
3. False. The cost of equity capital to the firm is the required rate of return received by the common stockholders. It is 10 percent for all four growth conditions. Only in the constant normal growth situation is the earnings-price ratio (reciprocal of price-earnings ratio) approximately equal to the required rate of return. If the dividend payout ratio had been 100 percent for the zero growth situation, the earnings-price ratio would also be equivalent to the required rate of return or cost of equity capital.
4. False. It certainly is an accurate and sound method of valuation, but other methods of valuation may be suitable depending on the purpose involved. For example, in bankruptcy the liquidation value may be the superior method to use in determining the current value of a firm.

If you missed any of the above, reread Frame 6¹³ before beginning Chapter 14 on page 109.

Frame 1¹⁴ continued

sheet—all sources of financing. Capital structure (capitalization) is financing from long-term sources, including long-term debt, preferred stock, and net worth. The capital structure or capitalization of the firm is therefore equal to total assets less current liabilities. Financial leverage is the ratio of total debt to net worth, called the debt-equity ratio. Business risk is the variability of the expected return resulting from the product-market mix activities of the firm. Operating risk reflects the degree of operating leverage employed by the firm—the relative proportion of fixed and variable costs in the firm's cost structure. Financial risk is the risk compounded on business and operating risk resulting from the use of financial leverage.

DESIGNING THE CAPITAL STRUCTURE OF THE FIRM

To determine the optimal capital structure of the firm requires an application of the theory of financial leverage. If the return on assets exceeds the cost of debt, leverage may increase the returns to equity. However, leverage also increases the degree of fluctuations in the returns to equity for any given degree of fluctuations in sales and the return on assets. Leverage increases the returns to owners if used successfully, but if leverage is unsuccessful, the result may be bankruptcy.

These generalizations are now illustrated. Table 14–1 provides data for calculating the re-

FIGURE 14–1
Return on net worth as a function of the return on assets under alternative leverage rates

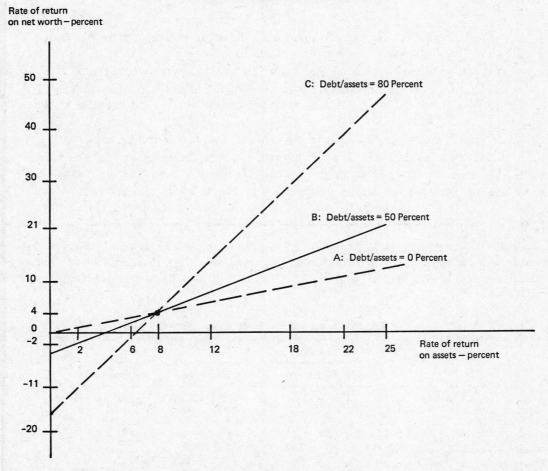

turn on equity under three alternative leverage and profitability conditions.

In line 1 of Table 14–1, the rates of return on total assets before interest and taxes are set forth under alternative profitability conditions ranging from very poor to very good. It is assumed that the firm has total assets of 100, hence the second row, entitled earnings before interest and taxes (EBIT), represents the first row with the percentage translated into dollars. The rate of interest on debt is 8 percent, and the tax rate is 50 percent.

The first line for each firm, EBIT, represents the data from the profitability conditions. Since Firm A employs no leverage, the interest expense is zero. The rate of return on common stock would be one half the rate of return on total assets because income would be reduced 50 percent by taxes, and the firm's net worth is equal to its total assets.

Firm B has a leverage factor of 50 percent so that its debt is 50 percent of total assets. At an 8 percent interest rate, its interest expense would be $4.00. The percent return on equity for Firm B ranges from −2 percent to +21 percent. Its range is 23 percentage points as compared with the range of 11.5 percentage points for Firm A. For Firm C the leverage factor is 80 percent—the ratio of debt to equity is four times. Its interest expense would be 8 percent times $80, or $6.40. The percentage return on common stock ranges from −11.0 percent to +46.5 percent, a total range of 57.5 percent. This example shows how leverage increases the variability of the return on common stock, also illustrated in Figure 14–1. The return on net worth degrees of leverage intersect the zero leverage return on net worth lines at the return on asset rate equal to the before-tax interest cost of debt.

Indicate whether each of the following statements is true or false by writing "T" or "F" in the space provided.

_____ 1. Financial structure and capital structure are synonymous terms.

_____ 2. Favorable financial leverage is defined as the variability of the expected return resulting from the product-market mix activities of the firm.

_____ 3. Unsuccessful financial leverage may lead to bankruptcy.

_____ 4. Table 14–1 shows how financial risk is increased by increasing the leverage factor from 0 percent to 80 percent.

Now turn to Answer Frame 1¹⁴, page 114, to check your answers.

Frame 2¹⁴

The effects of leverage on profitability are next expressed in terms of earnings per share under the assumption that at higher degrees of leverage, the cost of debt may increase. The data are set forth in Tables 14–2a and 14–2b. The right-hand side of the balance sheet is shown in Table

TABLE 14–2a

Financial structure from the balance sheet

	Case I	Case II	Case III	Case IV
	No leverage	Leverage 25%	Leverage 50%	Leverage 75%
Total debt....................................	0	$100	$ 200	$ 300
Interest rate applicable....................	5%	5%	10%	20%
Common stock, par $1.....................	$200	$150	$100	$50
Retained earnings.........................	200	150	100	50
Total equity................................	$ 400	$300	$ 200	$ 100
Total Assets...........................	$ 400	$400	$ 400	$ 400

TABLE 14–2b
Analysis of effects of leverage

	Probability of achieving indicated sales						
	5%	10%	30%	25%	15%	10%	5%
Sales...	$ 200	$ 400	$800	$1,000	$1,200	$1,400	$1,600
Total costs (400 + 0.5S)......................	500	600	800	900	1,000	1,100	1,200
Earnings before Interest and Taxes....	(300)	(200)	0	100	200	300	400
Effects on earnings per share							
Case I—no leverage:							
Interest expense...........................	0	0	0	0	0	0	0
Profit before taxes.........................	$(300)	$(200)	$ 0	$ 100	$ 200	$ 300	$ 400
Profit after taxes..........................	(150)	(100)	0	50	100	150	200
Earnings per share (200*).................	(.75)	(.50)	0	.25	.50	.75	1.00
Case II—leverage 25%:							
Interest expense...........................	5	5	5	5	5	5	5
Profit before taxes.........................	(305)	(205)	(5)	95	195	295	395
Profit after taxes..........................	(152)	(102)	(2)	48	98	148	198
Earnings per share (150*).................	($1.01)	(.68)	(.01)	.32	.65	.99	1.32
Case III—leverage 50%:							
Interest expense...........................	20	20	20	20	20	20	20
Profit before taxes.........................	(320)	(220)	(20)	80	180	280	380
Profit after taxes..........................	(160)	(110)	(10)	40	90	140	190
Earnings per share (100*).................	(1.60)	(1.10)	(.10)	.40	.90	1.40	1.90
Case IV—leverage 75%:							
Interest expense...........................	60	60	60	60	60	60	60
Profit before taxes.........................	(360)	(260)	(60)	40	140	240	340
Profit after taxes..........................	(180)	(130)	(30)	20	70	120	170
Earnings per share (50*).................	(3.60)	(2.60)	(.60)	.40	1.40	2.40	3.40

* Number of shares of common stock.

14–2a for four cases representing different degrees of leverage ranging from no leverage to a leverage ratio of 75 percent. In Table 14–2b, data are set forth for sales with the associated probabilities for achieving each indicated level of sales, and the total cost structure of the firm is also included. Sales less total operating costs would represent earnings before interest and taxes (EBIT). The effect on earnings per share of the four leverage situations is also developed in Table 14–2b. With no leverage, earnings per share range from a loss of $.75 per share to a gain of $1.00 per share. With leverage of 75 percent the range is from a loss of $3.60 per share to a gain of $3.40 per share.

The variability of returns is greater under the higher leverage case. But what is the profitability in relation to the variations in returns? This question is analyzed in Table 14–3. The probabilities set forth in Table 14–2b are applied to indicated earnings per share for each of the four cases. Thus, it can be seen that the expected return is highest under the 50 percent leverage factor. In addition, the variance and standard deviation of the earnings per share results are also calculated, and as before, the variability of earnings per share increases with increased leverage. In each case, the coefficient of variation is calculated by dividing the standard deviation by average earnings per share, and it rises from 2.43 in Case I to 17.06 in Case IV.

In Case IV the expected earnings per share drop to $.10 because the after-tax cost of debt capital is so high. Hence, we can rule Case IV out as a possible desired level of leverage. In Cases I through III, the expected earnings per share rises, but the standard deviation rises even more, so that the coefficient of variation increases as well. The choice among the three remaining possibilities would depend upon the influence of

Answer frame 1¹⁴

1. False. Financial structure refers to the entire right-hand side of the balance sheet; whereas capital structure includes everything on the right-hand side of the balance sheet except current liabilities. Capitalization refers to long-term financing sources or long-term debt, preferred stock, and net worth.

2. False. The variability of the expected return resulting from the product-market mix activities of the firm refers to business risk. Favorable financial leverage is where the return on assets exceeds the cost of debt. It also increases the return to equity but the fluctuation of these returns is magnified for any given degree of fluctuation in the sales level.

3. True. Unsuccessful financial leverage is where the return on assets is less than the cost of debt financing. This will reduce the returns to equity.

4. True. For example, at 0 percent leverage the variability of the return was 11.5 percent while at 80 percent leverage it was 57.5 percent.

If you missed any of the above, reread Frame 1¹⁴ before starting Frame 2¹⁴, page 112.

Frame 2¹⁴ continued

TABLE 14–3

Computation of expected EPS and measures of dispersion

Probability	EPS	pEPS	$(EPS - \overline{EPS})$*	$(EPS - \overline{EPS})^2$	$p(EPS - \overline{EPS})^2$
Case I—no leverage					
.05	(.75)	(.0375)	(.925)	.8556	.0428
.10	(.50)	(.0500)	(.675)	.4556	.0456
.30	0	.0000	(.175)	.0306	.0092
.25	.25	.0625	.075	.0056	.0014
.15	.50	.0750	.325	.1056	.0158
.10	.75	.0750	.575	.3306	.0331
.05	1.00	.0500	.825	.6806	.0340
	E(EPS) = .1750	CV = σ/E(EPS) = 2.43		$\sigma^2 = \overline{.1819}$ σ = .4260	
Case II—leverage 25%					
.05	(1.01)	(.0505)	(1.231)	1.5150	.0758
.10	(0.68)	(.0680)	(.901)	.8118	.0812
.30	(0.01)	(.0030)	(.231)	.0534	.0160
.25	0.32	.0800	.099	.0098	.0025
.15	0.65	.0975	.429	.1840	.0276
.10	0.99	.0990	.769	.5914	.0591
.05	1.32	.0660	1.099	1.2078	.0604
	E(EPS) = .221	CV = σ/E(EPS) = 2.57		$\sigma^2 = \overline{.3226}$ σ = .5680	
Case III—leverage 50%					
.05	(1.60)	(.080)	(1.85)	3.4225	.1711
.10	(1.10)	(.110)	(1.35)	1.8225	.1823
.30	(0.10)	(.030)	(0.35)	0.1225	.0368
.25	0.40	.100	0.15	0.0225	.0056
.15	0.90	.135	0.65	0.4225	.0634
.10	1.40	.140	1.15	1.3225	.1323
.05	1.90	.095	1.65	2.7225	.1361
	E(EPS) = .250	CV = σ/E(EPS) = 3.41		$\sigma^2 = \overline{.7276}$ σ = .8530	
Case IV—leverage 75%					
.05	(3.60)	(.18)	(3.70)	13.69	.6845
.10	(2.60)	(.26)	(2.70)	7.29	.7290
.30	(0.60)	(.18)	(0.70)	0.49	.1470
.25	0.40	.10	0.30	0.09	.0225
.15	1.40	.21	1.30	1.69	.2535
.10	2.40	.24	2.30	5.29	.5290
.05	3.40	.17	3.30	10.89	.5445
	E(EPS) = .10	CV = σ/E(EPS) = 17.06		$\sigma^2 = \overline{2.910}$ σ = 1.706	

* $\overline{EPS}$ is the same as E(EPS).

greater risk per dollar of expected return on the firm's cost of capital. Therefore, the groundwork has been established for turning to a considera- tion of the fundamental relationship between these two variables.

Label each of the following statements as true or false.

_____ 1. The variability of returns and the expected earnings per share are greatest under the highest leverage case.

_____ 2. The drop in expected earnings per share for the leverage factor of 75 percent is the result of the high-risk factor of increased variability of returns to equity holders.

_____ 3. The desired level of financial leverage is where the expected earnings per share are the greatest.

_____ 4. As illustrated in Table 14–3 it is best to use the variance (σ^2) or the standard deviation (σ) as the quantitative measure of financial risk.

Now turn to Answer Frame 2¹⁴, page 116, to check your answers.

Frame 3¹⁴

THE EFFECTS OF LEVERAGE ON THE COST OF CAPITAL

Professors Modigliani and Miller (referred to as MM) set forth two propositions for a world of pure and perfect competition, with no taxes:

$$\rho = \frac{\bar{X}}{V_u} \text{ (MM proposition I)} \tag{14-1}$$

$$k = \rho + (\rho - r)\frac{B}{S} \text{ (MM proposition II)} \tag{14-2}$$

Symbols are explained in Table 14–4.

TABLE 14–4

Symbols used in discussion of cost of capital theorems

ρ = The cost of capital of an unlevered firm.
$\bar{X}$ = expected EBIT.
V = Total value of a levered firm = $B + S = V_u + tB$.
V_u = The value of an unlevered firm.
π = Net income available to common stock holders.
k = Cost of equity capital for a levered firm.
r = Cost of debt.
S = Equity value of a firm.
B = Value of the debt of a levered firm.
t = Tax rate.
(WACC) = Weighted average cost of capital = $k\left(\frac{S}{V}\right) + r\left(\frac{B}{V}\right)$.

^ refers to after-tax measures.

Proposition I states that the cost of capital of an unlevered firm is equal to the net operating income (or earnings before interest and taxes) divided by the value of the firm. Proposition II states that the cost of equity capital rises linearly with the debt-to-equity ratio. These propositions are illustrated in Table 14–5.

Summary income statements and summary balance sheets for a levered and an unlevered firm are presented in Table 14–5. Proposition I is cal- culated by dividing EBIT by the total value of the firm to obtain 20 percent. Proposition II states that the return on equity is: Overall cost of capital of an unlevered firm plus the difference between this cost of capital and the cost of debt, weighted by the leverage ratio. This is 30 percent. Alternatively, the final profit term in the in- come statement of $60,000 can be divided by the equity value of $200,000 to again obtain 30 per- cent.

This illustration indicates the plausibility of the MM propositions: in a no-tax world, leverage has no influence on a firm's cost of capital. As shown in the table, the weighted average cost of capital remains constant regardless of the de- gree of leverage.

Answer frame 2¹⁴

1. False. According to Table 14–3 the greatest expected return, E(EPS) = 0.25, is under the 50 percent leverage factor. Notice that the greatest financial risk, CV = 17.06, is at the leverage factor of 75 percent.
2. True. The additional burden of fixed charges and the greater probability of bankruptcy have caused the cost of debt to be 20 percent. In addition, the increased variability of returns to equity holders will probably cause the market price of the common stock to fall.
3. False. The choice among the four cases illustrated in Table 14–3 would depend upon the trade-off between risk and return. The optimal capital structure depends upon the influence of greater risk per dollar of expected return on the firm's cost of capital.
4. False. The coefficient of variation is a better measure of risk in this example since it measures the risk per dollar of investment.

If you missed any of the above, reread Frame 2¹⁴ before beginning Frame 3¹⁴, page 115.

Frame 3¹⁴ continued

TABLE 14–5
Illustration of MM's propositions—no taxes

Facts	No leverage	50% leverage	75% leverage
Income statement			
Sales............	$800,000	$800,000	$800,000
Total costs.......	720,000	720,000	720,000
EBIT = $\bar{X}$.........	$ 80,000	$ 80,000	$ 80,000
Interest..........		20,000	30,000
Profit = π.......	$ 80,000	$ 60,000	$ 50,000
Balance sheet (at market values)*			
Value of debt (B).	0	$200,000	$300,000
Equity value (S)...	$400,000	$200,000	$100,000

Calculations:

No leverage

$$\rho = \frac{\$\,80,000}{\$400,000} = .20$$

50% leverage (r = 10%)

$k = .20 + (.20 - .10)1$
$\quad = .30$

$k = \frac{\pi}{s} = \frac{\$\,60,000}{\$200,000} = .30$

(WACC) = .30(½) + .10(½) = .20

75% leverage (r = 10%)

$k = .20 + (.20 - .10)3$
$\quad = .50$

$k = \frac{\pi}{s} = \frac{\$\,50,000}{\$100,000} = .50$

(WACC) = .50(¼) + .10(¾) = .125 + .075 = .20

* No leverage $\frac{B}{S}$ = 0; 50% leverage $\frac{B}{S}$ = 1; 75% leverage $\frac{B}{S}$ = 3.

COST OF CAPITAL WITH TAXES

The MM propositions for a world with taxes are set forth in Table 14–6 in equations (14–3) through (14–7). The facts are the same as in Table 14–5, with the addition of a corporate tax rate of 40 percent.

The calculation of the cost of equity capital for the unlevered firm begins with the relations between the value of an unlevered firm and the value of the levered firm set forth in equation (14–3). The value of an unlevered firm is smaller than the value of a levered firm by the amount of the tax shelter lost by not using debt, as measured by the term: the tax rate times total debt. Since the value of a levered firm is $400,000, the value of the unlevered firm would be this amount, less 0.4 × $200,000, or $320,000. The cost of equity capital for the unlevered firm can then be calculated as set forth in equation (14–4), yielding 15 percent.

The after-tax cost of equity capital for the levered firm can then be calculated by equation (14–5). Inserting the appropriate information yields an after-tax cost of equity for the levered firm of 18 percent, 3 percentage points higher than the cost of equity capital for the unlevered firm. Equation (14–5) yields a result consistent with that of equation (14–4). Since the unlevered firm has no leverage, the second term of equation (14–5) becomes zero, and the cost of

TABLE 14–6
Illustration of MM's propositions—with taxes

Facts*	No leverage	50% leverage
Income statement		
Sales	$800,000	$800,000
Total costs	720,000	720,000
EBIT = $\bar{X}$	$ 80,000	$ 80,000
Interest	0	20,000
PBT	$ 80,000	$ 60,000
Taxes	32,000	24,000
Profit after Tax	$ 48,000	$ 36,000

Calculations:

MM II. Cost of equity capital
No leverage

$$V_u = V - tB \qquad (14\text{-}3)$$
$$V_u = 400,000 - .4(200,000)$$
$$= 320,000$$

$$\hat{k} = \frac{\bar{X}(1 - t)}{V_u} = \hat{p}_u \qquad (14\text{-}4)$$

$$\hat{p}_u = \frac{(80,000)(.6)}{320,000} = \frac{48,000}{320,000} = .15$$

50% leverage

$$\hat{k} = \hat{p}_u + (\hat{p}_u - r)\frac{B(1 - t)}{S} \qquad (14\text{-}5)$$
$$= .15 + (.15 - .10)(0.6)$$
$$\hat{k} = .18$$

MM I. Cost of capital
No leverage

$$(\widehat{WACC})_u = \frac{\bar{X}(1 - t)}{V_u} = \hat{p}_u = .15 \qquad (14\text{-}4)$$

50% leverage

$$(\widehat{WACC})_L = \frac{\bar{X}(1 - t)}{V} \qquad (14\text{-}6)$$
$$= \frac{48,000}{400,000} = .12$$

$$(\widehat{WACC})_L = r(1 - t)\frac{B}{V} + \hat{k}\frac{S}{V} \qquad (14\text{-}7)$$
$$= .10(.6)(.5) + (.18)(.5)$$
$$= .03 + .09 = .12$$

* Same as Table 14–5 plus $t = 40\%$.

equity for the unlevered firm would be 15 percent.

Next, the overall cost of capital can be calculated. The overall cost of capital for the unlevered firm is the same as its cost of equity capital since the unlevered firm is all-equity financed. The weighted average cost of capital for the levered firm can first be calculated by using equation (14–6). This is the same as equation (14–4), except that the value of the levered firm is used in the denominator. The weighted average cost of capital for the levered firm is 12 percent, as shown in Table 14–6. A check on the calculation of the weighted average cost of capital for the levered firm can be achieved by using the weighted proportions of the cost of debt and the cost of equity capital. This is set forth in equation (14–7) in Table 14–6. Inserting the appropriate figures, the result confirms that the weighted average cost of capital is 12 percent. The weighted average cost of capital for the levered firm is lower than for the unlevered firm because of the tax shelter benefits achieved by the levered firm but not achieved by the unlevered firm.

The cost of capital comparisons for the levered and unlevered firms can be generalized under the alternative assumptions set forth in Figure 14–2. In panel 14–2a, the traditional view holds that the cost of debt or equity does not rise until leverage becomes "excessive." The solid lines in panel 14–2b reflect the assumptions of no taxes and no bankruptcy costs, also in the original MM propositions. The cost of capital is the same as previously described. Under these assumptions "leverage does not matter." The broken lines in panel 14–2b depict a world with corporate taxes but no bankruptcy costs. In this world, the cost of capital for a levered firm decreases as compared with the cost of capital for an unlevered firm: the more leverage the lower the cost of capital for the leveraged firm. This implies extremely high leverage ratios not observed in the actual world.

The actual world appears to be reflected in Panel 14–2c. For small amounts of debt well within the margin of safety to creditors and owners, the cost of debt and cost of equity functions are approximately linear. In this range, the overall cost of capital is declining, as in Panel 14–2b, because it is a world with corporate taxes, but bankruptcy costs have not yet affected the relationships. At some leverage, however, the risks of bankruptcy costs increase to the point where both the cost of debt and the cost of equity begin to rise. During some range, two opposing forces are operative. The tax effect tends to pull down the overall cost of capital for the levered firm. At some point, however, the in-

FIGURE 14–2

Alternative theories of cost of capital functions

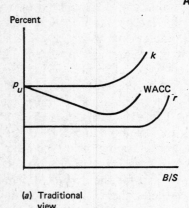

(a) Traditional view

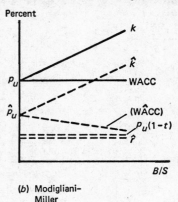

(b) Modigliani-Miller

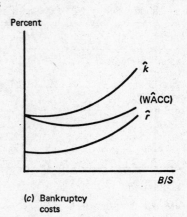

(c) Bankruptcy costs

creased risk of bankruptcy costs causes the cost of debt function and the cost of equity function to rise with sufficient steepness to begin to pull up the cost of capital for the levered firm. The weighted average cost of capital curve is relatively flat in the area of its minimum level.

True or false?

_____ 1. According to MM the WACC and ρ are always identical regardless of the leverage factor in a no-tax world.

_____ 2. The weighted average cost of capital for the levered firm is higher than for the unlevered firm because of increased tax liabilities.

_____ 3. With taxes, MM indicated that a firm's capital structure will consist of all debt.

_____ 4. In the real world the weighted average cost of capital curve is saucer shaped over some range of debt-to-equity ratios.

Now turn to Answer Frame 3¹⁴, page 120, to check your answers.

Frame 4¹⁴

THE COST OF CAPITAL AS AN INVESTMENT HURDLE RATE

The capital asset pricing model permits the criteria for asset expansion decisions to be set out unambiguously and compactly. It generalizes the more traditional weighted average cost of capital approach. In the case that follows, some illustrative materials for the application of the market price of risk (MPR) criteria, as compared with the WACC criteria, are provided.

Statement of the Mostin Company case. The Mostin Company is considering four projects in a capital expansion program. The vice president of finance has estimated that the firm's weighted average cost of capital (WACC) is 12 percent. The economics staff projected the future course of the market portfolio over the estimated life span of the projects under each of the four states of the world (first three columns in Table 14–7); it recommended the use of a risk-free rate of return of 4 percent. The Finance Department provided the estimates of project returns conditional on the state of the world (columns 4 through 7 in Table 14–7). Each project involves an outlay of approximately $50,000.

Assuming that the projects are independent and that the firm can raise sufficient funds to finance all four projects, which projects would be accepted using the WACC and MPR criteria?

Solution procedure for the Mostin Company case. The solution procedures for the Mostin case are as follows. The data provided by market relationships are utilized to calculate the expected return on the market along with its variance and standard deviation in Table 14–8. A similar procedure is followed in Table 14–9 for calculating the expected return and the covariance for each of the four individual projects.

In Table 14–10, the beta (β) for each project is calculated as the ratio of its covariance to the variance of the market return. The resulting betas in Table 14–10 range from a low of 0.60 to a high of 3.50.

Since the size of the beta is an index of the degree of risk or volatility of each individual investment project, it is used in Table 14–11 to

estimate the required return $(E(R_j) = Rf + [E(Rm) - Rf]\beta_j)$ on each project in terms of the market line relationship, where the risk-free rate of return is assumed to be 4 percent; hence the market risk premium is 6 percent $(E(Rm) - Rf = .10 - .04 = .06)$. The market risk differential is multiplied by each individual project beta and added to the pure rate of interest to obtain the required return on each project.

These required returns, as shown in column 2 of Table 14–11, are deducted from the estimated returns taken from column 4 of Table 14–9 for each individual project. The results, shown in column 4 of Table 14–11, are the estimated returns less the required returns, called the excess returns. These relations are depicted graphically in Figure 14–3.

The MPR criterion accepts the projects with positive excess returns, which appear above the MPR line. It rejects those with negative excess returns (plotted below the MPR line). The WACC criterion as portrayed in Figure 14–3 accepts projects with returns above 12 percent and rejects those with returns of less than 12 percent. The two criteria give conflicting results for Project

TABLE 14–7
Summary of information—Mostin case

(1) State of world (s)	(2) Subjective probability (p_s)	(3) Market return R_{ms}	(4) Project 1	(5) Rates of return Project 2	(6) Project 3	(7) Project 4
s = 1	.1	−.30	−.46	−1.00	−.40	−.40
s = 2	.2	−.10	−.26	−0.50	−.20	−.20
s = 3	.3	.10	.46	0.00	.00	.60
s = 4	.4	.30	.00	1.00	.70	.00

TABLE 14–8
Solution procedure for calculation of market parameters

(1) p	(2) R_m	(3) pR_m	(4) $R_m - E(R_m)$	(5) $[R_m - E(R_m)]^2$	(6) $p[(R_m - E(R_m)]^2$
.1	−.30	−.03	−.40	.16	.016
.2	−.10	−.02	−.20	.04	.008
.3	.10	.03	0	0	0
.4	.30	.12	.20	.04	.016
		$E(R_m) = .10$			Var $R_m = .040$
					$\sigma_m = .20$

Answer frame 3¹⁴

1. True. Table 14–5 illustrates this concept by showing the WACC $= \rho = .20$ in all three cases.
2. False. The weighted average cost of capital for the levered firm is lower than the unlevered firm because of the tax shelter benefits achieved by the levered firm. In Table 14–6 $(WACC)_u = .15$ whereas $(WACC)_L = .12$.
3. True. And this is where MM proposition I seems to be the most vulnerable—particularly when observing the marketplace. At extreme levels of leverage a firm's WACC in actuality seems to rise.
4. True. Even though MM theory is mathematically accurate, its assumptions seem vulnerable. Observations from the marketplace seem to corroborate the WACC as illustrated in Figure 14–2c

If you missed any of the above, restudy Frame 3¹⁴ before starting Frame 4¹⁴ on page 118.

Frame 4¹⁴ continued

TABLE 14–9

Calculation of expected returns and covariances for the four hypothetical projects

(1) Project Number	(2) p	(3) R_j	(4) pR_j	(5) $[R_j - E(R_j)]$	(6) $[R_m - E(R_m)]$	(7) $[R_j - E(R_j)] \times [R_m - E(R_m)]$	(8) $p[R_j - E(R_j)] \times [R_m - E(R_m)]$
P1......	.1	− .46	−.046	− .50	−.40	.200	.0200
	.2	− .26	−.052	− .30	−.20	.060	.0120
	.3	.46	.138	.42	.00	.000	.0000
	.4	.00	.000	− .04	.20	−.008	−.0032
		$E(R_1) = .040$				$Cov(R_1, R_m) =$	.0288
P2......	.1	−1.00	− .10	−1.20	−.40	.480	.0480
	.2	− .50	− .10	−0.70	−.20	.140	.0280
	.3	0	.00	−0.20	.00	.000	.0000
	.4	1.00	.40	0.80	.20	.160	.0640
		$E(R_2) = .20$				$Cov(R_2, R_m) =$	.1400
P3......	.1	− .40	− .04	− .60	−.40	.240	.0240
	.2	− .20	− .04	− .40	−.20	.080	.0160
	.3	.00	.00	− .20	.00	.000	.0000
	.4	+ .70	.28	.50	.20	.100	.0400
		$E(R_3) = .20$				$Cov(R_3, R_m) =$	.0800
P4......	.1	− .40	− .04	− .50	−.40	.200	.0200
	.2	− .20	− .04	− .30	−.20	.060	.0120
	.3	.60	.18	.50	.00	.000	.0000
	.4	.00	.00	− .10	.20	−.020	−.0080
		$E(R_4) = .10$				$Cov(R_4, R_m) =$	.0240

2 and for Project 4. The MPR criterion rejects Project 2 because it falls below the MPR line; but the WACC accepts it because the return is in excess of 12 percent. In addition, the MPR criterion accepts Project 4 while the WACC criterion rejects it.

The above example illustrates that the MPR criterion directly adjusts for risk differences and

TABLE 14–10

Calculation of the betas

$\beta_1{}^\circ = .0288/.04 = 0.72$
$\beta_2{}^\circ = .1400/.04 = 3.50$
$\beta_3{}^\circ = .0800/.04 = 2.00$
$\beta_4{}^\circ = .0240/.04 = 0.60$

develops the appropriate return-risk relations for making a determination of whether to accept or reject an individual project. However, the WACC criterion does not provide such a direct measure of the return-risk relation.

TABLE 14–11

Calculation of excess returns

(1) Project number	(2) Measurement of required return	(3) Estimated return	(4) Excess return
	$E(R_j{}^\circ) = R_f + MRP(\beta.)$		
P1.....................	$E(R_1{}^\circ) = .04 + .06(0.72) = .083$	.040	−.043
P2.....................	$E(R_2{}^\circ) = .04 + .06(3.50) = .250$	.200	−.050
P3.....................	$E(R_3{}^\circ) = .04 + .06(2.00) = .160$	.200	.040
P4.....................	$E(R_4{}^\circ) = .04 + .06(0.60) = .076$	.100	.024

FIGURE 14–3

Application of the asset expansion criterion

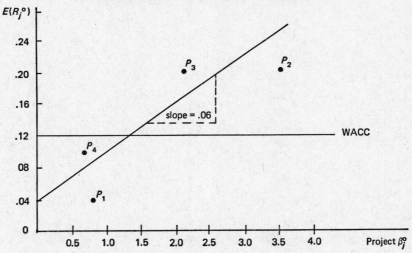

Is each of the following true or false?

_____ 1. The capital asset pricing model generalizes the traditional weighted average cost of capital approach by applying the market price of risk criteria.

_____ 2. The beta for any project is defined as the risk index of the comparison of the measurement of the variability or covariance of the returns of the individual security with that of the market returns.

_____ 3. According to Figure 14–3, projects 3 and 4 should be selected when selection is based on the capital market line (CML). Projects 2 and 3 should be selected when considering only WACC as the hurdle rate.

_____ 4. MPR is superior to WACC decision criterion in project selection because it provides a direct measure of the risk-return relationship.

Now turn to Answer Frame 4¹⁴, page 124, to check your answers.

chapter 15

DIVIDEND POLICY AND VALUATION

Frame 1[15]

Dividend policy determines the extent of a firm's internal financing—the major source of funds for financing business growth. Dividends are a source of cash flows that accrue to shareholders. Because dividend policy affects the financial structure, the flow of funds, corporate liquidity, and so on, it is an important decision area.

RESIDUAL THEORY OF DIVIDENDS

In theory, dividend policy is formulated simultaneously with the determination of the optimal capital structure, the marginal cost of capital, and the marginal return on investment. This has been referred to as the residual theory of dividends in that dividends are residual after investment needs have been met. The central principle is that shareholder wealth will be maximized if the firm retains and reinvests earnings as long as the return on reinvested earnings exceeds the rate of return the investor could obtain on other investments of comparable risk. This also reflects the idea that the cost of equity capital obtained from retained earnings is an opportunity cost which is the rates of return available from other alternatives. Thus, if a firm's shareholders could buy other stocks of equal risk yielding a 12 percent

dividend plus capital gains yield, 12 percent would be the firm's cost of retained earnings. If firms followed the theory briefly outlined, and if investors were indifferent to receiving their investment returns in the form of dividends or capital gains, shareholder wealth would be maximized.

SOME DIVIDEND GUIDELINES

Since the financial manager may not have all the information required to apply the theory, some guidelines are helpful. The following check list summarizes the major economic and financial factors influencing dividend policy:

A. Rate of growth and profit level. Economic theory suggests that high growth rates are associated with higher profit opportunities, and lower growth rates with smaller profit margins. The higher the growth rate and the larger the prospective margins, the lower the dividend payout is likely to be.

B. Stability of earnings. If earnings are relatively stable from the standpoint of both long-term growth and cyclical fluctuations, the dividend payout is likely to be higher. (This check list is continued in the next frame.)

Answer frame 4¹⁴

1. True. The capital asset pricing model—applying portfolio theory—sets out the criteria for capital project analysis considering both risk and return unambiguously and compactly.

2. True. It is calculated as the individual project's covariance divided by the variance of the market return and is illustrated in Table 14–10. Project 2 has the highest beta coefficient ($\beta_2 = .1400/.04 = 3.50$), which means it has the greatest degree of risk of the four example projects.

3. True. Project 3 is a unanimous choice, but conflicting rankings are obtained for projects 2 and 4. The MPR criterion rejects project 2 because it falls below the MPR line, or its level of risk is too high for its estimated return. WACC accepts project 2 because its estimated return is greater than the 12 percent hurdle rate.

4. True. The Mostin Company case shows how MPR criterion directly adjusts for risk differences and develops the appropriate risk-return relationship for making the accept-reject decisions on capital project analysis.

If you missed any of the above, restudy Frame 4¹⁴ before beginning Chapter 15 on page 123.

Frame 1¹⁵ continued

Indicate whether each of the following statements is true or false by writing "T" or "F" in the space provided.

_____ 1. The residual dividend policy states that shareholder wealth will be maximized when a balance is achieved in considering investment decisions, rate of growth and profit level, stability of earnings, age and size of firm, and so on.

_____ 2. Internally generated funds are free, which is the reason why they are the major source of funds for financing business growth.

_____ 3. The fact that retained earnings are free explains why firms with high growth rates in profits usually maintain low dividend payout ratios.

_____ 4. Dividend payout ratios are likely to be higher when earnings are relatively stable.

Now turn to Answer Frame 1¹⁵, page 126, to check your answers.

Frame 2¹⁵

C. Age and size of firm. A well-established, large firm has better access to capital markets than the new and small firm. Hence, the dividend payout, other things being equal, will be higher for the larger and older firm.

D. Cash position. The stronger a firm's cash or liquidity position in relation to its prospective future need for funds, the higher the probable dividend payout.

E. Need to repay debt. A firm that has heavy indebtedness has implicitly committed itself to a relatively high rate of earnings retention unless it seeks to prepare the markets for a common stock or debt-refunding issue. This factor may be reinforced by provisions in the debt contract that prevent the payment of cash dividends unless certain conditions are met.

F. Control. If maintenance of existing voting control is an important consideration, the dividend payout may be lower to permit financing from retained earnings. The procedure avoids issuance of additional securities, which would involve dilution of ownership or the increased risks of debt. However, if a struggle for control of the firm with opposition groups is in progress or is threatened, the dividend payout may be higher so as to appeal to stockholder goodwill.

G. Maintenance of a target dividend. The objective of a stable absolute dollar amount dividend policy will cause low payout ratios when profits are temporarily high, and high payout ratios when profits are temporarily depressed. Dividends will lag behind profit growth until the establishment of new earnings levels is strongly assured.

H. Tax position of stockholders. Corporations closely held by a few taxpayers in high-income brackets are likely to have a lower dividend payout because of the tax advantages of capital gains. Corporations widely held by small investors will tend to have higher dividend payouts.

I. Tax position of the corporation. Potential penalties for excessive accumulation of retained earnings may cause dividend payouts to be higher than economic and financial considerations alone would indicate.

Of the factors listed, some would result in higher dividend payouts, some in lower. It is not possible to provide a formula that can be used to establish the proper dividend payout for a given situation; an exercise of judgment is required. The considerations summarized above provide a check list for guiding dividend decisions.

Label each of the following statements as true or false.

———— 1. In determining dividend policy, an important consideration is the firm's flow of funds forecast.

———— 2. In small- to medium-sized firms, the factor of "voting control" is of paramount consideration in setting dividend policy.

———— 3. A fixed dividend payout ratio will lead to synchronization between dividends and earnings.

———— 4. Since capital gains are taxed at lower rates than ordinary income, small closely held firms tend to pay out as dividends a larger share of their earnings.

Now turn to Answer Frame 2¹⁵, page 126, to check your answers.

Frame 3¹⁵

DIVIDENDS AND VALUATION

Divergent points of view have been expressed with respect to the effect of the dividend payout ratio on the price of a firm's stock. One group holds that the capital gains which may result from earnings retention are more risky than dividends. Accordingly, this group would argue that for firms in comparable circumstances, a low payout firm will find that its earnings typically will be capitalized at higher rates (command a lower price) than the earnings of a high payout firm.

The second school argues that "dividends do not matter," indicating that investors are indifferent as to whether returns are in the form of dividends or of capital gains. This position also suggests that any effect that a change in dividends has on the price of a firm's stock results primarily from the information content provided about expected future earnings conveyed by a change in dividends. Thus an increase in the dividend payout indicates that higher earnings may be attained, and a drop in the dividend payout may signal a lower level of earnings.

A third group argues that the investment influence must be fully neutralized for dividend policy not to matter. The concept of neutralizing investment influence on dividend policy is illustrated in Table 15–1. Firm A pays an $11 dividend in Period 1 in which the cost of equity capital is 10 percent and pays a $12.32 dividend

Answer frame 1¹⁵

1. False. The element essential to the residual dividend policy is that the market price of a firm's common stock—the proxy for shareholder wealth—will be maximized when the firm retains and reinvests as long as the return on investment projects is greater than the return the investor could obtain on other comparable investments.
2. False. They are not free. If the return on reinvested earnings is greater than or equal to the required rate of return of its common shareholders, the market price of its common stock will probably either rise or remain constant. If the return is less than the stockholders' required rate of return, the common stockholders will switch to other investment opportunities and this will reduce the demand for the firm's stock and cause the price to fall. Thus, the cost of retained earnings is an opportunity cost which is the required rate of return demanded by the firm's common stockholders.
3. False. Firms with high growth rates in profits are those with many profitable investment opportunities. In fact, their cost of retained earnings is usually much higher than for slower growth firms.
4. True. When earnings are relatively stable from the standpoint of both long-term growth and cyclical fluctuations, dividend payout ratios tend to be higher.

If you missed any of the above, review Frame 1¹⁵ before starting Frame 2¹⁵, page 124.

Answer frame 2¹⁵

1. True. The firm's cash position or liquidity position is extremely important. Future growth opportunities, merger considerations, stock splits, debt refunding, and all other fund flows must be forecast in considering the outflow of funds for dividend payments.
2. True. Avoiding heavy dividend payments can eliminate the need for either a common stock or debt issue for acquiring needed funds. Dilution of control and the increased obligation of fixed interest charges are avoided.
3. True. But it will lead to widely fluctuating dividend payments—particularly for a firm with cyclical or widely fluctuating earnings. Therefore, it will consist of frequent dividend reductions. Many firms follow the objective of a stable absolute dollar amount of dividends. This causes low payout ratios when profits are high and high payout ratios when profits are low. When earnings are temporarily high and an increase in dividend is warranted, firms may pay an extra dividend in order not to diverge from their stable absolute dividend policy. General Motors, for example, will pay an extra dividend when profits are high.
4. False. Potential penalties for excessive accumulation of retained earnings will cause higher dividend payouts, but this is no problem if the small firm is growing so that it can justify earnings retention. Also, the tax structure on capital gains versus ordinary income is designed to encourage earnings to be plowed back into the firm for growth purposes.

If you missed any of the above, reread Frame 2¹⁵ before starting Frame 3¹⁵, page 125.

Frame 3[15] continued

TABLE 15–1
Neutralization of investment influence on dividend policy

$$P = \frac{D_1}{(1 + k_1)} + \frac{D_2}{(1 + k_1)(1 + k_2)}$$

$$P_A = \frac{\$11}{(1 + .10)} + \frac{\$12.32}{(1 + .10)(1 + .12)}$$

$$= \frac{\$11}{1.10} + \frac{\$12.32}{1.232} = \$20$$

$$P_B = 0 + \frac{\$11(1.12) + \$12.32}{(1 + .10)(1 + .12)} = \frac{\$11(1.12)}{(1.10)(1.12)}$$

$$+ \frac{\$12.32}{(1.10)(1.12)} = P_A$$

$$= \frac{\$12.32 + \$12.32}{1.232} = \$20$$

in Period 2 when the opportunity cost of equity capital is 12 percent. If the price of Firm A's stock is obtained by capitalizing the expected future dividends, P_A would be $20. Firm B pays no dividend in the first period. The expected dividend at the end of the second period is equal to $12.32 plus the dividend paid by Firm A in Period 1, augmented by the earning power Firm B would have had if it successfully employed the retained earnings at least at a rate equal to the opportunity cost of equity capital (12 percent) during Period 2. Thus the price of Firm B's stock would also be $20.

This example represents a special case of the general rule stated initially: that if the firm can earn at least the investor's opportunity cost of capital, it may retain earnings with no detriment to the investor. If the firm is unable to earn the investor's opportunity cost of capital, the earnings should be paid out in dividends. In practice, however, there are many special circumstances, of the type presented in the check list of factors, influencing dividend policy.

True or false?

_____ 1. One school of thought states that capital gains result from earnings retention, and this increased profitability is the reason why the earnings are typically capitalized at higher rates.

_____ 2. A second school of thought states that dividends are irrelevant to the firm's market valuation and suggests that dividends convey only information content about future earnings.

_____ 3. Firm X pays a $2.50 dividend in period 1 in which the cost of equity capital is 12 percent, and pays a $3.00 dividend in period 2 when the cost of equity capital is 14 percent. The price of Firm X's stock would be $4.58. Firm Y pays no dividend in the first period but pays [2.50(1 + .14) + 3.00] as the dividend in Period 2. Hence, the price of Firm Y's stock would be greater than $4.58.

_____ 4. The example in Question 3 illustrates a third school of thought which says that if a firm can earn the investor's opportunity cost of capital on retained earnings, the market price of its stock will not change.

Now turn to Answer Frame 3[15], page 128, to check your answers.

Frame 4[15]

The same considerations as mentioned above are involved in an analysis of share repurchase practices by business firms. If the firm is unable to earn as much as the shareholder's opportunity cost of equity capital with either its current cash flows or accumulated cash balances, share repurchase may be justified. Legal restrictions may limit the extent to which a firm may pay out cash dividends in excess of current year's earnings or accumulated retained earnings. Thus, one

Answer frame 3¹⁵

1. False. Typically, capital gains resulting from earnings retention are more risky than dividends, and thus capital gains may be capitalized at higher rates.
2. True. Therefore, a dividend reduction conveys bad news about future earnings, and a dividend increase conveys good news about future earnings.
3. False. The price of Firm Y's stock would also be $4.58 computed as follows:

$$P_X = \frac{2.50}{(1 + .12)} + \frac{3.00}{(1 + .12)(1 + .14)} = \$4.58$$

$$P_Y = 0 + \frac{2.50(1 + .14) + 3.00}{(1 + .12)(1 + .14)} = \$4.58$$

4. True. This is why the opportunity cost of capital is used as the cost of equity capital—so that if the firm cannot earn at least the investor's opportunity rate, the earnings should be paid out in dividends. Otherwise, the market price of the stock will probably decline.

If you missed any of the above, reread Frame 3¹⁵ before turning to Frame 4¹⁵, page 127.

Frame 4¹⁵ continued

justification for share repurchase would be to transfer funds from the firm unable to invest them at the shareholders' opportunity cost of capital to its shareholders who can. Other reasons for share repurchase relate to a variety of tax considerations, and also to the circumstances of individual shareholders and of individual companies.

Another principle of wide generality with respect to dividend policy is the sound rationale for a stable dollar amount of dividends. Fluctuations in the dollar amount of dividends may give rise to uncertainty as to what the future dividends are likely to be. Thus, a higher capitalization rate (lower price) may result. Firms may lag in raising dividends in years of good earnings and resist even more strenuously reductions in dividends as earnings decline. As a consequence,

empirical studies indicate that dividends are more stable than earnings.

The influence of stock splits and stock dividends on share prices have also been investigated. Neither have been found to exert more than a temporary influence on prices unless accompanied by a change in the effective dividend rate, in turn viewed as an indication of a change in expected future earnings. The fundamental determinant of the company stock price is its earning power compared with the earning power of other firms. However, both stock splits and stock dividends can be used as an effective instrument of financial policy. They are useful devices for reducing the price at which stocks are traded, and thereby may be helpful in broadening the ownership of a firm's shares.

Is each of the following true or false?

_____ 1. Share repurchase, which ends up on the balance sheet as treasury stock, is often conducted in lieu of paying out a cash dividend.

_____ 2. Empirical studies show that dividends fluctuate simultaneously with earnings, indicating that firms typically follow a fixed dividend payout ratio.

_____ 3. A stock split will usually place a firm's stock price in a more popular trading range, thereby increasing the demand for its stock. This will normally cause the adjusted market price of the stock to rise.

_____ 4. Another powerful rationale for a stock split or a stock dividend is the desire to broaden the ownership of the firm.

Now turn to Answer Frame 4¹⁵, page 130, to check your answers.

Frame 5[15]

With the background of dividend theory, we may now analyze the influence of internal versus external financing sources on the firm's cost of capital.

THE COST OF CAPITAL AS A FUNCTION OF THE QUANTITY OF FINANCING

Table 15–2 sets forth the data for an illustration of effects of the expansion rate of assets on the cost of capital. Part A shows that the Expanso Company has a capital structure with debt in the amount of $50 million with an 8 percent cost. An equal amount of common equity is held.

TABLE 15–2

Data for Illustration of the effects of the expansion rate on the cost of capital

Facts:

A. The Expanso Company has the following capitalization structure

Debt (at 8%).............		$50,000,000
Common stock........	$10,000,000	
Retained earnings.....	40,000,000	
Common equity........		$50,000,000

B. Earnings and price
 1. Earnings per share have grown 8% per year and are expected to be $4 in 1974.
 2. The dividend payment rate will be constant at 50%.
 3. Current market price is $50 per share of common based on the expectation of a continued 8% per year growth in earnings and dividends.
 4. The addition to retained earnings for 1974 will be $10 million.
 5. The tax rate is 50%.
 6. The firm believes that 50% debt in its capital structure is optimal and will be maintained.

C. Data on cost of sale of additional securities
 1. Bonds
  For additional up to: $10 million— 8%
  For additional up to: $20 million—10%
  For additional up to: $30 million—12%

 2. Common stock
  For additional up to: $10 million—flotation costs of: 10%
  For additional up to: $20 million—flotation costs of: 20%

D. Rate of return on investment opportunities
  For an amount of investment up to: first $20 million—11%
  For an amount of investment up to: second $20 million—10%
  For an amount of investment up to: third $20 million—9%

Part B in the table presents data on earnings, dividends, and price relationships. Part C sets forth the data on costs that would be incurred on the sale of additional securities. Flotation costs are defined to include not only the payments made to investment bankers for the underwriting and distribution of the securities, but also the price pressure influence. *Price pressure* refers to the pressure on the existing price of the firm's securities due to bringing more securities into the market without simultaneously increasing the quantity of securities demanded to the same degree. Part D of the table sets forth the schedule of investment opportunities of the firm.

The calculations for illustrating the effect of the expansion rate on the cost of capital are set forth in Table 15–3. In Step 1, the calculation of the weights to be employed is made. The weights reflect the capital structure of the firm with 50 percent in debt and 50 percent in equity. In

TABLE 15–3

Calculations for illustrating the effect of the expansion rate on the cost of capital

Step 1—Calculation of weights

		Percent of total
Debt....................	$ 50,000,000	50
Equity..................	50,000,000	50
Total capitalization.......	$100,000,000	100

Step 2—Calculation of component costs of capital
Component cost of debt
 Up to $10 million, $r = .08 \times (1 - .5) = .0400$
 From $10.01 million to $20 million, $r = .10 \times (1 - .5) = .0500$
 Over $20 million, $r = .12 \times (1 - .5) = .0600$

Component cost of common stock
Stockholders' approximate required rate of return equals:

$$\frac{D}{P} + g = \frac{2}{50} + .08 = .04 + .08 = .12$$

Up to $10 million new outside equity:

$$k_e = \frac{D}{P(1 - F)} + g$$
$$= \frac{2}{50(1 - .1)} + .08 = \frac{2}{45} + .08$$
$$= .044 + .08 = .124$$

Over $10 million new outside equity:

$$k_e = \frac{2}{50(1 - .2)} + .08$$
$$= \frac{2}{40} + .08 = .05 + .08 = .13$$

Answer frame 4¹⁵

1. True. But there also are other considerations in share repurchase decisions, such as the desire to accumulate shares for an employee or executive stock option plan, for a pending merger where a stock exchange is contemplated, and for a variety of tax considerations.

2. False. Firms lag in raising dividends in years of good earnings because of the fear of having to cut dividends when and if earnings decline. Hence, firms appear to follow a stable dollar amount of dividends and increase this stable amount only after the firm has clearly established a higher level of earnings. Consequently, dividends fluctuate less widely than do earnings.

3. True. However, empirical studies show that the price rise is only a temporary influence and the fundamental determinant of the firm's stock price is its relative long-term earning power in the marketplace.

4. True. A desire to broaden the ownership is a reason for issuing more shares. Another reason for a stock split or a stock dividend is to reduce the price to a more popular trading range. A third reason is to provide the opportunity for more even-lot (100-share) transactions with their concomitant smaller brokerage fees.

If you missed any of the above, reread Frame 4¹⁵ before beginning Frame 5¹⁵, page 129.

Frame 5¹⁵ continued

TABLE 15–4

The weighted marginal cost of debt for different rates of expansion

Up to $20,000,000

	Weight	×	Marginal cost	=	Product
Debt..................	.5	×	.04	=	.02
Equity................	.5	×	.12	=	.06
Weighted cost of new capital..........					.08
					8%

$20,000,000 *to* $40,000,000

	Weight	×	Marginal cost	=	Product
Debt..................	.5	×	.050	=	.025
Equity................	.5	×	.124	=	.062
Weighted cost of new capital..........					.087
					8.7%

$40,000,000 *to* $60,000,000

	Weight	×	Marginal cost	=	Product
Debt..................	.5	×	.06	=	.030
Equity................	.5	×	.13	=	.065
Weighted cost of new capital..........					.095
					9.5%

Step 2, a calculation is made of the component costs of capital. The first $10 million of equity funds utilized represent retained earnings. The required rate of return for internal financing is the dividend yield of 4 percent plus expected growth rate of 8 percent, totaling a required rate of return on equity capital of 12 percent. With a 10 percent flotation cost, the realized proceeds drop to $45. The current dividend yield rises to 4.4 percent, so the overall cost of equity capital rises to 12.4 percent. On the second $10 million of new outset equity financing, net proceeds are estimated to be $40 per share, so that the effective dividend yield rises to 5 percent. Therefore the required marginal return on equity capital becomes 13 percent.

The results in Table 15–3 are utilized next in Table 15–4, which sets forth the weighted marginal cost of debt for different rates of expansion. If the amount of expansion of a firm is $20 million, the weighted marginal (and average) cost of new capital is 8 percent. For an expansion of $40 million, the weighted marginal cost of new capital rises to 8.7 percent. For the expansion of $60 million, the weighted cost of the new capital becomes 9.5 percent.

Label each of the following statements as true or false.

———— 1. If we alter the Expanso Company's capital structure so that the target debt ratio is 25 percent of the incremental capital raised, the cost of debt will remain at 10 percent and the weighted marginal cost of capital at the $20 million expansion rate will be 10 percent.

———— 2. The after-tax cost of debt up to $10 million is likely to rise above 4 percent for the new capital structure as given in Question 1, assuming that the appropriate industry average is significantly below the 50 percent debt ratio.

———— 3. The weighted average cost of capital is primarily used to assist the firm in project selection.

———— 4. The equity capitalization rate is usually the easiest component of cost of capital to calculate.

Now turn to Answer Frame 5[15], page 132, to check your answers.

Frame 6[15]

What is relevant for the investment decision is a comparison of the marginal cost of capital with the marginal return from investments. The data reflecting this fact is set forth in Table 15–5 and graphed in Figure 15–1. The table and figure show that the Expanso Company could invest the first $20 million at a marginal return of 11 percent as compared with the marginal cost of 8 percent. Expanso Company could invest a second $20 million at a marginal return of 10 percent with a marginal cost of 8.7 percent. However, to invest any additional money at 9 percent would be to invest at a rate below the firm's 9.5 percent marginal cost of capital. Therefore, the rate of expansion for the firm in the year under analysis should be $40 million.

The decision process for determining the size of the firm's capital budget and its capital structure requires an iterated process used in planning and controlling the firm. The procedure includes the following steps:

1. The prospective investment opportunities of the firm must be assembled. Administratively,

this means compiling the capital outlay requirements and proposals from the individual divisions of the firm. Alternative capital budgets of different magnitudes are formulated based on a plausible range of costs of capital. Thus either the net present value approach (NPV), the net terminal value (NTV), or internal rate of return (IRR) approaches may be utilized, unless the multiple rates of return problem for the IRR method precludes its use.

2. Decide upon the tentative proportions of financing to be used for each of the alternative capital budgets.

3. Determine the cost of the various capital components under each alternative financing proportions and alternative amount of additional funds raised.

4. Use the alternative financing proportions and sizes of capital budget assumptions to calculate the alternative weighted marginal costs of capital.

5. Choose size of the capital budget along with the associated amount of additional financing required and the proportions of alternative forms of new financing which increases the wealth position of existing shareholders by the largest amount.

As the size of the capital budget increases, the amount of funds to be raised increases and the costs of each form of financing may increase for two reasons. The demand for each type of security form used by the firm relative to the

TABLE 15–5
Data for
determination of the expansion rate

Amount	Marginal return	Marginal cost
First $20 million............	11%	8%
Second $20 million.........	10	8.7
Third $20 million...........	9	9.5

Answer frame 5¹⁵

1. False. The calculation is as follows:

	Amount	Weighted A–T cost		Product
Debt..	$ 5	.25 × .050	=	.0125
Equity...	15			
Retained earnings............................	10	.50 × .120	=	.0600
New common stock.........................	5	.25 × .124	=	.0310
				.1035, or 10.35%

2. False. The debt to total asset ratio has declined from 50 percent to 25 percent so that financial risk has declined. Since the industry average debt ratio is significantly lower than 50 percent, it is probable that the firm's interest charge will decline rather than increase.
3. False. The weighted average cost of capital is primarily designed to assist a firm in determining its optimal capital structure. The marginal cost of new capital is primarily designed for project selection.
4. False. The required rate of return of equity holders is usually the most difficult of the cost of capital calculations. The future growth rates and dividend payments are the relevant components in this analysis. Past data may be so erratic that they are useless. High growth firms usually pay small dividends, and fantastic historical growth rates cannot be projected into the future indefinitely.

If you missed any of the above, restudy Frame 5¹⁵ before starting Frame 6¹⁵, page 131.

Frame 6¹⁵ continued

FIGURE 15–1

Prospective returns in relation to the weighted marginal and average cost of capital

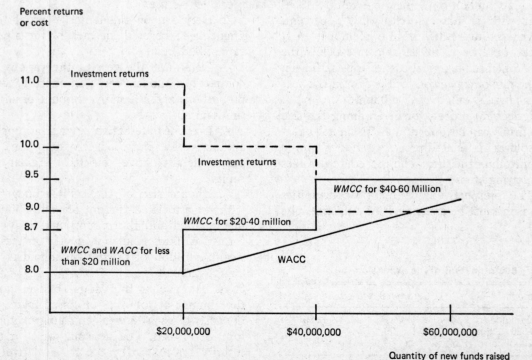

supply of funds increases more the greater the size of its capital budget for the period and the larger the amount of additional funds the firm seeks to obtain within a given time period. An increase in demand relative to supply is likely to cause the price to rise. Also, the risks that the firm may not be able to make all of the organization adjustments required to utilize the increased amount of funds increases the larger the amount by which the firm grows in a given time period. This increased risk increases fund costs.

Also at some point, as the amount of debt in the financial structure is increased, the tax advantage of debt will be dominated by the increased risks of bankruptcy.

Thus both the size of the capital budget and the forms of funds utilized to finance the capital budget will influence the firm's cost of capital. This presentation has sought to describe the general framework for such decisions. The analysis can be aided in various degrees by the new, sophisticated management sciences methods which show quantitatively the effects of alternative choices under alternative assumptions and models. But ultimately the decisions involve managerial judgments based upon balancing investment opportunities and costs of raising large amounts of funds. The benefits of using additional debt must be balanced against the increased risks. Also earnings retention must be balanced against the desires for some stockholders for present versus future income. The materials presented in this chapter seek to bring all these factors together in one framework.

True or false?

_____ 1. If the general level of interest rates declines in the marketplace, the firm's marginal cost of capital will be unaffected.

_____ 2. If the investment opportunity schedule of a firm remains the same with a decline in its marginal cost of capital, the stockholders' wealth will probably increase as more profitable opportunities become available to the firm.

_____ 3. For calculating the weighted marginal cost of capital, the actual amount of funds obtained from each financing source can be used to measure the firm's target financing mix on the additional funds raised. This approximates the use of market weights.

_____ 4. The marginal cost of capital is dependent upon operating and financial leverage as well as on the size of the capital budget.

Now turn to Answer Frame 6^{15}, page 134, to check your answers.

Answer frame 6¹⁵

1. False. This is a very important variable in forecasting future rates that the firm will have to pay for its capital. With a decline in interest rates it is probable that the firm's marginal cost of capital will decline also.
2. True. For example, if the marginal cost of capital for the Expanso Company declines below 9 percent, another 20 million of profitable projects will become available to the firm.
3. True. Except for the retained earnings, the external funds raised would be market values since they are being raised currently. Since the emphasis is on analyzing the costs of additional funds raised, this calculation of the weighted marginal cost of capital approximates market weights and current market costs of funds.
4. True. If the growth rate of a firm is very fast, the marginal cost of capital curve will rise rapidly.

If you missed any of the above, reread Frame 6¹⁵. Before beginning Chapter 16 turn to page 198 to work Examination 4, which covers Chapters 13–15.

chapter 16

FINANCIAL MARKETS AND THE TIMING OF FINANCING

Frame 1¹⁶

Money and capital markets refer to the mechanisms whereby short-term, intermediate-term, and long-term financing are obtained. This chapter will emphasize the markets in which equity and longer term debt instruments are traded, including the two broad types of security markets—the organized exchanges and the less formal over-the-counter markets. In addition, it encompasses the wide range of financial intermediaries such as commercial banks, insurance companies, and so on. This material provides a framework both for a discussion of the characteristics and uses of the long-term financing instruments described in subsequent chapters, as well as for the timing of financial decisions, some aspects of which were introduced in Chapter 9 dealing with working capital policy.

Business firms draw on money and capital markets to finance productive operations, increasing the real output and wealth of the economy. Also, allocations of real resources are improved in the process. A wide range of financial institutions have been developed to facilitate the redistribution of savings in the economy and to perform an important function in the financing of business firms. Three major categories include government institutions, private financial intermediaries, and institutions such as the securities markets. The role of each is briefly described.

CENTRAL BANK AND TREASURY POLICIES AFFECTING THE BUSINESS FINANCE ENVIRONMENT

An analysis of the role of the central bank, which in the United States is the Federal Reserve System, is fundamental to understanding the behavior of the money and capital markets. The Fed, as it is called, has a set of instruments with which to influence the operations of commercial banks, whose loan and investment activities in turn have an important influence on the cost and availability of money. The most powerful of the Fed's instruments, hence the one used most sparingly, is changing reserve requirements. Open-market operations, the purchase and sale of U.S. government securities, is a more delicate instrument used in "fine tuning" the economy and is the Fed instrument most often used.

The third method used by the Fed is to change the discount rate (the interest rate charged to commercial banks when they borrow from central banks). These changes are likely to have more psychological influence than direct quantitative effects. Discount rate changes represent an announcement by monetary authorities that changed economic conditions call for a tightening or easing of monetary policy.

When the Federal Reserve System purchases or sells securities in the open market, makes changes in the discount rate, or varies the reserve requirement, this produces a change in interest rates on most securities and in the availability of funds.

Indicate whether each of the following statements is true or false by writing "T" or "F" in the space provided.

_____ 1. Financial intermediation is the broad network of money and capital markets that facilitates the exchange of money and capital between savings surplus units and savings deficit units.

_____ 2. Redistribution of purchasing power improves resource allocation and thereby increases the real output and wealth of the economy.

_____ 3. The ability to change the discount rate is the most powerful of the Fed's instruments.

_____ 4. The focus of all the Fed's activities is to change the monetary aggregates and interest rates in order to accomplish the objective of the proper amount of stimulation for economic growth and price level stability.

Now check your answers by turning to Answer Frame 1[16], page 136.

Frame 2[16]

The government's fiscal policy has considerable impact on movements in interest rates. A cash budget deficit represents a stimulating influence by the federal government, and a cash surplus exerts a restraining influence from the government-spending sector of the economy. However, this generalization must be modified to reflect the way a deficit is financed and the way a surplus is used. To have the most stimulating effect, the deficit should be financed by sale of securities through the banking system, particularly the central bank—this provides maximum bank reserves and permits multiple expansion in the money supply. To have the most restrictive effect, the surplus should be used to retire bonds held by the banking system, particularly the central bank, thus reducing bank reserves and causing a multiple contraction in the money supply.

The impact of treasury financing programs will be different at different times. Ordinarily when the Treasury draws funds from the money market, it competes with other potential users of

Answer frame 1¹⁶

1. True. Since the savings and investment activities are performed by different groups, the efficient functioning of financial intermediaries is very important for the real growth of an economy.
2. True. This efficient redistribution of purchasing power is the primary function of financial intermediation. Hence, the real growth of a nation's GNP is enhanced.
3. False. The most powerful of the Fed's influences on interest rates is its ability to change reserve requirements. Changing reserve requirements has a multiple effect on the money supply provided by the nation's banks. Because of this multiple effect on the money supply, large or dramatic changes can be effected rapidly on the general level of interest rates.
4. True. The Fed's objectives are to achieve full employment, a high growth rate in the GNP, and price stability.

If you missed any of the above, reread Frame 1¹⁶ before starting Frame 2¹⁶, page 135.

Frame 2¹⁶ continued

funds, causing a rise in interest rate levels. However, the desire to hold down interest rates also influences Treasury and Federal Reserve policy. To ensure the success of a large new offering, Federal Reserve authorities may temporarily ease money conditions, a procedure that will tend to soften interest rates. If the Treasury encounters resistance in selling securities in the nonbanking sector and sells them in volume to the commercial banking system, reserves and the monetary base are expanded. This will lower interest rates unless it causes expectations of a booming economy which may cause interest rates to rise.

Price-level trends affect interest rates in two important ways. First, the nominal interest rate—the stated interest rate—reflects expectations about future price level behavior. If prices are rising and are expected to rise further, the expected rate of inflation is added to the interest rate that would have prevailed in the absence of inflation to adjust for the decline in purchasing power represented by price increases.

The second way that price inflation influences interest rates is through government actions. If prices are rising at a rate of more than 2 to 3 percent a year, restrictive monetary policy can be expected in an effort to reduce inflationary forces. As a consequence, relative tightness will prevail in monetary and credit markets, and nominal interest rate levels will be high.

Label each of the following statements as true or false.

_____ 1. The government's fiscal policy (the tax collector and spending arm of the government) also provides a considerable impact on the availability and cost of money.

_____ 2. A government deficit financed by sale of government securities through the Fed provides the most restrictive effect on economic growth.

_____ 3. When the Treasury (the arm of the government which finances the fiscal policy) draws funds from the money market, it effectively causes a decline in general interest rate levels.

_____ 4. Nominal interest rates generally include an amount to correct for the expected rate of inflation in order to prevent a decline in purchasing power as prices increase.

Now turn to Answer Frame 2¹⁶, page 138, to check your answers.

Frame 3[16]

FINANCIAL INTERMEDIARIES

In addition to the central bank and treasury operations, related federal government agencies and a large number of privately owned institutions perform important functions in the money and capital markets. These financial institutions as a group are involved in the processes of financial intermediation.

Financial intermediaries, such as commercial banks, savings and loan associations, insurance companies, pension funds, mutual savings banks, investment companies, and real estate investment trusts, increase the efficiency of the money and capital markets. Financial intermediaries transform primary securities (indirect claims). They substitute their own liabilities for others' liabilities they acquire. In addition, they transform financial claims into forms preferred by lenders and borrowers. For example, savings and loan associations take savings deposits and create home mortgage loans.

Financial intermediation is performed by dealings in newly issued securities and in securities after they have been issued. Securities are traded both on exchanges and in the over-the-counter market. Exchanges function as auction markets—buy and sell orders come in and what is primarily a brokerage function is performed to match these orders. For less frequently traded stocks, brokerage houses take a dealer's position, buying when individual investors wish to sell and selling when investors wish to buy. Thus as dealers, the transactions take place "over the counter." The stocks of larger industrial and utility companies are generally listed on an exchange; stocks of financial institutions, small industrial firms, and practically all bonds are traded over the counter. From the standpoint of the financial manager, listing on an exchange seems advantageous for seasoned issues, which are stocks of relatively large, well-established companies, which have been traded for some years. The over-the-counter market may aid in the seasoning process until a firm's securities can meet the requirements for listing.

The investment banker provides middleman services to both the seller and the buyer of new securities. He helps plan the issue, underwrites it, and handles the distribution function of selling the issue to the ultimate investors. The cost of the service to the issuer is related to the magnitude of the total job the banker must perform in placing the issue. The investment banker must also look to the interests of his brokerage customers; if these investors are not satisfied with the banker's products, they will deal elsewhere.

Flotation costs are lowest for bonds, higher for preferred stocks, and highest for common stocks. Also, larger companies have lower flotation costs than smaller ones for each type of security. For small common stock issues such as $1–5 million, flotation costs will range up from 10 percent; flotation costs will be only moderately lower for a $1 million issue of preferred stock or long-term debt. In contrast, on a common stock issue of $50 million or more, the costs of flotation will be in the range of 2.5 to 3.0 percent. On a large issue of debt or preferred stock, the cost of flotation is likely to be under 2 percent.

Financial managers must be familiar with the federal laws regulating the issuance and trading of securities because these laws, financing methods, and costs define his liabilities. Regulation of securities trading seeks (1) to provide information that investors can utilize as a basis for judging the merits of securities, (2) to control the volume of credit used in securities trading, and (3) to provide orderly securities markets. However, the laws do not prevent either purchase of unsound issues or wide price fluctuations. They raise somewhat the costs of flotation, but probably have decreased the cost of capital by increasing public confidence in the securities markets.

Answer frame 2[16]

1. True. Some economists hold that monetary policy as implemented by the Fed determines the availability and cost of money. However, it is generally believed that both fiscal and monetary policy working together will achieve optimal influence on the availability and cost of money.

2. False. If the deficit is financed by the sale of securities through the central bank, a stimulating effect is achieved by permitting multiple expansion in the money supply. Increasing the money supply pushes down the general level of interest rates which encourages greater capital investments.

3. False. When the Treasury draws funds from the money supply, the shortage of funds causes the general level of interest rates to rise.

4. True. Nominal interest rates reflect a risk-free rate, a premium for business and financial risk, and a premium for purchasing power risk. Obviously, the forecasting ability of the marketplace may or may not fully compensate for these various risk components.

If you missed any of the above, restudy Frame 2[16] before beginning Frame 3[16], page 137.

Frame 3[16] continued

True or false?

_____ 1. When financial intermediaries transform primary securities they are essentially substituting their own liabilities for other liabilities.

_____ 2. Many small, closely held firms resist listing their stocks on organized exchanges because of the necessity of making public the financial results of their operations.

_____ 3. In underwriting the distribution of a new issue of securities, the investment banker is assuming the risk of price fluctuations until the entire issue is sold.

_____ 4. The fundamental purpose of the federal security laws regulating the issuance of new securities is to prevent small investors from sustaining losses on the purchase of stocks.

Now turn to Answer Frame 3[16], page 140, to check your answers.

Frame 4[16]

FORECASTING INTEREST RATES

Within the framework of general economic and financial patterns, near-term interest rate forecasts are based on an analysis of the prospective demand and supply of funds. The framework is the Federal Reserve's flow of funds accounts which are set forth monthly in the *Federal Reserve Bulletin*. On the basis of the types of data provided in the flow of funds accounts, government agencies and financial firms develop interest rate forecasts by applying a number of approaches. The patterns of the sources and uses of funds in relation to the size and growth of the economy as a whole (as measured by gross national product) are developed. Whenever the demand for funds must be met by drawing on the commercial banking system to an unusually large degree, interest rates are likely to rise. When funds obtained from "private domestic nonfinancial investors" rise, pressure on interest rates is also indicated. For example, direct lending in credit markets in this category was $19 billion in 1966 as compared with $6 billion in 1967. Also, the direct lending in credit markets was $42 billion in 1969 as compared with $7 billion in 1970.

Predictably, there were strong upward interest rate pressures in 1966 and in 1969.

Of overriding significance in an interest rate forecast is the general economic forecast in relation to the full-employment potential of the economy. The critical variable here is the size of the indicated *full-employment gap*. Full-employment gap means the difference between the potential level of gross national product achievable by the economy in the forthcoming period as compared with the level of GNP likely to be achieved under current governmental and private policies and plans. A large full-employment gap indicates that there is some slack in the economy which would tend to result in lower interest rates. In addition, governmental policy is likely to be stimulative (e.g., increasing the monetary base), which could also make for an easing of interest rate levels.

On the other hand, when it appears that the full-employment gap may be minimal, reflecting "over-full" employment, these pressures will produce higher interest rates. Also, governmental policy is likely to be restrictive, resulting in higher interest rates. Since the early 1970s most predictions have been for continued high interest rate trends with only periodic moderate declines of relatively short duration. The major reason for this general forecast reflects governmental efforts throughout the world to achieve full employment and a high growth rate. As a consequence a worldwide capital shortage has resulted.

While the cost variations associated with interest rate fluctuations are substantial, the greatest significance of interest rates is their role as an index of the availability of funds. A period of high interest rates reflects tight money, which is in turn associated with tight reserve positions at commercial banks. At such times interest rates rise, of course, but there are conventional limits on interest rates. As a consequence, a larger quantity of funds is demanded by borrowers than banks are able to make available. Banks therefore begin rationing funds by giving preference to prospective borrowers who meet higher credit standards.

Is each of the following true or false?

_____ 1. Whenever the demand for funds must be met by drawing on the commercial banking system, interest rates are likely to decline.

_____ 2. During a full-employment gap the government's fiscal and monetary policy is likely to be restrictive and cause high interest rate levels.

_____ 3. The government's prime objective is to maintain a high growth rate in GNP with price stability.

_____ 4. GNP, the total value of goods and services produced in an economy, is an important variable for a financial manager to consider in the forecasts of his own firm as it will assist him in determining asset and financing requirements.

Now turn to Answer Frame 4[16], page 140, to check your answers.

Frame 5[16]

THE TERM STRUCTURE OF INTEREST RATES

An important element in the timing of financial decisions is an understanding of the relationship between long- and short-term interest rates. Short-term interest rates are those on securities with maturities of under one year; long term is here defined as pertaining to securities with maturities of longer than one year. In general, there is greater risk in holding long-term than short-term securities, so that the *uncertainty theory* suggests that long-term rates will be higher than short-term rates. For one thing, the longer the maturity of the security, the greater the risk that the issuer may not be able to meet its obligations in 10, 15, or 20 years. In addition, the prices of long-term bonds are much more volatile than

Answer frame 3[16]

1. True. Essentially, financial intermediaries are transforming their financial claims into forms preferred by lenders and borrowers. For example, a bank will take a demand deposit and create a commercial loan.
2. True. However, when a small entrepreneur is nearing retirement it may be to his advantage to list his stock. Thus, a valuation of his holdings for inheritance taxes is more readily ascertained as well as providing for ease of distribution.
3. True. This defines the underwriting function. This risk of price fluctuations is why the investment banker accomplishes a detailed study and financial analysis of each company and its securities. It is also the reason why a large fixed cost is involved in an underwriting.
4. False. The purpose of federal security laws is to make firms accurately represent their securities to the public. This is not the same thing as preventing small investors from speculating in stocks which may be overvalued.

If you missed any of the above, reread Frame 3[16] before starting Frame 4[16], page 138.

Answer frame 4[16]

1. False. Essentially, commercial banks are the balance wheel in the financial system, an increase in the demand for bank funds relative to money supply will tend to increase the general level of interest rates. Therefore, the forecasting of sources and uses of funds in relationship to the size and growth of the GNP is very important to financial managers.
2. False. During a full-employment gap, fiscal and monetary policies are likely to be expansionary, thereby causing a decline in interest rates. Hopefully then, reduced interest rates will encourage investments and more jobs.
3. True. Presumably the higher growth rate in GNP will also achieve a full-employment economy and help improve the quality of life.
4. True. Too often this variable escapes many small- to medium-sized firms, and their reactions to economic dips are slow. Thus, inventories tend to accumulate as sales fall and profits decline rapidly.

If you missed any of the above, restudy Frame 4[16] before starting Frame 5[16], page 139.

Frame 5[16] continued

those of short-term bonds when interest rates change.

Another theory of the relationship between the long-term and short-term interest rates, called the *expectations theory*, holds that current long-term rates represent an average of future expected short-term rates, as illustrated in Table 16–1.

In Section A it is assumed that short-term interest rates will rise 1 percent each year, beginning at 5 percent in year 1. The corresponding long-term interest rate in year 1 for a five-year period can be approximated by taking a simple arithmetic average of the five short-term rates: 7 percent. Thus, in year 1, the long-term rate is higher than the short-term rate. In Section B, a tight-money situation, in year 1 short-term rates are 9 percent, but they are expected to decline by

1 percent each year. The average of these rates is the same as in section A because the numbers are identical—but their time sequence is reversed. The current short-term rate is above the long-

TABLE 16–1

Relation between short-term and long-term interest rates

Year	A		B	
	Five-year note	Short-term rates	Five-year note	Short-term rates
1	7	5	7	9
2		6		8
3		7		7
4		8		6
5		9		5

FIGURE 16–1
Bond yields and interest rates

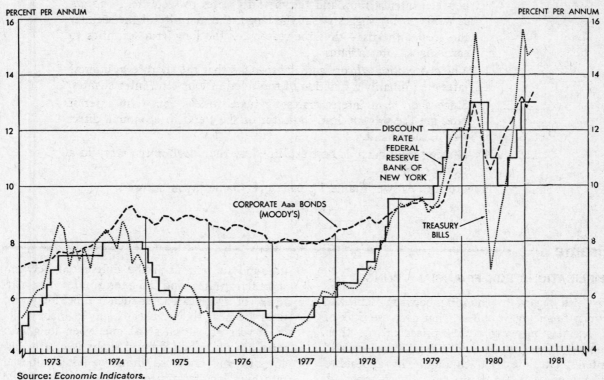

Source: *Economic Indicators.*

term rate of 7 percent. This table illustrates the pattern that would exist if the only factor operating was expected change in interest rate movement.

Recent patterns in long-term and short-term rates of interest are shown in Figure 16–1. Short-term interest rates show the widest amplitude of swings and generally lead movements in general business conditions. Long-term rates do not vary as greatly as short-term rates. Figure 16–1 illustrates periods during 1973–81 when short-term rates were above long-term rates and other periods when the more normal pattern of the term structure of interest rates existed.

"Term structure of interest rates" refers to the relation between the levels of interest rates on debt instruments with maturities ranging from short term to longer term. The characteristic pattern is a rising yield curve or interest rate structure. But the reverse may also be found, as well as other patterns such as an intermediate hump when the rates on intermediate-term debt instruments are higher than those for both short-term and long-term rates. This would occur when interest rates are currently low, are expected to be higher in the intermediate term, and then lower over a longer term.

Label each of the following statements as true or false.

_____ 1. The term structure of interest rates refers to the direct relationship between interest rates and the maturity dates of securities. The *uncertainty theory* suggests that the longer the maturity of the security the greater the risk—thus the reason for the long-term securities to carry higher interest rates.

_____ 2. The *expectations theory* actually specifies that the short-term interest rates are primarily a function of the trend in long-term interest rates.

_____ 3. Since short-term interest rates fluctuate widely, long-term interest rates are the primary lead indicator of the trend in economic direction or movement.

_____ 4. A rising yield curve is best explained by the *uncertainty theory* in a steady economy.

Now turn to Answer Frame 5[16], page 144, to check your answers.

Frame 6[16]

IMPLICATIONS FOR FINANCIAL TIMING

With regard to choosing between debt and equity financing, it appears that near the peak of a business upswing equity prices are at their highest (the cost of equity capital lower) and interest rates are relatively high. This appears to be the period when equity financing is most advantageous.

The relationship between short-term and long-term interest rates also indicates an important aspect of timing. As we have observed in Figure 16–1, long-term interest rates fluctuate only moderately while short-term interest rates have very wide swings. Thus in a tight money period usually brought on by efforts of governmental authorities to limit an overly strong economic upturn, short-term interest rates are above long-term interest rates. Conversely, in the effort to bring the economy out of a downturn, the easing of monetary and fiscal policy will bring short-term interest rates well below long-term rates.

Thus, near the start of a business upturn both long-term rates and short-term rates will be near their lows, but short-term rates will be well below long-term rates. Because short-term rates are near their lows, firms have a tendency to finance in the early stages of a business recovery with short-term financing rather than long-term financing. This is profitable if they do not wait too long to switch into longer term debt financing. But it is

unsound to wait until the differential between short-term rates and long-term rates has narrowed or disappeared. At such a time, long-term rates are near their cyclical high; to incur a 20- or 30-year obligation at a time when long-term rates are near their cyclical highs is clearly disadvantageous, because firms would be locked into high long-term rates of interest; they could have financed at lower long-term interest rates if they had financed with long-term debt at the early stages of a business upswing. Failure to recognize this pattern causes financial managers to get whipsawed by the pattern relationships. This is a very important practical implication of the material of this chapter.

But the cyclical aspects may increasingly be dominated by the strong underlying secular trends. As Figure 16–1 indicates, both short- and long-term rates have been in an upward trend since 1973, along with cyclical fluctuations. With continuing inflation, firms have increased their debt ratios so that on the average total debt is approximately equal to total equity for all manufacturing firms. Buyers of debt have increasingly sought potential equity participation and convertible debt financing therefore has risen.

The worldwide turmoil in the financing markets poses new challenges for financial managers. Increased uncertainties have given rise to new forms and patterns of financing. Increasingly, the arena for business finance is the global market.

At the start of each day, the corporate treasurer determines whether he will be borrowing or lending in the international financial market. He may be making investment decisions in the domestic product market or in foreign countries. The financial manager must consider the form and extent of protection against risks of devaluation on sales of his product to companies abroad. He must be concerned with the long-run political and commercial risks in his foreign sales and investments.

If he has surplus cash, he must compare the returns from investing in his domestic money market with utilizing the international financial market. Similarly, if short-term financing needs arise, he must make comparisons between financing sources abroad and domestic sources. He must consider the advantages and disadvantages of the more impersonal international financial markets and developing long-term financing relations with international commercial banks or financial groups in London, Paris, Zurich, and Bonn.

True or false?

_____ 1. If a financial manager were to finance the debt portion of a capital investment program near the peak of a business cycle, short-term funds should be used.

_____ 2. At the beginning of a tight money period while equity prices are still high, a financial manager would be motivated to use long-term funds obtained through the equity market.

_____ 3. With rampant inflation, firms would be wise to increase their leverage factor since the repayment of this debt obligation will be met at a future time with dollars that have a smaller purchasing value.

_____ 4. Because of inflationary psychology, bond investors have increasingly sought convertible features to meet these obligations.

Now turn to Answer Frame 6¹⁶, page 144, to check your answers.

Answer frame 5¹⁶

1. True. The longer the maturity of the security, the greater the risk that the issuer may not be able to meet its obligation in 15 or 20 years.
2. False. The example in Table 16–1 shows that the long-term interest rate reflects an average of future expected short-term rates. Other factors do exist in interest rate determination, however; this theory is a useful supplement to other theories in prediction of interest rate changes.
3. False. Short-term interest rates show the widest fluctuations and for this reason they lead movements in general business conditions. Figure 16–1 illustrates this phenomenon.
4. True. The uncertainty theory—also called the liquidity preference theory—will result in a rising yield curve when interest rates are expected to remain constant. The rise in yield or desired return on investment is explained by the increased risk of distant maturities.

If you missed any of the above, restudy Frame 5¹⁶ before starting Frame 6¹⁶, page 142.

Answer frame 6¹⁶

1. True. Even though short-term rates are usually higher than long-term rates, at this time it would be wise not to become locked-in to long-term obligations. Since long-term rates are expected to decline, it will usually be less expensive to finance current needs with short-term funds and wait until long-term interest rates have fallen.
2. True. Depending upon the firm's long-term capital investment plans and target capital structure, it may be wise to float a common stock issue when the cost of equity capital is low relative to the costs of debt funds.
3. True. Firms have significantly increased their leverage factor over the last several years. However, if the forecasts of inflation levels are accurately included as a premium in the general level of interest rates, the advantages to either the lender or borrower will have been nullified.
4. True. Convertible features are becoming more and more prevalent, and inflation psychology is only one of the many reasons for their increased popularity. Chapter 19 will treat convertible securities more extensively.

If you missed any of the above, restudy Frame 6¹⁶ before beginning Chapter 17 on page 145.

chapter 17

LONG-TERM FINANCING DECISIONS

Frame 1[17]

In the next three chapters the major forms of longer term financing instruments are discussed as a basis for choosing between alternative forms and sources of financing. An overview of the alternatives is set forth in Table 17–1, which shows how the forms of long-term financing are distinguished by their different positions with regard to risk, income, and control.

The common stockholders do not have a fixed claim on income: they receive the corporation's residual income. Owners of common stock are the legal owners and possess legal control of the corporation. Ordinarily, each share of common stock carries the right to cast one vote. However in cumulative voting, the stockholder is enabled to cast multiple votes for one director. For example, if eight directors are being elected, 100 shares can be cast as 800 votes for one director or 100 votes for each of eight directors. The number of shares required to elect a desired number of directors can be determined from the following:

$$\text{Nec.} = \frac{eN}{\# + 1} + 1$$

where:

Nec. is the number of shares required to elect a desired number of directors.

e is the number of directors desired to elect.

N is the total number of shares of common stock outstanding.

$\#$ is the total number of directors to be elected.

For example, if eight directors are to be elected, if a group's objective is to elect three of the eight, and 120,000 shares of common stock are outstanding, the number of shares required would be:

TABLE 17–1
Overview of position of financial instruments

	(1) Equity	(2) Debt	(3) Lease	(4) Subordinated debt	(5) Preferred stock	(6) Convertible debt
Risk..................	Residual claimant	Senior claim	Residual equity claimant	Junior to bank loans	Senior to common stock	Claim senior to equity
Income................	Variable	Fixed claim	Fixed claim plus ownership of the asset	Fixed claim	Fixed participation rate	Fixed plus option on equity
Control................	Voting	No voting indenture restrictions		No voting indenture restrictions	No voting, unless dividend arrearage	No voting unless convert to equity position

$$\text{Nec.} = \frac{3 \times 120,000}{8 + 1} + 1 = 40,001$$

The decision with regard to the use of common stock as a source of financing must balance a number of factors. The advantages of common stock as compared with debt forms of financing are: (1) no fixed charges are incurred, (2) there is no maturity date, (3) the credit worthiness of the firm is increased since common equity provides a cushion for creditors if liquidation of assets is required.

The common stock also carries disadvantages as compared with debt. There is dilution in the sense that unlike the fixed return to debt, additional shares of common stock participate fully in voting, earnings, and dividends. The cost of common stock ordinarily is higher than the cost of debt (common stock normally sells on a higher after-tax yield basis than debt). Also, flotation costs for common stock are higher than for debt, and dividends are not deductible as an expense for tax purposes. The junior position of common stock, both on earnings and on assets, increases the risk to the common stockholders in the event of liquidation.

The factors favoring the use of common stock reflect the firm's circumstances in relation to trends in the economic and financial environment. The firm should have a leverage policy or leverage target based on the principles set forth in previous chapters. The leverage policy of the firm may constitute a moving target as the economic environment changes. For example, during the six-year period following the onset of strong inflationary forces set off by the escalation of U.S. participation in the war in Southeast Asia, on the average, debt ratios have risen from approximately 50 percent of net worth to a level approximately equal to net worth for all manufacturing industries in the United States.

If a firm already has a debt ratio in excess of the leverage target considered appropriate for its line of business, the analysis in the next financing episode will favor the use of an equity issue. If the firm's sales and profits fluctuate widely, the use of debt will be risky. As a consequence, the target ratio will be lower and most of the financing used by the firm will be obtained through the sale of common stock. During a period of a strong bull market in common stocks, the firm's current price earnings ratio may be unusually high. To sell common stock at a high price level, based on investors' (overly) optimistic expectations in relation to the prospective long-term growth rate of company earnings, is to sell the common stock on an effective growth yield basis that is lower than the long-term internal profitability rate of the firm. The wealth position of the existing stockholders will be increased by the sale of common stock at favorable prices.

In some situations, the alternative of debt financing is not practical or feasible. The firm may be small and new without an established record of earnings. Long-term debt financing may therefore be unavailable or carry onerous restrictions. Current profit margins may not cover the cost of debt, but prospective profit rates may be favorable. Thus, risks of insolvency would make debt financing unavailable, but might make common stock financing more desirable because of its longer term potential. The influence of current versus prospective profit margin patterns may also be reinforced by the requirement of near-term debt amortization under debt financing, aggravating the firm's cash flow and insolvency risks.

For a large, well-established firm with a widely held common stock, the sale of additional equity shares does not pose the problem of dilution of control. If this circumstance is added to the considerations previously set forth, it may reinforce the decision to use common stock financing.

Indicate whether each of the following statements is true or false by writing "T" or "F" in the space provided.

_____ 1. The Milling Machine Company has 1 million common shares outstanding which have cumulative voting privileges. Four directors are to be elected. Thus, it would take 200,001 shares to elect one director to the board.

_____ 2. The cost of flotation for debt is greater than for common stock.

———— 3. If a firm has a debt-to-equity ratio in excess of its industry average, the marketplace will probably penalize a new debt offering sufficiently so that its weighted average cost of capital would rise dramatically.

———— 4. For a small, fast-growing firm the sale of additional equity shares does not pose the problem of dilution of control.

Now turn to Answer Frame 1¹⁷, page 148, to check your answers.

Frame 2¹⁷

RIGHTS OFFERINGS

When common stock financing is used, the new issue may be sold through a rights offering. A rights offering may be made either because it is legally required or because it is advantageous from a business standpoint. In some states, every corporate charter issued must include the provision of a *preemptive right* to the common stockholders. The preemptive right gives the existing common stock owners the option to purchase any additional new issues of common stock.

A right is an option to buy a newly issued share of common stock at a specified price during a designated period of time (a call). The preemptive right is designed to protect existing shareholders from dilution of their share of the firm's ownership and control if they so desire. Also, it seeks to protect the pro rata share of present stockholders in the earned surplus and future earning power of the firm.

When the sale of a new issue of common stock through a rights offering is discretionary on the part of the firm, the decision will be made on the basis of the following analysis. The central factor is the extent to which the use of rights will facilitate the sale of additional shares of common stock and thereby lower the cost of distributing the new issue. The main decision alternatives in a stock rights offering are (1) the size of the discount between the current market price and the subscription price offering and (2) the nature of the underwriting arrangement by the investment bankers. An example will help to clarify the issues involved.

Table 17–2 sets forth the facts for analysis of a rights offering by the Wrighton Company.

The following discussion of the effects of a rights offering with the alternative subscription prices of $20 versus $5 is keyed to the five-

TABLE 17–2
Facts for analysis of a rights offering by Wrighton Company

Liabilities and net worth position

Item	Before rights offering	After rights offering @ $20	After rights offering @ $5
Total debt at 10%....	$20,000,000	$20,000,000	$20,000,000
Common stock $1 par	1,000,000	1,250,000	2,000,000
Capital surplus......	9,000,000	13,750,000	13,000,000
Retained earnings...	10,000,000	10,000,000	10,000,000
Total Liabilities and Net Worth.......	$40,000,000	$45,000,000	$45,000,000

Earnings and market value before rights offering

EBIT................................	$ 6,000,000
Interest on debt.....................	2,000,000
Income before taxes.................	$ 4,000,000
Taxes at 50%........................	2,000,000
Income after Taxes............	$ 2,000,000
Earnings per share (1,000,000 shares)..	$2.00
Market price of stock.................	$25.00
Total Market Value.............	$25,000,000

numbered sections of Table 17–3. (1) The number of new shares is equal to the total dollar amount of new funds being raised divided by the subscription price at which the shares are offered. (2) The number of rights required to buy one share of stock at the subscription price is determined by the ratio of the number of old shares to the number of new shares being issued. Thus, four rights would be required to purchase one share of stock when the subscription price is $20, but only one right is required when the subscription price is $5.

(3) The new market value per share is equal to the total market value divided by the total number of shares. The initial assumption made here (which will be discussed further in appraising rights offering) is that the total $5 million of the additional market value received is added to

Answer frame 1¹⁷

1. True. It is calculated as follows:

$$\text{Nec.} = \frac{eN}{\# + 1} + 1 = \frac{1 \times 1,000,000}{4 + 1} + 1 = 200,001 \text{ shares}$$

2. False. Flotation costs for common stock are higher than for debt because common stocks are more risky and the underwriter investigation costs are higher.
3. True. An excessive debt-to-equity ratio can be expected to drive up the weighted cost of capital. Also, if the firm's sales and profits fluctuate widely, the analysis will favor the use of an equity issue even more.
4. False. Dilution of control usually is no problem for a large, well-established firm with a widely held common stock. Frequently a small firm's managers and equity owners are motivated to maintain absolute control for numerous reasons—i.e., pride of ownership and capital appreciation.

If you missed any of the above, reread Frame 1¹⁷ before beginning Frame 2¹⁷, page 147.

Frame 2¹⁷ continued

the existing market value of $25 million to obtain a new total market value of $30 million. Total market value is divided by the total number of (old plus new) shares to arrive at a new market value per share of $24 when the subscription price is $20, and $15 when the subscription price is $5. (4) The value of a right is the new market value per share less the subscription price

TABLE 17–3

Analysis of rights offerings of Wrighton Company

		Subscription price = $20	Subscription price = $5
(1)	Number of new shares = $\dfrac{\text{New funds}}{\text{Subscription price}}$	$\dfrac{\$5,000,000}{\$20}$ = 250,000 shares	$\dfrac{\$5,000,000}{\$5}$ = 1,000,000 shares
(2)	Number of rights required = $\dfrac{\text{Number of old shares}}{\text{Number of new shares}}$	$\dfrac{1,000,000}{250,000}$ = 4 rights	$\dfrac{1,000,000}{1,000,000}$ = 1 right
(3)	New market value per share = $\dfrac{\text{Total market value}}{\text{Total number of shares}}$	$\dfrac{\$30,000,000}{1,250,000}$ = $24	$\dfrac{\$30,000,000}{2,000,000}$ = $15
(4)	Value of a right = $\dfrac{\text{(New market value per share)} - \text{(Subscription price)}}{\text{Number of rights required}}$	$\dfrac{\$24-\$20}{4}$ = $1	$\dfrac{\$15-\$5}{1}$ = $10
(5)	Position of a stockholder with 100 shares:		
	Market value of 100 shares before rights offering......	$2,500	$2,500
	Sells rights:		
	Received from sale of rights.............................	$ 100	$1,000
	Market value of 100 shares, ex rights..................	$2,400	$1,500
	Total value after rights offering........................	$2,500	$2,500
	Exercises rights:		
	Additional investment..................................	$20(100/4) = $ 500	$5(100/1) = $ 500
	Total value after rights offering........................	125 × 24 = $3,000	200 × 15 = $3,000
	Total value less additional investment................	$2,500	$2,500

divided by the number of rights required to obtain the benefit. The result is the value of a right of $1 when the subscription price is $20 and $10 when the subscription price is $5.

(5) In every instance thus far, different results are obtained when the subscription price is $20 versus when it is $5. Does this affect a stockholder's position? To answer this question we analyze the position of a stockholder with 100 shares at an initial market value of $2,500. The shareholder has two alternatives when the rights are received: he may sell the rights or he may exercise them. If he sells the rights he receives $100 or $1,000. When these amounts are added to the new market value per share of the original 100 shares owned, in each case the total is $2,500. Alternatively, if the shareholder exercises his rights he will invest $500 in both cases. In each instance, the total value of his shareholdings after the rights offering will be $3,000, and the net value, subtracting the $500 investment he made, will be $2,500. Thus we can draw two conclusions. First, the rights offering as such neither benefits nor harms the shareholder. Second, it makes no difference arithmetically at what level the subscription price is set.

However, from a practical standpoint, there are some other considerations to take into account. It is clear that the value of a right will be much higher with the lower subscription price and there will be greater pressure on the existing shareholders to do something about the rights if they have substantial value.

The subscription price set and the fee required by the investment bankers are related. If the risks of having a large percentage of unsubscribed stocks is substantial, the underwriting fee will necessarily be larger. For this reason the subscription price is typically in the range of at least 15 percent to 20 percent below the prevailing market price to reduce the services required by the underwriter.

The final question with regard to the use of rights is: What is the ultimate effect upon the market price of the stock? The rights offering as such does not change the company's fundamentals; it is simply raising additional funds. If the additional funds are invested at an increased internal profitability rate, the future market price of the stock is likely to rise. Thus the ultimate effect on the market price of a rights offering (or any new financing) will be determined by the effects on the underlying earnings prospects of the company.

Label each of the following statements as true or false.

_____ 1. A preemptive right typically applies to all debentures.

_____ 2. The main decision alternatives in a rights offering involve the size of offering, the size of the discount between the current market price and the subscription price, and the nature of the underwriting arrangement.

_____ 3. When the new market value per share (ex rights) is $40, the subscription price is $28 and the number of rights required to purchase a new share is 4, the value of a right is $4.

_____ 4. If the subscription price is set relatively low in relation to the market price, the underwriting fee will necessarily be larger.

Now turn to Answer Frame 2¹⁷, page 150, to check your answers.

Frame 3¹⁷

LONG-TERM DEBT FINANCING

The second major form of long-term (i.e., funded) financing is debt financing. First, some technical terminology is covered. A *bond* is a long-term promissory note. A *mortgage bond* is secured by real property. An *indenture* is an agreement between the firm issuing a bond and the numerous bondholders, represented by a trustee.

Secured long-term debt differs with respect to (1) the priority of claims, (2) the right to issue

Answer frame 2¹⁷

1. False. A preemptive right applies to the common stockholders. It is designed to protect existing shareholders from dilution of their ownership and control of the firm.
2. True. These three alternatives determine the success of the offering and the overall cost to the firm.
3. False. The value of the right (VR) is calculated as follows:

$$VR = \frac{Me - S_b}{NR} = \frac{40 - 28}{4} = \frac{12}{4} = \$3$$

Me = New market value per share or market value of stock ex rights.
S_b = Subscription price.
NR = Number of rights required to purchase one common share.
[Note: $Mo = Me + R$ where Mo is market value of stock, rights on; $Me = Mo - R$ where Me is market value of stock, ex rights $VR = (Mo - S_b)/(NR + 1)$].
A date of record is set, much like for dividends, where prior to this date the rights go with the sale of the stock (rights on) and after this date the rights do not go with the sale of the stock (ex rights).
4. False. The value of a right will be much greater with the lower subscription price and there will be greater pressure on the existing shareholders to either exercise their rights or sell their rights. Thus, less selling effort is required to float the issue, resulting in a smaller percentage of unsubscribed stock with the concomitant lower underwriting fee.

If you missed any of the above, reread Frame 2¹⁷ before starting Frame 3¹⁷, page 149.

Frame 3¹⁷ continued

additional securities, and (3) the scope of the lien provided. These characteristics determine the amount of protection provided to the bondholder by the terms of the security. Giving the investor more security will induce him to accept a lower yield but will restrict the future freedom of action of the issuing firm. The main forms of unsecured bonds are (1) debentures, (2) subordinated debentures, and (3) income bonds. Holders of debentures are unsecured general creditors. Subordinated debentures are junior to other loans whose claims in liquidation must be fully satisfied before the subordinated debentures. Income bonds are similar to preferred stock in that interest is paid only when earned.

The characteristics of long-term debt include: The cost of debt is limited, but it is a fixed obligation. Bond interest is an expense deductible for tax purposes. Debt carries a maturity date and may require sinking fund payments to prepare for extinguishing the obligation. Bond indenture provisions are likely to include some restrictions on the freedom of action of the firm's management. Funding debt means replacing short-term debt with long-term debt.

The nature of long-term debt encourages its use under the following circumstances: (1) Sales and earnings are relatively stable. (2) Profit margins are adequate to make leverage advantageous. (3) A rise in profits or the general price level is expected. (4) The existing debt ratio is relatively low. (5) Common stock earnings/price ratios are high in relation to the levels of interest rates. (6) Control considerations are important. (7) Cash flow requirements under the bond agreement are not burdensome. (8) Restrictions in the bond indenture are not onerous. The list of factors is simply a check list of influences to consider in making the decision between equity financing and debt financing. The weighting of individual factors will vary.

True or false?

_____ 1. An indenture would most likely be found in a 90-day promissory note.

_____ 2. Priority of claims in liquidation would occur in the following sequence; senior mortgage bonds, debentures, subordinated debentures, preferred stockholders, income bonds, and common stockholders.

_____ 3. Since bond interest is deductible for tax purposes, financing by use of debt is usually the cheapest form of external financing for most industrial firms, if a sufficient equity base exists.

_____ 4. The list of factors to consider in making the decision between debt financing and equity financing is primarily the balancing of risk and return.

Now turn to Answer Frame 3^{17}, page 152, to check your answers.

Frame 4^{17}

PREFERRED STOCK FINANCING

Preferred stocks usually have priority over common stocks with respect to earnings and claims on assets in liquidation. Preferred stocks are usually cumulative; they have no maturity but are sometimes callable. They are typically nonparticipating and receive voting rights only on nonpayment of dividends for a specified number of quarters.

The advantages to the issuer are limited dividends and no maturity. These advantages may outweigh the disadvantages as compared with debt of higher cost and nondeductibility of dividends as an expense for tax purposes. But their acceptance by investors is the final test of whether they can be sold on favorable terms.

Companies sell preferred stocks when they seek the advantages of trading on the equity, but fear the dangers of the fixed charges on debt because of potential fluctuations in income. If debt ratios are already high or if the costs of common stock financing are relatively high, the advantages of preferred stock will be reinforced.

The use of preferred stock has declined significantly since the advent of the corporate income tax because preferred dividends are not deductible for income tax purposes, while bond interest payments are. However, in recent years there has been a strong shift back to a new kind of preferred stock—convertible preferred, used primarily in connection with mergers. If cash or bonds are given to the stockholders of the acquired company, they are required to pay capital gains taxes on any gains that might have been realized. However, giving convertible preferred stock to the selling stockholders constitutes a tax-free exchange of securities. The selling stockholders can obtain a fixed-income security and at the same time postpone the payment of capital gains taxes.

Is each of the following true or false?

_____ 1. A firm with a high debt ratio, control problems, high profit margins, and fluctuating sales and profits is more likely to issue preferred stock (than debt) to obtain the benefits of leverage.

_____ 2. Convertible preferred stock is used primarily in mergers because of tax advantages.

_____ 3. The major reason why many firms have retired their preferred stock is because it has a fixed obligation to make dividend payments regardless of fluctuations in profits.

_____ 4. Once issued, preferred stock can never be "retired" at the option of the issuer.

Now turn to Answer Frame 4^{17}, page 152, to check your answers.

Answer frame 3¹⁷

1. False. An indenture would most likely be used with debentures, mortgage bonds, convertible bonds, nonconvertible bonds, and possibly a line of credit.
2. False. Priority of claims in liquidation would be as follows: senior mortgage bonds, debentures, subordinated debentures, *income bonds*, preferred stockholders, and common stockholders. Common stockholders usually receive little or nothing in liquidation.
3. True. With marginal corporate tax rates near 50 percent, the cost of debt capital is significantly less costly than almost any other source of external long-term capital. This is why seeking an optimal capital structure becomes important in the decision-making process.
4. True. The optimal capital structure decision has as its main focus maximizing returns for a given level of risk or minimizing risk for a given level of return. Stability of sales and earnings, profit margins, existing debt ratios, and so on are all important factors in the long-term financing decisions of the firm.

If you missed any of the above, reread Frame 3¹⁷ before starting Frame 4¹⁷, page 151.

Answer frame 4¹⁷

1. True. A firm with such characteristics would tend to favor preferred stock over debt as a mechanism to employ financial leverage.
2. True. Preferred dividends are not deductible for income tax purposes, but giving convertible preferred stock to the selling stockholders in a merger constitutes a tax-free exchange of securities. Thus, the new holders of the convertible stock obtain a fixed-income security with the option to convert to common stock at some future time.
3. False. Nondeductibility of preferred dividends for tax purposes is the major reason why many firms have retired their preferred stock. Preferred dividends do not have to be paid unless they are declared.
4. False. Preferred stock is sometimes callable at the option of the issuer. This enables the issuer to "retire" the preferred stock.

If you missed any of the above, reread Frame 4¹⁷ before beginning Frame 5¹⁷ below.

Frame 5¹⁷

CHOOSING BETWEEN ALTERNATIVE FORMS OF FINANCING

To illustrate the application of the check lists for choosing between alternative major forms of financing, a case example will be used. The facts are the following: The Green Electrical Company produces a diversified line of electrical products sold to industrial users, including control equipment, switches, connectors, and so on. The company and its investment banker have determined to raise an additional $100 million during early 1974 to reduce short-term bank debt by $50 million and to provide for further future growth. Sales and profits have been growing at a rate between 7 percent and 8 percent per annum on the average during the past 10 years; future

growth is expected to continue at the same rate to support a growth in dividends and earnings per share of 7 percent per annum.

Two proposals have been presented. One would be the sale of common stock at a price slightly below its recent level of $52, which would be $50 per share, with underwriting costs 10 percent of gross proceeds. The second proposal was for 25-year, 8 percent sinking fund debentures, with underwriting expenses 2 percent of gross proceeds. The sinking fund payments of $5 million per year would begin in 1978. The total production cost function of the firm is $300 + .4S$ (in $million). Selling expenses are 10 percent of sales, while administrative and other expenses are assumed to be constant at $100 million for a range of sales from $600 to $1,500 million. Other financial information is presented in the financial statement in Tables 17–4 and 17–5.

In choosing between the two proposals, the following factors will be considered: A. Risk, B. Relative cost, C. Initial effects on earnings per share, D. Cash flow requirements, and E. Effects on control.

In analyzing the decision area of choosing between alternative forms and sources of financing,

TABLE 17–4

Green Electrical Company
Consolidated statement of income
Years ended December 31, 1971, 1972, 1973

	Percent of sales, 1973 industry standards	Dollar amounts in millions		
		1971	1972	1973
Revenues (net)........	100	$800	$900	$1,000
Cost of sales...........	70	550	620	700
Gross margin..........	30	$250	$280	$ 300
Selling expenses.......	10	$ 85	$100	$ 100
Administrative and other expenses......	10	85	90	100
Total of Other Expenses........	20	$170	$190	$ 200
Net operating income..	10	$ 80	$ 90	$ 100
Interest.................		9	13	17
Earnings before taxes..		$ 71	$ 77	$ 83
Income taxes..........		35	38	41
Profit after taxes...		$ 36	$ 39	$ 42
Dividends.............		$ 16	$ 19	$ 19
Earnings per share on common.............		$ 3.60	$ 3.90	$ 4.20
Cash dividends per share................		$ 1.64	$ 1.75	$ 1.87
Price range for common:				
High.................		$ 50	$ 60	$ 70
Low..................		30	30	30
Average.............		40	45	50

TABLE 17–5

Green Electrical Company
Consolidated balance sheets
Years ended December 31, 1971, 1972, 1973

	Percent of sales, 1973 industry standards	Dollar amounts in millions		
		1971	1972	1973
Current assets..............	35	$300	$325	$350
Investments...............	5	50	50	50
Net property...............	30	290	325	400
Total Assets............	80	$640	$700	$800
Total current debt*..........	10	$ 90	$130	$210
Long-term debt 5%..........	30	100	100	100
Total Debt...............		$190	$230	$310
Common stock par $10......		$100	$100	$100
Capital surplus..............		200	200	200
Retained earnings...........		150	170	190
Net Worth...............	40	$450	$470	$490
Total Claims on Assets.	80	$640	$700	$800

* Includes notes payable (8 percent interest rate) of $50 (1971), $100 (1972), and $150 (1973).

we draw on much of what has been developed before. The risk aspect in a financing decision relates to two aspects of leverage: one, the effects on the financial structure; and two, the effects on fixed charge coverage. We will first examine the effects on the financial structure.

In Table 17–6, the industry average for the financial structure is related to the data for the Green Electrical Company. As compared with the industry average, Green is relatively heavy in equity financing. It has not utilized debt to the same extent as the industry as a whole. Green has about the same financial structure that most manufacturing firms had in the United States before the serious inflation started in 1966. It

TABLE 17–6

A. Risk: Percentage of total assets

		Green Electric Company 1973					
		Now		Pro forma			
				Debt		Equity	
Category	Industry average	Amount	Percent	Amount	Percent	Amount	Percent
Current debt.....................	12%	$210	26%	$160	19%	$160	19%
Long-term debt....................	38	100	13	200	23	100	12
Total Debt......................	50%	$310	39%	$360	42%	$260	31%
Net worth........................	50	490	61	490	58	590	69
Total Assets....................	100%	$800	100%	$850	100%	$850	100%

TABLE 17–7
Coverage of fixed charges

| | At present | | Pro forma | | | |
| | | | Debt | | Equity | |
Net operating income, 1973, $100	Amount	Cost	Amount	Cost	Amount	Cost
Fixed charges:						
Short-term debt (8%)	$150	$12	$100	$ 8	$100	$ 8
Old long-term debt (5%)	100	5	100	5	100	5
New long-term debt (8%)	—	—	100	8	—	—
Total Fixed Charges		$17		$21		$13
Fixed charge coverage		5.9X		4.8X		7.7X

appears to have lagged in catching up with its industry in increasing its debt ratio. The financial structure analysis suggests the use of debt, but we have to consider other factors as well.

Another test of risk is analyzed in Table 17–7, which deals with coverage of fixed charges. If the profitability rate is low, a firm may have a high ratio of equity to debt but still have a poor fixed charge coverage, which could involve risk of inability to meet its financial obligations. The fixed charge coverage is calculated by dividing net operating income by total fixed charges. If the industry standard is a fixed charge coverage of five times, the data in Table 17–7 indicate that the firm meets this standard at present. However, if debt financing is used, the firm will fall slightly below the industry standard. The coverage ratio will have to be monitored if the firm chooses the debt financing alternative.

Table 17–8 next sets forth the relative costs. The estimated cost of retained earnings is 11 percent. With flotation costs of 10.0 percent the

cost of external equity financing would be 12.2 percent as shown. The after-tax cost (including flotation costs) of new debt would be 4.08 percent. Thus the cost of debt financing is substantially lower than the cost of equity financing.

TABLE 17–8
Relative costs

1. Estimated cost of retained earnings (k)

$$k = \frac{D_1}{P_0} + g = \frac{\$2.00^*}{\$50} + 0.07 = 0.04 + 0.07$$
$$= 0.11 = 11\%$$

2. Cost of external equity financing (k_e)

$$k_e = \frac{k}{(1-f)} = \frac{.11}{.90} = 12.2\%$$

3. Cost of new debt (r)

$$r = \frac{\text{Current bond yield}}{1 - \text{Percentage flotation cost}}(1-t)$$
$$= \frac{.08}{1 - .02}(1 - .50)$$
$$= 4.08\%$$

$^* D_1 = P_0(1+g) = \$1.87(1.07) = \$2.00$

Label each of the following statements as true or false.

_____ 1. Since the Green Company is relatively heavy in equity financing, its weighted average cost of capital is probably slightly lower than the typical industry company's cost of capital.

_____ 2. In evaluating the riskiness of any firm, it is useful to compare the firm's debt ratio and its fixed charge coverage ratio to the "norm" for the industry.

_____ 3. In trying to decide between equity or debt financing, it is important to compute the explicit cost of each source of financing and to favor the lowest cost alternative (which is almost always debt financing).

_____ 4. The cost of a new stock issue is always higher than the cost of retained earnings.

Now turn to Answer Frame 5¹⁷, page 156, to check your answers.

Frame 6[17]

In Table 17–9 the initial effects on earnings per share are calculated. The first line provides additional information on the probability of each of four alternative sales levels. The rest of Table 17–9 shows the usual pattern. At low rates of sales, earnings per share under the equity alternative are higher. At higher rates of sales, earnings per share under the debt alternative are higher.

These results are analyzed by probability analysis in Table 17–10. The expected return under the debt alternative is higher. But the variation of returns under the debt alternative is also higher. Hence, the influence of the return-risk relationship depends upon the attitudes toward risk of the firm's decision makers.

In Table 17–11 the cash flow requirements are analyzed. Cash flow is defined as net income plus depreciation (assuming this is the only expense which did not utilize cash), which is $82 million for the Green Company in 1973. Cash flow requirements must take into account sinking fund payments beginning in 1978. The cash flow coverage is much higher under equity financing than under the other alternatives. However, even during the period when the sinking fund payments must be made, the cash flow coverage still exceeds the industry average.

Finally, we analyze the effects on control if common stock is sold. The original number of shares is 10 million. Under equity financing $2 million in additional shares will be issued, representing a 20 percent increase. However, for a company with such widely held stock, the effects on control are not likely to be appreciable.

An overall assessment of the two alternatives may now be made. The advantage to the use of debt is that the costs are lower and the earnings will be greater if the firm's sales continue to grow. The main advantage of equity is that if debt is used, the fixed charge coverage is relatively tight, although the financial structure considerations favor the use of debt. Also, cash flow coverage will be close to the industry standard minimum if debt is utilized because of sinking fund requirements.

On balance, the board of directors of this company voted for the use of debt because they judged that the company's earnings would continue to increase and that some form of equity financing could then be utilized in the future. They felt also that they needed to get into line with industry financial structures to obtain the benefit of increased leverage and to adjust to the new economic and financial environment of in-

TABLE 17–9
Initial effects on EPS

	Probability of sales level			
	.1	.2	.3	.4
Sales	$ 400	$800	$1,000	$1,500
Total production cost (300 + .4S)	460	620	700	900
Gross margin	$ (60)	$180	$ 300	$ 600
Other expenses (100 + .1S)	140	180	200	250
Net operating income	$(200)	$ 0	$ 100	$ 350
Debt alternatives:				
Interest charges	21	21	21	21
Profit before taxes	$(221)	$(21)	$ 79	$ 329
Taxes at 50%	(110)	(10)	39	164
Earnings after taxes	$(111)	$(11)	$ 40	$ 165
EPS (10 million shares)	$ (11.1)	$ (1.1)	$ 4	$ 16.5
Equity alternative:				
Interest charges	$ 13	$ 13	$ 13	$ 13
Profit before taxes	$(213)	$(13)	$ 87	$ 337
Taxes at 50%	(106)	(6)	43	168
Earnings after taxes	$(107)	$ (7)	$ 44	$ 169
EPS (12 million shares)	$ (8.92)	$ (.58)	$ 3.67	$ 14.08

Answer frame 5¹⁷

1. False. Since the Green Company is using relatively smaller amounts of debt financing than the typical company in its industry, it may be operating to the left of the optimal debt/equity financing mix. If so, its weighted average cost of capital would be higher.
2. True. In looking at the Green Company's debt ratio and its fixed charge coverage ratio, it appears that it is less risky than the typical company in its industry.
3. False. It is true that debt financing may be the least cost alternative, but its impact is felt in other areas. Therefore, many factors must be considered in the decision to use debt or equity financing. Using excessive amounts of debt can substantially increase the risk of the firm, which could lead to an excessive cost of retained earnings as well as an excessive cost of external equity financing. Thus, the weighted cost of capital is the preferable cost to use in this decision process (as illustrated in Chapter 15).
4. True. The cost of a new stock issue is always higher than the cost of retained earnings because of the flotation costs.

If you missed any of the above, restudy Frame 5¹⁷ before starting Frame 6¹⁷, page 155.

Frame 6¹⁷ continued

flation, which would enable them to pay off debt with cheaper money in the future.

The Green Company case illustrates the general type of pattern that exists when debt financing is used. The circumstances that would make equity financing the preferred alternative would involve a number of changes. If the financial structure represented a debt ratio already in excess of the firm's target or industry standard, this would push the decision toward the use of equity. Also, if the coverage of fixed charges and the

coverage of cash flow requirements fell below industry standards, this would reinforce risk considerations in the direction of the use of equity. In general the cost of debt is below the cost of equity, but it involves greater risk. Hence, if the external financial environment were one in which the prices of equity securities in general were cyclically high, in conjunction with the other circumstances described, this would make the choice of equity financing a conclusive decision.

TABLE 17–10

Return-risk analysis of the debt versus equity alternatives

p	EPS	pEPS	[EPS − E(EPS)]	[EPS − E(EPS)]²	p[EPS − E(EPS)]²
Debt					
.1	(11.1)	(1.11)	(17.57)	308.70	30.87
.2	(1.1)	(0.22)	(7.57)	57.30	11.46
.3	4.0	1.20	(2.47)	6.10	1.83
.4	16.5	6.60	10.03	100.60	40.24
		E(EPS) = 6.47			σ^2 = 84.40
					σ = 9.187
				CV = [σ/E(EPS)] =	1.42
Equity					
.1	(8.9)	(0.89)	(14.64)	214.33	21.43
.2	(0.6)	(0.12)	(6.34)	40.20	8.04
.3	3.7	1.11	(2.04)	4.16	1.25
.4	14.1	5.64	8.36	69.89	27.96
		E(EPS) = 5.74			σ^2 = 58.68
					σ = 7.66
				CV = σ/E(EPS) =	1.33

TABLE 17–11
Cash flow requirements, 1973*

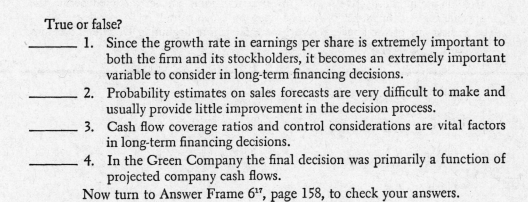

| Cash flow requirements | Industry standard | Now | Debt | | Equity |
			1973–77	1978–98	
Interest payments....................		$17	$21	$21	$13
Sinking fund.........................		—	—	5	—
		$17	$21	$26	$13
Cash flow coverage..................	3X	4.8X	3.9X	3.2X	6.3X

* Net income ($42) + Depreciation ($40) = Cash flow ($82)

True or false?

_____ 1. Since the growth rate in earnings per share is extremely important to both the firm and its stockholders, it becomes an extremely important variable to consider in long-term financing decisions.

_____ 2. Probability estimates on sales forecasts are very difficult to make and usually provide little improvement in the decision process.

_____ 3. Cash flow coverage ratios and control considerations are vital factors in long-term financing decisions.

_____ 4. In the Green Company the final decision was primarily a function of projected company cash flows.

Now turn to Answer Frame 6¹⁷, page 158, to check your answers.

Answer frame 6¹⁷

1. True. In addition, sales projections become the crucial input data in the calculation of earnings per share.
2. False. Probability estimates are difficult to make, but they usually do improve the decision process. Assigning probability estimates usually becomes easier when the firm has been in business several years and has some experience on which to base estimates.
3. True. Forecasting cash flow coverage ratios over recessionary periods is particularly helpful in determining the amount of leverage that a firm can safely employ. The control problem is particularly important to a small- to medium-size firm where its stock is not widely held.
4. True. However, risk, cost, earnings per share, cash flows, control considerations, and long-term prospective capital investments should all be evaluated before the specific form of financing is decided upon by a company.

If you missed any of the above, reread Frame 6¹⁷ before beginning Chapter 18 below.

chapter 18

INTERMEDIATE-TERM FINANCING

Frame 1¹⁸

Intermediate-term financing includes liabilities with maturities between one and five years. Anything shorter is a current liability, while obligations due in five or more years are thought of as long-term debt. The major forms of intermediate-term financing include (1) *term loans*, (2) *conditional sales contracts*, and (3) *lease financing*.

TERM LOANS

A term loan is a business credit with a maturity of more than one year but less than 20 years. Ordinarily term loans are retired by systematic repayments (amortization payments) over the life of the loan. While stronger companies can borrow on an unsecured basis, security, generally in the form of a chattel mortgage on equipment, is often employed. Commercial banks and life insurance companies are the principal suppliers of term loan credit. Commercial banks typically make smaller, shorter maturity term loans of 3 to 5 years; life insurance companies grant larger, longer term credits of 10 to 20 years.

The interest cost of term loans, like rates on other credits, varies with the size of the loan and the strength of the borrower. For small loans to small companies, effective rates may be as high as 15 to 20 percent; for large loans to large firms, the rate will be close to the prime rate. Since term loans run for long periods during which time interest rates can change radically, many loans have variable interest rates set at 1 to 4 percentage points above the prime rate or above the Federal Reserve rediscount rate.

Protective covenants are contained in most term loan agreements. The lender's funds are tied up for a long period during which the borrower's situation can change markedly. To protect himself, the lender will include in the loan agreement stipulations that the borrower will maintain his current ratio at a specified level, limit acquisitions of additional fixed assets, keep his debt ratio below a stated amount, and so on. These provisions are necessary from the lender's point of view, but they also restrict the borrower's freedom of action.

CONDITIONAL SALES CONTRACTS

Conditional sales contracts continue to be an important method by which firms obtain the use of equipment. Under the sales contract, the buyer agrees to buy a particular piece of equipment and to pay for it in installments over a one- to five-year period. Until payment is completed, the seller continues to hold legal title to the equipment; thus the completion of the sale is *conditional* upon completion of the payments.

The cost of financing under sales contracts is relatively high since the current borrowing rates are applied to the original balance discounted on the face amount of the contract—an effective rate of interest more than double the normal rate. However, on heavy machinery purchased by good credit risks, the rate may be close to the prime lending rate of banks.

A major advantage of conditional sales financing is that it increases the ability of small firms to purchase equipment, since the equipment itself provides security for the loan. Also, the equipment is often directly used in the production of income which provides for the repayment of the loan and thus is self-liquidating.

The interest costs on such borrowing are high, especially since the amount of interest paid is usually based on the initial amount borrowed, while the effective rate of interest should be related to the average loan balance outstanding. However, the cash flows generated by the equipment may make its acquisition profitable. In fact, the small business financing problem would be mitigated if working capital requirements could be financed as directly as equipment. Thus the main limitation of equipment financing is that its use is limited to the fixed asset portion of the investment requirements of firms.

Indicate whether each of the following statements is true or false by writing "T" or "F" in the space provided.

_____ 1. If interest rates are expected to decline in the future, a lender or commercial bank will want to set a floating interest charge.

_____ 2. Protective covenants on most term loan agreements are designed to prevent a firm from making decisions that would increase the riskiness of its prospective income stream.

_____ 3. Essentially, a conditional sales contract, from the standpoint of the lender, is a long-term accounts receivable financing arrangement with payments determined like those examined under the term loan arrangement.

_____ 4. A conditional sales contract increases the ability of a small firm to purchase fixed assets, but effective interest rates can be as high as 5 or more percentage points above the bank prime rate.

Now check your answers in Answer Frame 1[18], page 160.

Answer frame 1[18]

1. False. If interest rates are at a high level, the commercial bank will want to set a fixed interest rate and lock in the firm at this level—so as interest rates fall, the bank's profits will rise concomitantly. The borrowing firm would be desirous of arranging a floating interest charge under these conditions. Obviously, the accurate forecasting of interest rates may not be attained and the poorer forecaster will lose.
2. True. The lender wants to protect his investment, and by placing restrictions on the firm, he is attempting to preserve the firm's ability to repay the loan.
3. True. The terms of installment equipment financing are influenced mainly by the length of life of the equipment purchased. The down payment runs about one third of the purchase price, and the maturity usually runs from two to three years.
4. True. Hopefully, the fixed assets generate sufficient cash flows to make the installment payments. If so, this is a self-liquidating loan.

If you missed any of the above, reread Frame 1[18] before starting Frame 2[18] below.

Frame 2[18]

LEASING

Leasing has long been used in connection with the acquisition of equipment by railroad companies, and in recent years it has been extended to a variety of equipment. In the absence of major tax advantages, whether or not leasing is advantageous depends primarily on the firm's ability to acquire funds by other methods. Leasing may provide an advantage by increasing the firm's overall availability of nonequity financing and by changing the time pattern of its tax-sheltered payments as discussed in the illustrative example below. However, a leasing contract is very close to a straight-debt arrangement and uses some of the firm's debt-carrying ability. Also, the rental is a fixed obligation.

Because of the importance of residual value, it will generally be advantageous to a firm to own its land and buildings. But because of the obsolescence factor, the residual value considerations may be less important in connection with the acquisition of equipment. For this reason, leasing of equipment may be expected to continue to grow in relative importance in the future.

The statement is frequently made that leasing always involves higher interest rates. But this argument is of doubtful validity. First, when the credit-worthiness of the lessee is considered, there may be no difference. Second, it is difficult to separate the money cost of leasing from the other services that may be embodied in a leasing contract. Because of its specialized operations, the leasing company may perform nonfinancial services such as maintenance of the equipment, reconditioning, marketing used equipment, reduction of obsolescence losses—all at lower costs than the lessee or other institutions could perform them. If so, the effective cost of leasing may be lower than for the combination of funds and other services obtained from other sources. The efficiencies of performing specialized services may thus enable the leasing company to operate by charging a lower total cost than the lessor would have to pay for the package of money plus services on any other basis.

Two possible situations may exist to make leasing advantageous to firms seeking the maximum degree of financial leverage. First, it is frequently stated that firms can obtain more money for longer terms under a lease arrangement than under a secured loan agreement for the purchase of a specific piece of equipment. Second, leasing may not have as large an impact on future borrowing capacity as borrowing and buying equipment. Since the lease in most cases (there are some leases that must be capitalized) represents "off balance sheet" borrowing, a firm that is leasing will have lower debt ratios as conventionally measured. The amount of the annual rentals is shown as a note to the financial statements, but evidence suggests that many lenders give less weight to a lease obligation than to a loan obligation. To a considerable extent, the amount of borrowing by a firm that is leasing is more fully reflected by the "times-fixed-charges-covered" ratio in which the fixed charges include lease rental payments.

Label each of the following statements as true or false.

———— 1. Leasing may offer increased tax shelter benefits, increased borrowing capacity, increased financial leverage, and protection against a possible decline in residual values due to technological innovations.

———— 2. Leasing always involves higher interest rates over a straight purchase because of the insertion of a third party.

———— 3. The type of equipment best suited for leasing generally has unique features or a tailor-made design for the specific use of a given lessee.

———— 4. Dianne Plastics Company had a debt to total asset ratio of 40 percent. They leased a number of modern standardized machines whose purchase price was 25 percent of their existing total assets. Since the firm reports the effect of this lease arrangement in a footnote to its annual financial statement, its new debt to total asset ratio will be 52 percent.

Now check your answers in Answer Frame 2^{18}, page 162.

Frame 3^{18}

In Chapter 11, the logic of making capital budgeting decisions was set forth, and the chapter ended with a discussion of various types of investment decisions, one of which was mutually exclusive investments. This category can now be illustrated in comparing the lease versus purchase-loan method of acquiring the use of an asset. This will be done by the use of a case example. The facts for which are the following:

The Lessee Company is comparing two alternatives for acquiring a machine, with net cash inflows from cost reductions of $5,000 per year. It can buy the machine for $15,000 and borrow the amount to make the payment under an amortized 10 percent, five-year term loan arrangement. Its annual payments on the five-year loan would be $3,957. Alternatively, it can lease the equipment under a five-year lease for $4,000 per year. If the firm buys the machine, it will have to pay maintenance costs (included in the lease payment) estimated to be $500 per year. The salvage value of the machine at the end of its five-year use is forecasted to be $1,000.

Applying the capital budgeting principle for choosing between two mutually exclusive investment alternatives, we will select the alternative with the largest positive net present value (NPV). Since the present value of the net cash inflows will be the same whether the machine is leased or purchased, any difference in NPV will depend entirely on the present value of the costs of leas-

ing versus the present value of the costs of the borrow-purchase arrangement.

To calculate the NPV of the leasing alternative, we utilize the information and symbols below:

NPV_L is the net present value to the user if leasing is used.

c_t is the net cash flows in period t from the project = $5,000.

L_t is the lease payment in period t (maintenance charges are included) = $4,000.

τ is the corporate tax rate = 40%.

k is the weighted marginal cost of capital for the firm = 10%.

r^* is the after-tax cost of debt of the firm = $10(1 - .4) = 6\%$.

n is the number of years of the lease contract = 5.

This information is used in the following formula:

$$NPV_L = \sum_{t=1}^{n} \frac{c_t(1 - \tau)}{(1 + k)^t} - \sum_{t=1}^{n} \frac{L_t(1 - \tau)}{(1 + r^*)^t} \quad (18\text{--}1)$$

Equation 18–1 involves two expressions, both of which represent the present value of an annuity relationship. First, the net cash flows per period are reduced to an after-tax basis and discounted by the firm's cost of capital. From this is deducted the after-tax cost of leasing, discounted at the firm's after-tax cost of debt. From the information given in the statement of this case, we can insert

Answer frame 2¹⁸

1. True. However, with increased competition and sophistication, many of these advantages may well be priced out in the terms of the transaction. But, tax advantages may remain (particularly where one firm has tax losses and the transference of these tax benefits can be priced out in the terms of the transaction), and economies of scale or specialization of effort may also prevail.
2. False. In many cases the total taxes paid may be less, or tax payments may be delayed to future periods. Efficiencies of performing specialized services may also be significant, resulting in lower implicit interest charges on lease payments.
3. False. The standardized type of equipment is best suited for leasing, such as automobiles, airplanes, railroad cars, and so on. It should be a product that is easily identifiable and can be used by many different firms.
4. False. Since the equipment was not capitalized and placed in the body of the balance sheet, the debt ratio remains at 40 percent. A lender failing to capitalize a given firm's lease obligations would not obtain a true picture of the financial risk or fixed obligations of a firm. This failure is what gives rise to the illusion of a firm's increased borrowing capacity.

If you missed any of the above, restudy Frame 2¹⁸ before beginning Frame 3¹⁸, page 161.

Frame 3¹⁸ continued

the appropriate numbers in 18–1 as shown in 18–1a. Since the tax rate is 40 percent, the 0.6 in 18–1a represents the after-tax ratio. The interest factor for the present value of an annuity at 10 percent for five years is 3.791; the interest factor for the present value of an annuity at 6 percent for five years is 4.212.

$$NPV_L = \$5,000(0.6)(3.791) - \$4,000(0.6)(4.212)$$
$$= \$3,000(3.791) - \$2,400(4.212)$$
$$= \$11,373 - \$10,109 \qquad (18-1a)$$
$$= \$1,264$$

The present value of the net cash flows is \$11,373, the present value of the after-tax lease payments is \$10,109, and the NPV of leasing is \$1,264.

Now similarly we can calculate the net present value of the borrow-purchase alternative. The additional information and symbols required are first listed:

NPV_P is the net present value to the user if the machine is purchased.

A_t is the amortization payments on the loan = \$3,957.

m_t is the maintenance costs of the asset in period t = \$500.

f_t is the tax deductible interest costs per period under borrow-purchase (See Table 18–1).

d_t is the tax deductible depreciation charges under borrow-purchase = (\$15,000 − \$1,000)/5 = \$2,800.

V_n is the salvage value of the asset = \$1,000.

n is the useful life of the asset which is assumed to be the same as the life of the lease.

I_0 is the initial cost of the machine = \$15,000.

These factors are utilized in Equation 18–2.

$$NPV_P = \sum_{t=1}^{n} \frac{c_t(1-\tau)}{(1+k)^t} - I_0 + \sum_{t=1}^{n} \frac{\tau d_t}{(1+r^*)^t}$$
$$- \sum_{t=1}^{n} \frac{m_t(1-\tau)}{(1+r^*)^t} + \frac{V_n}{(1+k)^n} \qquad (18-2)$$

The net cash flows from the use of the asset will, of course, be the same as when the machine is acquired by leasing. But a deduction must be made for the after-tax costs of maintenance which were included in the lease payment. Additional positive cash flows come in the form of the tax shelter provided by the deductibility of the depreciation expenses and interest payments incurred. In Equation 18–2, the interest tax shelter is reflected in the *after-tax* cost of debt; in Table 18–2 it is set out explicitly. Both treatments give the same results. All of these flows take place during each of the years of the use of the machine and are discounted at the after-tax cost of debt as they are relatively certain, and little risk is attached to them. In addition, the estimated salvage value at the end of the five-year life is taken into account, discounted at 10 percent. The

TABLE 18–1

Schedule of debt payments

(1) Year	(2) Balance owed at end of year	(3) Payment	(4) Interest .10 × (2)	(5) Amortization of principal $3,957 − (4)
1.................	$15,000	$ 3,957	$1,500	$ 2,457
2.................	12,543	3,957	1,254	2,703
3.................	9,840	3,957	984	2,973
4.................	6,867	3,957	687	3,270
5.................	3,597	3,957	360	3,597
		$19,785	$4,785	$15,000

argument here is that an asset's salvage value at some future time is not at all certain, so that a risk adjusted discount rate should be used rather than the after-tax cost of debt.

In Tables 18–1 and 18–2, we analyze the cash flows of the borrow-purchase alternative to determine the present value of the after-tax cash flows. Table 18–1 separates the annual $3,957 loan payments into their interest and principal components. This is necesssary to determine the tax shelter from the interest payments which will reduce the cost of the borrow-purchase alternative.

Table 18–2 presents all of the costs and off-setting tax effects which would accrue to the firm as owner, but not as lessee.

We can now compare the costs of the two alternatives:

Costs of leasing............ $10,109
Costs of owning............. 10,923
Advantage to leasing........ $ 814

also,

$$NPV_L = \$11,373 - \$10,109 = \$1,264$$
$$NPV_P = \$11,373 - \$15,000 + \$4,717$$
$$- \$1,264 + \$621 = \$447$$
$$NPV_L - NPV_P = \$1,264 - \$447$$
$$= \$817 \approx \$814$$

We see that the advantage to leasing is over $800. There are a number of factors which might cause this result.

A firm in the leasing business sets the lease payment it will charge its customers in much the same way as a potential lessee analyzes the decision. That is, the lessor sets the lease rental payment such that, in equilibrium, the discounted receipts are exactly offset by the discounted costs of depreciation, maintenance, and so forth. If, as in the example above, a lessee finds that it will be advantageous to lease rather than to borrow and purchase, there must be differences in the situations of the two firms. The lessor may be able to provide maintenance service at a lower cost than the lessee could provide it. The lessor may have a

TABLE 18–2

Costs of owning

(1) Year	(2) Loan payment	(3) Annual interest	(4) Depreciation	(5) Maintenance expense	(6) Tax shield [(3) + (4) + (5)]0.4	(7) Cash flows after taxes [(2) + (5)] − (6)	(8) PV factor	(9) PV of costs
1..........	$3,957	$1,500	$2,800	$500	$1,920	$ 2,537	.943	$ 2,392
2..........	3,957	1,254	2,800	500	1,822	2,635	.890	2,345
3..........	3,957	984	2,800	500	1,714	2,743	.840	2,304
4..........	3,957	687	2,800	500	1,595	2,862	.792	2,267
5..........	3,957	360	2,800	500	1,464	2,993	.747	2,236
5..........						−1,000	.621	− 621
								$10,923

lower cost of capital than the lessee, or the lessor may be able to use accelerated depreciation or other tax credits which are unavailable to the lessee. Because of experience with many other users of similar machines, the lessor may be able to command a higher salvage value for the equipment. Any one or all of these factors could result in lower costs for leasing than for owning, and conversely, other factors would result in higher costs for leasing.

One of the critical factors in the comparison of the NPV of leasing versus purchase-borrow is the difference between the time pattern of the tax-sheltered expenses—the lease payments under leasing and the depreciation and interest expenses under purchase-borrow. Under either method of acquiring the use of an asset, there is considerable flexibility in arranging the time pattern of the tax-sheltered expenses which has an important impact on the results because of the time value of money. To illustrate this point, the tax shelter from accelerated depreciation using the sum-of-the-years'-digits method is shown in Table 18–3

TABLE 18–3

Tax shelter from accelerated depreciation

(1) SYD factors* and depreciation	(2) 0.4(1) Depreciation tax shelter	(3) PV factor at 6%	(4) (2)(3) PV of SYD depreciation tax shelter
5/15—$4,667............	1,867	.943	$1,761
4/15— 3,733............	1,493	.890	1,329
3/15— 2,800............	1,120	.840	941
2/15— 1,867............	747	.792	592
1/15— 933............	373	.747	279
Total....................................			$4,902
Straight-line depreciation: Tax shelter 1,120 × 4.212....................			$4,717
Increase in tax shelter from SYD depreciation method.....................			$ 185

*1 + 2 + 3 + 4 + 5 = 15, the denominator used.

and compared with the tax shelter under straight-line depreciation.

Column 1 shows the SYD factors and the annual depreciation charges based on the depreciable cost of $14,000 and 5 year life. In column 2 the 40 percent tax rate is applied, and in column 3 the present value factor is listed. In column 4 the present value of the sum-of-the-years'-digits depreciation tax shelter is shown and summed to the total amount of $4,902. Next the straight-line depreciation tax shelter of $4,717 used in the analysis is deducted to indicate an increase in the tax shelter from the SYD depreciation method, of $185. Since the previous advantage of leasing was $814, the addition of the $185 to the NPV of purchase-borrow reduces the advantage of leasing to $629.

The results of a comparison of the NPV of leasing versus purchase-borrow or other debt-forms will depend on the actual factors in each specific situation. A change in the extra maintenance costs of owning, a change in the time pattern of the leasing payments required, or a change in the forecasted salvage value could shift the advantage to the leasing or to the purchase-borrow alternative. Whatever the particular facts, the methodology set forth above is consistent with general capital budgeting analysis and provides a framework for making the comparison of alternatives.

The methodology proposed has general applicability. Different discount rates can be used if the cash flows have different levels of risk. Leasing, like other alternative sources of debt financing, may have characteristics which merit its inclusion as a part of the firm's financial plan. As illustrated in Chapter 15, the firm will seek to combine various proportions of debt forms and equity in relation to the prospective returns from capital budgets of alternative magnitudes, seeking to equate the marginal returns from investment to the marginal costs of capital. Thus, investment and financial structure decisions must be made in a simultaneous equation solution process.

True or false?

_____ 1. The Lessee Company procrastinated on the lease *versus borrow de-cision*, and the purchase price of the asset under consideration was increased from $15,000 to $15,972. If the estimated salvage value was zero and the interest rate on the term loan remains at 8 percent, the new loan payment will be $4,200.

_____ 2. When the sum-of-the-years'-digits (SYD) method of depreciation is employed, the net advantage to leasing is increased.

_____ 3. When salvage value is considered, this is always a plus value in cal-culating the NPV of purchasing the asset.

_____ 4. In some lease alternatives the relative size of the asset purchased (as compared to the total assets) may require the recalculation of the firm's marginal cost of capital.

Now turn to Answer Frame 3[18], page 166, to check your answers.

chapter 19

WARRANTS AND CONVERTIBLES

Frame 1[19]

The period since the end of World War II has been characterized by economic change and uncertainty, with continuous fear of recession and yet concern about inflation. Since mid-1966, in-flation has been experienced in varying degrees both in the United States and in the rest of the world, with concern that attempts to control it may lead to depression and deflation.

Thus, investors have sought to protect them-selves from both alternatives, giving rise to the development of new forms of financing, particu-larly expansion in the use of warrants and con-vertibles. Both represent forms of options de-signed to help investors deal with alternative future states of the world. They are typically associated with a fixed interest obligation to pro-vide the investor a degree of safety. The option to buy shares of common stock seeks to offer protection against inflation and to enable the in-vestor to participate in the growth of the econ-omy.

THE USE OF CONVERTIBLES

Convertible securities are bonds or preferred stock exchangeable for common stock at the holder's option. Typical terms of the conversion privilege include the conversion ratio: the num-ber of shares of common stock into which the convertible security may be exchanged. Given the par value of the convertible security, the con-version ratio also implies a conversion price, rep-resenting the effective price paid per share of common stock on conversion. The conversion

Answer frame 3¹⁸

1. False. The new payment is calculated as follows: let LP = Loan payment; and 3.992 = Interest factor for five-year annuity at 8 percent.

$$\$15,972 = LP3.993$$
$$LP = \frac{\$15,972}{3.993} = \$4,000$$

2. False. Accelerated depreciation (SYD) favors the buy alternative because of the higher depreciation tax shield and present value weights in the early years of the project's life. The illustrative case shows a net advantage to leasing of $814 using straight-line depreciation; whereas the net advantage to leasing of $629 was calculated using SYD depreciation. Thus, the decision is shifted toward the buy alternative using SYD depreciation.

3. False. The contribution of the salvage value to the net present value depends on when the salvage value will be received and on the discount factor applied. Since the salvage value is deducted from the investment on which the annual depreciation tax shelter is determined, the loss in the present value of the depreciation tax shelter may exceed the present value of the salvage value.

4. True. When the relative size of the assets obtained through a lease represents a sizable proportion of total assets, it becomes necessary to recalculate the marginal cost of capital. With a change in hurdle rate, other investment projects must be reevaluated. Thus, investment and financial structure decisions must be made in a simultaneous equation-solution process.

If you missed any of the above, restudy Frame 3¹⁸ before beginning Chapter 19 on page 165.

Frame 1¹⁹ continued

price can be obtained by dividing the par value of the convertible security by the conversion ratio. For example, for a par value bond of $1,000 if the conversion ratio is 20, the conversion price is $50. At the time a convertible security is issued, the conversion price is generally set above the stock's current market price by some 10 to 20 percent.

Convertibles always include a clause protecting the holder against dilution due to stock splits or stock dividends. In addition, some convertibles provide for decreasing conversion ratios, which would represent increasing conversion prices over time. The call provision is especially important in convertible bonds because it can be used by the firm to force conversion. The call price declines over the life of the bond. For example, on a 10-year convertible bond, the call price may be 110 during the first year. It could then decline by one point each year to 100 at the maturity date of the bond. Thus if the bond has a conversion ratio of 20 and the common stock is selling for $70, five years after the issue of the convertible bond, the market price of the bond will be at least $1,400.

The call price of the bond is now $1,050. If the firm calls the bond, the holders will convert into common stock. Thus the firm has *forced conversion*.

Since the convertible security represents an option to trade in the convertible security for common stock at a specified price or ratio, it represents a contingent claim to hold shares of common stock. In addition, the convertible bond has an investment value viewed as a form of straight debt. This is the price at which a convertible bond would sell if it did not carry the conversion option. The convertible bond's value as a straight debt instrument at time t can be determined by using equation 19-1.

$$B_t = \sum_{N=1}^{(T-t)} \frac{c}{(1+r)^N} + \frac{B_M}{(1+r)^{(T-t)}} \quad (19\text{-}1)$$

where:

B_t = Value as a straight debt instrument at time t
T = Original term to maturity = 20
t = Number of years after issue, reference year for valuation = 5

$N =$ Time subscript from year t to year $T = 1, 2, 3, \ldots 15$

$c =$ Dollar amount of interest paid at coupon rate each year $= \$60$

$r =$ Market rate of interest on straight debt issue of equivalent risk $= 8\%$

$B_M =$ Value of the bond at maturity $= \$1,000$

$$B_t = \sum_{N=1}^{15} \frac{60}{(1.08)^N} + \frac{1,000}{(1.08)^{15}} \qquad (19\text{--}1a)$$

$$= 60(8.559) + 1,000(0.315)$$

$$= 513.54 + 315.00 = \$828.54$$

As shown in equation 19–1a, a convertible bond with a 6 percent coupon, a current market rate of interest on straight debt of equivalent risk of 8 percent, and with 15 years to run to maturity, would have a value as a straight debt instrument of $828.54. This would represent a floor below which the value of the convertible bond is unlikely to decline under the facts assumed.

Indicate whether each of the following statements is true or false by writing "T" or "F" in the space provided.

_____ 1. Convertibles represent a security with a fixed return plus the option to exchange the security for a specified number of shares of common stock.

_____ 2. The conversion ratio is the par value of the security divided by the number of shares received.

_____ 3. Conversion prices are usually set 10 to 20 percent below the prevailing market price of the common stock at the time the security is sold.

_____ 4. A convertible bond has a floor value at date of issue of $871.26-$B_t$ when $T = 10$ years, $r = 9\%$, $B_M = \$1,000$, and $c = \$70$.

Now turn to Answer Frame 1[19], page 168, to check your answers.

Frame 2[19]

Now suppose the convertible debenture described in Frame 1[19] is convertible at $80 (its conversion ratio is 12.5). If the common stock into which the bond is convertible rises above an $80 price, the value of the convertible bond will rise above its par value. For example, if the market price of the stock rose to $100, the convertible bond would have a value of $1,250 plus some speculative premium.

From the standpoint of the firm issuing convertibles, one advantage is that it makes it possible to sell debt at interest rates lower than would have to be paid under straight debt. Since a conversion premium of 10 to 20 percent is also involved, convertibles provide a method of selling equity at "futures" prices higher than their current market prices. The inclusion of a call provision provides the company with flexibility for altering its financial structure. Whenever the market price of the stock exceeds the conversion price

sufficiently, the company is in a position to force conversion by issuing a notice that it will retire the bonds at their call price, which generally represents a modest premium over the maturity value of the convertible bonds.

From the standpoint of the issuer, the use of convertible bonds is not without its risks. If convertible bonds are issued in contemplation of making conversion attractive or forcing conversion into equity, there is a risk that the market price of the common stock might not rise above its conversion price. An overhanging issue exists when the firm is not able to force conversion because the market price of the common stock has not achieved the appreciation anticipated. As a consequence, a high debt-equity ratio would remain. Yet, the sale of straight debt plus a sale of equity financing, timed appropriately, might have enabled a firm to sell its equity shares at a much higher level than the conversion price specified in

Answer frame 1[19]

1. True. A convertible represents a security that is designed to help investors deal with alternative economic conditions. When the economy and the company are growing, the investor will hopefully be able to participate in this growth by converting the security into common stock. If the economy and firm are faltering, the investor will probably not convert his security and would continue to receive a fixed return.

2. False. The conversion ratio is the par value of the security divided by the conversion price. It is the number of shares to be received when the security is converted.

3. False. Conversion prices are usually set 10 to 20 percent *above* the prevailing market price.

4. True. The floor value is calculated as follows:

$$B_t = \sum_{N=1}^{10} \frac{70}{(1.09)^N} + \frac{1,000}{(1.09)^{10}}$$

$$= 70(6.418) + 1,000(0.422) = 449.26 + 422.00 = \$871.26$$

If you missed any of the above, reread Frame 1[19] before starting Frame 2[19], page 167.

Frame 2[19] continued

the terms of the sale of the convertible securities. Financial managers have viewed the increased use of convertibles in recent years as a method of raising equity capital at prices higher than those prevailing at the time the convertibles are issued.

Label each of the following statements as true or false.

———— 1. If a convertible bond of par $1,000 has a conversion price of $70, its conversion ratio is 14.285.

———— 2. If the common stock into which the bond is convertible, in question #1, rises to $90, the convertible bond would have a value of $1,285.65 plus a speculative premium.

———— 3. A convertible issue is not intended as a means of delayed equity financing.

———— 4. As a convertible bond approaches its maturity, whether its owners should convert before maturity will be influenced most by the current and prospective value of the common stock into which it is convertible.

Now turn to Answer Frame 2[19], page 170, to check your answers.

Frame 3[19]

USE OF WARRANTS

Warrants are long-term options to buy a specified number of shares of common stock during a designated period at a stated price. They differ from convertible bonds in that the warrants are characteristically separated from the debt issue that gave rise to them. The theoretical market value of warrants is equal to the following:

$$\text{Theoretical value of warrant} = \left[\text{Market price of common stock} - \text{Option purchase price} \right] \times \text{Number of shares each warrant entitles owner to purchase}$$

$$TVW = (P_{mkt} - O)N$$

The market value of a warrant tends to be higher when: (1) the duration of the period during which the option may be exercised is relatively long; (2) the current market price of the common stock relative to the price at which the option may be exercised is high; and (3) the earnings growth potential of the common stock that may be purchased with the option is relatively high.

A warrant generally sells above its theoretical value because of the speculative possibilities, the personal leverage factor, the limitation of loss, and the potential for capital gains. If there are optimistic expectations about the common stock, the premium above the theoretical value will be larger. The premium of the actual market price of a warrant above its theoretical value is largest when the price of common stock is at a low unit value, and it decreases as the absolute price of the common stock rises. The further potential increase in price is likely to be smaller as the price of the common stock rises substantially above the exercise price for the option. In addition, the leverage obtained by having a call on the underlying common stock, with a smaller investment than would be required if the common stock itself were purchased, diminishes as the price of the common stock rises.

For example, suppose a warrant enables the holder to buy one-half share of common stock at $10 when the common stock is selling at $12. While the TVW is $2(0.5) = $1, its actual price may be $3 to $5 because of the speculative po-

tential of a further rise in the value of the common stock. If the common stock were selling at $60, the TVW is $50(0.5) = $25. The premium of the actual price over the theoretical price is likely to be smaller than $2 because the common stock is not as likely to rise by as large a percentage as when the common was selling at $12 (given that the option price of $10 was meaningful). Further, the leverage potential of the warrant is smaller since it now sells in the $25 range as compared with around $3.

Warrants are characteristically used by growing firms as a sweetener to raise additional debt funds at reduced interest costs and with more favorable indenture provisions. Thus the use of warrants enables the firm to widen the market for its debt securities. In addition, when exercised, warrants bring additional equity funds into the company, helping to balance debt and equity financing over a period of time. Like convertibles, they provide for the sale of equity shares at price levels higher than those prevailing at the time the debt was issued.

The limitations on the use of warrants are similar to those described for the use of convertibles. In contrast to convertibles, the exercise of warrants does not extinguish the debt instruments. However, the increase in equity from the exercise of warrants moderates any previous debt-equity ratio.

True or false?

_____ 1. When the market price of a common stock is $50 and the option purchase price is $42 with one warrant, the theoretical value of that warrant is $8.

_____ 2. A warrant typically sells for more than its theoretical value because of the speculative value, the personal leverage factor, the limitation of loss, and the potential for capital gains.

_____ 3. Warrants, like convertibles, extinguish debt instruments when exercised, thereby reducing the financial leverage of the firm.

_____ 4. Warrants, like convertibles, bring additional equity funds into the firm when they are exercised.

Now turn to Answer Frame 3¹⁹, page 170, to check your answers.

Answer frame 2¹⁹

1. True. The conversion ratio (CR) is calculated as follows:

$$CR = \frac{\text{Par value}}{\text{Conversion price}} = \frac{1,000}{70} = 14.285$$

2. True. The conversion value (CV) when market price (P_{mkt}) is $90 is calculated as follows:

$$CV = CR(P_{mkt}) = 14.285 \times \$90 = \$1,285.65$$

3. False. Financial managers use convertibles as a method of raising equity capital at prices higher than those prevailing at the time of issue. In addition, it is a means of obtaining low-cost capital during the development phase of a project.

4. True. At maturity, the face value of the bond will be paid. However, as the maturity date of the bond approaches, the holders will convert to the common stock if the conversion value of the bond is significantly above its par value.

If you missed any of the above, restudy Frame 2¹⁹ before starting Frame 3¹⁹, page 168.

Answer frame 3¹⁹

1. True. The theoretical value (TV) of the warrant is calculated as follows:

$$TVW = (P_{mkt} - O)N = (50 - 42)1 = \$8$$

2. True. These reasons relate directly to the duration of the option, the relative market price of the common stock to the option purchase price, and the potential for growth in earnings.

3. False. Only convertibles extinguish the debt instrument and thus provide the greatest reduction in the debt-to-equity ratio, which is the measure of the firm's financial leverage. Exercise of the warrants, however, does moderate the debt-to-equity ratio as the equity base is increased.

4. False. Only warrants bring in additional equity funds when they are exercised. However, when convertibles are converted, the equity base is increased and additional debt can be sold more easily.

If you missed any of the above, restudy Frame 3¹⁹ before beginning Frame 4¹⁹ below.

Frame 4¹⁹

ILLUSTRATION OF THE USE OF CONVERTIBLES AND WARRANTS

To provide a concrete example of the relative roles of convertible debt and warrants, a composite case is described. The Jorden Specialty Chemicals Company is expecting further growth in the future. The price-earnings ratio of its common stock is now 22 and is expected to rise 25 or perhaps even 30 times. Jorden's earnings before interest and taxes is 20 percent of total assets. The financial position before Jorden's expansion is shown in balance sheet 1 and income statement 1.

Because Jorden expects its price-earnings ratio to be higher in the future, it will follow its investment banker's advice to finance its growth with convertible subordinated debentures or subordinated debentures with warrants. The convertible debentures carry an 8 percent interest rate and are convertible at $80. The debentures with warrants would have a 7 percent coupon with 20 warrants, each of which could buy a share of common stock at $75. Both have a 10-year maturity with an initial call premium of 10 percent, declining to zero in the 10th year. To help decide whether "converts" or debentures with warrants should be sold, an analysis is made of the effects of each on (1) the financial structure, (2) the earnings per share, and (3) the control

Balance Sheet 1

Current assets.........................	$2,400,000
Net fixed assets......................	1,600,000
Total Assets....................	$4,000,000
Notes payable 10%....................	$ 400,000
Other current debt....................	600,000
Long-term debt 10%..................	1,000,000
Common stock-$5 par.................	500,000
Paid-in capital.......................	500,000
Retained earnings....................	1,000,000
Total Liabilities and Owners' Equity...	$4,000,000

Income Statement 1

Earnings before interest and taxes......................		$800,000
Interest expense		
$0.1 \times 1,000,000$...........	100,000	
$0.1 \times 400,000$...........	40,000	140,000
Taxable income.............		$660,000
Taxes (assuming a 50% tax rate)..............		330,000
Net Income...........		$330,000

EPS = $330,000/100,000 = $3.30
$3.30 \times 22 = 72.60 price of stock

Balance Sheet 2

Current assets.........................	$3,000,000
Net fixed assets......................	2,000,000
Total Assets....................	$5,000,000
Notes payable—10%....................	$ 400,000
Other current debt....................	600,000
Debentures............................	1,000,000
Other long-term debt..................	1,000,000
Common stock—$5 par.................	500,000
Paid-in capital.......................	500,000
Retained earnings....................	1,000,000
Total Claims on Assets..........	$5,000,000

Convertibles Used—Income Statement 2a

Earnings before interest and taxes...................		$1,000,000
Interest expense		
$0.10 \times 400,000$............	40,000	
$0.08 \times 1,000,000$..........	80,000	
$0.10 \times 1,000,000$..........	100,000	220,000
Taxable income...........		$ 780,000
Taxes.....................		390,000
Net income........		$ 390,000

EPS = $390,000/$100,000 = $3.90
Price of common = $3.90 \times 25 = $97.50

Warrants Used—Income Statement 2b

Earnings before interest and taxes...................		$1,000,000
Interest expense..........		
$0.10 \times 400,000$......	40,000	
$0.07 \times 1,000,000$..........	70,000	
$0.10 \times 1,000,000$..........	100,000	210,000
Taxable income...........		$ 790,000
Taxes.....................		395,000
Net Income........		$ 395,000

EPS = $395,000/$100,000 = $3.95
Price of common = $3.95 \times 25 = $98.75

position of Jorden (who now owns 70 percent of the outstanding common stock).

The debentures are sold at $1 million and the firm continues to earn 20 percent on new total assets of $5 million. In balance sheet 2 and income statements 2a and 2b, a comparison is made between the use of convertibles versus warrants.

The earnings per share are somewhat lower for the use of convertibles at this stage since the interest rate assumed for the convertibles is somewhat higher. The price of common stock when convertibles are used is $97.50, well above the conversion price. Similarly, the price of common when the warrants are used is well above the exercise price of the warrants. The value of the convertible and the value of the warrant would therefore be the following:

Value of convertible. Value of convertible = Market price of common × Conversion ratio = $97.50 \times 12.5 = $1,218.75 plus some speculative premium.

Value of warrant. Value of warrant = (Market price—Option price) × (Number of shares each warrant entitles owner to purchase) = $(98.75 - 75.00) \times 1 = $23.75 plus some speculative premium.

At this point, if the firm wished to eliminate the fixed charges associated with the debentures sold. it could call the convertibles and thereby

force conversion into common stock. However, the firm cannot cause the warrants to be exercised. Thus, if the firm finances with warrants, it does not have the flexibility to eliminate debt and associated fixed charges.

Next it is assumed that the debentures are converted (balance sheet 3 and income statement 3), or alternatively that the warrants are exercised (balance sheet 4 and income statement 4). Therefore the new balance sheet, income statement, earning per share, and control position of Jorden are the following:

Convertibles:

A $1,000 debenture is convertible at $80. Therefore it is convertible into $1,000/80 = 12.5$ shares of common stock. 1,000 convertible debentures × 12.5 shares × $5 par value = $62,500 addition to common stock for value; funds raised of $1,000,000 − $62,500 = $937,500 addition to paid-in capital.

Conversion of Debentures
Balance Sheet 3

Notes payable—10%...............	$ 400,000
Other current debt.................	600,000
Long-term debt....................	1,000,000
Common stock—$5 par............	562,500
Paid-in capital....................	1,437,500
Retained earnings.................	1,000,000
Total Claims and Assets.....	$5,000,000

Income Statement 3

Earnings before interest and taxes..........		$1,000,000
Interest expense		
0.1 × 400,000.....................	$ 40,000	
0.1 × 1,000,000..................	100,000	140,000
Taxable income....................		$ 860,000
Federal income tax................		430,000
Net Income..................		$ 430,000

Earnings per share = 430,000/112,500 = $3.82

Warrants:

20 shares × 1,000 debentures = 20,000 new shares
20,000 shares × $5 par value = $100,000 addition to common stock par value
$75 option price × 20,000 new shares = $1,500,-000 funds raised
$1,500,000 − $100,000 = $1,400,000 addition to paid-in capital

Exercise of Warrants
Balance Sheet 4

Notes payable—10%...............	$ 400,000
Other current debt................	600,000
Debentures.......................	1,000,000
Long-term debt....................	1,000,000
Common stock—$5 par............	600,000
Paid-in capital....................	1,900,000
Retained earnings.................	1,000,000
Total Claims and Assets.....	$6,500,000

Income Statement 4

Earnings before interest and taxes............................		$1,300,000
0.1 × 400,000.....................	$ 40,000	
0.1 × 1,000,000..................	100,000	
0.07 × 1,000,000..................	70,000	$ 210,000
Taxable income....................		$1,090,000
Federal income tax................		545,000
Net Income..................		$ 545,000

Earnings per share = $545,000/120,000 = $4.54

Control Position of Jorden

Before financing, total common shares......................	100,000
Owned by Jorden 70% = 70,000..	
New shares if convertibles exercised....................	12,500
Total shares if convertibles exercised....................	112,500
Percent owned by Jorden...... $\frac{70,000}{112,500} = 62.2\%$	
New shares if warrants exercised....................	20,000
Total shares if warrants exercised....................	120,000
Percent owned by Jorden...... $\frac{70,000}{120,000} = 58.3\%$	

If common stock had been sold originally at $70 (slightly below its market at the time) to raise $1 million, the number of shares sold would have been 14,286. Jorden's ownership position would have been 70,000/114,286 = 61.2% (versus 62.2%). If enough common was sold at $70 to raise the $2,500,000 that was raised by debentures with warrants, the number of shares would have been 35,714. In this case Jorden's control position would have been: 70,000/135,714 = 51.6% (versus 58.3%). Thus Jorden's control position is somewhat better when the converts or warrants are used.

We are now in a position to appraise the comparative characteristics of the two alternatives. The convertibles would be employed under the following assumptions:

1. Debt ratios are already high.
2. A prospect of near-term prosperity, when converts sell well above par, offers the opportunity to force conversion into common. (Provides Jorden Company with discretion on timing of conversion.)
3. If the firm could raise additional new funds on terms equivalent or better than the increased amount of funds obtained under the debt-plus-warrants alternative.

The circumstances under which the warrants would be advantageous are the following:

1. The firm could use more debt.
2. The firm could utilize profitably the larger amounts of capital received when the warrants are exercised.
3. The uncertainty of adverse developments in

the economy and stock market make it uncertain that an opportunity will arise to force conversion of convertible debt, and the firm must be prepared to live with the additional debt raised.

In general, the control position of Jorden is best with converts, and the earnings per share are greater if warrants are used. Warrants give investors more flexibility, but provide the company with less flexibility. In general, warrants offer higher returns to the firm but involve greater risk—so again a return-risk trade-off comparison would be required for the final decision.

Is each of the following true or false?

_____ 1. If Jorden forces the conversion of its converts when the market price of the common stock is $97.50, many investors will accept the call and receive a 10 percent premium.

_____ 2. Jorden has the flexibility to force conversion with the debentures with warrants, but the premium is usually around 20 percent.

_____ 3. Financing of debentures with warrants rather than with convertibles generates $1,500,000 additional assets on which $300,000 additional earnings before interest and taxes are produced.

_____ 4. Debentures with warrants provide the greatest amount of funds and the greatest number of shares outstanding for Jorden. The dividend policy and cash flow projections also become important along with financial structure, earnings per share, and the control position of Jorden.

Now turn to Answer Frame 4[19], page 174, to check your answers.

chapter 20

MERGERS AND CONGLOMERATES

Frame 1[20]

Growth is vital to the well-being of a firm, for without it a business cannot attract able management by promotions and challenging creative activity. Mergers have played an important part in the growth of firms, so financial managers are required both to appraise the desirability of prospective mergers and to participate in evaluating the respective companies involved. In a sense, a merger is like any other investment decision—assets with potential earning capacity are ac-

Answer frame 4¹⁹

1. False. Most investors will convert to common stock since the conversion value is $1,218.75. Only $1,100 will be received if they accept the call.
2. False. Jorden cannot cause the warrants to be exercised—hence, it does not have the flexibility to eliminate debt and the associated fixed charges. Warrants could be given a limited life, and by setting the exercise price low enough, Jorden could be fairly certain of the warrant's timing. But the call provision on convertibles gives Jorden the most flexibility.
3. True. Actually, the comparison in earnings per share between the two alternative financing plans would be more valid if the total assets were of the same size. Thus, perhaps it would be reasonable to assume that Jorden could raise an additional $1,500,000 through a sale of other securities so that total assets would be the same for either method of financing.
4. True. If dividends are maintained at previous levels, the total cash outflow will be greater under debentures with warrants than with convertibles. The bond interest will be paid in addition to dividends on an increased number of shares of common stock outstanding after the warrants are exercised to buy common stock.

If you missed any of the above, reread Frame 4¹⁹ before beginning Chapter 20, page 173.

Frame 1²⁰ continued

quired. From this point of view, the merger decision should be analyzed in a capital budgeting framework: The acquisition should be made if it increases the acquiring firm's net present value as reflected in the price of its common stock.

HOLDING COMPANIES

In a merger, one or more firms may disappear. An alternative, however, is for one firm to buy all or a majority of the common stock of another and to run the acquired firm as an operating subsidiary. When this occurs, the acquiring firm is said to be a holding company. A number of advantages arise when the holding company form is used. (1) It may be possible to control the acquired firm with a smaller investment than would be necessary if a merger were to occur. (2) Each firm in a holding company is a separate legal entity, so the obligations of any one unit are separate from the obligations of the other units. (3) Stockholder approval is required before a merger can take place, but not necessary to establish a holding company relation. There are also some disadvantages to holding companies. (1) Some multiple taxation is likely to occur at the different layers of firms. (2) Holding companies can employ debt at each stage so that the mul-

tiple leverage effects subject them to the increased risks of amplifying any earnings fluctuations of its operating companies.

A variant on the holding company arrangement is the use of *financial groups*, an important source of financing in developing countries. Built around a nucleus of a commercial bank or an industrial finance company, several enterprises carry on a variety of activities. These activities do not represent a formal conglomerate firm as has developed in the United States in the 1960s. Nor do they represent a formal holding company relationship. Rather the group is held together primarily by personal and financial ties. The coordinating device seems to be effective interaction among the financial principals involved.

FINANCIAL ACCOUNTING FOR MERGERS

A merger may be treated as either a purchase or a pooling of interest. In a *purchase*, a larger firm generally takes over a smaller one and assumes all management control. The amount actually paid for the smaller firm is reflected in the acquiring firm's balance sheet. If more is paid for the acquired firm than the fair (market) value of its net assets, a goodwill account is created to make up the difference and is reflected in the acquiring firm's financial statements. Goodwill should be amortized by systematic charges to income over the periods estimated to be benefited, but the period of amortization cannot exceed 40 years.

In a *pooling of interests*, the merged firms generally are about the same size, both managements should carry on important functions after the merger, and common stock rather than cash or bonds should be used in payment. (For a full description of the necessary criteria see Ac-

counting Principles Board Opinion No. 16, *Business Combinations*, August 1970, published by the American Institute of Certified Public Accountants.) The total assets of the surviving firm in a pooling are equal to the sum of the assets of the two independent companies, so no goodwill is created. The difference between the purchase price and the book value of net worth acquired is reflected in adjustments to the capital accounts of the newly created firm.

Indicate whether each of the following statements is true or false by writing "T" or "F" in the space provided.

————— 1. Mergers can be the quickest way of achieving a desired growth rate by a firm and are properly analyzed in a capital budgeting framework.

————— 2. By employing the holding company concept, it is possible to obtain control of another firm with a smaller investment than would be necessary for a merger.

————— 3. In a merger that is treated as a purchase, a goodwill account is created to reflect the difference in value between the large firm and the small firm.

————— 4. In a merger that is treated as a pooling of interests, the goodwill account is usually very small since the merged firms are of approximately the same size.

Now turn to Answer Frame 1²⁰, page 176, to check your answers.

Frame 2²⁰

VALUATION IN MERGERS

In a merger, the value of each entity must be established to arrive at merger terms. The greatest weight in arriving at valuations in mergers is accorded earnings: the past earnings patterns, the expected future earnings, and the potential contributions of each entity in the merger to the rate of future earnings growth of the surviving firm. Current market prices are the second most important determinant of prices in mergers. Depending on whether or not asset values are indicative of the earning power of the merged firm, book values also may exert an influence on the terms of the mergers. Net current assets, an indication of the amount of liquidity being purchased in a merger, may be accorded some weight if important to the merged firm. These are all quantitative factors.

But qualitative, less measurable, factors are sometimes the overriding determinants of merger terms. The qualitative factors include (1) the respective research and development capabilities of the companies; (2) the quality and breadth of management experience; (3) the extent to which each of the firms has management capabilities in the specific management functions, such as manufacturing, marketing, and personnel; (4) the respective capabilities in the more general management functions of financial planning and control, research staffs, legal staffs, advertising and marketing staffs; and (5) the degree to which one firm's capabilities or operations complements the capabilities and operations of the other firm. One firm may be strong in research, the other in marketing; a merger may be the least expensive method of adding the required capability. Or firm A may be

Answer frame 1[20]

1. True. It is much faster to buy an existing firm in an existing industry than it is to start from scratch to build a plant, product, customers, and so on. A capital budgeting framework should be used.
2. True. This is one of the primary advantages of a holding company. It is possible to pyramid a series of holding companies to obtain maximum leverage with a minimum investment. For example, holding company X may own 20 percent of holding companies Q, R, and S, which own 20 percent in nine subsidiaries. (Assume that 20 percent ownership represents controlling interest.) Hence, for every dollar of capital in each of the subsidiaries, company X controls them with an investment of $.36 or 4 percent of the total capital of the nine subsidiaries.
3. False. Goodwill is the difference between the market price paid and the fair market value of the net assets of the acquired firm.
4. False. Goodwill is nonexistent in a pooling of interests. The total assets at book value of the acquired firm are added to the assets of the acquiring firm.

If you missed any of the above, reread Frame 1[20] before starting Frame 2[20], page 175.

Frame 2[20] continued

strong in all areas but have some capacities not fully utilized, yet not posessed by firm B; a merger may enable firm A to achieve economies of scale not otherwise attainable or attainable only after the long period required to increase its sales substantially. Or two firms may each have volume sufficient only for one-shift operations; a merger would make two-shift operations possible, permitting the sale of excess facilities. Such complementarities may make possible economies through cost savings or revenue increases, making synergy (the $2 + 2 = 5$ effect) a potentiality. Opportunities for synergy are represented by complementarities, possible economies of scale, and reenforcement of capabilities of the type described by the examples.

A consideration of the quantitative and the qualitative factors may produce merger terms representing unequal price-earnings ratios for the firms involved. The consequences are illustrated by a case example. Table 20–1 sets forth the basic facts for two companies. Firm A acquires firm B

with the stockholders of A and B receiving shares on the basis of their respective market prices before the merger. Thus shareholders of the B company receive two thirds share of A for each share of B stock held. Assuming no immediate increase in earnings, the effects on earnings per share are shown in the tabulation in Table 20–2.

Thus, on the basis of the old shares held, the earnings per share will decrease by 40 cents per share for the B shareholders; but will increase by 40 cents per share for the A shareholders. The example illustrates how firms could increase their growth in earnings per share by acquiring firms with lower price-earnings ratios. The results are also summarized in Table 20–4 below, which is designed for utilization in subsequent examples. The precise effects on market value are less certain, depending upon whether A's or B's price-earnings ratio will prevail after the merger, but A's stock prices are likely to increase because of the apparent 20 percent growth in its earnings per share.

TABLE 20–1

	Company A	Company B Case I	Company B Case II
Total earnings...	$30,000	$30,000	$1,000
Number of shares of common stock.....................	15,000	15,000	500
Earnings per share of stock.............................	$ 2.00	$ 2.00	$ 2.00
Price-earnings ratio per share..........................	15X	10X	30X
Market price per share.................................	$ 30.00	$ 20.00	$60.00

TABLE 20–2

Stockholders	Shares of Company A owned after merger	Earnings before merger		After merger	
		Total	Per share	Per new shares	Per old shares
A..................... 15,000		$30,000	$2	$2.40	$2.40
B (Case I)............. 10,000		30,000	$2	$2.40	$1.60
Total............ 25,000		$60,000			

Label each of the following statements as true or false.

_____ 1. Some of the most important variables in arriving at quantitative valuations in mergers are past earnings, expected future earnings, and the contribution of the future growth to the surviving firm.

_____ 2. One of the most important qualitative consideration in a merger is the appraisal of management personnel in the firm to be acquired.

_____ 3. The combination of two firms may generate more total earnings than could be obtained by the individual firms operating as separate entities, but it may also result in combined earnings that are less than the sum of the individual components.

_____ 4. The acquiring firms can increase their growth in earnings per share by buying firms with lower price earnings ratios.

Now turn to Answer Frame 2²⁰, page 178, to check your answers.

Frame 3²⁰

The earnings per share increase for A will not necessarily be offset by the earnings decrease per share for B. This particular result followed because the respective sizes, as measured by the total earnings of the two companies, were the same. The effect of size on earnings accretion and dilution can be illustrated by assuming that company B's earnings were $1,000 with 500 shares of common stock outstanding as shown in Table 20–1, Case II. The new results would be as shown in Table 20–3.

These results are summarized in Table 20–4,

under the column Case II, in a form to facilitate comparisons with the effects of other sets of circumstances. Since the B shareholders received two shares for each share they currently hold, the total number of shares outstanding becomes 16,000. The earnings per share on the new shares would, therefore, be $1.94. To the B shareholders, this would represent $3.88 per old share that they had held. Thus, with unequal sizes, the earnings appreciation and earnings dilution will not be equal and offsetting on a per share basis. For the A shareholders the earnings dilution is $.06 per

TABLE 20–3

Shareholders	Shares of Company A owned after merger	Earnings before merger		After merger	
		Total	Per share	Per new share	Per old share
A..................... 15,000		$30,000	$2	$1.94	$1.94
B (Case II)............. 1,000		1,000	2	1.94	$3.88
Total................ 16,000		$31,000			

Answer frame 2²⁰

1. True. There may be unique situations where a tax benefit, unusual net asset value, or some other aspect of an acquired firm may dominate, but not in the typical merger.
2. True. In fact, this element may dominate all quantitative analysis. The management of the acquired firm may be strong in research, marketing, production, or some other aspect; and to hire this talent may not be possible except by acquiring a company.
3. True. The result depends on whether synergy takes place or does not. In cases where it does not, the acquiring firm may have been misled by practices that had temporarily inflated the acquired firm's earnings before the merger. Also, difficulties may arise from attempting to coordinate different management policies and styles.
4. True. The example illustrated in Table 20–2 represents such a situation and shows that the new firm's earnings per share growth is an apparent 20 percent.

If you missed any of the above, restudy Frame 2²⁰ before starting Frame 3²⁰, page 177.

Frame 3²⁰ continued

TABLE 20–4
Calculation of new earnings per share

	Case I	Case II	Case III	Case IV	Case V
Combined EBIT	$120,000	$62,000	$120,000	$120,000	$180,000
Interest on bonds of A (5% × $540,000)	—	—	27,000	—	—
Earnings before income taxes	$120,000	$62,000	$ 93,000	$120,000	$180,000
Income taxes at 50%	60,000	31,000	46,500	60,000	90,000
Earnings after tax	$ 60,000	$31,000	$ 46,500	$ 60,000	$ 90,000
Number of shares of common stock	25,000	16,000	15,000	15,000	18,000
EPS, before merger A, B	$2.00	$2.00	$2.00	$2.00	$2.00
EPS, new shares, A	2.40	1.94	—	—	5.00
EPS, new shares, B	2.40	1.94	3.10	4.00	5.00
EPS, per old shares, A	2.40	1.94	1.80	—	5.00
EPS, per old shares, B	1.60	3.88	3.10	4.00	5.00

share, for the B shareholders there is an accretion of $1.88. This example of unequal sizes indicates how a firm with a low price-earnings ratio could develop a strategy for making initial acquisitions by buying smaller firms in glamour industries with high price-earnings ratios. Their hope would be that at some point the financial community would view Company A as a glamour stock and attach a higher price-earnings ratio to the combined earnings of company A (the acquirer) and the smaller companies merged into its operations.

But more generally, in recent years the aggressive acquiring firm had a higher price-earnings ratio than the firm it acquired. If it started with a lower price-earnings ratio, it could increase its earnings per share growth by merger in order to

be able subsequently to have a higher price-earnings ratio than the companies it acquires. Hence we next illustrate how firm B in Case I, the lower price-earnings ratio company, would increase its earnings per share growth by use of other financial strategems.

In Table 20–4, Case III, B acquires A by paying 5 percent convertible bonds in an amount representing the present market value of A's stock of $450,000 plus a 20 percent premium to total $540,000. The effect on earnings per share is shown in the Case III column. The combined EBIT is $120,000, the same as in Case I. The interest on the bonds to the A shareholders is $27,000. Earnings after taxes are $46,500. The number of shares remains unchanged at 15,000, so the earnings per share for the B shareholders becomes $3.10. The $27,000 interest paid represents an equivalent of $1.80 for each of the old shares of Company A, only slightly below the previous $2.00. But firm B's earnings per share have increased to $3.10, an increase of 55 percent. With such growth in earnings per share, the price of its stock will rise, after which the convertible bonds paid to the old A shareholders could profitably be converted into firm B's common stock.

Another practice used by aggressive conglomerate firms in recent years is illustrated in Case IV. In this instance B buys A by paying convertible preferred stock, paying a 5 percent stock dividend in its own common stock annually, beginning one year later. We may analyze the immediate effect of this acquisition in Table 20–4. Since no cash outlay will be involved in this instance, there is no interest deduction and the number of B shares remains unchanged. The new earnings per share for the B shareholders rises to $4.00.

In Case V, the Case IV situation is examined four years later. At that time the shares of common stock have increased by 20 percent (simple basis) of 15,000 shares so that 18,000 are now outstanding. However, during the four-year period of time it can reasonably be assumed that the company's earnings also would have grown. If the earnings of the company have grown at a 5 percent simple basis, or by 20 percent over a four-year period of time, the earnings per share of the B shareholders will remain constant at $4.00. Therefore, to continue future growth in earnings per share in Case V would require that the growth rate of earnings be greater than 20 percent over the four-year period.

If the growth rate in earnings over the four-year period were a 9 percent compound annual rate (this represents a doubling in eight years), this would be a 50 percent growth in four years. The combined EBIT would, therefore, be $180,000 and the earnings after tax would be $90,000. The new earnings per share would be $5 (of course, at this point the shares of stock received by the A shareholders would also be earning $5 per share). For earnings per share for the B shareholders to have increased from $4 to $5 in four years (an increase of 25 percent), an increase in overall earnings of 50 percent was required. Thus, to achieve continued growth in earnings per share subsequent to transactions such as Case IV necessitated a substantial improvement in the underlying earnings ability of the conglomerate firm. This suggests the requirements for the success of mergers from a business standpoint.

True or false?

_____ 1. An acquiring firm with a low price-earnings ratio could buy smaller firms that had high price-earnings ratios with the hope that the marketplace would attach a higher price-earnings ratio to the combined surviving company.

_____ 2. Case III in Table 20–4 illustrates how an acquiring firm with a low price-earnings ratio can purchase another firm with a high price-earnings ratio with convertible bonds—resulting in about the same income to the shareholders of the acquired firm as well as increased earnings per share for the acquiring firm.

_____ 3. Case IV and Case V as shown in Table 20–4 illustrate how the use of convertible preferred stock with a 5 percent stock dividend produces superior earnings when compared to Case I, Case II, and Case III. Thus, convertible preferred stock is the preferable means of merger financing.

_____ 4. To achieve continued growth in earnings per share a vigorous acquisition program is recommended.

Now turn to Answer Frame 3²⁰, page 180, to check your answers.

Answer frame 3[20]

1. True. This would be a strategy to try to raise the combined earnings growth so that the marketplace would increase the company's price-earnings ratio.
2. True. But you must recognize that financial risk is greater with the introduction of the convertible debt. It is true that growth in earnings per share is enhanced, but the new surviving firm must continue this growth pattern in earnings per share in order for the market price appreciation of the common stock to continue.
3. False. These cases are independent illustrations designed to show practices used by aggressive conglomerates, and are not designed to be a comparative analysis. Differing time periods, financial risks, sizes, and so on are just a few of the variables that make comparative results across these cases invalid.
4. False. Many aggressive firms do enhance growth in earnings per share, but long-term growth in earnings must come from the underlying earnings ability of each of the firms involved in the conglomerate firm.

If you missed any of the above, reread Frame 3[20] before beginning Frame 4[20] below.

Frame 4[20]

REQUIREMENTS FOR SUCCESSFUL MERGERS

During the height of conglomerate merger activity in the 1960s, with a rising stock market and with emphasis by investors on growth in earnings per share, many mergers were motivated by financial factors. As illustrated above, companies with a high price-earnings ratio could engage in self-levitation of earnings growth by merging with companies with a lower price-earnings ratio. While some conglomerate firms had a solid conceptual basis and were well managed, others emphasized financial devices. Pooling of interests accounting could be used almost without restrictions—in addition to earnings growth by playing the differential price-earnings ratio game, firm A could buy firm B at a market value of $10 million, record its book value of $6 million in its accounting records as a pooling, then sell the assets of firm B at $9 million, recording $3 million (selling price less recorded book value) as a gain included in reported earnings per share. A number of such financial conglomerates suffered great declines in earnings and market value when they could no longer continue their merger activity.

From a business standpoint, the basic requirements for the success of mergers are that they fit into a soundly conceived long-range company plan and that the quality of the managerial organization created is such that the resulting firm will have greater efficiency than attainable by the previously independent entities. Indeed, the timing of the conglomerate merger movement can at least partially be explained by the acceleration of changes in managerial technology that occurred after the mid-1950s. Enterprise planning began to develop and advances in computer technology began to be adapted to business management. Financial planning and control systems were extended with further improvements in the use of balanced centralized-decentralized management control systems. Further, World War II and the Korean conflict stimulated new technologies, resulting in an uneven diffusion and wide variations in advanced technological capabilities among firms. The major conceptual point emphasized here is that the role of the general management functions (planning, control, organizing, information systems) and functions centralized at top management levels, (research, finance, legal) increased in importance and effectiveness in the management of business firms. In consequence, the potential economies in performing general management functions in large, diversified firms were substantially increased relative to operating economies. This is the broader theoretical basis explaining the ability of the conglomerate firms as a group to raise their average (actual) returns on economic resources during the decade of the 1960s.

Mergers without synergy cannot provide permanent gains to investors. While some potentials for synergy appear to be present, conglomerate mergers in the United States during the 1960s were stimulated by diverse motives. Whether synergy can in fact be achieved in a particular merger depends upon the characteristics of the merging firms and the quality of managerial abilities achieved in seeking to realize whatever potentials for synergy that may be present.

SELLER MOTIVATIONS AND TENDER OFFERS

To this point the presentation has been primarily from the standpoint of acquiring firms. But the viewpoint of the seller also needs to be taken into account. Why are firms sometimes sellers? A number of factors may lead the acquired firm to take the initiative in selling to another firm.

Small- and medium-sized firms may reach a stage when a broader range of capabilities is required. Often the initial thrust of a firm comes from an individual entrepreneur who has strength in one or two specific management functions. His capability may be in research, manufacturing, marketing, or finance. In the early stages of a rapidly growing industry, a firm may achieve successful performance with strength in one of these areas. But at some stage in industry development and at some firm size, a broader range of management competence becomes necessary.

The firm may add such capabilities by hiring executives. But it takes time and skill to build a strong organization, so the owners may be interested in selling to a larger firm that already has a broad range of management expertise. Or sometimes, small- and medium-sized firms will join together to complement their specific abilities. The desire to sell out may also be influenced by recognition that the industry growth rate is slowing down and that the potentials for maintaining the high rate of growth for the individual firm have substantially diminished.

Is each of the following true or false?

_____ 1. The basic requirement for the success of a merger is a soundly conceived long-range plan with a managerial organization that will achieve greater efficiency than attainable by the previously independent entities.

_____ 2. The conglomerate merger movement in the last decade can be partially explained by the application of computer technology to the management functions of the firm.

_____ 3. Synergy must be present before investors are able to achieve any permanent gains.

_____ 4. Small- and medium-sized firms usually possess strength in one or a few specific management functions. A merger may be the way for a company to gain strength in other areas of management in order to continue its rapid growth rate.

Now turn to Answer Frame 4[20], page 182, to check your answers.

Frame 5[20]

A combination of factors may be involved in the decision to sell. The firm recognizes that it needs a broader range of management capabilities; its perceived growth opportunities are diminishing; and to achieve some growth momentum, the amount of financing required might dilute the control position of the owners and jeopardize the wealth position already achieved. In addition, there may be much doubt about the availability of the requisite additional financing.

These considerations may be reinforced by related financial and tax considerations. If the firm can be sold at 10 times earnings or more, the uncertainty of future earnings is thereby eliminated:

Answer frame 4²⁰

1. True. Preoccupation with short-term growth in earnings per share will not achieve long-term maximization of shareholder wealth. Conglomerate firms must have a solid conceptual basis and be well managed.
2. True. Because of computer technology and accelerated advances in managerial technology, the ability of the conglomerate firms to increase their actual returns on economic resources was enhanced.
3. True. Opportunities for synergy are represented by complementarities, possible economies of scale, and reinforcement of capabilities of either or both of the merged firms.
4. True. Small- and medium-sized firms do join together and with larger firms to complement their specific abilities. There seems to be a size beyond which a broader range of management competence becomes necessary.

If you missed any of the above, reread Frame 4²⁰ before beginning Frame 5²⁰, page 181.

Frame 5²⁰ continued

the owner-seller has locked up 10 or more years of future earnings. In addition, he has converted what would be ordinary income into capital gains, which are subject to lower tax rates. Furthermore, if the firm has been privately held, there are uncertainties in connection with inheritance and estate taxes such as the value the Internal Revenue Service will place upon the ownership of the firm. This problem can be removed by selling the firm to one with publicly traded stock. Also, the necessary liquidity to meet inheritance tax payments is provided by publicly traded shares of stock.

The foregoing are a sample of the circumstances under which the owner of a firm may be favorably disposed toward being acquired. There are also some reasons the owner may not wish to sell out. The owner may value his entrepreneurial freedom. The acquiring firm may require that his operations fit into the general pattern of the larger firm so that the owner-manager must change his previous style of operations. He may recognize that such a change would have unfavorable effects on sales and profits. In addition, the owner-manager may judge that the freedom and flexibility to pursue new opportunities will be diminished with unfavorable effects upon performance. For these reasons, the owner-manager may judge that he will achieve a greater flow of profits and a greater increase in wealth if he continues to conduct his operations independently.

Most acquisitions of small- and medium-sized firms are made with the acquiescence, indeed enthusiasm and initiative, of the owner-manager. Such acquisition and sales activity represents the effective operations of the market for capital assets. On the other hand, if a firm wishes to avoid being acquired, and if it hopes to successfully withstand an involuntary take-over, it should avoid the circumstances under which it becomes vulnerable. A tender offer is when Firm A makes an appeal directly to the shareholders of Firm B inviting them to sell, or tender, their shares at a firm price usually somewhat above the existing market level for a specified period of time. A brief check list of factors that make a firm vulnerable to a tender offer include the following:

1. A small fraction of ownership by management.
2. A growth rate smaller than that of the product-market.
3. A growth in earnings per share lower than that for the industry.
4. A reduction in recent dividend payments.
5. A return on net worth lower than that of the industry average.
6. A market value below book value; further aggravated if book value is below realizable or liquidating value.
7. A strong working capital and liquidity position.
8. Relatively free of debt.

If a number of the above conditions exist, the firm is particularly vulnerable to being acquired involuntarily. Such a situation may offer opportunities for both "asset and management redeployment" to the profit of the acquiring firm.

True or false?

_____ 1. A strong motivation for an individual entrepreneur to sell to a large firm is the possibility of immediately obtaining future earnings which would be taxed at the capital gains rate.

_____ 2. Inheritance taxes and estate planning problems are also important motivations for a privately held firm to sell out to a publicly held firm.

_____ 3. The owner-manager will usually have more freedom and flexibility if he joins with a larger firm with greater resources.

_____ 4. If a firm wishes to avoid a take-over it should attempt to reduce growth in earnings per share below that for the industry so that the firm will be unattractive.

Now turn to Answer Frame 5²⁰, page 184, to check your answers.

Answer frame 5²⁰

1. True. If the firm can be sold at 10 times earnings or more, the uncertainty of future earnings is eliminated. Thus, a capital gains tax on the immediate gain is taken rather than the higher ordinary income tax rate on the future yearly earnings.
2. True. It is very difficult to attach a valuation on a nonlisted, privately held stock. Indeed, the market valuation established and the marketability of a publicly held stock is very important in estate settlements.
3. False. Typically, the owner-manager must fit into the mold as cast by the acquiring firm. Particularly, the financial functions will no longer be performed by the owner-manager and the entity must be operated consistent with the financial planning and control system of the acquiring firm.
4. False. To reduce the vulnerability to a tender offer, an important factor is to perform well in relation to the goal of the firm—to maximize shareholder wealth. Thus, a fine growth rate in earnings per share is probably the best way to please your stockholders and thereby convince them to stick with the present management.

If you missed any of the above, restudy Frame 5²⁰ before beginning Chapter 21 below.

chapter 21

REORGANIZATION AND BANKRUPTCY

Frame 1²¹

The major cause of failure is incompetent management which, in a high percentage of cases, results from lack of proper training and experience for the line of business. Technical insolvency occurs when a firm cannot meet its current obligations as they come due even though its total assets may be in excess of its total liabilities. A firm is a failure in a bankrupt sense if its total liabilities exceed a fair valuation of its total assets, indicating that the net worth position of the firm has become negative. Bankruptcy is also the term used in a legal sense to describe the procedures for the liquidation of a firm. But even though a firm may be insolvent in a bankrupt sense, it may be reorganized and rehabilitated rather than liquidated.

If failure has occurred, a number of remedies are open to the interested parties. The quality of management must be improved, the policies of the firm must be changed, and perhaps the firm's product-market emphasis must be altered. Frequently when a firm is facing difficulties, the remedy proposed is to inject more money into the firm. But financial difficulties are likely to be a consequence of the disease rather than a cause of the firm's problems. However, sometimes when a firm is having difficulties, time and money are critical factors in enabling conditions to be corrected.

The first question to be answered when a firm encounters financial difficulties is whether the firm is better off alive or dead—whether it should be rehabilitated or whether it should be liquidated. The critical test is whether greater value could be realized by selling the firm's assets before further deterioration takes place, as compared with what would be obtained in rehabilitation and continued operations.

INFORMAL ADJUSTMENT ARRANGEMENTS

In general, reorganization represents procedures for rehabilitating the firm, while bankruptcy represents procedures for liquidating the firm. Under reorganization there are both informal and formal procedures. The informal procedures used in reorganization are (1) *extension*, which postpones the date for required payment of obligations, and (2) *composition*, which reduces the amount owed to creditors. Both represent voluntary concessions made by creditors when the debtor appears to be a good moral risk and has indicated ability to make a recovery in the future.

To illustrate reorganization and bankruptcy, a specific case analysis is presented. Procedures will be illustrated under the assumptions that would result in (1) informal reorganization, (2) formal reorganization, and (3) alternative assumptions that would call for bankruptcy.

Table 21–1 sets forth the balance sheet for the Failow Company before financial readjustment and after an informal financial readjustment. Table 21–2 sets forth a partial income statement for the Failow Company under similar alternative circumstances.

Before financial readjustment, the Failow Company earns $3.1 million before depreciation, interest, and taxes. Depreciation is 5 percent of

the gross value of plant and equipment of $40 million, or $2 million. EBIT is $1.1 million. The interest expense is shown in Table 21–1.

Hence, the earnings before taxes before financial readjustment represent a loss of $.9 million. It is assumed that the firm has been suffering losses for a long period of time so that there are no longer any tax credits from previous profits to include in the current income statement. The firm has a small number of supplier firms which hold most obligations due to trade creditors. After meeting with the two banks which have been lenders to Failow and with the four insurance companies which own all of the 8 percent subordinated debentures, all parties agree on a financial readjustment plan for Failow.

Inventories are written down by $6 million, and fixed assets are written down by $10 million. With a $16 million write-off, total assets become $14 million, as shown in Table 21–1. The banks agree to forgo interest on the notes payable loans for five years as a part of their contribution to the hoped-for work-out plans and to receive 20 percent of the firm's cash flow in loan repayments beginning in the sixth year. In return for their claims, the subordinated debenture holders and the trade creditors are each given 500,000 shares of stock. Thus, they own shares of stock approximately equal in total to those held by the existing stockholders before financial readjustment. The total liabilities and capital therefore become $14 million, equal to total assets as shown in the balance sheet in Table 21–1.

The income statement after readjustment is shown in Table 21–2. For the first five years, depreciation expense is reduced to $1.5 million, and interest expense is the $.3 million due on the mortgage bonds. Hence, the Failow Company will be earning $1.3 million per year during the first five years. Earnings per share would be $.65 per share for the first five years.

Thus, by the write-down of the depreciable fixed assets, and by changing the nature of some of the liability claims into equity claims, the Failow Company has been turned from an unprofitable company into a profitable one. The expectation is, of course, that the previous management errors still must be corrected so that the underlying earning power of Failow will also be improved. If improvement occurs, potentially the

TABLE 21-1

FAILOW COMPANY
Balance Sheet
March 31, 1981
(in $ millions)

	Before financial readjustment		After financial readjustment	
Current assets..	$12		$ 6	
Net property...	18		8	
Total assets.....................................		$30		$14
Accounts payable....................................	$ 5		$—	
Taxes..	1		1	
Notes payable to banks at 8%.......................	5		5	
Notes payable to trade creditors at 10%.............	5		—	
Accrued Wages.......................................	1		1	
Total current liabilities......................		$17		$ 7
6% first mortgage bonds, due 1990....................	$ 5		$ 5	
8% subordinated debentures, due 1990.................	10		—	
Total long-term debt............................		15		5
Common stock ($1 par)...............................	$ 1		$ 2	
Paid-in capital......................................	4		—	
Earned surplus.......................................	(7)		—	
Net worth......................................		(2)		2
Total liabilities and capital..................		$30		$14

Memo:
Notes payable to banks...................................	$ .4 million	—
Notes payable to trade....................................	.5	—
First mortgage bonds......................................	.3	.3
Subordinated debentures...................................	.8	—
Total interest expense.............................	$2.0 million	$.3 million

TABLE 21-2

FAILOW COMPANY
Partial Income Statement
Year ended March 31, 1981
(Income statement items in $ millions;
memo items as shown)

	Before financial readjustment	After financial readjustment
Earnings before depreciation, interest and taxes........	$ 3.1	$3.1
Depreciation (5% of $40)................................	2.0 (5% of $30)	1.5
EBIT...	$ 1.1	$1.6
Interest expense..	2.0	.3
Earnings before taxes...................................	$(0.9)	$1.3
Taxes..	—	—
Earnings after tax......................................	$(0.9)	$1.3
Memo:		
Number of shares....................................	1 million	2 million
Earnings per share..................................	($.90) per share	$.65 per share

earnings per share could result in marked improvement in the value of its common stock. This would enable the trade creditors and the former subordinated debenture holders to realize, in the form of the market value of their common stock holdings, amounts greater than they could have achieved under alternative actions that might have been taken. For example, if the company had been forced into bankruptcy, the trade creditors and subordinated debenture holders as general creditors might have received at most 15 to 20 cents on the dollar, or $2 to $3 million. If the market value of the common stock sells at 10 times earnings, the market value of their stock will be $6.5 million. If the earning power of the company is further rehabilitated, the market value of their equity holdings might even exceed the dollar amount of their original debt claims.

Indicate whether each of the following statements is true or false by writing "T" or "F" in the space provided.

_____ 1. Technical insolvency occurs only when total liabilities exceed total assets.

_____ 2. When a firm encounters financial difficulties it should be liquidated.

_____ 3. Extension and composition are informal procedures used in reorganization.

_____ 4. In the Failow Company illustration, the creditors could eventually recover an amount even greater than the original amount of debt.

Now turn to Answer Frame 1²¹ on page 188 to check your responses.

Frame 2²¹

REORGANIZATION

If voluntary settlement through extension or composition is not possible, the matter is thrown into the courts. If the court decides on reorganization rather than liquidation it will appoint a trustee to (1) control the firm while it is going through reorganization and (2) prepare a formal plan for reorganization. The plan must meet the standards of fairness to all parties, and of feasibility in the sense that the reorganized enterprise will have a reasonable probability of being able to meet its future obligations. If the dollar amounts involved are large, the plan is reviewed by the Securities and Exchange Commission which provides an advisory opinion on the plan.

In the somewhat more formal reorganization procedure, the company first files a petition for reorganization with the federal court. The court, in accordance with the law, appoints a disinterested trustee. Subsequently, the trustee files a plan of reorganization with the court which obtains an advisory opinion from the Securities and Exchange Commission. In the Failow case referred to above, the trustee found that the company could not be rehabilitated by management changes, so concluded that the only feasible program would be to combine Failow with Successow, an established producer of a similar line of product whose characteristics would make the combination of the operations more efficient.

Successow then made a formal proposal: (1) to assume the obligations for the 6 percent first-mortgage bonds of Failow, (2) to pay its $1 million back wages and $1 million back taxes, and, in addition, (3) to offer 200,000 shares of Successow common stock, which had a current market value of $5.00 per share. Thus, Successow offered an amount equivalent to the following:

Mortgage bond obligation.........	$5,000,000
Payment of wages................	1,000,000
Payment of taxes.................	1,000,000
Value of common shares.........	1,000,000
Total.......................	$8,000,000

The trustee's plan allocated the claims of the unsecured creditors as set forth in Table 21–3. The Securities and Exchange Commission made an evaluation of the proposal from the standpoint of fairness. On the basis of estimates set forth in Table 21–4, the SEC arrived at an evaluation of net value. First, sales estimates based on the underlying properties of the Failow Company were made. These ranged from $18 to $20 million. The earning power of companies in this line of business is 4 to 5 percent of sales. Applying the 4 percent to the $18 million of sales gives an earnings estimate of $720,000; applying the 5 percent estimate to $20 million of sales gives earnings of $1 million. It was agreed that an eight times price-earnings ratio was reasonable. Utilizing the eight times price-earnings ratio, they arrived at a total value less the $7 million mortgage assumed

Answer frame 1²¹

1. False. It occurs when a firm cannot meet its current obligations as they come due even when its total assets may be in excess of its total liabilities.
2. False. In some cases it should be rehabilitated and in others it should be liquidated. It all depends on which action will lead to greater value.
3. True. Extension postpones the date for required payment of obligations. Composition reduces the amount owed to creditors. Both are informal procedures used in reorganization.
4. True. The market value of their new equity holdings could eventually exceed the dollar amount of their original debt claims.

If you missed any of the above, you should restudy Frame 1²¹ before turning to Frame 2²¹ on page 187.

Frame 2²¹ continued

TABLE 21–3
Trustee's plan for Failow Company

Prior claims	Amount	Receives
1. Wages..	$1,000,000	Cash paid by Successow
2. Taxes...	1,000,000	Cash paid by Successow
3. First mortgage, 6%, 1990.........................	5,000,000	Assumed by Successow
	$7,000,000	

Remainder of Claims	Amount	4 percent × amount of claim	Claim after subordination	Number of shares of common stock
1. Notes payable to banks..........................	$ 5,000,000	$ 200,000	$ 600,000	120,000
2. Notes payable to trade..........................	5,000,000	200,000	200,000	40,000
3. General unsecured creditors.....................	5,000,000	200,000	200,000	40,000
4. Subordinated debentures........................	10,000,000	400,000	0	0
	$25,000,000	$1,000,000*	$1,000,000	200,000

* Valuation based on 200,000 shares at $5 equals $1 million, or 4% of $25 million liabilities.

plus the cash paid ranging from a negative $1.24 million to a positive $1 million. Thus, the amount paid by Successow is at the high end of the range of the indicated value of the Failow Company. The SEC therefore recommended the approval of the trustee's plan for reorganization as meeting the test of fairness.

LIQUIDATION

The analysis in Table 21–4 provides a basis for moving to the analysis of bankruptcy and liquidation. Suppose that an analysis of the liquidating values of the Failow Company indicated that the amount that could be realized would be $10 million. Therefore, if $10 million could be realized

on liquidation, it would be preferable to liquidate the company if reorganization would yield a value of only $6 to 8 million as indicated in Table 21–4.

If liquidation is decided upon, again two alternative procedures are available. Assignment is a liquidation procedure that can be used to achieve full settlement of claims but does not require going through the courts. The common law provides for an assignment whereby a debtor transfers title of the assets to a third person known as an assignee or trustee. The trustee liquidates the assets and distributes the proceeds among the creditors on a pro rata basis. The creditors then sign a release for the debtor from all his unpaid obligations.

However, more formal procedures may also be

TABLE 21–4
Failow Company,
SEC evaluation of fairness

Valuation	
Estimated sales of Failow Company properties....................	$18,000,000 –$20,000,000 per year
Earnings at 4% to 5% of sales......................................	720,000 – 1,000,000
Price earnings ratio of 8 times earnings..........................	5,760,000 – 8,000,000
Cash paid and mortgage assumed..............................	7,000,000 – 7,000,000
Net value...	($ 1,240,000)–$ 1,000,000

involved in bankruptcy. A voluntary petition of bankruptcy may be filed by the debtor. But if the creditors wish to file an involuntary petition of bankruptcy, three conditions must be met:

1. The total debts must be $1,000 or more.
2. The creditors filing must be owed $500 or more.
3. Within the four preceding months the debtor must have committed one or more of the six acts of bankruptcy.

The six acts of bankruptcy are: (1) the debtor conceals, or fraudulently conveys assets; (2) the debtor gives preferential transfer of assets to one or more creditors; (3) the insolvent debtor permits any creditor to obtain a lien or to seize property that has been pledged as security; (4) the debtor makes a general assignment; (5) the insolvent debtor permits the appointment of a receiver or trustee; (6) the debtor admits in writing the inability to pay debts and the willingness to be judged bankrupt.

If the court determines that the debtor is in fact bankrupt, the case is transferred by the court to a referee in bankruptcy. This referee is a lawyer apointed for a specified period of time by the judge of the bankruptcy court to act in his or her place after the adjudication or determination of bankruptcy has been made by the court. In addition, on petition of the creditors, the referee in voluntary proceedings, or the judge in involuntary proceedings, may appoint a receiver. A receiver serves as a custodian of the property of the debtor until the election of a trustee at the first creditors' meeting. The trustee then seeks to convert all assets into cash. The property may not be sold without the consent of the court at less than 75 percent of the appraised value set by the court-appointed appraisers.

When the assets have been converted into cash to the extent possible, the cash is paid out on the basis of the following order of priority of claims:

1. Costs of administering and operating the bankrupt estate.
2. Wages due workers if earned within three months prior to the filing of the petition in bankruptcy. The amount of wages is not to exceed $600 per person.
3. Taxes due the United States, state, county, or any other governmental agency.
4. Secured creditors with the proceeds of the sale of specific property pledged for a mortgage.
5. General or unsecured creditors. This claim consists of the remaining balances after payment to secured creditors from the sale of specific property and includes trade credit, bank loans, and debenture bonds.
6. Preferred stock.
7. Comon stock.

The order of priority of claims can be illustrated by drawing on data from the previous example for the Failow Company, for which the following amounts were realized on liquidation:

Current assets...........	$ 6,000,000
Net property.............	4,000,000
Total..............	$10,000,000

In Table 21–5 we see that the amount available to general creditors is $3.5 million. The total general claims are $26 million. Thus, only 13.5 percent of the total claims can be met. Since the debentures are subordinated to the bank notes payable, the full amount of the claim of the sub-

TABLE 21–5

Order of priority of claims for the Failow Company

Cash received from sale of current assets...............................		$6,000,000
1. Fees and expenses of bankruptcy proceedings......................	500,000	
2. Wages due workers earned three months prior to filing of bankruptcy petition..	1,000,000	
3. Unpaid taxes..	1,000,000	
Total of priority claims from current assets.........................		$2,500,000
Available to general claims......................................		$3,500,000
Cash received from sale of net property................................	$4,000,000	
First mortgage claim..	5,000,000	
Unsatisfied portion of first mortgage claim.........................	$1,000,000	

Claims of general creditors	(1) Claim	(2) Application of 13.5 percent*	(3) After sub-ordination adjustment*	(4) Percentage of original claims received
Unsatisfied portion of first mortgage...........................	$ 1,000,000	$ 135,000	$ 135,000	82.7%
Notes payable to bank................	5,000,000	675,000	2,025,000	40.5
Notes payable to trade................	5,000,000	675,000	675,000	13.5
Accounts payable.....................	5,000,000	675,000	675,000	13.5
Subordinated debentures.............	10,000,000	1,350,000	0	0.0
	$26,000,000	$3,500,000	$3,500,000	

* Does not add to the total because of rounding.

ordinated debentures must be transferred to the claim of the notes payable to banks. The total amount realized on liquidation (after preferred claims) is the first mortgage claim of $4 million plus the $3.5 million available to the general creditors, a total of $7.5 million. This represents, of course, the $10 million proceeds less the prior claims of $2.5 million for bankruptcy fees, wages owed, and taxes owed. Thus, the creditors on total claims of $26 million plus the $4 million first-mortgage claim satisfied, have total claims of $30 million. For these total claims of $30 million, a net of $7.5 million was available. Thus, the creditors as a group received $0.25 cents on the dollar on liquidation.

But the percentages realized varied among the individual claimants; they ranged from 82.7 percent for the first mortgage holders and 40.5 percent for the banks down to 13.5 percent for the

other general creditors and nothing for the subordinated debenture holders. This illustrates the value of the first-mortgage security as well as the subordination agreement. It also illustrates the generally unfavorable position of the general creditors on liquidation. It is for this reason that they are often willing to work out some informal financial readjustment as described earlier, in hopes that they may do better than the average of 15 to 20 percent on the dollar received by general creditors.

These variables indicate the opportunities for creative finance for an alert financial manager, even in the event of business failure. The manager must understand the realistic alternatives when a business firm becomes insolvent in either a liquidity sense or in terms of the size of its total debt obligations in relation to the book value of its assets.

Indicate whether each of the following statements is true or false by writing "T" or "F" in the space provided.

———— 1. If voluntary settlement through informal procedures is not possible, the courts must decide on reorganization or liquidation.

———— 2. The Securities and Exchange Commission has a role in the formal reorganization procedure if the dollar amounts involved are large.

———— 3. Liquidation can only be brought about by a voluntary petition of bankruptcy filed by the debtor or an involuntary petition of bankruptcy filed by the creditors.

———— 4. Common stockholders are last in line when the cash is paid out in a liquidation.

Now turn to Answer Frame 2²¹ on page 192 to check your responses.

Frame 3²¹

THE NEW BANKRUPTCY LAW

The new bankruptcy law became effective October 1, 1979. It revised procedures of the old bankruptcy law in a number of ways. Old Chapter X covered reorganization procedures for large corporations with public investors in the bonds and common stock of the firm. Chapter XI proceedings were devised for use with smaller firms with no public participation in the financing or ownership of the firm. The processes were more flexible and informal than the Chapter X requirements.

Under the new bankruptcy law, Chapters X and XI are blended into a single procedure. Cases can be initiated either on a voluntary or involuntary basis. Involuntary petitions must be commenced only under Chapter VII which deals with liquidation or Chapter XI dealing with reorganization. The debtor company remains in possession of its business and continues to operate it unless the court orders otherwise. However, under a Chapter VII liquidation case, the court may appoint an interim trustee to operate the business to avoid loss. The debtor, however, may regain possession from the trustee by filing an appropriate bond as required by the court. The trustee has very broad powers and discretion if so authorized by the court. He may retain or replace management as well as augment management with additional professionals. The trustee may also obtain additional financing on an unsecured credit basis.

The consolidated approach under the new bankruptcy law eliminates disputes over whether Chapter X or XI will be used. This speeds up the proceedings, reduces costs, and hopefully shortens the time until the firm is operating profitably again. Since the debtor remains in control of the operations of the business, informal negotiations between the debtor company, the creditors, and the stockholders become more feasible. The absolute priority rule is relaxed under the new law. Negotiations may provide for a restructuring of debt involving a rescaling or time extensions including all creditors and stockholders. Hence, claims from unsecured creditors and stockholders have an increased probability of realizing cash or receiving some contingent claims on the reorganized companies. If it can be established that claimants receive as much as they would under a straight liquidation program, a reorganization plan can be approved by a vote of the parties who would be affected by it.

Since management will continue to be in control, the debtor and the large prime creditors may be the major influence. Sometimes this means institutions such as banks and insurance companies will dominate the proceedings. It is said that the SEC loses a strong weapon under the new consolidated procedure. Formerly, the threat to convert a Chapter XI to a Chapter X made debtors and large creditors willing to make concessions to avoid such a conversion. Under the new bankruptcy law, the SEC can still sue to have a trustee appointed. However, to be successful in such a suit aparently will require demonstrating management incompetence.

Thus, overall, the new bankruptcy law with respect to business firms provides for greater flexibility in the procedures. Greater flexibility avoids rigid processes that can often be very expensive and time consuming. On the other hand, greater flexibility may provide opportunities for

Answer frame 2²¹

1. True. And, if it decides on reorganization, it will appoint a trustee to control the firm during reorganization and to prepare a formal plan for reorganization.
2. True. For instance, in the Failow case illustrated, the SEC determined that the trustee's plan for reorganization met the test of fairness. The SEC provides an advisory opinion on such plans.
3. False. In addition to these two formal procedures there is a less formal liquidation procedure. It is called assignment and does not involve going through the courts. The debtor transfers title to a third party, who liquidates the assets and distributes the proceeds among the creditors on a pro rata basis. The creditors then release the debtor from all unpaid obligations.
4. True. All others rank before the common stockholders. In the example provided, they received nothing.

If you missed any of the above, you should restudy Frame 2²¹ before turning to Frame 3²¹ on page 191.

Frame 3²¹ continued

increased leverage by some of the parties involved. This may be to the detriment of other parties. Until we have more actual experience with the new bankruptcy law, it is not possible to make a definitive evaluation.

Indicate whether each of the following statements is true or false by writing "T" or "F" in the space provided.

_____ 1. Under the old bankruptcy law, Chapter X was used for large, public corporations and Chapter XI was used for smaller, private companies.

_____ 2. Chapters X and XI have been blended into a single procedure under the new law.

_____ 3. Under the new law, a trustee appointed by a court may have only very limited powers.

_____ 4. The precise effects of the new law on the various types of parties involved in a bankruptcy is difficult to determine.

Now turn to Answer Frame 3²¹ on page 194 to check your responses.

chapter 22

INTERNATIONAL BUSINESS FINANCE

Frame 1[22]

The multinational corporation may be defined as a firm which owns and manages business operations in two or more countries. It has direct investments in foreign countries which involve the ownership and management of physical assets as well as the managerial and worker personnel to make these physical assets productive. This is in contrast to portfolio investments in securities which do not involve active participation in management.

Almost every large enterprise has experienced some effects of international forces on its operations. Its inputs may include imported materials and its products may be exported or become a part of some export products. It may have agents or representative offices abroad; it may even license foreign firms to manufacture some of its products. However, a firm takes on the important characteristics of a truly multinational enterprise only when it must carry out the responsibilities of financing, producing, and marketing products within foreign nations.

Multinational operations may be achieved by moving through a number of stages in the development from a domestic firm to a truly international operation:

1. Development of a strong product for domestic sales.
2. Import of some products.
3. Use of export brokers.
4. Direct export sales.
5. Branch sales office abroad.
6. Licensing.
7. Licensing with joint venture.
8. Joint venture.
9. Wholly-owned manufacturing subsidiary.
10. Multinational management organization.
11. Multinational ownership of equity securities.

In multinational organizations, corporate headquarters normally makes the final decisions on strategic policy such as the determination of product lines and capital budgets. The chief executives of its foreign affiliates are given broad authority to operate within the general policy guidelines within their respective countries. The main pattern of planning and control parallels that of domestic operations. Periodic budgets initiated by the foreign affiliate set forth goals and targets for operations. There is also a periodic review and evaluation of progress. The review is performed jointly by corporate headquarters and affiliate managers.

With more firms moving through the stages, the field of international business finance has become an increasingly important aspect of financial management. Sales or investments abroad involve a wide range of new risks to a business firm. Exchange rate fluctuations are pervasive risks. An important tool of analysis in developing the methodology for forecasting future exchange-rate movements is the balance-of-payments information.

THE BALANCE OF PAYMENTS: CONCEPTS AND USES

A nation's balance of payments is a double-entry accounting statement of its international economic transactions for a designated period of

Answer frame 3²¹

1. True. And the processes under Chapter XI were more flexible and informal than under Chapter X.
2. True. This eliminates disputes over whether Chapter X or Chapter XI should be used. This speeds up the proceedings, reduces costs, and hopefully shortens the time until the firm is operating profitably again.
3. False. While it may be less likely that a trustee will be appointed, if one is appointed, the trustee may have very broad powers if so authorized by the court. For instance, the trustee may take such actions as replacing management and obtaining additional financing.
4. True. Until more experience is gained under the new law, it is difficult to determine the effects on the various parties. For instance, the absolute priority of claims is relaxed under the new law. Precisely how common stockholders and others will be treated is still somewhat unclear.

If you missed any of the above, you should restudy Frame 3²¹ before beginning Chapter 22 on page 193.

Frame 1²² continued

time. Since it is a double-entry system, there are two sides to the account:

Favorable changes	Unfavorable changes
Credits	Debits
Receipts	Payments
Plus	Minus
Exports	Imports

The receipts or plus side is equivalent to exports. The payments or minus side is equivalent to imports. In one sense, the balance of payments is always in balance—the debits always equal the credits. But in another sense the balance of payments is an analytical tool for studying the trends in a nation's economic and financial positions.

The key account balance is the balance on current account. It represents the basic balance on goods and services plus unilateral transfers along with U.S. government grants as shown in Table 22–1. It regards these main items as the basic economic transactions. It excludes the influence of capital movements.

TABLE 22–1

Selected U.S. international transactions, 1979

Exports of goods and services....................	$287
Imports of goods and services...................	− 282
Balance on goods and services..................	+$ 5
Government and private unilateral transfers......	− 2
Balance on goods, services, and remittances......	+$ 3
U.S. government grants.........................	− 4
Balance on current account.....................	−$ 1

Of the different ways of measuring the balance-of-payments position, no one method is best by all criteria. What is most useful depends upon the nature of the important international financial transactions that are taking place. The financial manager must study the balance-of payments relationships and their trends to determine the implications for exchange rates and for predicting government policies affecting the flow and convertibility of funds.

Indicate whether each of the following statements is true or false by writing "T" or "F" in the space provided.

_____ 1. A multinational corporation is one which owns business operations in two or more countries.

_____ 2. In multinational organizations, strategic policy decisions are generally made by the chief executives of its foreign affiliates.

_____ 3. A nation's balance of payments is favorably affected by exports and unfavorably affected by imports.

———— 4. Capital movements are excluded in deriving the balance on current account.

Now turn to Answer Frame 1²² on page 196 to check your responses.

Frame 2²²

EXCHANGE RATES

A fundamental difference between international business finance and domestic business finance is that transactions and investments are conducted in more than one currency. For example, when an American firm sells goods to a French firm, the American exporter normally desires to be paid in dollars and the French importer or French firm normally expects to pay in French francs. The buyer can pay in one currency and the seller receive payment in another currency because of the existence of a foreign exchange market in which individual dealers and many banks trade.

Since two different currencies are involved, a rate of exchange must be established between them. The conversion relationship between two different currencies is expressed in terms of their price relationship. If foreign exchange rates did not fluctuate, it would make no difference whether a businessman has dollars or any other currency. However, since exchange rates do fluctuate, a firm is subject to exchange-rate fluctuation risks if it has a net asset or a net liability position in a foreign currency. If net claims exceed liabilities in a foreign currency, the firm is said to be in a "long" position because it will benefit if the value of the foreign currency *rises*. If the firm is in a net debtor position with regard to foreign currencies, it is said to be in a "short" position because the firm will gain if the foreign currency *declines* in value.

Because of the risks of exchange-rate fluctuations, transactions have developed in a forward or futures foreign exchange market. The forward or futures market enables a firm to engage in hedging in the attempt to reduce the risk of exchange-rate fluctuations. Individuals also speculate by means of transactions on the forward market. Forward contracts are normally for a 30-, 60-, or 90-day period, though special contracts for longer periods can be arranged by negotiation.

The cost of this protection is the premium or discount that is required over the spot rate—the exchange rate in effect when the forward contract is purchased. The premium or discount required varies from 0 to 2 or 3 percent per annum for currencies that are considered reasonably stable. For currencies undergoing devaluation in excess of 4 to 5 percent per year, discounts required may be as high as 15 to 20 percent per year. When there are strong probabilities that future devaluations may exceed 20 percent per year, forward contracts are usually no longer available.

The magnitude of the premium or discount required depends upon the forward expectations of the financial communities of the two countries involved and upon the supply-and-demand conditions in the foreign exchange market. Since members of the financial communities in the two countries are usually well informed as to the expected forward exchange values of their respective currencies, the premiums or discounts quoted are very closely related to the probable occurrence of changes in the exchange rates. As a result, the forward market is chiefly used as protection against *unexpected* changes in the foreign exchange value of a currency.

To illustrate how the forward market works, let us start with the basic situation that in September 1981 the USP Company has made a sale of goods to a foreign firm and will receive FC 380,000 in December 1981. The USP Company incurred costs in dollars and wishes to know the definite amount of dollars it will receive in December 1981. It is considering three alternatives to avoid the risk of exchange-rate fluctuations.

The first alternative is to buy now a forward contract which provides for the sale of FCs for dollars at the 90-day forward rate quoted in September. The USP Company will then utilize the FC 380,000 it receives in December to pay for the dollars it has contracted to buy at the 90-day

Answer frame 1²²

1. False. It must own *and manage* business operations in two or more countries to be considered a multinational corporation.
2. False. Corporate headquarters normally makes the final decisions on strategic policy. The chief executives of its foreign affiliates must operate within these general policy guidelines.
3. True. The receipts or plus side is equivalent to exports. The payments or minus side is equivalent to imports.
4. True. The balance on current account is found by adding exports, deducting imports, deducting government and private unilateral transfers, and deducting U.S. government grants. Capital movements are excluded from the computation.

If you missed any of the above, you should restudy Frame 1²² before turning to Frame 2²² on page 195.

Frame 2²² continued

forward rate. Under this arrangement the USP Company will receive a definite amount in dollars in December.

The second alternative is to borrow now from a foreign bank the amount the USP Company will be receiving in December. By borrowing, the USP Company receives the FC 380,000 immediately and can immediately purchase dollars with the FCs received at the September spot rate. When the USP Company receives the FC 380,-000 in December, it uses the funds to liquidate the loan it has incurred in September.

The third alternative is to make no attempt to cover the exchange risk involved in waiting the three months for receipt of the FC 380,000. Un-

der the third alternative the USP Company will convert the FC 380,000 into dollars at whatever spot rate prevails in December.

Which alternative is better will depend upon the pattern of relationships between the spot rate and the 90-day forward rate in September and in December. To illustrate this, the three alternatives will be analyzed for a pattern of spot and forward rates for September and a set of illustrative rates as of December 1981. First we shall consider the pattern of rates that was characteristic of Latin American countries in past years. The basic facts are set forth in the following tabulation:

	September 1981		December 1981	
	Value of $ in FC	Value of FC in $	Value of $ in FC	Value of FC in $
Spot rate.............................	FC 1.90	$0.53	FC 2.10	$0.48
Ninety-day forward rate................	FC 2.00	$0.50	FC 2.20	$0.45

We can now analyze the three alternatives. The first alternative involves the purchase of a forward contract in which the USP Company agrees to pay FC 380,000 to receive dollars at the September 90-day forward rate, which is FC 2.00. Therefore, under the first alternative the USP Company has contracted to definitely receive $190,000. Typically the customer would arrange

the forward contract with his bank or a trader with whom he has conducted operations in the past so that he is known to them. The fee charged by the bank is already reflected in the exchange rate. For example, if the expected spot rate in the future is as indicated, FC 2.10, then the September 90-day forward rate would be lower by the amount of the fee built in. If the normal difference between the September forward rate and the December spot rate were 0.07, the spread of 0.10 that we have illustrated here might represent an additional 0.03 as compensation to the bank or the foreign exchange trader.

Under alternative two, the USP Company borrows FC 380,000 from a foreign bank and converts it immediately into dollars at the spot rate of 1.90 receiving $200,000. Of course, it will have to pay interest on the loan obtained from the foreign bank. On the other hand, the USP Company will have the funds three months earlier and can invest those funds at its opportunity cost. Since in this example we are focusing on the influence of different patterns of spot and forward exchange rates, we will assume that the firm's opportunity cost on the use of the funds is such that the profitability and the interest factor cancel out.

Under the third alternative, in December 1981 the FC 380,000 would be converted into dollars at the spot rate then in effect. This would represent FC 380,000 divided by 2.10, or $180,952. The $180,952 represents an expected amount to be received in December 1981.

Among the three alternatives the largest number of dollars is received under alternative two, in which the FC 380,000 were borrowed and

$200,000 is received. This is definitely better than the $190,000 received under alternative one. But in comparing alternative two with alternative three we cannot be certain which is better. The expected spot rate for December 1981 represents a decline of the foreign currency unit in dollars from $0.50 at the forward rate of September 1981 to $0.48 at the spot rate in December 1981. However, if the December spot rate turned out to be exactly the same as the September spot rate, or if the value of FCs in dollars actually rose, alternative three could become the best of the three alternatives. In general, if a management is almost certain that the value of the foreign currency will decline over time, the logic is to make the arrangements to convert the foreign currency into the domestic currency as soon as possible. This is achieved by using either alternative one or two, which enables the USP Company to protect the value of its sales volume.

Now we turn to the alternative type situation characteristic of the relationship between the United States and Western European countries in recent years. This is the pattern in which the value of the foreign currency unit is expected to be rising in relationship to the U.S. dollar as time goes on. Such a pattern is illustrated in the table that follows:

	September 1981		December 1981	
	Value of $ in FC	Value of FC in $	Value of $ in FC	Value of FC in $
Spot rate	FC 2.00	$0.50	FC 1.70	$0.59
Ninety-day forward rate	FC 1.90	$0.53	FC 1.50	$0.67

The same three alternatives are assumed to be available to the USP Company, but the pattern of analysis for the three alternatives will be different. Under alternative one the USP Company buys a forward contract to receive $200,000 in December. Under alternative two the Company obtains FC 380,000 and buys dollars immediately. The spot rate is FC 2.00 so that the USP Company receives $190,000. Again we will assume the relationship between the interest cost and the opportunity profit rate is such that they will exactly cancel out.

Under alternative three, where no action has

been taken, the conversion will take place at the FC 1.70 spot rate expected to exist in December. The USP Company will, therefore, receive FC 380,000 divided by FC 1.70 or $223,529.

Among the three alternatives, using the numbers given in the illustration, alternative three is better than alternative one, which in turn is better than alternative two. This result obtains because the number of FC units to buy $1 is expected to drop over time, which is to say that the value of one FC in dollars is rising over time. But again this result is based on expectations being close to reality. It could very well be for any period of time that instead of the spot rate in December representing a smaller number of FCs required per dollar, if international monetary conditions change, the spot rate in December might actually be above the spot rate in September. If the spot rate in December resulted in an FC rate equal to or higher than the spot rate in September, the third alternative would be the worst rather than the best of three possible actions. Alternative one would then be the best because it yields $200,000 as compared to receiving $190,000 under alternative two.

In summary, among the alternative available in seeking to protect a firm's exchange-rate position, an unequivocal choice cannot be made. The answer is dependent upon judgments about what future exchange rates will be in comparison with current exchange rates. Choice among alternatives depends upon the relationship between the current forward rate and the future spot rate as well as the relative opportunity cost of money in the two countries involved. The decision is basically a businessman's judgment which heavily depends upon a forecast of future foreign exchange rates.

Indicate whether each of the following statements is true or false by writing "T" or "F" in the space provided.

   _____ 1. A "long" position is when liabilities exceed net claims in a foreign currency.

   _____ 2. Hedging allows firms to protect against the risks of exchange-rate fluctuations.

   _____ 3. If the management of a firm believes that the value of the foreign currency will rise over time it will want to convert the foreign currency into the domestic currency as soon as possible.

   _____ 4. The choice of the best course of action cannot be made unequivocally.

Now turn to Answer Frame 2[22] on page 200 to check your responses.

Frame 3[22]

MONETARY BALANCE

In addition to using the forward markets to protect against exchange-rate risks, monetary balance may be employed. Monetary balance is having a net monetary creditor position in a country for which exchange rates are expected to rise and a net monetary debtor position in a country for which exchange rates are expected to fall. Monetary assets and liabilities are those items whose value, expressed in foreign currency, does not change with devaluation. A partial listing follows:

Monetary assets	Monetary liabilities
Cash	Accounts payable
Marketable securities	Notes payable
Accounts receivable	Tax liability reserve
Tax refunds receivable	Bonds
Notes receivable	Preferred stock
Prepaid insurance	

As a general rule, branches and foreign subsidiaries of U.S. firms operating in foreign areas are monetary creditors. Among their assets are cash in the foreign currencies and accounts receivable from foreign customers. Indebtedness, if any, is usually owed to the parent company in terms of U.S. dollars—debts which do not offset monetary assets in terms of the foreign currency. Therefore, the achievement of monetary balance requires borrowing of foreign currency and the spending of these funds for business purposes. The cost of obtaining monetary balance in reducing exchange-rate risk is the interest that must be paid on the borrowed funds.

Consider the dollar value of a foreign subsidiary at the present to be:

$$\text{Value}_0 = \frac{\text{Net real assets}}{X_0} + \frac{\text{Net monetary assets}}{X_0} \tag{22-1}$$

where X_0 is the present spot rate. A year later the value will be:

$$Value_1 = \frac{\text{Net real assets}}{X_1} + \frac{\text{Net monetary assets}}{X_1}$$

$$(22-1a)$$

where X_1 is the spot rate one year hence. The change in dollar value during the year is given by:

$$Value_0 - Value_1 = \frac{\text{Net monetary assets}}{X_0}$$
$$- \frac{\text{Net monetary assets}}{X_1} \quad (22-1b)$$

This represents the change in the dollar value of the foreign subsidiary due to the change in the foreign exchange value of the foreign currency. It is assumed that the real assets will not lose value since their foreign currency value will increase with the decrease in the foreign exchange value of that currency.

Net monetary assets (if plus, a net monetary creditor) are defined as monetary assets minus monetary liabilities. If this value is equal to a quantity A, then the loss would be:

$$\text{Loss} = A(1/X_0 - 1/X_1)$$

If instead of taking this loss the subsidiary borrows an amount equal to A locally and spends this money on equipment or inventory, then the subsidiary's net monetary position would be equal to zero, and neither gain nor loss would result with changes in the foreign exchange value of the foreign currency. The cost of this protection is the interest that would have to be paid on the additionally borrowed funds to achieve monetary balance.

Thus, borrow foreign if:

$$(r_F - r_{US}) < [(X_1 - X_0)/X_0] (1 + r_{US}) \quad (22-2)$$

where r_{US} is the U.S. borrowing rate.

Monetary balance provides an exchange risk protective device because if there is any downward change in the value of the foreign currency in relation to the U.S. dollar, losses incurred due to the possession of monetary assets are balanced by profits resulting from the possession of an equal amount of monetary liabilities.

In countries whose exchange rates are likely to fall, local management of subsidiaries should be encouraged to follow these policies:

1. Never have excessive idle cash on hand. If cash accumulates it should be used to purchase inventory or other real assets.

2. Attempt to avoid granting excessive trade credit or normal trade credit for extended periods. If accounts receivable cannot be avoided, an attempt should be made to charge interest high enough to compensate for the loss of purchasing power.

3. Avoid, wherever possible, giving advances in connection with purchase orders unless a rate of interest is paid by the seller on these advances from the time you, the buyer, pay them to the time of delivery, at a rate sufficent to cover the loss of purchasing power.

4. Borrow foreign currency funds from banks or other sources whenever these funds can be obtained at a rate of interest equal to or smaller than the anticipated rate of devaluation.

5. Make an effort to purchase materials and supplies on a trade-credit basis in the country in which the foreign subsidiary is operating, extending the final date of payment as long as possible.

The opposite set of policies should be followed by subsidiaries operating in countries whose exchange rates are likely to rise.

Indicate whether each of the following statements is true or false by writing "T" or "F" in the space provided.

_____ 1. Monetary balance may be used to protect against exchange-rate risks.

_____ 2. Monetary creditors must borrow foreign currency to obtain monetary balance and reduce exchange-rate risk.

_____ 3. In countries where exchange rates are likely to rise, local management of subsidiaries should never have large amounts of idle cash on hand.

_____ 4. Charging a sufficient amount of interest can offset losses which would result from changing exchange rates.

Now turn to Answer Frame 3²² on page 200 to check your responses.

Answer frame 2²²

1. False. The situation described is a "short" position. A "long" position is when net claims exceed liabilities in a foreign currency.
2. True. One of two alternatives may be followed to hedge against exchange-rate fluctuations. A firm may buy now a forward contract which provides for the sale of FCs for dollars at the 90-day forward rate quoted presently. Alternatively, it may borrow now from a foreign bank the amount the company will be receiving in the future. A third alternative is to make no attempt to cover the exchange risk.
3. False. It would do this only if it expected the foreign currency to *fall* over time.
4. True. The best choice depends upon expectations about future exchange rates.

If you missed any of the above, you should restudy Frame 2²² before turning to Frame 3²² on page 198.

Answer frame 3²²

1. True. The firm may establish a net monetary creditor position in a country for which exchange rates are expected to rise and a net monetary debtor position in a country for which exchange rates are expected to fall.
2. True. If the monetary creditor borrows enough to make its monetary position equal to zero, neither gain or loss results from changes in the foreign exchange value of the foreign currency. The cost of this protection is the interest cost on the borrowed funds less the earnings on the borrowed funds.
3. False. This advice applies to situations where exchange rates are likely to *fall*. Where they are expected to rise, a gain would be realized.
4. True. For instance, if accounts receivable cannot be avoided in a country where exchange rates are likely to fall, sufficient interest can be charged to offset the loss of purchasing power.

If you missed any of the above, you should restudy Frame 3²² before turning to Frame 4²² below.

Frame 4²²

PROJECT EVALUATION IN FOREIGN INVESTMENT DECISIONS

In project evaluation the basic principles are similar for foreign investment decisions and domestic investment decisions. Hence, the same general pattern of analysis applies to both. This involves comparing cash inflows and outflows of the project and applying a relevant cost of capital to determine its net present value. With no capital rationing, for independent investments, all projects with positive net present values are accepted. For mutually exclusive investments, the project with the highest net present value is selected. With capital rationing, mathematical programming techniques must be used to achieve a formally correct decision.

Project analysis. For project analysis of foreign investment decisions, there are at least three distinctive aspects: (1) the range of variables to be considered in the analysis is expanded; (2) the estimates of both inflows and outflows may be subject to wider margins of error; and (3) the analysis of risks and returns is likely to be more complex. The broad outlines of the patterns for project analysis of foreign direct investments parallel those for domestic investments. However, some distinctive elements reflect the characteristics of foreign investments. Some elements of cost are introduced in the cash outflow section. Costs of hedging against foreign exchange losses may represent the use of forward exchange markets or the use of swaps. In addition, costs of insuring against expropriation may be required.

Additional taxes in the foreign country may also be involved, including local fees, taxes on income, and withholding taxes on dividends. An additional cost to the subsidiary may be supervisory fees charged by the parent company. However, such fees may be involved in parent-subsidiary relations in domestic investments as well.

Sometimes, in the establishment of a foreign subsidiary, it may be advantageous for the parent company to transfer used equipment from its domestic operations. This used equipment may provide an adequate volume of operations for its foreign demand, enabling the parent to substitute new and modern equipment for its domestic operations, realizing higher salvage values than otherwise possible for the older equipment. The used equipment may have a depreciated value in the accounting records of $200,000. However, the opportunity costs of acquiring such equipment in Mexico may be (for illustration) $500,000. Hence the appropriate charge to the project is $500,000.

The asset-acquisition requirements will then be reflected in the summary inflow and outflow analysis. Additional items involved in foreign investments may also be noted. The firm may have been exporting instruments from its U.S. or other manufacturing operations, and some sales of the new subsidiary may substitute for these export sales. Hence an item is introduced to reflect this offset—the after-tax decline in cash flows caused by the decline in export sales, resulting from the substitution of sales by the new foreign subsidiary.

In addition, foreign investments utilize parent company management know-how capabilities built up over a period of years. A portion of this know-how is inevitably shared with the nationals who will be employed in the foreign operations. Thus a portion of this valuable investment know-how is likely to be "used up" and should therefore be a charge to the foreign project. The pattern of analysis then follows the standard form for capital budgeting decision models.

Risk considerations in project analysis. Risk considerations are especially important in foreign investment decisions. Hence, the models for the treatment of investment under uncertainty take on special importance. Because of the wider range and severity of possible risks in the foreign environment that can only be partially hedged or insured against, the range of possible outcomes may be much greater for the foreign investment.

The appropriate procedure is to set forth the cumulative NPVs that would occur under alternative possible future states and outcomes for the investment project. A firm must consider expected returns and the dispersion of expected returns as measured by the variance and standard deviation of alternative outcomes. On a return-risk basis, some different choice combinations may be involved. Domestic investments are likely to offer lower expected returns and lower standard deviations, whereas foreign investments offer higher expected returns and higher standard deviations of possible returns. In addition, the covariance characteristics of domestic investments and foreign investments may differ, offering new opportunities for diversification.

Indicate whether each of the following statements is true or false by writing "T" or "F" in the space provided.

_____ 1. While the basic principles are similar for foreign and domestic investment decisions, the project analysis for foreign investment decisions is more complex.

_____ 2. When a parent company transfers used equipment from its domestic operations to a foreign project, the equipment should be charged to the project at its depreciated value.

_____ 3. Both foreign and domestic projects are likely to offer the same expected returns and standard deviations.

_____ 4. Covariance characteristics may differ between domestic and foreign projects.

Now turn to Answer Frame 4²² on page 202 to check your responses.

Answer frame 4²²

1. True. It is more complex because the range of variables is expanded, estimates of cash flows may be subject to wider margins of error, and the analysis of risks and returns is likely to be more complex.
2. False. It should be charged to the foreign project at its opportunity cost.
3. False. Domestic investments are likely to offer lower expected returns and lower standard deviations than do foreign investments. The foreign environment has a wider range and severity of possible risks.
4. True. And this offers new opportunities for diversification.

If you missed any of the above, you should restudy Frame 4²² before turning to Frame 5²² below.

Frame 5²²

INTERNATIONAL FINANCING

Decisions by international firms on alternative forms, sources, places, and timing of financing are influenced by a large number of variables. Of primary importance are the characteristics of the individual firms with respect to products produced and sold, the firm's absolute size, its share of the markets in which its products are sold, and the age of the firm. In addition, the life cycles of industries and changes in general economic environmental conditions will influence the costs of financing.

International financing forms. Some financing operations are distinctive to international business finance. For example, overdrafts represent a form of commercial bank financing widely used in Europe. An overdraft agreement permits a customer to draw checks up to some specified maximum limit. The practice is similar to a line of credit arrangement in the United States.

Another form of financing which, until recent years, was much more widespread in Europe than in the United States, is the discounting of "trade bills" in both domestic and foreign transactions. The increased use of banker's acceptances in the United States has been associated with the growth of the movement of goods in international trade.

A third variation from U.S. financing practices is the broader participation of commercial banks in the medium- and long-term lending activities found in Europe. Commercial banks in Europe carry on considerable activity of the kind that would be described as investment banking in the United States. However, the Banking Act of 1933 required the divestiture of investment banking operations by commercial banks in the United States, so that this difference is the result of a legal requirement.

A fourth financial area distinctive to international financing includes arbi-loans and link financing, both functioning to equalize the supply of and demand for loanable funds in relation to sensitive interest-rate levels among different countries. Using arbi-loans (international interest arbitrage financing), a borrower obtains loans in a country where the supply of funds is relatively abundant. These borrowings are then converted into the required local currency. Simultaneously, the borrower enters into a forward exchange contract to protect himself on the reconversion of local currency into foreign currency that will be required at the time the loan must be repaid. Commercial banks are typically involved in arbi-loan transactions both as lenders and as intermediaries in foreign exchange trading.

In link financing, the commercial banks take an even more direct role. A lender in a foreign country deposits funds with a bank in the borrower's country, where interest rates are higher. This deposit then may be earmarked for a specified borrower, or it may be channeled through a money broker to borrowers of good credit standing. In the latter case, the foreign lender generally receives a portion of the broker's premium in addition to the interest rate differential. The lender, of course, will hedge his position in the foreign exchange markets, since he will be repaid in the currency of the country in which the bank deposit was made. Because of the risk associated with foreign lending and with foreign exchange fluctuations, the maturity of link financing transactions are short term, leaving open the possibility of renewal at maturity.

Eurodollar and Eurocurrency markets. Instead of transferring funds from the United States, American companies may borrow Eurodollars for conversion into foreign currencies to meet financing needs abroad. Thus they are able to obtain funds for use abroad without a transfer of funds from the United States.

In addition, Eurodollars can increase the amount of available financing in the United States. For instance, during tight money periods U.S. money-center banks have used the Eurodollar deposits of their foreign branches to increase their loanable funds in the United States. Similarly, for both foreign and U.S. corporations, international financing may be utilized when the capital markets of a particular country do not provide sufficient equity financing or are not of sufficent breadth to make local funds available. Or international financing may be used when government controls restrict the borrowing of foreign currency. Thus, Eurodollar financing may be applied for both working capital purposes and for longer-term investment.

The Eurocurrency market offers a number of advantages to the U.S. company whose affiliate is seeking financing abroad. The Eurocurrency market encompasses any currency available in the international marketplace to finance U.S. industries. The choice may be among dollars, pounds, French francs, Swiss francs, Deutsche marks, or Dutch guilders. The analysis must take into consideration the exchange-rate risks as well as interest costs. Many methods of financing are available in European currency. One that has been a major source of financing by individual business firms has been bank credit lines under a medium-term commitment, with interest rates tied to the cost of deposits to Eurocurrency market banks. An operating and profit margin is also added to the cost of time deposits paid by these Eurocurrency market banks.

Historically, the revolving Eurodollar or Eurocurrency credit line has ranged from one to five years. Medium-term credits, of course, are appropriate for financing temporary working capital,

but they are not appropriate for financing long-term investments. These revolving credits have generally been arranged on a syndicated basis through London-based banking houses or the London branches of large U.S. banks. Credit obtained in the Eurocurrency market is arranged through European banking houses. The objective is not only to raise funds but also to develop relationships with banking houses in a number of countries to provide various forms of assistance to firm operations.

Using commercial paper as a vehicle for providing Eurocurrency financing to U.S. industry has been growing. This represents a recent major breakthrough which has enabled U.S. industry to tap capital in the hands of private foreign investors. This enables private investors to purchase the U.S. borrower's short-dated debt notes. The Eurocurrency commercial paper market has grown to the point where some 15 issuing companies have been utilizing it, and all of them have at least an A bond rating in the United States. Their commercial paper has been successfully placed at rates of interest which are consistently below the interest cost associated with borrowing under the Eurodollar revolving bank credit line.

Eurobond market. The Eurobond market is a very important segment of the Eurocurrency market. It is available in a range of currencies both on a straight-debt basis and through the use of convertible securities. The Eurobonds are usually denominated in dollars and have a fixed maturity of between 12 to 15 years, with annual sinking-fund requirements commencing after 2 to 4 years. And in recent years increasing use has also been made of convertible securities.

International financing subsidiaries. Subsidiaries engage in international financing to raise funds abroad. The major reason U.S. companies adopt this financing vehicle is that interest payments made to foreign lending institutions from U.S.-based companies are subject to a 30 percent U.S. withholding tax. But this tax can be eliminated or reduced, depending upon reciprocal tax treaties between the United States and the country of the lending bank. This problem can be completely overcome, however, by establishing an international financing subsidiary. The best known of these are domiciled in Delaware and the Netherlands Antilles.

FINANCIAL MANAGEMENT IN A WORLD DIMENSION

The multinational firm operates in widely diverse environments and obtains financing from a wide diversity of sources. While some degree of autonomy may be granted to international subsidiaries, at some point the financing activities must be coordinated at the central headquarters of the multinational enterprise. Tax considerations, investment decisions, and cash-flow management must be centralized. Management information systems take on increased importance. To control cash throughout its operations, the multinational firm requires frequent reports to headquarters from subsidiaries. Some firms have established "mobilization points" as centers for transferring funds on a semidecentralized basis.

Multinational corporate treasurers must achieve efficient worldwide corporate cash management. To this end, large multinational banks have expanded their operations to provide services to multinational corporations. These banks help to achieve maximum speed in moving funds, and they cooperate with corporate management in establishing daily control over the firm's international cash flow.

Thus, increasingly, the arena for business finance is the global market. At the start of each day, the corporate treasurer determines whether the corporation will be borrowing or lending in the international financial market. The treasurer may be making investment decisions in domestic product markets or in foreign countries. The financial manager of the multinational corporate enterprise must consider the form and extent of protection against risks of devaluation on sales of the company's product to companies abroad. The financial manager must be concerned with the long-run political and commercial risks in the company's foreign sales and investments.

If there is surplus cash, the financial manager must compare the returns from investing in the domestic money market with utilizing the international financial market. Similarly, if short-term financing needs arise, comparisons must be made between financing sources abroad and domestic sources. The advantages and disadvantages of the more impersonal international financial markets must be considered, and consideration must be given to developing long-term financing relations with international commercial banks or financial groups in London, Paris, Zurich, and Bonn.

Indicate whether each of the following statements is true or false by writing "T" or "F" in the space provided.

———— 1. Overdrafts are illegal in Europe.

———— 2. Commercial banks in Europe are more involved in medium- and long-term lending than are commercial banks in the United States.

———— 3. Link-financing transactions are generally short-term.

———— 4. The Eurocurrency market consists entirely of currencies available in the international marketplace.

———— 5. Cash management activities are very critical for the multinational firm.

Now turn to Answer Frame 5^{22} on page 206 to check your responses.

Answer frame 5²²

1. False. Overdrafts are widely used in Europe and are similar to a line-of-credit arrangement in the United States.
2. True. The Banking Act of 1933 required the divestiture of these investment banking operations by commercial banks in the United States.
3. True. This is because of the risk associated with foreign lending and with foreign exchange fluctuations.
4. False. Long-term financing, such as Eurobonds, as well as currencies, are an important part of the Eurocurrency market.
5. True. Inefficient management of cash can be very costly to the firm. The financial manager must spend considerable time on this activity.

If you missed any of the above, you should restudy Frame 5²². Then turn to page 222 and work Examination 5 which covers Chapters 16–22.

Appendix: Compound Interest Tables

TABLE A–1
Compound sum of $1; $S_n = P(1 + r)^n$

Year	1%	2%	3%	4%	5%	6%	7%	8%
1	1.010	1.020	1.030	1.040	1.050	1.060	1.070	1.080
2	1.020	1.040	1.081	1.082	1.102	1.124	1.145	1.166
3	1.030	1.061	1.093	1.125	1.158	1.191	1.225	1.260
4	1.041	1.082	1.126	1.170	1.216	1.262	1.311	1.360
5	1.051	1.104	1.159	1.217	1.276	1.338	1.403	1.469
6	1.062	1.126	1.194	1.265	1.340	1.419	1.501	1.587
7	1.072	1.149	1.230	1.316	1.407	1.504	1.606	1.714
8	1.083	1.172	1.267	1.369	1.477	1.594	1.718	1.851
9	1.094	1.195	1.305	1.423	1.551	1.689	1.838	1.999
10	1.105	1.219	1.344	1.480	1.629	1.791	1.967	2.159
11	1.116	1.243	1.384	1.539	1.710	1.898	2.105	2.332
12	1.127	1.268	1.426	1.601	1.796	2.012	2.252	2.518
13	1.138	1.294	1.469	1.665	1.886	2.133	2.410	2.720
14	1.149	1.319	1.513	1.732	1.980	2.261	2.579	2.937
15	1.161	1.346	1.558	1.801	2.079	2.397	2.759	3.172
16	1.173	1.373	1.605	1.873	2.183	2.540	2.952	3.426
17	1.184	1.400	1.653	1.948	2.292	2.693	3.159	3.700
18	1.196	1.428	1.702	2.026	2.407	2.854	3.380	3.996
19	1.208	1.457	1.754	2.107	2.527	3.026	3.617	4.316
20	1.220	1.486	1.806	2.191	2.653	3.207	3.870	4.661

Year	9%	10%	11%	12%	13%	14%	15%	16%
1	1.090	1.100	1.110	1.120	1.130	1.140	1.150	1.160
2	1.188	1.210	1.232	1.254	1.277	1.300	1.322	1.346
3	1.295	1.331	1.368	1.405	1.443	1.482	1.521	1.561
4	1.412	1.464	1.518	1.574	1.631	1.689	1.749	1.811
5	1.539	1.611	1.685	1.762	1.842	1.925	2.011	2.100
6	1.677	1.772	1.870	1.974	2.082	2.195	2.313	2.436
7	1.828	1.949	2.076	2.211	2.353	2.502	2.660	2.826
8	1.993	2.144	2.305	2.476	2.658	2.853	3.059	3.278
9	2.172	2.358	2.558	2.773	3.004	3.252	3.518	3.803
10	2.367	2.594	2.839	3.106	3.395	3.707	4.046	4.411
11	2.580	2.853	3.152	3.479	3.836	4.226	4.652	5.117
12	2.813	3.138	3.499	3.896	4.335	4.818	5.350	5.936
13	3.066	3.452	3.883	4.363	4.898	5.492	6.153	6.886
14	3.342	3.797	4.310	4.887	5.535	6.261	7.076	7.988
15	3.642	4.177	4.785	5.474	6.254	7.138	8.137	9.266
16	3.970	4.595	5.311	6.130	7.067	8.137	9.358	10.748
17	4.328	5.054	5.895	6.866	7.986	9.276	10.761	12.468
18	4.717	5.560	6.544	7.690	9.024	10.575	12.375	14.463
19	5.142	6.116	7.263	8.613	10.197	12.056	14.232	16.777
20	5.604	6.728	8.062	9.646	11.523	13.743	16.367	19.461

TABLE A–2

Present value of \$1; $P = S_n(1 + r)^{-n}$

Periods until Payment	1%	2%	2½%	3%	4%	5%	6%	8%	10%	12%	14%	15%	16%	18%	20%	22%	24%	25%	26%	30%	40%	50%
1	0.990	0.980	0.976	0.971	0.962	0.952	0.943	0.926	0.909	0.893	0.877	0.870	0.862	0.847	0.833	0.820	0.806	0.800	0.794	0.769	0.714	0.667
2	0.980	0.961	0.952	0.943	0.925	0.907	0.890	0.857	0.826	0.797	0.769	0.756	0.743	0.718	0.694	0.672	0.650	0.640	0.630	0.592	0.510	0.444
3	0.971	0.942	0.929	0.915	0.889	0.864	0.840	0.794	0.751	0.712	0.675	0.658	0.641	0.609	0.579	0.551	0.524	0.512	0.500	0.455	0.364	0.296
4	0.961	0.924	0.906	0.888	0.855	0.823	0.792	0.735	0.683	0.636	0.592	0.572	0.552	0.516	0.482	0.451	0.423	0.410	0.397	0.350	0.260	0.198
5	0.951	0.906	0.884	0.863	0.822	0.784	0.747	0.681	0.621	0.567	0.519	0.497	0.476	0.437	0.402	0.370	0.341	0.328	0.315	0.269	0.186	0.132
6	0.942	0.888	0.862	0.837	0.790	0.746	0.705	0.630	0.564	0.507	0.456	0.432	0.410	0.370	0.335	0.303	0.275	0.262	0.250	0.207	0.133	0.088
7	0.933	0.871	0.841	0.813	0.760	0.711	0.665	0.583	0.513	0.452	0.400	0.376	0.354	0.314	0.279	0.249	0.222	0.210	0.198	0.159	0.095	0.059
8	0.923	0.853	0.821	0.789	0.731	0.677	0.627	0.540	0.467	0.404	0.351	0.327	0.305	0.266	0.233	0.204	0.179	0.168	0.157	0.123	0.068	0.039
9	0.914	0.837	0.801	0.766	0.703	0.645	0.592	0.500	0.424	0.361	0.308	0.284	0.263	0.225	0.194	0.167	0.144	0.134	0.125	0.094	0.048	0.026
10	0.905	0.820	0.781	0.744	0.676	0.614	0.558	0.463	0.386	0.322	0.270	0.247	0.227	0.191	0.162	0.137	0.116	0.107	0.099	0.073	0.035	0.017
11	0.896	0.804	0.762	0.722	0.650	0.585	0.527	0.429	0.350	0.287	0.237	0.215	0.195	0.162	0.135	0.112	0.094	0.086	0.079	0.056	0.025	0.012
12	0.887	0.788	0.744	0.701	0.625	0.557	0.497	0.397	0.319	0.257	0.208	0.187	0.168	0.137	0.112	0.092	0.076	0.069	0.062	0.043	0.018	0.008
13	0.879	0.773	0.725	0.681	0.601	0.530	0.469	0.368	0.290	0.229	0.182	0.163	0.145	0.116	0.093	0.075	0.061	0.055	0.050	0.033	0.013	0.005
14	0.870	0.758	0.708	0.661	0.577	0.505	0.442	0.340	0.263	0.205	0.160	0.141	0.125	0.099	0.078	0.062	0.049	0.044	0.039	0.025	0.009	0.003
15	0.861	0.743	0.690	0.642	0.555	0.481	0.417	0.315	0.239	0.183	0.140	0.123	0.108	0.084	0.065	0.051	0.040	0.035	0.031	0.020	0.006	0.002
16	0.853	0.728	0.674	0.623	0.534	0.458	0.394	0.292	0.218	0.163	0.123	0.107	0.093	0.071	0.054	0.042	0.032	0.028	0.025	0.015	0.005	0.002
17	0.844	0.714	0.657	0.605	0.513	0.436	0.371	0.270	0.198	0.146	0.108	0.093	0.080	0.060	0.045	0.034	0.026	0.023	0.020	0.012	0.003	0.001
18	0.836	0.700	0.641	0.587	0.494	0.416	0.350	0.250	0.180	0.130	0.095	0.081	0.069	0.051	0.038	0.028	0.021	0.018	0.016	0.009	0.002	0.001
19	0.828	0.686	0.626	0.570	0.475	0.396	0.331	0.232	0.164	0.116	0.083	0.070	0.060	0.043	0.031	0.023	0.017	0.014	0.012	0.007	0.002	
20	0.820	0.673	0.610	0.554	0.456	0.377	0.312	0.215	0.149	0.104	0.073	0.061	0.951	0.037	0.026	0.019	0.014	0.012	0.010	0.005	0.001	
21	0.811	0.660	0.595	0.538	0.439	0.359	0.294	0.199	0.135	0.093	0.064	0.053	0.044	0.031	0.022	0.015	0.011	0.009	0.008	0.004	0.001	
22	0.803	0.647	0.581	0.522	0.422	0.342	0.278	0.184	0.123	0.083	0.056	0.046	0.038	0.026	0.018	0.013	0.009	0.007	0.006	0.003	0.001	
23	0.795	0.634	0.567	0.507	0.406	0.326	0.262	0.170	0.112	0.074	0.049	0.040	0.033	0.022	0.015	0.010	0.007	0.006	0.005	0.002		
24	0.788	0.622	0.553	0.492	0.390	0.310	0.247	0.158	0.102	0.066	0.043	0.035	0.028	0.019	0.013	0.008	0.006	0.005	0.004	0.002		
25	0.780	0.610	0.539	0.478	0.375	0.295	0.233	0.146	0.092	0.059	0.038	0.030	0.024	0.016	0.010	0.007	0.005	0.004	0.003	0.001		
26	0.772	0.598	0.526	0.464	0.361	0.281	0.220	0.135	0.084	0.053	0.033	0.026	0.021	0.014	0.009	0.006	0.004	0.003	0.002	0.001		
27	0.764	0.586	0.513	0.450	0.347	0.268	0.207	0.125	0.076	0.047	0.029	0.023	0.018	0.011	0.007	0.005	0.003	0.002	0.002	0.001		
28	0.757	0.574	0.501	0.437	0.333	0.255	0.196	0.116	0.069	0.042	0.026	0.020	0.016	0.010	0.006	0.004	0.002	0.002	0.002	0.001		
29	0.749	0.563	0.489	0.424	0.321	0.243	0.185	0.107	0.063	0.037	0.022	0.017	0.014	0.008	0.005	0.003	0.002	0.002	0.001			
30	0.742	0.552	0.477	0.412	0.308	0.231	0.174	0.099	0.057	0.033	0.020	0.015	0.012	0.007	0.004	0.003	0.002	0.001	0.001			
40	0.672	0.453	0.372	0.307	0.208	0.142	0.097	0.046	0.022	0.011	0.005	0.004	0.003	0.001	0.001							
50	0.608	0.372	0.291	0.228	0.141	0.087	0.054	0.021	0.009	0.003	0.001	0.001	0.001									

TABLE A–3

Present value of \$1 received annually; $A_{\overline{n}|r} = \$1 \left[\frac{1 - (1 + r)^{-n}}{r}\right] = \$1P_{n,r}$

Periods to Be Paid	1%	2%	2½%	3%	4%	5%	6%	8%	10%	12%	14%	15%	16%	18%	20%	22%	24%	25%	26%	30%	40%	50%
1	0.990	0.980	0.976	0.971	0.962	0.952	0.943	0.926	0.909	0.893	0.877	0.870	0.862	0.847	0.833	0.820	0.806	0.800	0.794	0.769	0.714	0.667
2	1.970	1.942	1.927	1.914	1.886	1.859	1.833	1.783	1.736	1.690	1.647	1.626	1.605	1.566	1.528	1.492	1.457	1.440	1.424	1.361	1.224	1.111
3	2.941	2.884	2.856	2.829	2.775	2.723	2.673	2.577	2.487	2.402	2.322	2.283	2.246	2.174	2.106	2.042	1.981	1.952	1.923	1.816	1.589	1.407
4	3.902	3.808	3.762	3.717	3.630	3.546	3.465	3.312	3.170	3.037	2.914	2.855	2.798	2.690	2.589	2.494	2.404	2.362	2.320	2.166	1.849	1.605
5	4.853	4.713	4.646	4.580	4.452	4.330	4.212	3.993	3.791	3.605	3.433	3.352	3.274	3.127	2.991	2.864	2.745	2.689	2.635	2.436	2.035	1.737
6	5.795	5.601	5.508	5.417	5.242	5.076	4.917	4.623	4.355	4.111	3.889	3.784	3.685	3.498	3.326	3.167	3.020	2.951	2.885	2.643	2.168	1.824
7	6.728	6.472	6.349	6.230	6.002	5.786	5.582	5.206	4.868	4.564	4.288	4.160	4.039	3.812	3.605	3.416	3.242	3.161	3.083	2.802	2.263	1.883
8	7.652	7.325	7.170	7.020	6.733	6.463	6.210	5.747	5.335	4.968	4.639	4.487	4.344	4.078	3.837	3.619	3.421	3.329	3.241	2.925	2.331	1.922
9	8.566	8.162	7.971	7.786	7.435	7.108	6.802	6.247	5.759	5.328	4.946	4.772	4.607	4.303	4.031	3.786	3.566	3.463	3.366	3.019	2.379	1.948
10	9.471	8.983	8.752	8.530	8.111	7.722	7.360	6.710	6.145	5.650	5.216	5.019	4.833	4.494	4.192	3.923	3.682	3.571	3.465	3.092	2.414	1.965
11	10.368	9.787	9.514	9.253	8.760	8.306	7.887	7.139	6.495	5.938	5.453	5.234	5.029	4.656	4.327	4.035	3.776	3.656	3.544	3.147	2.438	1.977
12	11.255	10.575	10.258	9.954	9.385	8.863	8.384	7.536	6.814	6.194	5.660	5.421	5.197	4.793	4.439	4.127	3.851	3.725	3.606	3.190	2.456	1.985
13	12.134	11.348	10.983	10.635	9.986	9.394	8.853	7.904	7.103	6.424	5.842	5.583	5.342	4.910	4.533	4.203	3.912	3.780	3.656	3.223	2.468	1.990
14	13.004	12.106	11.691	11.296	10.563	9.899	9.295	8.244	7.367	6.628	6.002	5.724	5.468	5.008	4.611	4.265	3.962	3.824	3.695	3.249	2.478	1.993
15	13.865	12.849	12.381	11.938	11.118	10.380	9.712	8.559	7.606	6.811	6.142	5.847	5.576	5.092	4.676	4.315	4.001	3.859	3.726	3.268	2.484	1.995
16	14.718	13.578	13.055	12.561	11.652	10.838	10.106	8.851	7.824	6.974	6.265	5.954	5.668	5.162	4.730	4.357	4.033	3.887	3.751	3.283	2.488	1.997
17	15.562	14.292	13.712	13.166	12.166	11.274	10.477	9.122	8.022	7.120	6.373	6.047	5.749	5.222	4.775	4.391	4.059	3.910	3.771	3.295	2.492	1.998
18	16.398	14.992	14.353	13.754	12.659	11.690	10.828	9.372	8.201	7.250	6.467	6.128	5.818	5.273	4.812	4.419	4.080	3.928	3.786	3.304	2.494	1.999
19	17.226	15.678	14.979	14.324	13.134	12.085	11.158	9.604	8.365	7.366	6.550	6.198	5.878	5.316	4.844	4.442	4.097	3.942	3.799	3.311	2.496	1.999
20	18.046	16.351	15.589	14.877	13.590	12.462	11.470	9.818	8.514	7.469	6.623	6.259	5.929	5.353	4.870	4.460	4.110	3.954	3.808	3.316	2.497	1.999
21	18.857	17.011	16.185	15.415	14.029	12.821	11.764	10.017	8.649	7.562	6.687	6.312	5.973	5.384	4.891	4.476	4.121	3.963	3.816	3.320	2.498	2.000
22	19.660	17.658	16.765	15.937	14.451	13.163	12.042	10.201	8.772	7.645	6.743	6.359	6.011	5.410	4.909	4.488	4.130	3.970	3.822	3.323	2.498	2.000
23	20.456	18.292	17.332	16.444	14.857	13.489	12.303	10.371	8.883	7.718	6.792	6.399	6.044	5.432	4.924	4.499	4.137	3.976	3.827	3.325	2.499	2.000
24	21.243	18.914	17.885	16.936	15.247	13.799	12.550	10.529	8.985	7.784	6.835	6.434	6.073	5.451	4.937	4.507	4.143	3.981	3.831	3.327	2.499	2.000
25	22.023	19.523	18.424	17.413	15.622	14.094	12.783	10.675	9.077	7.843	6.873	6.464	6.097	5.467	4.948	4.514	4.147	3.985	3.834	3.329	2.499	2.000
26	22.795	20.121	18.951	17.877	15.983	14.375	13.003	10.810	9.161	7.896	6.906	6.491	6.118	5.480	4.956	4.520	4.151	3.988	3.837	3.330	2.500	2.000
27	23.560	20.707	19.464	18.327	16.330	14.643	13.211	10.935	9.237	7.943	6.935	6.514	6.136	5.492	4.964	4.524	4.154	3.990	3.839	3.331	2.500	2.000
28	24.316	21.281	19.965	18.764	16.663	14.898	13.406	11.051	9.307	7.984	6.961	6.534	6.152	5.502	4.970	4.528	4.157	3.992	3.840	3.331	2.500	2.000
29	25.066	21.844	20.454	19.188	16.984	15.141	13.591	11.158	9.370	8.022	6.983	6.551	6.166	5.510	4.975	4.531	4.159	3.994	3.841	3.332	2.500	2.000
30	25.808	22.396	20.930	19.600	17.292	15.372	13.765	11.258	9.427	8.055	7.003	6.566	6.177	5.517	4.979	4.534	4.160	3.995	3.842	3.332	2.500	2.000
40	32.835	27.355	25.103	23.115	19.793	17.159	15.046	11.925	9.779	8.244	7.105	6.642	6.234	5.548	4.997	4.544	4.166	3.999	3.846	3.333	2.500	2.000
50	39.196	31.424	28.362	25.730	21.482	18.256	15.762	12.233	9.915	8.304	7.133	6.660	6.246	5.554	4.999	4.545	4.167	4.000	3.846	3.333	2.500	2.000

Source for Tables A–2 and A–3: Jerome Bracken and Charles J. Christenson, *Tables for Use in Analyzing Business Decisions* (Homewood, Ill.: Richard D. Irwin, Inc., 1965), except for the data on 2½%, the source for which is *Mathematical Tables from Handbook of Chemistry and Physics*, 6th ed. (Cleveland: Chemical Rubber Publishing Co., 1938).

TABLE A–4

Sum of an annuity of $1 for n years

$$S_{\overline{n}|\,r} = \$1 \left[\frac{(1+r)^n - 1}{r} \right] = \$1 C_{n,r}$$

Year	1%	2%	3%	4%	5%	6%	7%	8%
1	1.000	1.000	1.000	1.000	1.000	1.000	1.000	1.000
2	2.010	2.020	2.030	2.040	2.050	2.080	2.070	2.080
3	3.030	3.060	3.091	3.122	3.152	3.184	3.215	3.246
4	4.060	4.122	4.184	4.246	4.310	4.375	4.440	4.506
5	5.101	5.204	5.309	5.416	5.526	5.637	5.751	5.867
6	6.152	6.308	6.468	6.633	6.802	6.975	7.153	7.336
7	7.214	7.434	7.662	7.898	8.142	8.394	8.654	8.923
8	8.286	8.583	8.892	9.214	9.549	9.897	10.260	10.637
9	9.369	9.755	10.159	10.583	11.027	11.491	11.978	12.488
10	10.462	10.950	11.464	12.006	12.578	13.181	13.816	14.487
11	11.567	12.169	12.808	13.846	14.207	14.972	15.784	16.645
12	12.683	13.412	14.192	15.026	15.917	16.870	17.888	18.977
13	13.809	14.680	15.818	16.627	17.713	18.882	20.141	21.495
14	14.947	15.974	17.086	18.292	19.599	21.051	22.550	24.215
15	16.097	17.293	18.599	20.024	21.579	23.276	25.129	27.152

Year	9%	10%	11%	12%	13%	14%	15%	16%
1	1.000	1.000	1.000	1.000	1.000	1.000	1.000	1.000
2	2.090	2.100	2.110	2.120	2.130	2.140	2.150	2.160
3	3.278	3.310	3.342	3.374	3.407	3.440	3.473	3.506
4	4.573	4.641	4.710	4.779	4.850	4.921	4.993	5.066
5	5.985	6.105	6.228	6.353	6.480	6.610	6.742	6.877
6	7.523	7.716	7.913	8.115	8.323	8.536	8.754	8.977
7	9.200	9.487	9.783	10.089	10.405	10.730	11.067	11.414
8	11.028	11.436	11.859	12.300	12.757	13.233	13.727	14.240
9	13.021	13.579	14.164	14.776	15.416	16.085	16.786	17.518
10	15.193	15.937	16.772	17.549	18.420	19.337	20.304	21.321
11	17.560	18.531	19.561	20.655	21.814	23.044	24.349	25.733
12	20.141	21.384	22.713	24.133	25.650	27.271	29.002	30.850
13	22.953	24.523	26.212	28.029	29.985	32.089	34.352	36.786
14	26.019	27.975	30.095	32.393	34.883	37.581	40.505	43.672
15	29.361	31.772	34.405	37.286	40.417	43.842	47.580	51.659

Examination 1: Chapters 1–6

CHAPTER 1

Select all correct answers for each question.

1. The duties of financial officers include:
   _____ *a)* A role in controlling cash flows.
   _____ *b)* Participation in planning and control such as production or research and development
   _____ *c)* The overseeing of planning and control functions.
   _____ *d)* Responsibility for obtaining outside financing for the company.

2. Financial officers are at a high level in the organization structure of firms because:
   _____ *a)* Of the importance of planning analysis and control operations for which they are responsible.
   _____ *b)* Significant economies can be achieved by centralizing financial operations.
   _____ *c)* They are always in-laws of the president.
   _____ *d)* Many financial decisions are crucial to the survival of the firm.
   _____ *e)* Money is always more important than anything else in a company.

3. The following finance functions contribute to the efficient utilization of resources:
   _____ *a)* Planning and control.
   _____ *b)* Determining factory layouts.
   _____ *c)* Selecting advertising copy.
   _____ *d)* Determining the channels of distribution.
   _____ *e)* Valuation decisions.
   _____ *f)* Management of cash flows.
   _____ *g)* All of the above.

4. The size and riskiness of expected future earnings are influenced by:
   _____ *a)* Product-market mix of the firm.
   _____ *b)* Liquidity position of the firm.
   _____ *c)* Size of the firm.
   _____ *d)* Tax status of major stockholders.

_____ *e)* Rate of growth of the firm.
_____ *f)* Debt-to-equity proportions of the firm.

CHAPTER 2

Fill in the blanks with the correct words or phrases.

1. When cash is acquired through the issuance of common stock, current assets increase as well as _____ and _____ _____.

2. When raw materials are purchased on credit, both _____ and _____ increase.

3. As work is performed on raw materials, _____ decrease and work-in-process inventories _____.

4. When finished goods are sold, total assets will further increase because _____ are valued at selling price, whereas the _____ are valued on a cost basis.

5. When sales have been made and accounts receivable increased, _____ will change by the amount of net profit on sales.

6. Although the total assets of a firm will increase with the purchase of raw materials on credit and the recording of sales reflected in increases in accounts receivable, the firm may encounter a _____ or _____ problem because of the need to meet _____.

CHAPTER 3

1. Match the ratio category with the proper definition below.

   Ratio category
   (1) Activity ratios.
   (2) Cost-structure ratios.
   (3) Leverage ratios.
   (4) Liquidity ratios.

(5)   Profitability ratios.
(6)   None of the above.

Definition

———— Measures the ability to meet near-term maturing liabilities.

———— Measures how effectively the firm is managing the control of its costs.

———— Measures the firm's overall effectiveness of operations and policies.

———— Measures how effectively the firm is managing its investments in assets.

———— Measures the extent to which the firm finances its investments and operations by the use of debt.

2. The ———— and ———— ratios reflect management policies. Up to a point, decreasing ———— and increasing ———— will increase the profitability of the firm.

3. Name the ratio.

Ratio   *Formula for calculation*

———— *a.* Net income/Sales

———— *b.* (Current assets–Inventories)/Current liabilities

———— *c.* Receivables/Sales per day

———— *d.* Total debt/Total assets

———— *e.* (Sales–Cost of goods sold)/Sales

———— *f.* Net income/Net worth

———— *g.* (EBIT + Rentals)/Fixed charges

4. Financial ratios of companies are evaluated by three main methods: ————, ————, and ————, used in conjunction with both of the preceding.

5. ———— is the basic forecasting variable in financial ratio analysis, budgeting, and financial forecasting.

6. If inventory turnover is low (select all correct answers):

———— *a)* Profits will be depressed.

———— *b)* Sales are lost because of the lack of a sufficient quantity of inventories.

———— *c)* Some inventories may be obsolete and current assets are overstated.

———— *d)* Fixed assets may be underutilized.

7. An average collection period in excess of the industry average may indicate (select all correct answers):

———— *a)* Credit terms are liberal.

———— *b)* Collection policies are lax.

———— *c)* Bad-debt writeoffs may occur.

———— *d)* Sales are too small.

———— *e)* Balance sheet value of accounts receivable is overstated.

———— *f)* Current assets are too small.

8. A firm's total asset turnover is influenced by (select all correct answers):

———— *a)* Lease of plant or equipment.

———— *b)* Nature of the industry.

———— *c)* Size of the firm.

———— *d)* Total sales.

9. When the current ratio is two to one, this means that current assets may shrink by ———— percent before the firm cannot meet maturing short-term liabilities.

10. The Dun and Bradstreet industry ratios (select all correct answers):

———— *a)* Group ratios by size of firm.

———— *b)* Present 14 different ratios.

———— *c)* Are useful for comparison against similar ratios of the individual firm.

———— *d)* Should be used mechanically in judging a firm.

———— *e)* Show historical trends.

11. Financial ratios are used for (select all correct answers):

———— *a)* Time-trend analysis.

———— *b)* Comparisons with industry averages.

———— *c)* Planning and control functions.

———— *d)* Aiding the evaluation by outside creditors and security analysts.

12. Determine the cost of goods sold from the following: Inventory turnover = 4; Gross profit margin = 30%; Current ratio = 2.5; Quick ratio = 1.1; Current liabilities = $350,000.

CHAPTER 4

1. The du Pont chart system of planning and control (select all correct answers):

———— *a)* Is used in planning and control of divisions in multidivisional firms.

———— *b)* Is concerned with return on investment.

———— *c)* Shows all factors that measure the efficiency of managing company's investments and controlling costs.

———— *d)* Should be employed to judge the financial policy of the company.

2. In the duPont system, division managers are held responsible for (select all correct answers):

———— *a)* Leverage of the firm.

———— *b)* Liquidity of the firm.

———— *c)* Areas of activity for which they have authority.

———— *d)* Use of assets under their control.

———— *e)* Net income available to equity holders.

———— *f)* Activity ratios.

3. Return on net investment (total assets net of the reserve for depreciation) is particularly sensitive to ———————— and ———— policies.

4. Return on total investment is the product of ———— and ————————————.

CHAPTER 5

1. The balance sheet for the Huggies Company is shown below for sales of $300,000. Using the percentage of sales method, assuming no long-term debt is paid off, how much outside financing is required? (Assume net profit to sales is 5 percent, payout ratio is 40 percent of net income, and sales increase 50 percent during 1974).

HUGGIES COMPANY
Balance Sheet as of 12/31/7A

Cash............................	$ 15,000
Accounts receivable............	60,000
Inventory.......................	90,000
Current assets..................	$165,000
Fixed assets....................	30,000
Total Assets..............	$195,000
Accounts payable...............	$ 30,000
Accruals.......................	15,000
Notes payable..................	0
Total current debt liabilities.....	$ 45,000
Long-term debt.................	90,000
Total debt.....................	$135,000
Capital stock..................	60,000
Retained earnings..............	0
Total debt and Net Worth.......	$195,000

2. The first and most important step in developing a financial forecast is the firm's forecast of ————.

3. The percentage of sales method of financial forecasting can be in error for extended period projections because (select all correct answers):

———— *a)* The sales forecast was incorrect.

———— *b)* The rate of profitability was not as projected.

———— *c)* Relationships between balance sheet items and sales did not remain unchanged.

———— *d)* Costs increased.

4. In order to make a financial forecast we need to know (select all correct answers):

———— *a)* The industry the firm is in.

———— *b)* The age of the company.

———— *c)* The size of the company.

———— *d)* The estimated sales volume.

———— *e)* The expected growth rate in sales.

5. Long-term growth should normally be financed by (select all correct answers):

———— *a)* Short-term debt.

———— *b)* Long-term debt.

———— *c)* Equity.

6. ———————————————— and ———— ———— are methods used to produce financial forecasts.

7. For the data given below, the slope of the regression line would be ————————.

Year	(X) Sales	(Y) Inventory
197A.................	$ 750,000	$100,000
197B.................	1,500,000	125,000
197C.................	2,250,000	150,000
197D.................	3,000,000	175,000
197E.................	3,750,000	200,000
197F.................	4,500,000	225,000

8. In Problem 7, the intercept of the line is

———— *a)* $ 25,000.

———— *b)* 45,000.

———— *c)* 75,000.

———— *d)* 90,000.

———— *e)* 100,000.

9. In Problem 7, the ———————— of the line is the base to which additional amounts of inventory are added as sales increase.

———— *a)* Slope.

———— *b)* Intercept on the inventory axis.

_____ c)   Intercept on the sales axis.
_____ d)   Length.
_____ e)   None of the above.

CHAPTER 6

1. A budget is a (select all correct answers):
    _____ a)   Planning and control device.
    _____ b)   Tool.
    _____ c)   Guide.
    _____ d)   Method to improve operations.

2. Budgets are developed (select all correct answers):
    _____ a)   For every significant activity of the firm.
    _____ b)   To provide an integrated picture of the firm's operations as a whole.
    _____ c)   From forecasts of types of assets required to support sales.
    _____ d)   To allow managers to trace the effect of a particular decision on the outlook for the firm.

3. The _____ indicates the combined effect of the budgeted operations on the firm's _____.

4. If an increase in the volume of a firm's operations results in a _____ cash flow, the cash budget will show the amount of _____ and its _____ as well.

5. Break-even analysis is used to determine the point at which sales will just cover _____ _____.

6. The degree of _____ is defined as the percentage change in operating income that results from a percentage change in units sold.

7. The Granite Quarry sells granite blocks to artists for $1,000 each. It now sells 5,000 blocks a year with variable costs of $750 per unit. It realizes a net profit of $500,000. What is the amount of fixed costs?

8. The break-even point for the facts in Problem 7 is a quantity sold of _____.

9. The degree of operating leverage for Granite Quarry in Problem 7 is _____.

10. Assume that variable costs rise by $50 a unit. If sales stay at 5,000 units, to what level would the price have to rise for the same $500,000 profit to be realized?
    _____ a)   1,025.
    _____ b)   1,050.
    _____ c)   1,075.
    _____ d)   1,100.
    _____ e)   1,125.
    _____ f)   1,150.

11. If the price rises to $1,200, what would the quantity sold have to be to maintain the $500,000 profit when variable costs have risen to $800 per unit?
    _____ a)   2,875.
    _____ b)   3,000.
    _____ c)   3,125.
    _____ d)   3,250.
    _____ e)   3,750.
    _____ f)   4,000.

12. A greater degree of operating leverage:
    _____ a)   Magnifies the percentage change in profits in response to a percentage change in sales.
    _____ b)   Decreases the percentage change in total costs by its value.
    _____ c)   At any one point is the difference between sales and variable cost divided by profit.
    _____ d)   Has no significance.

Now compare your answers with those on page 229.

Examination 2: Chapters 7–9

CHAPTER 7

Select all correct answers to each question.

1. Current assets are composed of:
   _____ *a)* Equipment.
   _____ *b)* Inventory.
   _____ *c)* Cash.
   _____ *d)* Investment tax credits.

2. Net working capital is:
   _____ *a)* Current assets.
   _____ *b)* Cash, inventories, and accounts receivable.
   _____ *c)* Current assets − Fixed assets.
   _____ *d)* Current assets − Current liabilities.
   _____ *e)* Cash + Marketable securities.

3. Cash and cash equivalent include:
   _____ *a)* Currency on hand.
   _____ *b)* Time deposits in banks.
   _____ *c)* Demand deposits at commercial banks.
   _____ *d)* Holdings of officers' five-year promissory notes.
   _____ *e)* Marketable securities.

4. Cash is held because of:
   _____ *a)* Transaction requirements.
   _____ *b)* Precautionary motives.
   _____ *c)* Speculative motives.
   _____ *d)* Distrust of banks.
   _____ *e)* Businessmen make poor investments.

5. Float is:
   _____ *a)* Checks written on a demand account not yet cashed.
   _____ *b)* Collateral.
   _____ *c)* Liquidity.
   _____ *d)* Funds in transit.
   _____ *e)* None of the above.

6. To reduce float:
   _____ *a)* Use a "lock-box plan."
   _____ *b)* Increase cash outflow.
   _____ *c)* Sell fixed assets.
   _____ *d)* Increase accounts receivable.
   _____ *e)* Wear weights while swimming.

7. Level of receivables is influenced by:
   _____ *a)* Seasonality of sales.
   _____ *b)* Volume of sales.
   _____ *c)* Collection policies.
   _____ *d)* Terms of sales and credit policies of individual firms.
   _____ *e)* The liquidity of the firm.

8. The five Cs of credit are:
   _____ *a)* Capacity.
   _____ *b)* Capital.
   _____ *c)* Care.
   _____ *d)* Cash.
   _____ *e)* Character.
   _____ *f)* Collateral.
   _____ *g)* Conditions.
   _____ *h)* Continuity.

9. Terms of 2/20, net 30, mean:
   _____ *a)* Discount of 30 percent if bill is paid within 2 to 10 days.
   _____ *b)* Discount of 2 percent if payment is made within 20 days, otherwise full payment is due within 30 days.
   _____ *c)* Discount of 20 percent and payment is due within 30 days.
   _____ *d)* The supplier will provide 20 percent of an order within 10 days and the rest within 30 days.
   _____ *e)* Nothing.

10. The basic inventory model recognizes that:
    _____ *a)* Carrying costs rise as average inventory holdings increase.
    _____ *b)* Safety stock is necessary.
    _____ *c)* Anticipation stocks are required.
    _____ *d)* Ordering costs and stock-out costs rise as average inventory holdings rise.

11. If a firm sells on terms of net 30 days and its accounts are an average of 30 days overdue, what will its accounts receivable be? (Credit sales = $600,000/year)

12. A firm has sales of 1 million units a year at a cost of $5 a unit. It costs $6,000 to process an order with carrying costs of $.30. The optimal number of orders per year is:

_____ a) 5.
_____ b) 15.
_____ c) 25.
_____ d) 50.
_____ e) 60.

CHAPTER 8

1. Short-term credit is defined as debt:
_____ a) To be repaid within five years.
_____ b) To be repaid within one year.
_____ c) That is small.
_____ d) Carrying low interest rates.

2. The terms on Barnes Supply Company's purchasing of nails is 2/8, net 20. If Barnes does not take the discount, what is its cost of credit?
_____ a) 57.99%.
_____ b) 74.87%.
_____ c) 47.35%.
_____ d) 61.22%.
_____ e) 39.68%.

3. If a firm is able to take advantage of available cash discounts at all times, which credit terms would it find most desirable, all other things constant?
_____ a) 1/10, net 20.
_____ b) 3/10, net 30.
_____ c) 1/10, net 30.
_____ d) 2/10, net 30.

4. A firm should not take advantage of cash discounts when (select all correct answers):
_____ a) It does not have the cash.
_____ b) The borrowing rate is above the implicit interest rate of the discount.
_____ c) The return on other investments is greater than the cost of credit of the discount.
_____ d) When it can spend the cash on executive recreation.

5. If a firm borrows $20,000 from a bank requiring a compensating balance of 15 percent on the loan at a simple interest rate of 12 percent, what is the effective interest rate?

6. Hose Manufacturing borrows $50,000 for a year, having to pay $5,000 in interest. If the bank discounts the loan 20 percent and the company pays the loan off in monthly installments, what is the cost of the loan?
_____ a) 10%.
_____ b) 25%.
_____ c) 16%.
_____ d) 31%.
_____ e) 20%.

7. The two most common collateral used for short-term credit are:
_____ a) Accounts receivable.
_____ b) Land.
_____ c) Inventories.
_____ d) Demand deposit accounts.

8. The factor performs which one(s) of the following?
_____ a) A credit-checking function.
_____ b) A field warehousing function.
_____ c) A risk-bearing function.
_____ d) A lending function.
_____ e) An algebraic function.

CHAPTER 9

1. Working capital policy involves decisions with respect to which one(s) of the following?
_____ a) Inventories.
_____ b) Mix of current versus fixed assets.
_____ c) Fixed assets.
_____ d) Relation between current assets and liabilities.

2. Although both _____ and _____ assets are functions of expected sales, only _____ assets can readily be adjusted to actual sales in the short run.

3. A conservative working capital policy is slack in the sense that there is ample investment in _____ and _____; in addition there is _____ by current liabilities as compared with financing by _____.

4. Under a tight or aggressive working capital policy, _____ are held to a minimum, _____ are very tight, and _____ are vigorously pursued.

5. Under a conservative working capital policy, the _____ is much _____ than under an aggressive working capital policy.

6. While the state of the economy will affect the level of sales, under a conservative (slack) working capital policy, sales are likely to be _____ than under a more _____ working capital policy.

7. A conservative working capital policy is likely to involve _____ fixed costs because of larger investment costs of holding more inventories; a tighter working capital policy will involve higher _____.

8. One risk of heavy reliance on short-term debt is that during a period of _____, the firm may _____ _____ its loans.

Now compare your answer with those on page 230.

Examination 3: Chapters 10–12

CHAPTER 10

1. A firm's earnings are $5,000, at a 10 percent growth rate. How many years will it take for earnings to triple?

2. What would an investor who demands a 6 percent yield pay for a $1,000 five-year bond which pays $40 interest semiannually?

3. An item of equipment is expected to have a salvage value of $20,000 at the end of 10 years. What is its present value at a 12 percent interest rate?

4. An item of equipment costs $50,000 and will achieve savings of $20,000 for five years. What is the rate of return on the investment?

5. An item of equipment will provide savings of $10,000 for eight years. The firm's cost of capital used in discounting is 12 percent. What is the most the firm could pay for the equipment to earn its cost of capital?

6. A firm invests $35,000 in a piece of equipment which will bring in savings of $10,000 per year for six years. At a cost of capital of 12 percent what is the net present value of this project?

CHAPTER 11

1. Each of two projects requires an $800 investment. The firm's cost of capital is 10 percent. The cash flow patterns (income returns after taxes plus depreciation) for each project follows:

Year	Project A	Project B
1	400	100
2	400	200
3	200	200
4	100	200
5	10	300
6	10	400

For projects A and B, respectively, the net present values are:

_____ a) $100 and $155.
_____ b) $112 and $112.
_____ c) $124 and $155.
_____ d) $198 and $155.

2. For projects A and B, respectively, the internal rates of return are:

_____ a) 13% and 15%.
_____ b) 15% and 14%.
_____ c) 18% and 20%.
_____ d) 18% and 15%.

3. Ranking the two projects according to NPV, IRR, and payback period:

_____ a) All methods give the same ranking.
_____ b) IRR gives a different ranking from the other two.
_____ c) Payback period gives a different ranking from the other two.
_____ d) NPV gives a different ranking from the other two.

4. The payback method is defective in that it ignores _____ _____ and _____ of money: it is useful in providing information on an aspect of _____.

5. In general, the theoretically correct method of ranking investment proposals is provided by the _____ method.

CHAPTER 12

1. In two-asset diversification, the least beneficial effect of diversification is achieved if the correlation between the two products is:

_____ a) +1.
_____ b) +0.5.
_____ c) 0.
_____ d) −0.5.
_____ e) −1.

2. The probability distribution of cash flows from a project with high risk would be:

_____ a) Exponential.

_____ b) Relatively flat.
_____ c) Relatively peaked.
_____ d) Skewed.
_____ e) None of the above.

3. A risk averter would have what kind of marginal utility for money?
_____ a) Diminishing.
_____ b) Constant.
_____ c) Increasing.
_____ d) Exponential.

4. Your company can invest $4,000 in one of two possible projects, each of which would yield the following returns for four years.

Project A		Project B	
Probability	Cash flow	Probability	Cash flow
.1	$2,000	.1	$ 100
.4	$3,000	.4	$3,500
.2	$3,600	.2	$7,500
.3	$3,400	.3	$6,500

If the riskier project is evaluated at a 12 percent cost of capital versus 9 percent for the less risky project, the NPV's for A and B, respectively, are:
_____ a) $8,858 and $7,818.
_____ b) $10,700 and $9,990.
_____ c) $3,572 and $14,000.
_____ d) $6,174 and $10,760.

5. Returns on investments j and k are not correlated but they have equal expected returns. To minimize the risk of a portfolio containing only j and k, where $\sigma_j = 8\%$ and $\sigma_k = 12\%$, the proportion of k should be:
_____ a) .69.
_____ b) .60.
_____ c) .40.
_____ d) .31.

6. The standard deviation is divided by the mean to calculate the _____ _____; this normalizes the _____ _____ for the size of the units measured.

7. The element of risk not eliminated by diversification is the _____ _____ between securities.

8. The nature of covariance is illuminated by recognizing that it is equal to _____ _____ _____ _____.

9. Generally, it is considered that investors can diversify _____ than business firms.

10. Since investments usually involve a choice between _____ and _____, the choice of the appropriate combination depends upon _____ _____.

Now compare your answers with those on page 231.

Examination 4: Chapters 13–15

CHAPTER 13

1. Union Electric is expected to earn $2.80 a share and it currently pays $1.40 annual dividend. Its current price is $28 per share.
   a) Its dividend yield is _____.
   b) Its price to earnings ratio is _____.

2. A firm's stock is selling for $40 a share. The firm is earning $4 per share and paying a $3 dividend.
   a) At what rate must earnings, dividends, and price all grow if investors require a 12 percent return?
   b) If retained earnings are reinvested at the required rate of return, what will be the new earnings per share?

3. Company A issues $1,000 consols with an 8 percent coupon rate. If investors expect to earn 7 percent on this type of bond, what will they pay?

4. Risk units of market returns are measured by the _____ _____. Risk units of company (or inefficient portfolio) returns equal _____ _____.

5. The capital market line for efficient portfolios indicates that the required return on a portfolio is equal to the _____ _____ plus _____ _____ times _____ _____.

6. The capital market line for individual securities has a different measure for the _____ and for the _____.

7. For an individual security, the market risk premium is divided by the _____ of market return instead of its _____.

8. The CML for individual securities is linear when the measure of risk employed is the _____

_____.

9. The beta or volatility of the returns to an individual security is the _____ _____ divided by the _____ _____.

10. The current earnings-price ratio does not represent the _____ since the E/P ratio varies inversely with the _____ _____ _____.

11. The cost of equity may be estimated from the sum of the _____ plus _____ _____.

CHAPTER 14

1. The capitalization of a firm is equal to _____ less _____.

2. Financial risk is the risk compounded on business and operating risk resulting from the use of _____.

3. The leverage ratio is the ratio of _____ to _____.

4. Increased leverage will _____ fluctuations in the returns to equity.

5. If used successfully, leverage will _____ _____ to owners.

6. In a no-tax world, leverage will _____ _____ on a firm's cost of capital.

7. In a no-tax world, the cost of equity is _____ _____ _____ plus the difference between _____ and the _____ weighted by the _____.

8. In a world of taxes, the use of leverage will _____ the value of a firm.

9. In a world with corporate taxes, the value of a leveraged firm is equal to _____ _____ plus _____ _____ _____ .

10. The weighted average cost of capital is equal to the _____ weighted by the ratio of _____ _____ plus the _____ weighted by the ratio of _____ _____; this is also equal to _____ _____ times one minus the tax rate all divided by _____ _____ .

11. The increase in the total cost of financing caused by an increment in the amount of financing represents _____ _____ .

12. At some degree of financial leverage, the increasing risks of _____ cause both the cost of equity and of debt to _____; at this point the value of the firm would _____ with increasing leverage.

13. Both the marginal price of risk approach and the weighted cost of capital approach can be used to estimate a _____ _____ or _____ _____ .

CHAPTER 15

1. An increase in which one(s) of the following is likely to decrease a firm's ability or willingness to pay dividends?
_____ *a)* Current ratio.
_____ *b)* Target growth rate of assets.
_____ *c)* Debt ratio.
_____ *d)* Rate of return on assets.

2. The residual theory of dividend policy asserts that:
_____ *a)* Total dividend payments are constant. Residual earnings are invested internally.

_____ *b)* Dividend payout ratio is constant. Residual earnings are invested internally.
_____ *c)* Dividends are residual after investment needs have been met.
_____ *d)* Dividends are a constant percentage of residual investments in the firm.

3. Before a 3-for-1 split, **X** Company stock sold for $45 a share, earning $12 and paying $6 dividend per share. After the split, the dividend per share becomes $2.40. By what percentage has the payout increased?

4. If the investment influence is neutralized, the effect of dividend policy on the value of a firm depends upon _____ _____ .

5. Share repurchase may have a useful function to perform if the firm _____ _____ as much as the shareholders' _____ .

6. One rationale for paying out a stable amount of dividends is that fluctuations in the amount of dividends may cause _____ _____ _____ _____ .

7. Neither stock dividends nor stock splits will have a lasting effect on the market value of a firm's stock unless they indicate _____ _____ .

8. The greater the amount of funds raised externally in a given period of time, the higher the _____ is likely to be.

9. The investment decision requires a comparison of _____ with _____ .

10. Investment and financing decisions _____ each other and therefore must be made _____ or in an _____ .

Now compare your answers with those appearing on page 232.

Examination 5: Chapters 16–22

CHAPTER 16

For each of the questions indicate all correct answers:

1. Financial intermediation:
_____ a) Facilitates the exchange for real goods by lowering transaction costs.
_____ b) Increases real output by redistribution of purchasing power.
_____ c) Is a new development during the past 10 years.
_____ d) Operates between savings surplus and savings deficit units.

2. Financial institutions include which of the following?
_____ a) Securities markets.
_____ b) Manufacturing corporations.
_____ c) Private financial intermediaries.
_____ d) Government institutions.
_____ e) The United Nations.

3. Which of the following are methods the Fed uses to control the money supply?
_____ a) Change reserve requirements.
_____ b) Change tax rates.
_____ c) Conduct open-market operations.
_____ d) Determine the degree of progression of personal income tax rates.
_____ e) Determine the demand for loans by business firms.
_____ f) Discount securities offered by commercial banks.

4. A federal cash deficit is most stimulating to the economy when:
_____ a) Government bonds held by the banking system are retired.
_____ b) Interest rates rise.
_____ c) Securities are sold to the banking system.
_____ d) Interest rates fall.
_____ e) None of the above.

5. Investment bankers' functions include which of the following?

_____ a) Selling a new security issue to permanent investors.
_____ b) Making long-term loans to corporate clients from its own funds.
_____ c) Underwriting new issues.
_____ d) Arranging private financing for a client.

6. Flotation costs for which of the following are greater than for preferred stock?
_____ a) Convertible bonds.
_____ b) Mortgage bonds.
_____ c) Cumulative preferred.
_____ d) Subordinated debentures.
_____ e) Common stock.

7. Regulation of securities trading seeks to:
_____ a) Provide orderly securities markets.
_____ b) Control the use of credit in securities trading.
_____ c) Prevent wide price fluctuations.
_____ d) Provide information to guide investors.
_____ e) Prevent purchase of issues on which price declines may subsequently take place.

8. Interest rate forecasts for the short term:
_____ a) Are based on an analysis of prospective supply and demand of funds.
_____ b) Are affected by the size of the full-employment gap.
_____ c) Are affected by the rate of price level increases on commodities.
_____ d) Are affected by the expected level of interest rates in the longer term future.

9. Long-term securities:
_____ a) Are less risky to hold than short-term securities.
_____ b) Have maturities longer than 10 years.
_____ c) Have more volatile prices than short-term bonds when interest rates change.

_____ *d*) Have interest rates that reflect the expected short-term rates within one year.

10. _____ term interest rates are higher than _____ term and _____ term rates when there is a "hump" in the yield curve.

11. Near the peak of a business upturn:

_____ *a*) Equity prices are at their highest points.

_____ *b*) All interest rates are low.

_____ *c*) Long-term rates are always higher than short-term rates.

_____ *d*) Long-term rates are near their highs.

_____ *e*) Businesses should switch financing from long-term to short-term securities.

CHAPTER 17

1. The board of directors of Ajax industries is being elected. A group of minority stockholders with 750,000 shares seeks to elect some members of the board of 12 directors. The company has 2,500,000 shares outstanding. How many directors can they elect with cumulative voting?

2. The advantages of common stock financing include (select all correct answers):
   a) There is no maturity date.
   b) Flotation costs are cheaper than debt.
   c) No fixed charges are incurred.
   d) There is no dilution of owners' equity as with debt.
   e) The cost of common stock is always lower than the cost of debt.

3. A firm will tend to use equity financing (select all correct answers):
   a) If it has a debt ratio in excess of its leverage target.
   b) If its sales and profits fluctuate widely.
   c) During a "bear" market, when price-earnings ratio is low.
   d) If it is a young firm and long-term debt financing is unavailable.

4. If a corporate charter includes a provision for preemptive rights, the stockholders:
   a) Must sell their stock to the company.
   b) Receive the first option to buy additional issues of common stock.

   c) May purchase existing treasury stock.
   d) Must first attempt to sell their stock.
   e) Cannot utilize cumulative voting procedures.

5. An important feature of the preemptive right is that the rights:
   a) May be sold for profit.
   b) Are negotiable.
   c) Afford stockholders' protection against dilution.
   d) May be cumulatively voted.
   e) Are nontransferable.

6. The preemptive right typically applies to:
   a) All debentures.
   b) All bank loans.
   c) New issues of common stock.
   d) Preferred stock.
   e) All of the above.

7. A rights offering will most likely fail:
   a) If the new issue is small compared to the total common outstanding.
   b) If the issue has shown price stability over the past year.
   c) If the stock is very widely held.
   d) If the subscription price is close to the market price and market prices are fluctuating.
   e) If the stock appears likely to increase in price.

8. The Morrocan Oil Company C.S. is selling on the NYSE @ $16.50. There are 300,000 shares outstanding. The company wishes to raise $800,000 by a rights offering by selling 100,000 new shares at $8 a share.
   a) Disregarding flotation costs, what is the theoretical new market value per share?
   b) What is the theoretical value of one right?

9. Characteristics of long-term debt include (select all correct answers):
   a) The cost of debt is limited but also a fixed obligation.
   b) The amount of debt financing is inversely proportional to the firm's liquidity.
   c) There is a maturity date.
   d) Management has freedom of action.
   e) Bond interest is deductible.

10. For the following list of securities, from one

firm, rank them as to risk for holder [(1) is the safest]

		Rank
a)	Subordinated debenture.	1
b)	Income bonds.	2
c)	First mortgage bonds.	3
d)	Preferred stock.	4
e)	Debentures.	5
f)	Common stock.	6
g)	Second mortgage bond.	7

11. Major factors distinguishing the different positions of alternative forms of financing are _____, _____, and _____.

12. Secured long-term debt issues differ with respect to _____, _____, _____, and _____.

13. Preferred stocks generally have _____ _____, but are usually _____.

14. Taxes have tended to reduce the use of preferred stocks because the dividends paid are _____; however, in mergers, convertible preferred stock has been used to pay selling stockholders since this represents _____ _____.

15. In choosing between alternative forms of financing, two factors of major importance are _____ and _____ _____.

16. In analysis of alternative forms of financing, if the use of debt will increase the leverage ratio far above _____ _____, this will weigh heavily against the use of debt because of _____.

17. The analysis of the initial effects of new financing on indicated earnings per share _____ the relative costs of alternative forms of financing, but does not provide _____ _____ of alternative forms of financing.

CHAPTER 18

1. Term loans (select all correct answers):
   a) usually have financing costs with 14–18 percent effective rates of interest.
   b) are not secured.
   c) are principally supplied by commercial banks and life insurance companies.
   d) may have variable interest rates that are 1–4 percentage points above the Fed's rediscount rate.
   e) are callable at any time.

2. For a term loan of $10,000 due in four years with a stated interest rate of 9 percent, how much is an annual payment?

3. In problem 2, what is the balance of the loan after two years?

4. A conditional sales contract (select all correct answers):
   a) represents accounts receivables financing.
   b) transfers the title of the purchased equipment upon initiation of payments.
   c) can be terminated because it is a conditional contract.
   d) is usually an expensive means of financing compared to unsecured loans.
   e) in default provides for repossession of equipment.

5. Advantages of leasing are (select all correct answers):
   a) Protection against obsolescence.
   b) The increase in firm's availability of nonequity financing.
   c) The ability to obtain financing for longer periods.
   d) Savings because lease payments are tax deductible.
   e) The possibility of obtaining financing at lower cost.

6. Simpson fabrics had a debt-to-equity ratio of 1.1. The company then leased new store equipment which cost 50 percent of total assets. What is the debt to equity ratio of the firm after leasing?
   a) 2.3.
   b) 2.0.
   c) 1.7.
   d) 1.1.
   e) .6.

7. The Henderson Company has an opportunity to purchase a new conveyor line for $200,000. They can borrow $180,000, paying $20,000 down with annual payments for five years and an interest rate of 12 percent. They also have an opportunity to lease the

line for $58,000 a year. At the end of five years, the estimated salvage value is $40,000. If owned, the cost of maintenance is expected to be $8,000 per year. Assume straight-line depreciation, a 50 percent tax rate, an after-tax cost of capital of 16 percent, and an after-tax cost-of-debt of 6 percent. What is the present value of the after-tax cost of leasing for the five-year period?

Questions 8–15 are also based on the statement of facts given in Problem 7.

8. What are the yearly payments required to amortize the loan? What is the present value of these payments?

9. How are the yearly payments divided between interest and amortization of principal? What is the present value of the interest tax shelter?

10. What is the depreciation tax shelter under the borrow-purchase arrangement?

11. What is the present value of the maintenance costs?

12. What is the present value of the estimated salvage that will be realized?

13. What is the total net after-tax cost of the borrow-purchase alternative?

14. Which method of acquiring-financing the use of the equipment has the lower net outflows?

15. What effects would accelerated depreciation have had on the net disadvantage of leasing?

CHAPTER 19

1. The Marsh Company stock is selling at $80. It has convertible bonds outstanding with a conversion ratio of 20. If there is 10 years to maturity on the 20-year convertibles (par value = $1,000 with coupon of 12 percent) and the market rate of interest is 8 percent, compare the straight-debt value of the bond and the conversion value of the bond.

2. The conversion price is usually set _____ the prevailing market price of the common stock at the time the bond issue is sold.
   a) At.
   b) 20 to 30 percent below.
   c) 45 to 50 percent above.

   d) 10 to 15 percent above.
   e) 0 to 5 percent above.

3. Convertibles (select all correct answers):
   a) Permit the sale of debt at lower interest rates than on straight debt.
   b) Are utilized as a sweetener when selling debt.
   c) Might never be converted because of low stock prices.
   d) Can be used when there is little demand for straight debt.
   e) Sell equity at prices higher than present.

4. The warrants of the Stonehead Company are selling for $60, which is an $18 premium over the theoretical value. They allow the purchase of 10 common shares of stock for $10 each. What is the market price of the common stock?

5. Factors to be examined in choosing the use of convertibles or warrants are (select all correct answers):
   a) Financial structure.
   b) Market price of stock.
   c) Earnings per share.
   d) Control position.
   e) Interest rates.

6. The Harrison Company is controlled by John Jacob Harrison who owns 510,000 of 800,000 outstanding shares. In order to insure control which of the following alternatives should be chosen to raise $10 million? The tax rate is 50%.
   (1) Sell convertible bonds with 10 percent coupon rates which are convertible at $50.
   (2) Sell 8 percent debentures with warrants attached that would allow purchase of 15 shares of stock at $40.
   (3) Sell common stock to net $35 per share. Presently the stock is selling for $40.

7. Suppose for Problem 6 EBIT is $20 million and interest expense is originally $2 million, what is initial EPS for each approach?

CHAPTER 20

1. A disadvantage(s) of holding companies is (are):
   a) Partial multiple taxation.

b) Economies of scale.

c) Control with fractional ownership.

d) Isolation of risks.

e) Stockholder approval not required.

2. Which of the following conditions is indicative of a purchase rather than a pooling of interests?

a) Acquired firm's stockholders continue ownership.

b) Accounting methods are unchanged.

c) Total assets of surviving firm are equal to the sum of the assets of the combining firms.

d) Contingent payouts are not permitted.

e) Excess of market value over book value acquired is set up as good will.

3. The Paul and John Company and the Dandy Company have agreed to merge their competing ice cream vending services into one organization, retaining the Paul and John name. The following premerger financial data is given:

	Paul and John	Dandy
Total earnings.........	$120,000	$100,000
Outstanding shares....	30,000	5,000
Earnings per share.....	$ 4.00	$ 20.00
Price-earnings ratio.....	25X	10X
Stock price.............	$ 100.00	$ 200.00

Paul and John will acquire the shares of Dandy by a two-for-one exchange of stock. Assume that combined earnings remain at the premerger level and there are no synergistic effects.

a) How will the merger affect the EPS of Paul and John stockholders?

b) How will the merger affect the EPS of Dandy stockholders?

c) If Paul and John had been growing at 15 percent per year and Dandy at 6 percent, what will be the expected yearly growth rate in total earnings?

4. A firm might be vulnerable to a tender offer if (select all correct answers):

a) It is in a strong liquidity position.

b) Dividend payments have been reduced.

c) Its growth rate is larger than that of the product market.

d) Market value is above book value.

e) None of the above.

5. The following are not sound social reasons for mergers (select all correct answers):

a) Easy entry into a new market.

b) Economies of scale.

c) Risk reduction through diversification.

d) Stock price manipulation.

e) Monopoly control over markets.

f) None of the above.

6. In a _____, the merged firms should be about the same size, both managements should carry on important functions after the merger, and common stock rather than cash or bonds should be used in payment.

7. The total assets of the surviving firm in a pooling are equal to the _____ _____ of the two independent companies.

8. The greatest weight in arriving at valuations in mergers is accorded the _____ _____, _____, and the _____ _____ _____.

9. _____ are sometimes the overriding determinants of merger terms.

10. _____ are represented by complementarities, possible economies of scale, and re-enforcement of capabilities.

11. Generally, in recent years the aggressive acquiring firm had a _____ _____ than the firm it acquired.

12. The basic requirements for the success of mergers are that _____ _____, and that the resulting firm _____ than attainable by the previously independent entities.

CHAPTER 21

Select all correct answers for each question.

1. The primary causes of business failure are:
   _____ a) Technology.
   _____ b) Lack of managerial skill.
   _____ c) Poor location.
   _____ d) Business cycles.
   _____ e) Lack of funds.
   _____ f) Lack of experience.

2. A cash settlement of creditor claims on a pro rata basis is:
   _____ a) An extension.
   _____ b) Creditor control.
   _____ c) A consolidation.
   _____ d) A trust agreement.
   _____ e) A composition.

3. Reorganization procedures consist of several steps including:
   _____ a) Appointment of a trustee.
   _____ b) Approving the reorganization plan.
   _____ c) Filing.
   _____ d) Compensation.
   _____ e) All of these steps are included.

4. In liquidation, the objective is:
   _____ a) To ignore the shareholder claims.
   _____ b) To liquidate as rapidly as possible.
   _____ c) To repay as much as possible of the debts owed.
   _____ d) To make the auctioneer a sizeable commission.
   _____ e) None of the above are correct.

5. The standards of any reorganization plan include:
   _____ a) Fairness.
   _____ b) Tortness.
   _____ c) Feasibility.
   _____ d) Risibility.
   _____ e) All of the above are correct.

6. In order that there be an involuntary petition of bankruptcy, the debtor must have committed one or more of the six acts of bankruptcy. Indicate which of the conditions listed below is not one of the six acts of bankruptcy.
   _____ a) Assignment.
   _____ b) Appointment of receiver or trustee.
   _____ c) Hedging.
   _____ d) Fraudulent conveyance.
   _____ e) Concealment.

7. Technical insolvency occurs when:
   _____ a) Losses occur.
   _____ b) Income is below projected levels.
   _____ c) A firm's liabilities exceed its assets.
   _____ d) Assets exceed liabilities, but a firm cannot meet current obligations.
   _____ e) Revenues do not cover costs.

CHAPTER 22

Select all correct answers for each question.

1. The Transnational Food Corporation has a subsidiary in LDC, a small foreign country. LDC has just devalued its currency against the U.S. dollar. Assuming that TFC is in a net creditor position,
   _____ a) The cost of bribes increases.
   _____ b) The nationalized subsidiary has to be written off.
   _____ c) On translation, the value of the parent company's equity in the subsidiary will decrease.
   _____ d) On translation, the value of the parent company's equity in the subsidiary will increase.

2. When evaluating a capital budgeting decision where investment in a foreign country is contemplated, which of the following are important:
   _____ a) Tax laws in both countries.
   _____ b) OFDI restrictions on direct foreign investments.
   _____ c) Cash flows in the foreign country and cash flows to the parent firm.
   _____ d) Possible currency devaluations.

3. In September 1981, the USP Company has made a sale of goods to a foreign firm and will receive payment in the foreign currency in

December 1981. To avoid the risk of exchange rate fluctuations, USP can:

_____ a) Buy now a forward contract which provides for the sale of dollars into foreign currency units at the 90-day forward rate quoted in September.

_____ b) Buy now a forward contract which provides for the sale of foreign currency units for dollars at the 90-day forward rate quoted in September.

_____ c) Buy now government bonds in the denomination of the foreign currency units in which USP will be paid in December and in the amount that is due.

_____ d) Borrow now in foreign currency from a bank in the country in which the buyer is located and in the amount that USP will be receiving in December 1981.

_____ e) Convert the foreign currency units into dollars at the spot rate prevailing in December 1981 when the payment is received.

4. In September 1981, the UST Company has made a purchase of goods from a foreign firm and must make payment in the foreign currency in December 1981. To avoid the risk that the value of the foreign currency units will rise by the time payment is due in December 1981, UST can:

_____ a) Buy now a forward contract which provides for the sale of dollars into foreign currency units at the 90-day forward rate quoted in September.

_____ b) Buy now a forward contract which provides for the sale of foreign currency units for dollars at the 90-day forward rate quoted in September.

_____ c) Buy now government bonds in the denomination of the foreign currency units in which UST will pay in December and in the amount that is due.

_____ d) Borrow now in foreign currency from a bank in the country in which the seller is located and in the amount that UST will be paying in December 1981.

_____ e) Convert the foreign currency units into dollars at the spot rate prevailing in December 1981 when the payment is received.

5. The following are monetary assets:

_____ a) Cash.

_____ b) Notes receivable.

_____ c) Equipment.

_____ d) Land.

_____ e) Notes payable.

6. The following are monetary liabilities:

_____ a) Cash.

_____ b) Bonds payable.

_____ c) Notes payable.

_____ d) Accounts receivable.

_____ e) Machinery.

_____ f) Inventory.

Now compare your answers with those appearing on page 233.

Answers to examinations

EXAMINATION 1: CHAPTERS 1–6

Chapter 1

1. *a, b, c, d*
2. *a, b, d*
3. *a, e, f*
4. *a, b, c, e, f*

Chapter 2

1. net working capital; current ratio
2. current assets; current liabilities
3. cash and raw materials; increase
4. accounts receivable; finished goods inventories
5. retained earnings
6. financing or liquidity; maturing obligations

Chapter 3

1. 4, 2, 5, 1, 3
2. liquidity, leverage; liquidity, leverage
3. *a.* profit margin on sales
   b. quick ratio
   c. average collection period
   d. leverage ratio
   e. gross profit margin
   f. return on net worth
   g. fixed charges coverage
4. historical trends, comparisons with composite ratios, judgment
5. sales
6. *a, c, d*
7. *a, b, c, e*
8. *a, b, c, d*
9. 50
10. *b, c*
11. *a, b, c, d*
12. 2.5 × $350,000 = Current assets of $875,000;

($875,000 less inventories)/Current liabilities = 1.1; inventories = $490,000.
Sales = 4 × $490,000 = $1,960,000.
Cost of goods sold = 0.7 sales = $1,372,000.

Chapter 4

1. *a, b, c*
2. *c, d, f*
3. rate of asset replacement; depreciation
4. turnover; profit margin on sales

Chapter 5

1. *Solution:*

	Percent of sales
Cash	5%
Accounts receivable	20
Inventory	30
Current assets	55
Fixed assets	10
Total assets	65

	Percent of sales
Accounts payable	10%
Accruals	5
Notes payable	X
Long-term debt	X
Capital stock	X
Retained earnings	—

Percent of sales

  65% Total assets
−15 Spontaneous financing
  50% Financed by notes payable, long-term and equity

Sales increase by 50% to $450,000
Increase of $150,000
To be financed = 0.5 × $150,000 = $75,000
Net profit = 0.05 × $450,000 = $22,500
Retained earnings = 0.6 × Net profit = 0.6 × $22,500 = $13,500
Additional financing required = $75,000 − $13,500 = $61,500

2. sales
3. *a, b, c, d*
4. *a, b, c, d, e*
5. *b, c*

6. percent of sales method, regression method
7. *Solution:* $Y = A + BX$

$B =$ Change in Y/Change in X

$$= \frac{(225,000 - 100,000)}{(4,500,000 - 750,000)}$$

$B = 1/30 = 0.033$

8. *c. Solution:* $Y = BX + A$

$100,000 = 750,000 \, (1/30) + A$

$A = 75,000$

9. *b*

Chapter 6

1. *a, b, c, d*
2. *a, b, c, d*
3. cash budget; cash flows
4. negative; additional financing required; timing
5. total costs
6. operating leverage
7. *Solution:*

Let   Q = Quantity sold = 5,000;   FC = Fixed costs = SP = Sales price = $1,000; VC = Variable costs = $750.

Q(SP − VC) − FC = Profit = $500,000

5,000 (1,000 − 750) − 500,000 = FC

FC = $750,000

8. *Solution:*

Q(S − VC) − FC = 0

Q($1,000 − $750) − $750,000

Q = $750,000/$250 = 3,000

9. *Solution:*

OL_Q = (S − VC)/(S − VC − FC)

   = (5,000,000 − 3,750,000)/(1,250,000 − 750,000)

   = 1,250,000/500,000 = 2.5

10. *Solution: b*

5,000 (SP − $800) − $750,000 = $500,000

5,000 SP − $4,000,000 − $750,000 = $500,000

5,000 SP = $5,250,000

SP = $1,050

11. *Solution: c*

Q(SP − VC) − FC = Profit

Q($1,200 − $800) − $750,000 = $500,000

$400Q = $1,250,000

Q = 3,125

12. *a*

EXAMINATION 2: CHAPTERS 7–9

Chapter 7

1. *b, c*
2. *d*
3. *a, c, e*
4. *a, b, c*
5. *a, d*
6. *a*
7. *a, b, c, d*
8. *a, b, e, f, g*
9. *b*
10. *a, b*
11. ($600,000)[60/360] = $100,000
12. *Solution: a*

$$EOQ = \sqrt{\frac{2FS}{C}}$$

EOQ = Economical order quantity

s = Sales/per period in units = = 1,000,000

p = Price per unit = $5

F = Purchasing cost per order = $6,000.000

c = Inventory carrying charge = $.30

$$EOQ = \sqrt{\frac{2(6,000)(1,000,000)}{\$.30}}$$

   = 200,000/order

Optimal numbers of orders = S/EOQ = 1,000,000/200,000 = 5

Chapter 8

1. *b*
2. *Solution: d*

$$Cost = \frac{Discount\ percent}{(100 - Discount\ percent)}$$

$$\times \frac{360}{(Final\ due\ date - Discount\ period)}$$

$$= \frac{2}{98} \times \frac{360}{20 - 8} = 61.22\%$$

3. *b*
4. *b, c*
5. *Solution:*

Annual interest = 0.12 × 20,000 = $2,400

Amount of loan = $20,000

Compensating balance = 0.15 × 20,000

   = $3,000

$$\text{Cost} = \frac{\$2,400}{\$20,000 - 3,000} = 14.12\%$$

6. *Solution: b*
   Amount of loan = \$50,000
   Annual interest = \$5,000
   Discount amount = $0.2 \times 50,000 = 10,000$

   Amortized loan—has use of $\dfrac{50,000 - 10,000}{2}$
   for a year.

   $$\text{Cost} = \frac{\$5,000}{\dfrac{\$50,000 - 10,000}{2}} = \frac{\$5,000 \times 2}{\$40,000}$$

   Cost = 25%
7. *a, c*
8. *a, c, d*

Chapter 9

1. *a, b, d*
2. current; fixed; current
3. inventories; accounts receivables; relatively less financing; long-term debt
4. inventories; credit terms; collections
5. current ratio; higher
6. higher; aggressive
7. higher; variable costs
8. tight money; not be able to renew

EXAMINATION 3: CHAPTERS 10–12

Chapter 10

1. *Solution:*
   On a compound sum table under 10%, 3.0 appears halfway between the 11th year (2.853) and 12th year (3.138). Therefore, it requires 11.5 years to triple money earning 10%.

2. *Solution:*

\$1,000	Maturity value of bond
×0.744	Present value factor, 3% for 10 semi-annual periods
\$ 744	
\$ 40.000	Semiannual
× 8.530	Present value of an annuity factor, 3% for 10 semiannual periods
\$341.200	
\$ 744.00	
+341.20	
\$1,085.20	\$1,085

3. $(\$20,000)(0.322) = \$6,440$
4. $(\$50,000/\$20,000) = 2.5 =$ Present value of annuity factor for 5 years $\cong 28\%$
5. \$10,000 × Present value of annuity at 12% for 8 years
   $\$10,000 \times 4.968 = \$49,680$
6. Present value of savings = Present value of annuity of 12% for 6 years times \$10,000 = $4.111(\$10,000) = \$41,111$
   Cost of investment = \$35,000
   Net present value = Present value of savings less cost of investment
   $= \$41,111 - \$35,000$
   $= \$6,111$

Chapter 11

1. *Solution: c*
   Using present value tables under 10%:

Year	Interest factor	PV of A	PV of B
1	.909	\$364	\$ 91
2	.826	330	165
3	.751	150	150
4	.683	68	137
5	.621	6	186
6	.564	6	226
Total present value		\$924	\$955
Less initial investment		800	800
		\$124	\$155

2. *Solution: d*
   By trial and error determine the discount rate to equate the present values of cash inflows to the cost of the investment.

	Project A		
Year	Interest factor at 18%	Cash inflows	PV of A
1	0.847	\$400	\$338.8
2	0.718	400	287.2
3	0.609	200	121.8
4	0.516	100	51.6
5	0.437	10	4.4
6	0.370	10	3.7
Total Present Value			\$807.5
Less Initial Investment			800.0

Project B			
Year	Interest factor at 15%	Cash inflows	PV of B
1	.870	$100	$ 87.0
2	.756	200	151.2
3	.658	200	131.6
4	.572	200	114.4
5	.497	300	149.1
6	.432	400	172.8
Total Present Value			$806.1
Less Initial Investment			800.0

3. *Solution: d*

Payback period for A is 2 years. Payback period for B is $4\frac{1}{3}$ years.

Rank	NPV	IRR	Payback
1	B	A	A
2	A	B	B

Only NPV gives a different ranking from the other two.

4. returns beyond the payback period; time value; liquidity

5. net present value (NPV)

Chapter 12

1. *a*
2. *b*
3. *a*
4. *Solution: d*

Expected cash flow (A)

$$
\begin{aligned}
&= \$2{,}000 \times .1 = \$2{,}200 \\
&+ \ 3{,}000 \times .4 = \ 1{,}200 \\
&+ \ 3{,}600 \times .2 = \ \ \ 720 \\
&+ \ 3{,}400 \times .3 = \ 1{,}020 \\
&\phantom{+ \ 3{,}400 \times .3 = } \overline{\$3{,}140}
\end{aligned}
$$

Expected cash flow (B)

$$
\begin{aligned}
&= \$ \ \ 100 \times .1 = \$ \ \ \ 10 \\
&+ \ 3{,}500 \times .4 = \ 1{,}400 \\
&+ \ 7{,}500 \times .2 = \ 1{,}500 \\
&+ \ 6{,}500 \times .3 = \ 1{,}950 \\
&\phantom{+ \ 6{,}500 \times .3 = } \overline{\$4{,}860}
\end{aligned}
$$

Project B, with greater variability, is more risky and evaluated at 12%. From present value of an annuity table for 4 years, if (9%) = 3.240 and if (12%) = 3.037:

$$
\begin{aligned}
\text{NPV (A)} &= \$3{,}140 \times 3.240 - \$4{,}000 \\
&= \underline{\underline{\$6{,}174}} \\
\text{NPV (B)} &= \$4{,}860 \times 3.037 - \$4{,}000 \\
&= \underline{\underline{\$10{,}760}}
\end{aligned}
$$

Project B is preferable.

5. *Solution: d*

Use the equation for proportion:

$$
X_k = \frac{\sigma_j(\sigma_j - \text{COR}_{jk}\sigma_k)}{\sigma_j{}^2 + \sigma_k{}^2 - 2\text{COR}_{jk}\sigma_j\sigma_k}
$$

where:

$$
\sigma_j = .08
$$
$$
\sigma_k = .12
$$
$$
\text{COR}_{jk} = 0
$$

$$
X_k = \frac{.08(.08 - 0)}{(.08)^2 + (.12)^2 - 0} \approx 0.31
$$

6. coefficient of variation; risk measure

7. covariance of returns

8. correlation coefficient times the product of the standard deviation of each security

9. more efficiently

10. return; risk; the investor's attitude toward risk (the shape of his utility function relating risk and return).

EXAMINATION 4: CHAPTERS 13–15

Chapter 13

1. *Solution:*

a) Dividend yield = $\dfrac{\text{Paid dividend per share}}{\text{Price per share}}$

$$
= \frac{\$1.40}{\$28.00} = .05 = 5.0\%
$$

b) P/E = $\dfrac{\text{Price per share}}{\text{Total earnings per share}}$

$$
= \frac{\$28}{\$2.80} = 10\text{X}
$$

2. *Solution:*

a) $K = \dfrac{D}{P} + g$

$$
12\% = \frac{\$3}{\$40} + g
$$
$$
= 7.5\% + g
$$
$$
g = 4.5\%
$$

b)
	$ 4	Earnings per share
−	3	Dividends per share
	1	Retained earnings per share
×	.12	Rate of return
	$.12	Increase in EPS
	$4.00	Old EPS
+	.12	Increase in EPS
	$4.12	New EPS

3. *Solution:*

   $\$1,000$ Face value of bond

   $\times\ \ 0.08$ Coupon rate

   $\overline{\$80.00}$ Interest per year

   $\dfrac{\$80}{.07} = \$1,143$

4. standard deviation of market returns; covariance of firm with market returns

5. risk-free return; price of risk reduction for efficient portfolios; standard deviation of portfolio returns

6. market price of risk; risk of the security

7. variance; standard deviation

8. covariance of the returns of the individual security with the market

9. covariance of the individual security returns with the market; variance of market returns

10. cost of equity; expected future growth rate in earnings and dividends

11. expected dividend yield; expected growth rate in income from the security

Chapter 14

1. total assets; current liabilities
2. financial leverage
3. debt; equity or total debt to total assets
4. increase
5. increase the returns
6. have no influence.
7. cost of capital of a leverage-free firm; this cost of capital; cost of debt; leverage ratio
8. increase
9. the value of an unlevered firm; the amount of debt multiplied by the tax rate
10. cost of debt; debt to total assets; cost of equity; equity to total assets; net operating income (EBIT); value of the firm.
11. weighted marginal cost of financing
12. bankruptcy costs; rise; fall
13. required cost of capital; investment hurdle rate

Chapter 15

1. *b, c*
2. *c*

3. *Solution:*

   Payout before the split $\dfrac{6.00}{12.00} = 50\%$.

   Payout after the split $\dfrac{2.40}{4.00} = 60\%$.

   $\dfrac{60\% - 50\%}{50\%} = \dfrac{10\%}{50\%} = 20\% =$ Percent increase in dividend payout.

4. earnings rate in company versus earning opportunities of stockholders

5. is unable to earn; opportunity cost of equity capital

6. increased uncertainty about what future dividends will be

7. a change in expected future earnings

8. marginal cost of financing

9. marginal cost of capital; marginal returns from investments

10. influence; simultaneously; iterated process

EXAMINATION 5: CHAPTERS 16–22

Chapter 16

1. *a, b, d*
2. *a, c, d*
3. *a, c, f*
4. *c*
5. *a, c, d*
6. *e*
7. *a, b, d*
8. *a, b, c, d*
9. *c*
10. intermediate; short; long
11 *a, d*

Chapter 17

1. *Solution:*

   $$e = \frac{(\text{Nec.} - 1)(\# + 1)}{N}$$

   Nec. = Number of shares required

   e = Number desired to elect

   N = Total number of shares of common stock outstanding

   \# = Total number of directors to be elected

   $$e = \frac{(750,000 - 1)(12 + 1)}{2,500,000} = 3.9$$

2. *a, c*

3. *a, b, d*

4. *b*

5. *c*

6. *c*

7. *d*

8. *Solution:*

   a) | 300,000 | Current shares |
× $16.50	Market price
$4,950,000	Market value of firm
+800,000	Additional funds to be raised
$5,750,000	Total value of firm after rights issue
300,000	Original shares
+100,000	Additional shares to be sold
400,000	Total shares outstanding after rights issue

   $$\frac{5,750,000}{400,000} = \$14.375 = \$14.38$$ Theoretical new market value of one share after rights offering

   b) $\frac{300,000 \text{ Old shares}}{100,000 \text{ New shares}} = 3$ rights per new share

   $$R = \frac{M - S}{N} = \text{Value of one right}$$

   M = New market value of share
   S = Subscription price
   N = Number of rights required

   $$R = \frac{\$14.38 - \$8}{3} = \frac{\$6.38}{3} = \$2.13 \text{ value of one right}$$

9. *a, c, e*

10. 1) *c*
    2) *g*
    3) *e*
    4) *a*
    5) *b*
    6) *d*
    7) *f*

11. risk; income; control

12. priority of claims; right to issue additional securities; scope of lien.

13. no maturity; callable

14. not a tax deductible expense; a tax-free exchange of securities

15. relative costs; effects on risk

16. industry standards or norms; increased risk

17. reflects in some degree; a measure of costs

Chapter 18

1. *c, d*

2. *Solution:*
   Loan = Annual payment × (PV factor for 4-year annuity at 9%)

   $$\text{Annual payment} = \frac{\$10,000}{3.24} = \$3,086$$

3. *Solution:*

	First year	Second year
Balance..................	$ 10,000	$ 7,814
Interest rate..............	× .09	× .09
Interest payment.........	$ 900	$ 703
Total payment............	$ 3,086	$ 3,086
Interest payment.........	− 900	− 703
Loan repayment..........	$ 2,186	$ 2,383
Initial loan balance.......	$ 10,000	$ 7,814
Loan repayment..........	−2,186	−2,383
Final loan balance........	$ 7,814	$ 5,431

4. *d, e*

5. *a, b, d, e*

6. *d*

7. *Lease:*
   After-tax cost of leasing = 0.5 × $58,000 × 4.212 = $122,148

8. *Solution:*
   Amortization of loan: Present value of 5 annual payments

   $$\$180,000 = P \times (IF @ 12\% \text{ for 5 years})$$
   $$180,000 = P \times (3.605)$$
   $$P = \$49,931 = \text{Yearly payments}$$

   PV of $49,931 @ 6% = 49,931 × 4.212
   = 210,309

9

Year	Balance owed	Interest 12%	Amortization	Interest tax shelter	PV Factor @ 6%	PV of interest tax shelter
1............	$180,000	$21,600	$28,331	$10,800	.943	$10,184
2............	151,669	18,200	31,731	9,100	.890	8,099
3............	119,938	14,393	35,538	7,196	.840	6,045
4............	84,400	10,128	39,803	5,064	.792	4,011
5............	44,597	5,352	44,579	2,676	.747	1,999
						$30,338

10. Depreciation tax shelter:

$$\text{Yearly depreciation} = \frac{200,000 - 40,000}{5}$$

$$= \$32,000$$

Tax savings = (.5)(32,000) × IF @ 6% for 5 years

$$= 16,000 \times 4.212$$

Depreciation tax shelter = $67,392

11. Maintenance costs-discounted at 6%
$4,000 × IF @ 6% = $4,000 × 4.212

$$= \$16,848$$

12. Salvage value = IF @ 16% in 5 years from now × $40,000

$$= .476 \times 40,000 = \$19,040$$

13. Borrow-purchase outflows:

Down payment...	$ 20,000	
Loan............	180,000	
Maintenance costs.	16,848	$216,848
Less:		
Interest tax shelter.	$ 30,338	
Depreciation tax-shelter........	67,392	
Salvage value.....	19,040	116,770
Total Net Out-flows		$100,078

14. Cost of purchase-borrow
arrangement. $100,078
After-tax cost of leasing......... 122,148
Net Disadvantage of Leasing... $ 22,070

15. Would have increased it because of greater PV of depreciation tax shelter.

Chapter 19

1. *Solution:*

B_t = Value of bond as straight debt $(T - t)$

$$B_t = \sum_{N=1}^{T-t} \frac{c}{(1+r)^N} + \frac{B_M}{(1+r)^{T-t}}$$

$T - t = 20 - 10 = 10$
$r = 0.08$
$c = \$120$

$$B_t = \sum_{N=1}^{10} \frac{\$120}{(1.08)^N} + \frac{\$1,000}{(1.08)^{10}}$$

$$= 6.710(\$120) + \$1,000\,(0.463)$$

$$= \$805.20 + \$463$$

$B_t = \$1,268.20$

Conversion value = 20 × $80 = $1,600

2. *d*

3. *a, b, c, d, e*

4. *Solution:*

$$\text{Theoretical value} = \begin{array}{l}(\text{Market price of} \\ \text{common stock})\end{array} -$$

$$\begin{array}{l}(\text{Option} \\ \text{price})\end{array} \times \begin{array}{l}\text{Number of shares} \\ \text{per warrant}\end{array}$$

$$\text{Market price of common stock} = \frac{\$42}{10\ \text{shares}}$$

$$+ \$10/\text{share}$$

$$= \$4.20 + \$10$$

$$= \$14.20$$

5. *a, b, c, d, e*

6 *Solution:* (1) or (2)

(1) Before financing, total common shares.. 800,000
Owned by Harrison...................... 510,000
Percent owned by Harrison............. 63.75%
New shares if convertibles exercised
($1,000/$50 = 20; 20 × 10,000 = 200,000). 200,000
Total shares if convertibles exercised... 1,000,000
Percent owned by Harrison (510,000/1,000,000).................................. 51%

(2) New shares if warrants exercised
(15 × 10,000 + 150,000)................. 150,000
Total shares if warrants exercised....... 950,000
Percent owned by Harrison (510,000/950,000).................................. 53.7%

(3) New shares if stock sold at $35 (Number of shares = 10,000,000/35 = 285,714).... 286,000
Total shares............................. 1,086,000
Percent owned by Harrison (510,000/1,086,000).................................. 47.0%

7. *Solution:*

Convertibles

EBIT.....................	$20,000,000
Interest expense $2,000,000 +	
(.1 × 10,000,000)........	3,000,000
Taxable income...........	$17,000,000
Taxes....................	8,500,000
Net Income...............	$ 8,500,000

$$EPS = \frac{\$8,500,000}{800,000} = \$ \qquad 10.60$$

Common stock

EBIT.....................	$20,000,000
Interest..................	2,000,000
Taxable income...........	$18,000,000
Taxes....................	9,000,000
Net Income...............	$ 9,000,000

$$EPS = \frac{9,000,000}{1,086,000} = \$ \qquad 8.29$$

Warrants

EBIT	$20,000,000
Interest expense $2,000,000 +	
(.08 × 10,000,000)	2,800,000
Taxable income	$17,200,000
Taxes	8,600,000
Net Income	$ 8,600,000

$$EPS = \frac{\$8,600,000}{800,000} = \$ \qquad 10.75$$

Chapter 20

1. *a*
2. *e*
3. *a*

$120,000	Earnings, Paul and John
100,000	Earnings, Dandy
$220,000	Combined earnings
30,000	Premerger shares
10,000	Shares created by merger
40,000	Postmerger shares outstanding

$$\frac{\$220,000}{40,000} = \$5.50 \text{ EPS after merger}$$

$5.50	EPS after merger
4.00	EPS before merger
$1.50	Increase

b EPS after merger adjusted for two-for-one exchange $5.50 × 2 = $11.00

$20.00	EPS before merger
11.00	EPS after merger
$ 9.00	Decrease in adjusted EPS

c Weighted by respective total earnings before merger

Paul and John $\dfrac{\$120,000}{\$220,000}$ .15 = .545 × .15 = .08175

Dandy $\dfrac{\$100,000}{\$220,000}$ .06 = .454 × .06 = .02724

.10899

Approximately 11%.

4. *a, b*
5. *d, e*
6. pooling of interests
7. sum of the assets
8. past earnings patterns; expected future earnings; contributions to the rate of future earnings growth of the surviving firm.
9. qualitative factors
10. opportunities for synergy
11. higher price-earnings ratio
12. they fit into a soundly conceived long-range company plan; will have greater efficiency

Chapter 21

1. *b, f*
2. *e*
3. *e*
4. *c*
5. *a, c*
6. *c*
7. *d*

Chapter 22

1. *c*
2. *a, c, d*
3. *b, d*
4. *a, c*
5. *a, b*
6. *b, c*